AF581308

Other Books by Jeff Wright

THE GHOST OF SAGE GREY - Classic Ghost Story

MR. BONES TRILOGY - Thriller/Horror

1. Mr. Bones I - From Out of the Darkness
2. Mr. Bones II - Goldilocks
3. Mr. Bones III - Den of Scorpions

YETI - Alaskan Thriller

THE MYSTERIOUS ABIGAIL ROSE

JEFF WRIGHT

Library of Congress Registration Number: TXu 1-879-089

ISBN - 13 9781492381396

ISBN - 10 149238139X

This book was printed in the United States of America - 1st Edition.

To my beautiful sisters -
Barb, Carolyn, Joanne, Kathy, and PJ

Special thank you to Laurel Kenny
for her meticulous efforts and support.

1

The Enchanting Tale Begins

In the beautiful countryside of Laurence, Maine, Abigail Rose awoke with a ray of sunlight streaming through her bedroom window. She pulled her covers up over her shoulders, turned sideways, and looked out through her drawn curtains. She smiled with delight seeing that spring was finally here to chase the winter blues away. At her tender age of ninety-nine, the cold winter months seemed to make her fragile bones feel as if they were covered in wet cement. And no matter how many pairs of clothes she put on, she always seemed to be freezing. Today, however, was the first day of spring, and there was so much to do. She tossed the covers over, sat up, and removed her ear warmers.

"Theodore," she bellowed.

Theodore pushed open her door and pranced in. "Good morning, Madam Rose. Did you sleep well?"

"Yes, Theodore. Please go down and tell the kitchen that I'm up."

"Yes, me lady," he replied, turning and prancing out.

Abby stepped inside her slippers and walked into the bathroom.

"Good morning, Madam Rose," Brenda greeted her.

"Good morning, Brenda. I think today I'll soak for awhile."

"Would you like a nice bubble bath?"

"Yes please, with a little spice."

"Spice it is," Brenda replied, reaching toward the bottles on the windowsill.

After removing her nightgown, Abby looked into the mirror and sighed staring at the wrinkly old lady looking back at her. "Time sure has flown by," she grumbled. "Yesterday I was five and today I am almost one hundred years old."

Brenda looked over and shook her head. "You don't look a day over fifty, Madam Rose. And, I must confess, you're still as beautiful as your mother, Amelia, and you certainly have her gorgeous eyes as well."

Abby paused with Brenda's outward pleasantry. She gazed into the eyes of the old woman in the mirror. *My mother was stunning,* she thought. *All she had to do was waltz into a room, and the room would fall silent.* Abby smiled with that thought. Her father, Derek Von Haussler fell in love with Amelia

Eichmann the moment he laid eyes on her. She was the belle of the ball while being escorted by her father, Lord Eichmann, at one of his extravagant parties outside of Berlin.

It was Derek's luck that he was invited to such an event - for only those wealthy enough attended such trappings. However, what got him the break to attend, was that he was fortunate in meeting Lord Eichmann at another eventful party put on by none other than Hans Wolfgang - who had invited Derek to stand up and perform some of his magic. Not just any kind of magic, Derek was years ahead of the game. Pulling rabbits out of a hat was not his style – no, Derek took his profession even further. One of his favorite tricks was having someone come up on stage, draw a card out of his deck, look at it and then slip it back in. Afterward, Derek would simply wave his wand and a beautiful mourning dove would fly into the room carrying the card strapped to the undercarriage of its wing.

Another one of his famous tricks was a disappearing act. He would stand in the center of the room wearing a black tuxedo, a black top hat and cape, and begin to spin in a circle; covering *himself* with the cape. Then suddenly, a flash of smoke would engulf him. The guest would step back alarmed, seeing that Derek was no longer standing there. The room would fall silent, except for the whispering to where he had gone. Then out of nowhere, a man - wearing a totally different outfit would walk into the room. Derek would stand there until the guests all noticed him and they'd all start clapping. Derek would raise his brow, splash on a boyish grin, and then tip his top hat to the crowd. However, it was more than just magic – it was a family secret to Derek's extraordinary abilities.

The room full of guests always sighed in awe with his brilliant display of magic – one of them being Lord Eichmann. He was awestruck by Derek's abilities. Therefore, Lord Eichmann invited Derek to perform his magic at his opening summer party. That moment would change his life forever. He met Amelia, and they fell madly in love with one another. And, as the saying goes - the rest was history. Well, not quite….

Derek's parents frowned on the budding love affair between Amelia and their son. Marriages outside the inner circle were absolutely forbidden. You see, Derek's grandmother, Hilda - who resided in the deep forest region within the Austrian mountains, a stone's throw away from a little village called Transylvania - was a witch. The inner circle comprised of Hilda, her four sisters and husbands and their children, and five other families. They were a clan of witches that resided in the small village called Nome; a village populated with tall canopy trees, dense forest vegetation, moss covered ground and they lived in round stone huts with grass roofs.

After receiving the news of Derek's love affair with Amelia, Hilda summoned her grandson to come and present himself before the clan, which was a day's journey by horse and buggy.

Upon his arrival, she could see the love in her grandson's eyes for Amelia as he spoke about Amelia inside her tiny stone hut. As the matriarch of the clan, she had no other choice but to call a meeting in the center of the village. She had Derek stand in the middle and proclaim his love for Amelia. There were immediate hollers from the females and shouts from the males cast upon him. Hilda raised her hands as she walked out from the circle and approached Derek. "Are you sure?" she asked. "Yes. I want to marry her," was his reply. Hilda turned in a circle looking at each of her clan members. All she saw was fire and brimstone etched in their faces.

"What about all these fair maidens standing before you, Derek? Is there not one that fancies your eye?" Gertrude yelled out.

Derek turned and faced her, and then cast his eyes down the row of fair maidens standing there. "They are all stunning in their own right. However, love..." he said and then paused, turning to face his grandmother. "...love has no rhyme or reason. It does not think, but only feels. All of you," he continued, turning in a circle looking at each one, "all of you know what I am talking about. Love just happens, and when it does, the heart simply wins out."

He took three steps out toward the gathering of clan members and began slowly walking around the group. "I've always been proud of being born into this clan. Moreover, I figured that one day I too would marry one of these beautiful maidens. However, if it wasn't for my parents who wanted me schooled, I would have never left Nome," he said, stopping in front of Gertrude.

"What do you mean?" Magdalene, the children's superintendent harshly replied, stepping out of the circle to confront him. "You were schooled in reading and writing and the art of witchcraft."

"That is not what I meant. There's more to just reading and writing."

Magdalene stepped back shaking her head.

"Please, everyone, and pardon my expression, but I've seen and experienced the world out there beyond these forests," Derek said, pointing through the trees toward the mountain ridge. Magdalene's eyes followed his finger outward through the forest. She looked back at him.

"Amelia is from the outside world and she comes from a good family," Derek continued, walking again. "Her father is not a peasant – his name is Lord Eichmann. He's a British Noble who holds court with the Chancellor of Germany."

"We heard of your performances," Adler shouted. "Magic tricks performed with witchcraft. You have them all fooled, young man."

Derek walked over and stared into his eyes. "We are not a clan of evil doers," he replied. He then turned and faced the crowd. "Our witchcraft has never been used for casting spells to hurt someone. I use my gifts simply to entertain the people of Germany. What is wrong with that, may I ask?" he said waiting to hear if anyone had anything else to say. No one spoke up to refute his comment. They all trained their attention on Hilda knowing that she would have the final say in this.

Derek turned toward his grandmother. He could see the love within her eyes for him. In that moment, she decided on what course to take. "There is only one way to decide this," she said to her clan members' disapproving stares. "I want the men folk to fill the cauldron with water and light a fire underneath. You women folk - please return to your huts and get dressed. Tonight, we'll call on Shadow to give us his answer."

With that, Hilda departed to get dressed herself. When all the women of the clan returned, they were wearing black robes with hoods. As the water started to boil, Hilda began placing all kinds of spices and herbs into the cauldron. She then added animal parts such as powdered shavings from an Elk antler, one foxtail, a bat wing and two dead horny toads. "Tonight, with no moon in the night sky I'll call out on the wind to Shadow, the Alpha male of the Timber Wolf Pack. Are there any objections?"

"No, call the wolf and let him decide," they shouted back, knowing the ritual. Wolves never howled during a moonless night. On moonless nights, the pack would hunt. So tonight, Hilda was going to call upon Shadow. If Shadow howled, Derek could marry Amelia. If Shadow did not howl, Derek would then have to decide to either stay with the clan and not marry Amelia, or leave the clan forever if he decided to make her his wife.

"*Fire and brimstone, coal and wood, I call upon Shadow to let us know if Derek should,*" Hilda sang out, tossing white powder into the cauldron that produced flames and smoke.

The wind suddenly picked up, sending the tree branches swaying as Hilda's request went out through the forest and hillside. Everyone silently stood there waiting for Shadow.

Shadow stopped on a trail along the ridge. His pack stopped behind him. His ears went up and then he lifted his nose into the wind. He looked back at his pack and gave a low growl – telling them to stay back. He turned his head, walked out onto a bluff and looked down upon the small village below. Without hesitation, he gave a mighty howl.

Hilda smiled at her clan members. They all nodded their approval, walked up to Derek and hugged him. Before Derek left the village, they presented him with all kinds of pouches filled with spices and herbs and one very special jar - one that held a magic seed inside.

Hilda then gave him her prized possessions - a book containing all the potions and spells, which was a family heirloom from her great uncle, the Black Knight, and also, her uncle's beautiful porcelain swan, Brenda. She then instructed Derek to guard and protect both items with his life. Afterwards, the clan of witches and warlocks saw him out of the village.

When he returned to Berlin, Lord Eichmann enticed him into performing on stage at the Berlin Theater. After that splendid performance, Derek took Berlin and then the whole of Germany by storm – becoming the most famous man in all of Germany. However, Derek wanted more. He set his sights on America. In the year 1900, Derek and Amelia packed up their belongings and traveled to England by train. There, they went on board the 'Knight and Gail', a British Cruise Liner bound for Boston. From Boston, they eventually settled in a small town called Cloverdale in the foothills of Pennsylvania. In 1904, Amelia and Derek had a baby girl. They named her Abigail Von Haussler.

"Nineteen hundred and four," Abby whispered, stepping out of her thoughts. "It's amazing how time seems to fly by so quickly," she continued, gazing at herself in the mirror. "And you're right, Brenda, I do have my mother's beautiful eyes."

"That you do, me lady."

"Well," Abby beamed, spinning around. "It's time – my first bicentennial is almost here."

"You'll find him. I am sure of that."

"You're right, Brenda," she quipped, walking over and stepping inside the tub.

After her bath, she waltzed out like a summer breeze and got dressed. After pulling open the curtains, she stretched out her arms and greeted the day with a long whimsical sigh, “Ha… my beautiful Butterfly Weeds and Forget-Me Not’s… my Black-Eyed Susans and Yellow Daisies… and all those wonderful, Crimson Clovers and Hollyhocks… they make my head spin like crazy. Today before I go, they’ll all sprout up and smile at me,” she continued, turning and walking out the door.

At the bottom of the staircase, Grandfather greeted her. “Good morning, Madam Rose.”

“Good morning, Grandfather. It’s the first day of Spring you know,” she replied, strolling past him.

“Yes. I am well aware of that. I am the time keeper around here, and by my time, you must know this is the year.”

She spun around, slid her hands down the side of her dress and replied, “I’m well aware of that, Grandfather. Our time here is up. We must move back to Cloverdale.”

“Cloverdale!? You’re not saying we must move…” his voice trailed off.

“Yes, we need to purchase my father’s estate back on Cherry Hill, or it won’t work. You heard him when I was a child.”

“Yes, I heard every word, but I thought you could do this here.”

“No, I’m sorry to say. My father’s spell will only work inside that Manor. And today being the first of May – I must purchase it before someone else does.”

“But what if it’s not there anymore?”

“Oh, I’m sure it is. My father’s Manor was given to the town of Cloverdale and I know they’d never tear down a stately place like that. Trust me. I’ll make the call right now.”

Grandfather watched her leave. He cast his brawny, silvery eyes sideways. “Psst… Sir Henry, are you awake?”

“Yes, I heard every word.”

“Then why didn’t you speak up?”

Sir Henry raised his brow. “Speak up? Why, you heard Madam Rose,” he replied and then was abruptly interrupted.

“Yes, I was just speaking to her,” Grandfather scoffed.

“Well then, we must move.”

Grandfather rolled his eyes.

"You can roll your eyes all you want, but I remember quite clearly what her father said to her on her tenth birthday while sprinkling his magic dust in her hair."

"Oh, what would you know, you're just a stick."

"Mind your manners. You're speaking to royalty you know."

"Royalty! I've heard that before," Grandfather chuckled.

"That's right. I was handcrafted from the finest timber in all of England as a gift to King Louie III on his thirtieth birthday."

"Finest timber in all of England did you say?"

"That is correct."

"Well, you don't look like fine timber to me. You look more like an old coat rack."

"Oh now… you hush. At least the house respects my title. I am Sir Henry of Knotting Wood.

"Knotting Wood," Grandfather laughed. I think you're confused, old timer. To me, you look like Sir Knucklehead from Five and Dime."

"Oh… poppycock, Grandfather. Someday you'll be missing me."

"And when will that be? Soon I hope."

"When we move back into the Manor, I'll be putting in my request to be placed where I'll be respected."

"And where will that be? At the back door?" Grandfather quipped.

Abby drifted down the hallway toward the kitchen while listening to Grandfather and Sir Henry quarreling. They seemed to be arguing more and more these days. *I wish they'd just settle their differences and become friends again. Maybe Theodore could assist in that. He is, after all, Lord of the household.*

"Good morning, Hansel," she greeted the large serving spoon, walking into the kitchen.

"Good morning, Madam Rose. The kitchen is preparing you eggs, toast, hash browns and blueberry muffins."

"That will be fine. May I have a glass of orange juice please?"

"Why of course," she replied, tapping her handle on the counter. Simon opened his doors, pardoned himself, and then allowed the orange juice to float out toward the table. A glass tipped itself so the orange juice could pour. "There you go," Hansel continued, shooing the orange juice back into the fridge.

"Thank you, Hansel. I don't know what I'd do without you around here. You run this kitchen like a captain at sea."

Hansel spun on her handle looking at all the busy utensils, pots and pans, and sighed. "Well, we all have our place and everyone knows their jobs. I just make sure things are done properly."

"That you do. Oh my, I almost forgot… Theodore," she yelled.

"Yes, Madam Rose," he replied, prancing in.

"Fetch me the phone please. I would tell you where it is if I only could remember."

"You left it in the lounge, Madam Rose. I'll be right back."

When Theodore returned with the phone, she smiled taking it from him. "Now let me see," she said, bringing her hand up and waving her fingers. The top kitchen drawer opened on its own and a small black leather binder floated up and over to the table. Abby turned the pages until she came to - Meek's Real Estate Company in Cloverdale. She picked up the phone and dialed the number.

"Meek's Real Estate. Sid Peterson speaking, may I help you?"

"Good morning Mr. Peterson. My name is Abigail Rose. I'm calling in regard to the Von Haussler Manor on Cherry Hill. Is it still there?"

Sid looked over at his partner, Don Reed. He quickly nodded his head for Don to walk over. Don wrinkled his brow getting up. Sid jotted down 'Von Haussler Manor'. Don shifted his eyes on him confused.

"Yes, Mrs. Rose, the Manor is still there. From what I know, the owner...," he said and then paused, frantically pulling out the paperwork from his bottom desk drawer and looking for the past owner's name "...Derek Von Haussler had given the Manor to the town of Cloverdale for a set time," he continued, glancing at the dates within the contract. "Until the First of May, Twenty - twelve," he gasped, staring up at Don. *Today was the 1st of May, 2012!* Don leaned over Sid's desk scratching his head. *Unbelievable,* he thought.

"Well, isn't that a hoot that I am calling you now, Mr. Peterson. I'd like to purchase it if I may," Abby replied.

Sid looked at Don and mouthed, "She wants to buy it." Don leaned off the desk, stunned. "Well, Mrs. Rose, I don't know if you are aware of the condition the Manor is in. The town has actually done nothing with it except to use it as a museum of sorts. We get lots of visitors in town that go up and check out the place, especially around Halloween."

"I see, well – I honestly don't care about the condition it's in right now, as long as it's still standing. When can I come to purchase it?"

"Before I say yes to your arrival, I need to tell you that all the services will have to be restored. You know, like water, electrical and gas. It was built in 1904 by a tycoon by the name of Derek Von Haussler."

"How wonderful," she quipped, "built by a real tycoon. It must have been a grand Manor in its day."

"Yes, how wonderful," Sid repeated. "I guess you can come anytime you'd like. Where do you live?"

"I live in Laurence, Maine. I can have a moving company here by tomorrow and drive out myself. I'll be there on the Fifth of May – say around noon-ish."

"OK, Mrs. Rose. We'll see you then. Have a great day," Sid replied and then hung up. He looked up at Don with a question mark over his brow.

"What?" Don asked.

"She never even asked about the price," Sid replied, rubbing his chin.

The following day, the moving company pulled in with two large moving vans. Abby turned over the keys to the real estate agent, Mark Hammer, who would oversee and manage the place for her. As she saw Mr. Hammer out, she requested to walk the place one more time, ensuring him that she'd lock up. After he left, Abby shut the door, set Theodore down on the floor and waved her hand over him. *WHOOSH* - Theodore came alive. "Are they gone," he asked.

"Yes. I would like you to go outside and wake up Wilfred while I walk the place one more time. I am sure Wilfred will need a good dusting off."

"Yes, Madam Rose," Theodore replied, turning for the back door.

Abby spent close to an hour walking about the house. She sat a spell in each room upstairs looking out the windows overlooking the manicured lawns and gardens. *It certainly is a splendid place to live,* she thought, turning and walking out of the dayroom with its large glass windows and bay doors leading out to the upper balcony overlooking the back property.

Theodore gingerly walked toward the garage, past the maple tree at the side and pushed the door open. "Wilfred," he said, walking up to the old 1907 Ford K, which Derek had purchased right off the assembly line and then gave to his daughter, Abigail, as her twenty-first birthday present.

Wilfred opened his big round eyelids seeing Theodore standing there. He gave a huge yawn. "What time is it?"

"Wake up, Wilfred, it's time to go."

"Is Madam Rose finally taking me for a drive? I sure hope my wooden spokes, wheel bearings and axles hold out. They haven't been lubed in years," he replied, slowly moving his front tires. "Thank God my tires are hard rubber. They'd certainly be flat by now."

"You look splendid, Wilfred. Maybe seeing the light of day and feeling the fresh air through your grill will bring you back to life."

"And where, my fine friend, is she taking me?"

"We are not going for a drive."

"What – don't be kidding me now?!"

"No, you can count your lucky stars. We're not going for a drive – we're going on a trip. Madam Rose has just turned over the keys to a real estate man. We are moving back to Cherry Hill."

"Cherry Hill!" Wilfred gushed, rolling his headlight shields and tooting his horn. "I loved that manor. I can still remember the day Baron Von Haussler drove me up the long driveway. Oh… that garage. It was a marvelous place to sit. Back then, the Baron had mechanics that looked after me. It made me feel as grand as the day I rolled off the assembly line. Now, however, I just sit here looking out through the cracks in the boards," he moaned.

Theodore shook his head walking around to the side of Wilfred. He pulled the old tarp off and slowly shook his head. Wilfred's paint was faded, the seats were now battered and brittle and both sideboards were covered in rust. The only thing that had been using Wilfred in the last few years were spiders that had come and gone, leaving their webbing all over him, plus the dust that had settled on his faded, metal body. "You are a sight, my old friend," Theodore gasped.

"Well, you would be too if you sat in an old garage for years on end. Now open the doors and let me roll out, then go and fetch me the hose. I've got to clean myself off."

Twenty minutes later, Theodore returned to the house and informed Madam Rose that Wilfred was ready. "OK, jump up into my arms and let's get you into the car when he pulls up out front."

Wilfred rolled up to the front of the house and waited for Madam Rose to come out. When she did, Wilfred heard her sigh as she walked down the steps. She placed Theodore on the front seat, went back up and then waved her hand over her blue suitcase. It lifted off the ground, floated down the steps and then settled on the rumble seat in back. With everything packed and ready to go, Abby waltzed down to the driver's side door. She took one last look up at the house and then got in.

“Wilfred,” Abby said, buckling her seat belt, “do you remember how to get to Cherry Hill?”

“Yes, Madam Rose,” he replied, starting his engine. On the way down the driveway, she promised to get him fully restored as soon as they got back to Cherry Hill. The very place she grew up.

2

Home Sweet Home

Cloverdale was a quaint little cottage town built by migrants that streamed in and settle down in the lush, green valley, starting up families and laboring in the rock quarries that were discovered along the mountains and rolling hills of Pennsylvania in 1905.

The town itself began with just one street and a few shops, selling items that the new arrivals needed and gradually grew over time. The one main street through the center of the town was called just that - Main Street - which was cobbled from the rocks dug out from the quarry. The buggy trails throughout the countryside began connecting onto Main Street as the homes in the area started to spread outward.

By the time Abby was five years old, the town had a population of two hundred people. More shops were added, a bakery, a grocery store and one small service station for those who could afford a car. Today, however, Cloverdale was now a bustling town with a beehive of activities.

The beautiful Victorian homes built back then, with long decorative verandas, still sat at the edge of town along with the Mayor's office, library and schools. Even though the town grew up, it never lost its place as one of Pennsylvania's most distinguished historical towns with some shops dating all the way back to its beginning.

As Abby drove down Main Street, she noticed right away that the town had gone through many transformations since she was a child growing up there. Some shops she recognized like Fletchers Five & Dime, Jim's Hardware, Susan's Dress Shop and Bender's Soda Fountain which her father loved taking her there to enjoy the wonderful ice cream dishes.

Her favorite place to sit was right up front at the counter on one of those high, round stools with red vinyl seat coverings. She felt big sitting there amongst the adults that sat and talked about the price of seed, fertilizers, live stock and farm machinery. Her father, on occasion, would do magic tricks for them.

The small town back then prided itself in having such a distinguished resident by the name of Baron Von Haussler. The Baron's dream of taking America by storm was so sudden that even he was surprised. All it took was performing three shows in New York and his name went up in lights. After becoming famous, he preferred to live in a place hidden from the world which would help him in keeping his secret. Thus, he picked Cloverdale to settle in.

One of his favorite tricks at Bender's was unscrewing the top off a small sugar container, pouring the contents into his closed fist and then he'd put his fist up to his mouth. In one swift motion, he would blow into his fist while tossing his hand outward in front of him and the sugar would just disappear. The owner, Frank Bender, never liked that trick because he always worried the sugar would be mess to clean up. She would laugh when Mr. Bender's face contorted seeing her father make the sugar simply disappear. Customers begged to know how he did it. Some even wagered bets that it went down his long-sleeved jacket. He'd then politely take if off and show them that the sugar wasn't there.

What made her laugh even more was when they were driving home from town and her father would glance over with big wide eyes, wink at her and then extend his hand out the side of the car and pour all the sugar onto the road. She remembered asking him when she could have a crack at it. His answer was simply, "In time my dear, you'll be greater than me."

As Abby continued driving down Main Street, drifting back to those wonderful days, she was unaware of the looks she was getting from people walking by and those sitting under the shop awnings, stunned at the spectacle passing before them. Some even commented, "*Which was older - the car or the old lady driving it?*"

"There it is!" Abby said with excitement, seeing the Meek's Real Estate sign in the window. When she pulled up along the curb, Wilfred shut off his engine. After getting out, Abby walked around to the opposite side of the car. She picked up Theodore and placed him on top of her suitcase on the back-rumble seat. "Now you look after my belongings while I go in and introduce myself, Theodore," she said, turning and walking up to the door.

Across the street, Shaun Stevenson, a handsome young man with wavy black hair which he liked to slick back as they did in the 50s, stepped out of Olson's Service Station. He reached around, pulled out the white cloth from out of his back pocket and began wiping his greasy hands while staring in awe at the old car sitting there parked across the street.

"Will you look at that?" Todd Olson, Shaun's boss, said, walking up behind him.

"That's a nineteen hundred o' seven Ford K, Mr. Olson," Shaun replied. "They don't make them like that anymore."

Mr. Olson laughed. "That it is. You certainly know your vehicles young man."

Shaun turned his head and looked at him. "It would be awesome to work on that, don't you think?"

"It sure would. Right now, however, we have a Buick inside needing a new fuel line."

Shaun nodded, still eyeing up the old car. He turned and followed Mr. Olson back in.

When Abby entered the small real estate office, the two men working at their desks stood up. "Good afternoon. My name is Abby. I called a few days ago about the manor."

Sid rounded his desk, pulled up a chair for her to sit down and then introduced himself. "Good day, Mrs. Rose. I'm Sid Peterson, the one you spoke with over the phone. And this is my partner, Don Reed."

Abby smiled taking the other man in. He was tall, slender and wearing a brown pinstripe suit. She also noticed that he was losing a bit of his hair up top. Sid, however, was a short, round little man, wearing a light blue shirt and navy blue pants.

"Please, please – have a seat," Sid said, gesturing to the chair in front of his desk.

"Why, thank you," Abby replied, sitting down. She folded her hands in her lap still holding her smile.

"I wanted to start off by saying that we've spoken to Mayor Sam Bumpkin about this sale."

"Mayor Bumpkin," she quipped. "Yes, please go on."

"Well, the Mayor was worried about you being able to bring the manor up to city code."

"Oh, yes. That's no problem. As you said, just restoring the water, electrical and gas. They can start today."

Sid glanced over at Don. Don raised his brow thinking of the cost. He was sure that when Mrs. Rose heard the price of the manor, she'd just stand up and walk out. Or worse, she'd simply faint.

"Alright," Sid replied, "after speaking with the Mayor and the city council, they have set the price on the manor at $500,000.00. And to bring it up to city code, the total price would be $520,000.00."

"$520,000.00… Why, you'll have it today," Abby replied without even blinking an eye.

Sid almost fell off his chair. Don quickly sat down before he did fall over. Abby looked at the two as if they had just stepped into a cow pie.

Sid reached up, ran his fingers through his hair and calmly asked, "Will that be a wire transfer from your bank, or simply a bank check?"

"Oh no… I never use banks and I can't remember the last time I wrote a check. I have it in the suitcase out front. Cold hard cash is the best, don't you think?"

Sid shifted his eyes on the front glass door. Mrs. Rose's car looked older than she did. He glanced back at Abby. "You have it in the car?" he asked startled.

"Yes, Theodore is watching it for me."

Sid and Don both looked out - there was no one sitting in the car. They glanced back at the old lady. Sid thought she was possibly a sandwich short of a picnic. Don thought she had escaped from the Funny Farm. However, before they could grab their composure, Abby sat up and asked, "Now where do I sign?"

Sid looked at Don. Don rolled his eyes as if to say – *get the contract*. Sid opened his top drawer and pulled out the paperwork. He pushed it across his desk toward Mrs. Rose and then handed her a pen. Abby leaned over, jotting her name down at the bottom and then allowed Don to sign under her name as a witness.

"Now, before we settle and the money is handed over, which I would assume that you two would like to deposit as soon as possible, do you mind if we walk the shops a bit? I just love small country stores," Abby said.

"Yes, I'd be glad to escort you around town, Mrs. Rose. Is there any shop in particular that you have in mind?"

"Yes, Fletcher's Five and Dime. I just love browsing. Most old ladies do."

"I've noticed that in this small town," Sid replied standing up. Don stood up when Abby did.

"It was nice meeting you, Don," she said, turning and heading for the door. She suddenly stopped and turned around. "This might be a tad forward

Don, but I remember reading in my great grandmother's old recipe and remedies book about a remedy for baldness."

Don glanced over at Sid. Sid smiled raising his brow. Don cast his eyes back on Abby. "Yes, go on," he said more so to humor the old gal.

"Take a pinch of barley, three clover leaves, one egg white, a lemon peel and one dandelion stem and blend it with a half cup of vinegar. Then rub it into your hair and leave it on for one hour every night before you go to bed. In a week, you'll see your hair coming back."

Sid laughed. Abby looked at him. "You may laugh, Mr. Peterson, but my great grandmother was a remarkably wise woman," she remarked.

"I'm sure she was," Don spoke up.

"Well then, take my advice and try it," she replied, turning for the door.

Sid opened the door for her and then looked back at Don. Don smiled and shrugged.

When Sid stepped outside, he stared at the old car. "Will you look at that," he said, amazed.

"That's a nineteen o'seven Ford K. My father gave it to me on my twenty first birthday."

"You don't say," Sid replied, looking at the rumble seat in back. He saw a stuffed white lion sitting on top of a blue suitcase. "That wouldn't be Theodore, would it?" he questioned.

"Yes, that's Theodore. He's another gift from my father. I've had him since I was a child. He watches over everything for me."

Forget about being a sandwich short of a picnic, Sid thought. *The old lady was dancing on Mars.* "I see. And I suppose that's where you keep your money," he jokingly inquired.

"Yes I keep all my money in there."

Sid's face went slack. He wanted to ask how much but decided against it. "Would you like Don to come out and watch it while you do a bit of shopping?"

"No… that's why I have Theodore with me. Now shall we?" she replied, walking down the sidewalk toward Fletcher's.

Sid took one more look back at Theodore, shook his head and then raced up alongside Abby.

Todd Olson, at the service station, stepped out of his garage. He leaned up against the bay doorframe watching Sid escorting Abby down the street. Shaun walked up to Mr. Olson.

"Pretty classy, don't you think?" Mr. Olson remarked, keeping his eyes on Abby.

"What's pretty classy?"

"That old woman and that car sitting there," Mr. Olson replied, nodding his head toward the car across the street.

"Yeah, I see what you mean. They certainly go together."

"They certainly do," Mr. Olson replied, lifting his backside off the doorframe and walking back in. Shaun stood there for a moment watching the old woman and Sid heading down to Fletcher's Five and Dime. As he was about to turn and go back inside, he spotted Willy Myers, Molly Dutton and Bobby Ray riding their Stingray bicycles down the sidewalk on the other side of the street. Willy was better known as the town's hooligan, just like his brother Ernie used to be. Some just called Willy unruly, a prankster and/or non-parented. His sidekick, Bobby Ray, was certainly heading in the wrong direction too. Molly Dutton, on the other hand, was simply a tomboy, who'd rather be out catching frogs and snakes down by the river than dressing up and playing with dolls like the other girls her age. Why she liked Willy was beyond Shaun. Willy, in his mind, was nothing but trouble.

Shaun stood there as the three slowly rode up to the old Ford K. Willy looked in the back and spotted the stuffed lion sitting on top of the suitcase. He looked over at Shaun standing there watching. The look on Shaun's face was – touch it and your dead. Willy gave him a smug look and continued riding up the street with his two comrades.

Shaun watched them do a skid in front of Fletcher's and get off their bikes. *I sure hope they don't give that old lady any grief,* he thought, walking back into the garage.

When the three kids opened the door, they saw Mr. Fletcher assisting an old woman in the sewing section. They strolled up to the counter looking through the large candy jars on the counter.

"What-cha going to buy, Willy?" Bobby Ray asked, eyeing up the watermelon sticks.

"I'm not sure. How about you, Molly?"

"I only have a nickel. That's all my mother would give me," she replied, reaching into her front overall pocket. She couldn't feel it and searched the other pocket. "Hey, my nickel is gone," she frantically said.

"It can't be gone," Bobby Ray exclaimed.

"It's gone," she fumed, checking all her pockets.

Hank Fletcher looked over to see the commotion up at the counter. "I'll be right back, Mrs. Rose," he said, excusing himself and hurrying over to the kids. "OK, what seems to be the problem with you three!?"

"I can't find my nickel," Molly replied.

"Well, I can't help you there. Please hurry up and pick out what you want."

Abby turned, hearing Mr. Fletcher scolding the kids. She looked at Sid who rolled his eyes. She sighed walking up to the counter. "Now Mr. Fletcher," she started to say. "I guess you're too old to remember when you were just a child."

Hank leaned against the counter looking at her surprised. "Mrs. Rose…"

"Why, Mr. Fletcher, you're not going to disrespect me too, are you?!" she interrupted, placing her hands on her hips.

Hank cleared his throat trying to remain calm. Mrs. Rose knew nothing of these three youngsters – *always causing trouble,* he thought. He wasn't going to try to explain; not with that fiery look Mrs. Rose was displaying.

"I was just trying to help, that's all."

"Well, I see that you're not very good at it," she snapped, looking down at the girl wearing pigtails. She was a charming little thing with brownish blonde hair, light green eyes and a splash of freckles across her nose.

"Now, my dear, what seems to be the problem?"

"I lost my nickel."

"You did? Where did you have it last?"

"It was in one of these pockets," Molly replied, pressing her hands down the sides of her overalls.

"Well, that certainly is a dilemma, isn't it?" Abby replied.

Sid walked up to watch. He was curious to see what Mrs. Rose was going to do.

"Yes, I was really aching for one of those strawberry sticks."

Abby looked up at the jars on the counter. She flashed back to when she came in and picked one out herself. She gave a sigh looking down at Molly. "I know a simple trick that just might work," she said with a wink.

"Really?" Molly replied, shifting her eyes on her friends.

"Yes. Now what you have to do is turn slowly in a circle while closing your eyes real tight and then think back – back to when you placed it in your pocket."

Molly looked at her then at Mr. Fletcher, who seem more agitated now with this show. She closed her eyes and began turning in a circle.

"Think back," Abby whispered. "Keep thinking back."

After three turns, Abby told her to stop and open her eyes. "Now, which pocket did you put it in?"

"This one," Molly replied, slipping her hand inside that pocket. She was surprised to feel something round and hard. She pulled it out. It was her nickel. "Will you look at that?" she said surprised, holding her hand out.

"You see, it works every time," Abby beamed, glancing up at Mr. Fletcher. He slightly shook his head.

Molly looked down at her nickel. Something was odd. It was shinier than the one her mother had given her. "This isn't my nickel," she said, wrinkling her nose.

"No?" Abby said.

"No, mine was dirty and this one is shiny."

Abby smiled. "It looks like your lucky day. Now, how about picking something out and you three be on your way," she replied, glancing at the boys with awe in their eyes.

"May I have the strawberry stick?" Molly pleasantly asked Mr. Fletcher, handing him the nickel.

"I'll take the apple stick," Willy said, slapping his nickel on the counter.

"I'll have the watermelon, please," Bobby Ray added.

After the three got their candy and walked out, Mr. Fletcher looked at Mrs. Rose. "How did you do that?"

"Simple," she replied, opening her purse and pulling out a small coin pouch inside. "Hold my purse, Sid."

Sid smiled taking it. Abby then looked at all the candy jars and saw the one she wanted. The price on the jar was a dime. She pulled out a dime, handed Sid the pouch and then placed the dime in her left palm. "Now watch carefully," she said, rubbing her hands together with the dime in the middle. She then closed her two hands into fists. "Which hand's it in?" she asked, Mr. Fletcher.

Hank looked at Sid, who just shrugged. He shifted his eyes on Abby and then down at her closed fists. "It's in that hand", he said, pointing to the right one. Abby opened it – nothing. She then opened her left hand – nothing. Hank stood back amazed. Abby smiled, walked up to the counter and opened a jar. She pulled out a large Tootsie Roll. "Come, Sid, it's time we get back," she said, walking toward the door.

"Hey, that will be a dime," Hank yelled after her.

She turned her head slightly and replied, "It's right behind you on the counter. Have a good day Mr. Fletcher."

Hank slowly turned and looked down at the counter. He sighed, seeing the dime sitting there. He picked it up, turned around as the front door closed. "How in blazes did she do that?" he gasped, looking down at the dime and then back up at the door again.

Sid handed Abby her purse and coin pouch outside. "You mind me asking you how you did that?"

Abby smiled. Sid was like playing with a kindergartener. "It was simple. The dime was already sitting there," she lied.

Sid shook his head. *Maybe she is smarter than I thought.*

Abby glanced up the street just in time to see the three kids racing off on their bikes. They rode past Wilfred and then darted around the corner. Willy was out front, as he rounded the corner first. They were taking a path between the last shop on the street and a small wooded area toward the river. Bobby Ray caught up to him behind the shop and raced Willy across an open field to the river. Molly just tagged along in the rear until she caught up to them. She got off her bike seeing Bobby Ray and Willy walking up to a large boulder overlooking the river.

"Gee, Molly, you're slow," Bobby Ray said, taking in gulps of air.

"If I were a boy, I'd of beat-cha both," she replied, taking a seat on the rock. Willy looked over at her as she sat down. "Are you sure that wasn't your nickel," he asked, pulling out his candy stick.

"I'm as sure as I am a girl," she replied, sticking out her tongue at Bobby Ray.

Bobby Ray shook his head. "How do you think she slipped it into your pocket while you were turning in a circle?" he asked.

"She didn't slip it into Molly's pocket, Bobby Ray," Willy said. "I was watching her the whole time, and she never even put a hand on Molly."

"Willy's right, Bobby Ray, I would have felt it for sure."

"Then how did she do it?" Bobby Ray asked.

"Beats me," Molly quipped. "I'm just glad she was there. Besides, it was nice to see her tug on that old windbag's ear. Mr. Fletcher is as mean as an old dog that's been kicked too many times."

Willy lay down upon the rock with his Apple stick hanging out of his mouth. "I wonder where she came from?" he asked, looking up into the trees.

"I don't know, but my mother certainly will," Molly said. "She hangs out with Karen Bloom who's in the Women's Club. That club always gets the latest gossip," she continued, pulling out her Strawberry stick.

"Well, let us know, will ya?" Bobby Ray replied, removing the wrapper from his Watermelon Stick and lying back.

"I will," Molly said, lying back herself.

Back at the real estate office, Abby requested Sid to drive with her down to the bank so she could deposit the money for the manor into Meek's Real Estate account. When Sid got in her car, he looked at the simple dashboard, the long clutch and gearshift on the outside running board. *It's amazing how far we've come since this was built,* he thought, watching Mrs. Rose place the key into the ignition. "Weren't these cars hand cranked?" he asked.

Abby laughed. "Yes, but I had it changed over. I'm certainly too old to be doing that."

"Yes, I suppose," he replied, nodding. He looked at the gas gauge. The needle was on empty. "You look low on gas. We could pull across the street if you'd like."

Abby glanced over at the service station. She could not recall the last time Wilfred rolled into one. "Maybe the gas needle is stuck, you know these old cars - there's always something to fix," she replied, tapping on the instrument panel. The needle floated over to *full.* "There, now let's get going. I'd like to make the purchase before my moving company shows up today," she replied, turning the key.

Sid shook his head seeing the gas tank was full.

One block down, Sid told Abby to turn left at the corner and the bank would be on the right-hand side of the street. After getting out, he picked up Theodore and handed him to Mrs. Rose. Upon lifting the suitcase, he realized it was heavier than it looked.

The Cloverdale bank manager, Bart Hornsby, noticed Sid hauling in the suitcase with an elderly woman carrying a stuffed toy lion. "May I help you with that?" he asked, meeting them at the door.

"Yes, please. This is Mrs. Rose. She just purchased the manor up on Cherry Hill - and inside this suitcase is the money," he huffed, setting the suitcase down.

Bart's dentures almost fell out of his mouth hearing that. "You must be joking?" he replied.

"No, the money's all there," Abby answered.

Bart glanced down at the suitcase then looked up at Sid as if to say - how much.

"Five hundred and twenty thousand dollars," rolled off Sid's tongue. Bart sighed thinking of the time it would take to count that much. He glanced down at the suitcase again. "Are you sure you have that much in there, Mrs. Rose?"

"Yes, and possibly more," Abby remarked.

"OK..." he slowly replied. "Follow me, please."

Forty-five minutes later, with one hundred dollar bills stacked to the ceiling, Bart, and his assistant manager, Anny Hasting, had it all counted. Bart saw Abby and Sid out and then shut the door. "Call the Mayor, Anny," he deeply sighed, shaking his head.

"I have the Mayor on line one, Mr. Hornsby."

"Good," Bart replied, walking up to the counter and taking the phone from her.

"Hello, Bart. What can I do for you?" Mayor Bumpkin asked.

"I just wanted you to know that Sid just brought down a Mrs. Rose who has just purchased the old manor up on Cherry Hill."

"Yes, I'm well aware of that, Bart."

"Well, maybe you should sit down before I tell you how she paid for it."

Mayor Bumpkin raised his brow. "Please, I'm all ears."

"She paid in cash right out of a suitcase."

Mayor Bumpkin sat down. "All of it?"

"Every penny and that's not all. There was plenty more inside when she closed it."

"You don't say! Did she tell you when she's moving in?"

"She said that the moving vans would be pulling in some time this afternoon so I would imagine today, Mayor."

Mayor Bumpkin gasped. "Well then, I better get over there. I cannot allow an elderly woman to be moving into a creepy old place like that without running water or electricity. What would the town folk think of me?"

Bart smiled knowing he had a fantastic comeback. "I can just see it now, Mayor – you being dragged through the streets by your heels as people toss eggs and tomatoes at you for allowing an old lady to move into absolute squalor."

Mayor Bumpkin cringed with that thought. "You're right, I'd better get moving," he replied and then hung up.

Bart laughed hanging up the phone.

Don shook his head when Sid walked in.

"What's that look for?" Sid asked, rounding his desk and sitting down.

"You – don't you have any morals?" Don snidely remarked.

"Morals?"

"Yes, we both know that it only cost ten thousand dollars to bring the manor up to city code. You went and added another ten thousand on top of that. How could you do that to that charming old lady?"

Sid sat back lifting his shoes up on his desk. "Man, you really know how to thank me. Kevin Meeks, the owner of this fine real estate agency just made a cool fifteen thousand on *our sale!* And what do we get? A measly two hundred dollars each for selling a forty-room estate," he replied and then paused. "Now you know we've never had any problems with tampering with the sale profits. Why, Mr. Meeks trusts us with his very soul."

Don shook his head. "I don't like this one, Sid. It's too much money to hide and then siphon out of the account."

"Oh, will you stop worrying? I have it all figured out. Tomorrow I'll simply transfer the ten thousand into the real estate general account and then we'll draw it out over a period of a few days. Mr. Meeks will never suspect a thing," he said and then paused, thinking of another angle to stop Don from worrying. "Just imagine being able to give your darling sweet wife, Sue, something nice. I'm sure a five-thousand-dollar present would make her happy enough to do just about anything," he continued, raising his brow.

Don sat back listening to Sid rambling on. Sure, he knew his wife would like something nice, and she'd probably do tricks for him receiving a nice lavish present. On the other hand, though, screwing a buyer out of that much money was absolutely crazy. *One hundred here – two hundred there was OK. But five thousand dollars each. That's jail time.*

"You look like you're dreaming about all that money, Don," Sid said.

Don shifted his eyes on him. "If we get caught, Sid, you can bet your sweet ass that I'll confess to not knowing a thing. Well, that's what I'll say when they slap us in cuffs."

Sid laughed. "No one is going to be slapping us in cuffs – certainly not Roy Roger and his sidekick, Tonto."

Don smiled hearing those names. Roy Roger was Roy Collins, the Cloverdale Sheriff, and Tonto was Larry Oxford, Collins' trusted Deputy. They were two bumbling idiots.

"Besides, Don," he continued, taking Don out of his thoughts, "you should have seen the money still left inside that suitcase."

"No…." he gasped, seeing the look in Sid's eyes. "Don't even think about it, Sid."

"Well just remember, my fine-feathered friend, who's minding the store."

Don wrinkled his brow.

"That white stuffed lion, Theodore."

Don shook his head thinking - *a stuffed lion of all things to be guarding a suitcase full of money.*

3

A Surprise Visit

Mayor Bumpkin drove up the long manor driveway with Claudia Hornsby, who, for all practical matters, ran the town of Cloverdale through the Women's Club. She was tall, boxy and full of vinegar. Mayor Bumpkin put up with her obnoxious demeanor because her husband, Bart, managed the Cloverdale bank.

"I just can't see an old lady so pleased to want to move right in," Claudia spewed, looking at the dilapidated place with its round bell tower standing higher than any other part of the roof.

"Well, it looks like she is," Mayor Bumpkin replied, looking at the movers hauling Mrs. Rose's things inside. He pulled in behind the huge trucks, got out and walked around to the other side opening Claudia's door. "Now, Mayor Bumpkin," Claudia said, getting out. "Let me do all the talking. I'm sure I can convince her not to move in until the city contractors come out and at least hook up some power and turn the water back on."

"Claudia," he replied, fixing his tie. "I am the Mayor and it's my job to do the talking."

"Oh poppycock, Mayor Bumpkin. When you start talking even the pigeons laugh."

"Nonsense," he scolded, turning and walking toward the door. "Excuse me," he asked, stopping one of the men walking out. "Where is Mrs. Rose?"

"She's standing in the parlor directing the men carrying in her items."

"You'd better get in there fast," Claudia scolded, giving his backside a shove.

Through the door and around some boxes, Mayor Bumpkin and Claudia spotted Mrs. Rose pointing this way and that as the movers came through the door with her items. "Please be extremely careful with that crate. It needs to go upstairs in the master's chambers near the terrace," Abby ordered, looking at the small crate. It was her father's miniature tree – a very special tree.

While standing there looking at the small crate going up the stairs, she flooded back in time; back to when her father had her close her eyes and spin in a circle during her tenth birthday party. She remembered feeling spices and herbs falling on her head as her father whispered, '*Red belly frog legs jump over me –*

when you're in need of money - just sing to the tree.' She didn't know then what he was doing, but over time her parents sat her down and told her a secret – a very big secret which went all the way back to when her father was summoned to the village of Nome before he married her mother, Amelia.

After the clan of witches accepted Derek's decision to marry Amelia, Derek's grandmother, Hilda, gave him a jar with a truly special seed inside. It was a money tree seed. You see… the clan of witches never had to work. It was one of the reasons they didn't need to send their children off to a proper school like Derek's parents wanted for him.

"Good afternoon, Mrs. Rose, I'm Mayor Bumpkin and this is Claudia Hornsby from the Women's Club," he greeted her, shifting his eyes to the stuffed white lion in her arms.

Abby stepped out of her thoughts looking at the Mayor. "Oh, I'm sorry. I didn't see you two coming through the door. Glad to make your acquaintances," she replied, pointing to another mover coming in with a box. "That goes in the den over here," she continued and then turned to face the Mayor. "Now, what can I do for you, Mayor Bumpkin?"

"Mrs. Rose," Claudia replied, stepping up. "You may not know this, but this place needs to be brought up to code before you can move in."

Gee, that's a great way to start, Mayor Bumpkin thought. Abby looked at the little man who seemed out of place with this woman standing next to him. Claudia was twice his size in every department. She glanced up at Claudia. "Well, I am aware of that. However, after signing the contract with Sid and handing over the money, the place is rightfully mine, is it not?"

"Yes, yes, the place is now yours," Mayor Bumpkin agreed.

"But you still have to follow the rules, Mrs. Rose," Claudia added.

"Oh now, rules are just rules – and as you can see, all my belongings have arrived and with that I must move in."

"Yes, you can move your belongings in." Mayor Bumpkin replied, "However, where are you going to be staying while I can have the city contractors come in?"

"Here with Theodore, where else would I go?" Abby sprouted back, rubbing Theodore's head.

"Here?!" Claudia gasped. "What if something happens to you while you're all alone up here, Mrs. Rose? Will *he* rescue you?" she continued, pointing at the stuffed toy lion in her arms.

"Now, Claudia, I'm not worried about anything happening to me up here. And besides...," Abby replied, turning around when a mover walked in.

"Excuse me, ma'am, the crate containing the huge tub, I was told that it's going upstairs."

"Yes, and please be very careful handling it. It's a family heirloom purchased in the late seventeen hundreds."

"Well, we're afraid of these stairs, ma'am. We could have a crane hoist it up to the master's chambers windows."

Abby sighed. "For now, let's just store it in the ballroom with all the other non-essential items."

Claudia's temper was about to ignite with all this ridiculous nonsense.

"Hold on," she bellowed, raising her hand in the air. "I want all you men outside, right now."

Mayor Bumpkin glared at her.

"You too, Mayor if you're going to stand there and pout," she scolded, turning and looking at Mrs. Rose. "Do you have any idea how big this place is?"

Abby sighed under her breath. *This place,* she thought. *Call it what you want - a manor, a mansion, or just a place, it's still my home - the home I grew up in.* "Yes, I know how big it is. It has approximately forty rooms in all. And, if I may be so inclined my dear child, the manor has one master's chambers, eight guest bedrooms with baths, a ballroom, two studies, a parlor, dining area, a kitchen, a den, a billiard room, an indoor pool and sauna, two maid's quarters, one butler's quarter, a sewing room, and lastly, four pantries, and that doesn't include the wine cellar and the carpentry workshop down in the basement."

Claudia almost fell over hearing her rattling off such details. "Mrs. Rose, my husband and I live in a two-story, three bedroom home with one full bath, one half bath, a small dining room, kitchen and front room, At our age, that's getting too much to manage. So how on earth are you going to manage all this on your own?"

Abby smiled. "One room at a time, I suppose."

"One room at a time!?" Claudia gasped, staring at Mayor Bumpkin. She could tell by the expression on his face that he wasn't going to step into this argument.

"It feels like home already," Abby beamed, looking about the interior. "Why, with just a little cleaning and painting, this manor will look brand new. You'll see."

Claudia looked at the enormous parlor and then up the grand staircase. She wondered if rats would even move into this dilapidated monstrosity. "Now, Mrs. Rose," her voice softened. "Do you honestly think that Mayor Bumpkin and I would allow such a fragile woman like yourself to live up here all alone without electricity or running water?"

"I..." Abby went to speak.

Claudia raised her hand - she wasn't through. "And besides," she continued, leaning over. "What would the town folks think of us if we did allow you to stay?"

Abby was about to reply when she saw a mover poking his head into the parlor. "Excuse me, please. We'd like to finish sometime today," the man said, looking at the big woman and the Mayor standing there.

Abby cast her eyes on Claudia. Claudia shook her head.

"Please continue," Abby said to the man.

The next thing coming through the door was a tall crate strapped to a dolly. "Please be extremely careful with that. That's also a family heirloom," Abby said. Inside the tall crate was Grandfather.

"Certainly, ma'am, where would you like it?"

"Set it down over there," she replied, pointing at the wall next to the

foyer. After the men unstrapped the crate and left, Abby turned and faced Mayor Bumpkin and Claudia. "Now, where were we?"

"We were deciding on where you'll be staying. Now, before we came up, I called Karen Bloom who said she'd love to have you stay with her and her husband, Albert. They live just down the hill on Daisy Lane," Claudia said. Abby gave that a thought. She stepped in between the pair. "Look you two - I'll make you a bet. Let me stay here tonight, and if anything happens… then you have a deal," she said, with a sly wink.

Mayor Bumpkin's face went flush. *The old lady must be a kook,* he thought, looking about the place. *I wouldn't stay in this rundown heap - even with the lights on all night.*

"Now, Mrs. Rose," Claudia started to say.

Abby raised her hand to the big woman. "That's the deal, now if you please," she replied, turning and facing the men coming through the door. "That goes in the dining area, gentlemen."

Mayor Bumpkin glanced at Claudia. She saw the look his eyes; they were not going to persuade Mrs. Rose. *What else can we do?* she thought. *Wait a minute,* her thoughts spun. *We'll go along with Mrs. Rose's deal. Why, one night sleeping in this run down shack Mrs. Rose will be begging to move in with Karen and Albert.* “Alright, Mrs. Rose. We’ll take you up on your bet,” she said.

Mayor Bumpkin cleared his throat. Claudia raised her brow to him.

“Good.” Abby replied, smiling.

“OK,” Claudia said. “We’ll be here at dawn. I am sure you’ll be waiting out front for us to come get you. Now let’s go, Mayor Bumpkin. Mrs. Rose has a lot to get organized.”

4

Three Little Mice

Abby saw them out and then finished up with the movers. After the trucks had left, she set Theodore down, shut the door and sighed. "We have so much to do," she said, waving her hand over Theodore. WHOOSH - he came to life. "We have a big night ahead of us."

"I can see that, Madam Rose," Theodore replied, looking at all the boxes and crates. "But where to start," he continued.

"Mm mmmm…" a muffled sound came from within the tall crate next to the wall.

"Oh dear me…. Grandfather!" Abby gasped, hustling over to him. "Hurry, Theodore, open the crate."

Theodore pulled on the boards until the nails came out. "Ah… fresh air," Grandfather sighed.

"By your minute hand spinning I can tell that you're upset," Abby said.

Grandfather rolled his eyes watching his minute hand going around and around. It slowed then stopped. "What time is it?" he asked.

Abby looked down at her watch. "It's seven p.m."

Grandfather slowly moved his minute and hour hand to meet the time. Then suddenly, there was a knocking sound coming from the tall box across the parlor. Abby shook her head walking over. She pulled open the box. "Well, it's about time," Sir Henry gasped.

"I'm sorry, Sir Henry. Today has just been a mess."

"I can see that," he replied, seeing all the boxes stacked to the ceiling. He looked over at Grandfather. Grandfather lifted his chin. It made Abby pout. "Now listen you two," she started to say, walking to the center of the parlor and folding her arms. "Theodore is Lord of this house."

They looked at Theodore raising his head up high with that comment - as if he were king.

"Now, I want you two to settle your differences or, Theodore will," she continued, turning and winking at him. Theodore knew it was just a bluff to get them to stop bickering amongst themselves. He walked over and looked up at Grandfather. He then turned and looked at Sir Henry. Sir Henry stared into

Theodore's dazzling, blue eyes. Theodore tightened his brow glaring back at him. Sir Henry swallowed.

"Alright now, no more squabbling, we have lots to do," she said, turning around. "Theodore, let's bring them out and have them placed by the door where they can supervise," she continued, smiling at him.

By her smile, Theodore knew that she was trying to make Grandfather and Sir Henry feel better.

With Sir Henry and Grandfather standing in their places, Abby gave the orders: "I want Madelyn and Rebecca with their cleaning crew: buckets, mops and scrub brushes front and center." Madelyn, Abby's blue broom and Rebecca, Abby's red broom, along with their crew, all scampered out of their boxes and stood in a line. "Grandfather," Abby said, wanting him to put them to work.

Grandfather cleared his throat. "The master's chambers and kitchen will be done first. Rebecca and the red team will clean the master's chambers and Madelyn and the blue team will start with the kitchen."

"Why do we always get the kitchen?" Madelyn complained.

"Sir Henry," Grandfather said.

"If I recall," Sir Henry said and then paused. "Grandfather is in charge of maintenance cleaning around here. In the future, I will suggest to him that you take turns cleaning certain parts of the manor. Fair enough?"

"In the future," Madelyn harshly remarked, turning and looking at Madam Rose. All she got back was a stiff upper chin. "Come, cleaners, we have a job to do," she continued, walking toward the corridor.

"Madam Rose," Theodore said.

She turned and looked at him. "Nightfall is approaching. We'll need candles."

"Oh yes," she replied, knowing they'd be working throughout the night. "Come, I think they put those boxes in the dining area," she continued, walking toward the corridor.

After Abby and Theodore had left, Grandfather looked over at Sir Henry standing opposite of him in the foyer. "Did you notice that they placed me inside a crate and put you inside a box?"

"And what is the meaning of that, may I ask?"

"You heard Madam Rose - she called me a family heirloom," Grandfather commented.

Sir Henry gave a long sigh to his snide remark. *He's trying to goad me,* he thought. *Right after Madam Rose cut the discord between us - or more so - Theodore. Now Grandfather wants to continue the bickering.* "Since I'm from Royalty, I will not debate with you about such nonsense, Grandfather."

Grandfather rolled his eyes.

"That will not help your cause either."

"You know, Sir Henry. You really wind me up with your outdated English accent and grammar. Did King Louie the Third speak like that too?"

"He most certainly did."

"Most certainly, you say."

"Of course. In our time, proper grammar was a sign of intelligence, which I see you harbor none."

"There you go again."

When Abby and Theodore retrieved the candleholders and candles, she snapped her finger and flames appeared on the wicks. "There, now let's place these about the house," she said, walking into the kitchen.

"How are we supposed to work in here with all these boxes," Madelyn asked, sweeping a pile of dust into the dustpan.

"Just have the bucket and scrub brushes do the counters, cupboards and sink then Hansel will start organizing the kitchen. We'll do the floor last after everything is done."

"Yes, Madam Rose."

Abby set a candle in a holder near the sink and walked out with Theodore. She went into the parlor and placed a candle upon the mantelpiece. As she entered the den, she looked up and was surprised to see Boris, her father's favorite moose head, hanging over the wood-grained mantelpiece. She stepped back, raised her candlestick high in the air and looked at Boris. *How did I not see him this afternoon?* she thought, looking at the dust and cobwebs draped all over him. *"Moonlight dancing upon a stream - it's time to wake up and come out of your dreams, Boris,"* she said, waving her hand.

Boris blinked and then sneezed, "Achoo."

"Well, bless you."

He looked down to see someone standing there.

"Hello, Boris."

"Hello to you - whoever you are."

"It's me, Abigail."

"Abigail?"

"Yes."

Boris shifted his eyes on Theodore sitting there. "Well, will somebody pull my antlers? Abigail, you look…" his voice trailed off.

"Old?"

"That wasn't the word I was going to use," he replied and then sneezed again, "Achoo."

"My, my, there must be a ton of dust up there."

"There sure is," he replied and then sneezed again. "Now, where was I?"

"Something about being old, I think."

"You're not old."

"Oh now, let's not be kidding ourselves. I'm older than when you saw me last."

Boris cocked his head. "That means," he started to say, "I've must have been asleep for a very long time?"

"Yes, you have, and you look as if you've been asleep since the dinosaurs roamed the earth with all those cobwebs hanging off you."

Boris shifted his eyes from side to side looking at the dust and spider webs. He shook his massive antlers. Dust and webbing flew everywhere.

"Achoo," he sneezed.

"Bless you again."

"Thank you. Now can you tell me what has been going on around here since I've been asleep?"

"That, my dear moose, would take days and weeks. I'll have a team of cleaners come in and dust you off soon. Right now, I'm heading upstairs."

"I am glad you've come back, Abigail, which means…" his voice trailed off, looking toward the foyer. "Are Grandfather and Sir Henry here too?"

"We're standing over here, Boris. It's so nice to see you again," Grandfather spoke up.

Sir Henry turned and cleared his throat. "Boris, my mighty friend from the forest, I've missed the sight of you," he greeted him.

"Missed the sight of you," Grandfather spewed, rolling his eyes.

Boris looked down at Abby. "I see nothing has changed," he remarked.

"Not at all, they're still fighting like cats and dogs," she replied, walking toward the stairs. "See you all in the morning."

Before taking the stairs up, she had a thought. "I think we better go down and check the basement and wine cellar, Theodore."

Theodore nodded, following her through the corridor. When Abby opened the basement door in the kitchen, she stretched her candlestick out over the steps leading down. "Those steps look pretty steep. Maybe you should go first."

"My pleasure, Madam Rose," Theodore replied, heading down.

"Shh… did you hear that?" a little mouse whispered.

"What?" another one said.

"It sounds like someone's coming down the basement steps."

"Oh will you stop with the nonsense. There hasn't been anyone here in years."

"No, listen. Someone is coming down."

As Theodore proceeded down, one little mouse looked up to see big paws, huge legs and then the majestic face of a lion. "It's Theodore! Run for your lives!!"

"It can't be!" another mouse replied, looking up the steps and seeing the big cat. "Runnnnnnnnn…" he yelled.

As Abby nervously took the steps down, she thought she heard little voices. Then suddenly, she saw Theodore pick up his pace and ran down the remaining steps toward the basement floor. Abby hurried down pushing the cobwebs aside just in time to see three little mice scampering across the floor toward the corner. She lifted her candlestick high in the air and caught sight of them jumping up onto old crates that were stacked in the corner near the basement window which was open. She quickly waved her hand. The window shut just as two were about to escape. "Hold it right there," she ordered, looking at the two and then down at the one still standing on one of the crates. "Turn around," she scolded.

All three slowly turned. Their little legs were shaking seeing Theodore standing there licking his chops.

"And who might you three be?" she asked.

"I'm Wilson."

"I'm Cracker."

She looked at the one still standing on the crate. "I'm Benjamin," the little mouse nervously replied.

Abby caught her breath. "You can't be," she gasped, setting her candlestick down on a small dust covered table. She looked at the three grey mice - one in particular, the one with the small, black marking around his eye - *Cracker*. She focused on the one standing alongside him. He had a white marking on his belly - *Wilson.* She cast her eyes down at the one on the crate with just the tip of his tail black – *Benjamin.*

"Who are you may I ask?" Wilson said.

Abby stood there in awe. They were her father's mice. The ones he used in his magic acts. "I can't believe I'm seeing the three of you. It's me, Abigail."

"Abby," the three replied, stunned. "The last time we saw you, you were just a little girl," Benjamin spoke up.

"Well, we all grow up you know. So, tell me, how are you still here?"

Wilson looked at her and frowned. "After your father passed away, his manager, Thomas Pain, let us loose in the backyard. We didn't want to leave. We honestly had nowhere to go, so we thought we'd slip back in and live down here in the basement," he replied.

Abby looked at him, then at Cracker and then she cast her eyes down on Benjamin. He gave her a charming little smile back. "Well now, isn't this a hoot," she said. "After my father passed away, I asked Mr. Pain what had happened to you. He said that you three took off for New York. He said something about you three going there and trying to find Max the piano player. And now I can see that surely wasn't the case. Mr. Pain simply let you go and then told me that fib so as not to break my little heart back then."

"Well, he may have saved your little heart from pain, but what about ours," Benjamin whimpered. "He certainly broke our little hearts, didn't he fellas?"

She looked up at Wilson. He slowly nodded with a disapproving look. Abby felt the sorrow she saw in his soft little eyes. She stepped up and asked, "I don't understand how you're all still here though? That was many years ago."

Cracker and Benjamin looked at Wilson. Wilson raised his small bushy eyebrows. She could see he had a story to tell – he always did when they got into trouble. "By the look in your eyes, Wilson, I'm sure to be hearing another one of your mischief stories?"

"Well, Abby…" his voice trailed off. "You see…" he started to say, taking a seat on the windowsill and folding his hands. "As you know, your father took us everywhere he went."

Abby sighed, knowing she was in for a treat. If these three weren't into the cookies and/or the jam, they'd certainly be up to something. She turned her attention back on Wilson.

"Your father liked to take us everywhere he went. However, the times we spent at the manor we were free to frolic and play."

"I know all too well," she sighed. "Go on."

"Well, our favorite place to play was with your father up in his study. He'd always be tinkering with new magic acts with us. Once he had an idea, he'd tell us to stay there while he went up into the bell tower. That's where he kept your great grandmother's Potion and Spells book."

Abby's ears shot up. She needed to know where that book was now. It was extremely important. "Did you three actually ever see the book back then?" she asked.

"Yes. This is the good part, right Wilson," Cracker spoke up.

Abby looked at Cracker. *There were never any 'good parts' in their mischief.*

"Yes, we did. You see, it was on one of those cold and rainy days and your father decided to leave us at the house when he went into town. We were bored… so… we thought we'd climb into the bell tower. That's when we saw the book. It was sitting there on your father's desk. We each took a hold of the cover and opened it, and that's how we got into trouble."

"Trouble!? You three… never," she shockingly professed.

"Yes, but this time it was more than trouble. We came across a certain spell. It was confusing at first. Then Cracker came up with a way it had to be said in order for it to work," Wilson confessed.

"Work?" she questioned.

"Yes. It was a riddle of sorts. So, the three of us held hands and said the words aloud. Then Wham! It felt as if the whole sky fell on top of us. When we woke up lying there, your father was standing over us looking as mean as ever," Wilson replied.

"He was awful mad," Cracker whispered.

"I'm sure he was. So… what was the spell?" she asked, folding her arms.

"It was a spell for long… for long… I'm trying to remember.... oh, what was it again?"

"Longevity," Benjamin said.

"That's it. For longevity, whatever that means," Wilson repeated.

"Longevity!" she gasped.

"Yes. It went like this: "*Dribble drabble, dribble drum, a cork barrel full of Rum… go to sleep and…."*

"Stop, stop!" she shouted and then sighed. "You must be careful with those spells. Repeating them can cause all kinds of headaches.

"Headaches?" Benjamin questioned.

"Not those kind of headaches, Benjamin. I meant trouble."

"Oh…" he replied, holding his little paws over his mouth.

"Yes," she scolded, looking at Wilson. "Longevity means long life."

"Oh…" Cracker replied and then chuckled. "*That's* why we haven't aged."

Abby shook her head looking at the three. *Cracker is right - they haven't aged at all.* "Now if I may ask," she said, stepping forward. "How many times have you used that spell?

They all looked at one another. Wilson put out his paw and started counting his fingers. He then held up four fingers. "This many, I think."

"That many! No wonder you're still young," she replied, thinking. *I've got to find that book. Without it, my plans will never work.* She looked at her three little friends and smiled while raising her brow. "You three wouldn't, by any chance, know where that book is right now, would you?"

The three glanced at one another and then looked at her. "No. You see, when your father found us, that was more trouble than a headache, Abby. Your father scolded us something terrible for using that spell. After he kicked us out of the bell tower, we never saw the book again," Wilson said, with a long drawn expression.

Abby slowly nodded while shifting her eyes at Theodore sitting there. She looked up at the mice. "OK, gentlemen. I have a mission for you three," she said.

"Really?" Cracker replied.

"Yes. I want you three to find that book for me."

They all looked at one another again wondering where it could be.

"Theodore," she said, bringing Wilson, Benjamin and Cracker out of their thoughts. "Let's see if we can find those old cigar boxes and that little house," she continued, smiling at her little friends. "Welcome home, fellas," she delightfully beamed.

Wilson and Cracker jumped down from the windowsill and stood next to Benjamin. "We'll search every nook and cranny for that book, Abby," Wilson assured her, while shifting his eyes on Theodore. Wilson's smile disappeared, drifting back to when Theodore used to chase them about the house at night while Abby was asleep. *I'm certainly not going to put up with that anymore,* he thought. "Can we finally be friends, Theodore?" he asked.

Abby gazed at Wilson and then cast her eyes down on Theodore.

"Theodore?" she said in a questioning manner. Theodore glared at Wilson and then slowly turned his head and looked up at her. "They were fun to play with at night."

"Play with?!" Cracker spat. "You were always scaring the daylights out of us!"

Abby knew the game oh so well – cat and mouse. It made her mad. She folded her arms. "I'm sorry. I was just a little girl and I did not know that Theodore was acting that way while I was asleep. However, now that I am Queen Bee around here, there will be none of that," she said, eyeing up Theodore. Theodore could feel her stare. It made him angry. "From now on, Theodore will be your protector – isn't that right, Theodore?"

Theodore swallowed his pride. "As you command, Madam Rose," he replied.

Wilson looked at Benjamin. Benjamin turned and looked at Cracker. Then they all cast their eyes on Theodore. "No more games at night?" Wilson asked.

"Certainly not," Theodore replied.

"Good," Abby said, heading toward the wine cellar. After she had left, Theodore stepped up to the little runts. "You three together wouldn't even be a morsel," he whispered, then turned and followed Abby into the cellar.

Wilson patted Benjamin on the back. "It looks like we're finally home, fellas."

"Yeah, and on a mission to boot. Where shall we start searching?" Cracker asked.

Wilson smiled at his comrades. "Let's start up in the bell tower and work our way down. But, before we start, let's go and see Wilfred out in the garage."

"Yeah," Benjamin spouted. "It's been a long time since we've chatted with him."

Just down the hill from the manor, Karen Bloom, who lived on Daisy Lane, got up from her bed and made her way through the dark to the bathroom. She stopped at the window, stunned to what she saw. She opened the drawn curtain to see lights on inside the manor up on Cherry Hill. "Albert," she whispered. Her husband rolled over snoring. "Albert," she whispered again.

"What, what?" he said, still in a haze.

"There are lights on up in the manor."

"Did you slip and fall? There haven't been lights on in that old place for close to a hundred years."

"No, I'm serious. Come take a look."

Albert sat up, rubbed his eyes and got out of bed. "Well I'll be. I thought the old woman was going to be staying with us after Mayor Bumpkin and Claudia went up to talk with her?"

"Claudia called me afterward," Karen replied. "They'll be going back up there in the morning to see if Mrs. Rose has changed her mind."

Albert looked at his wife and then slowly turned and looked out the window again. He hated the place looming there - as if it were watching them. The sight of it crawled up his backside like spiders dancing on his skin. "What person in their right mind would want to live up there?" he said more to himself than to his wife.

"I don't know, Albert. But you wouldn't catch me in that place without an army going in first."

"Me either! Now let's go back to sleep before the sun comes up," he replied, turning for the bed.

Karen watched him slip under the covers. She turned and glanced out the window one more time. *That old woman must be half out of her mind, or,* she thought, *completely stir-crazy*. She let the curtain go and headed into the bathroom.

5

Rekindling Friendships

Wilson nudged his friends then jumped down to the floor. “Come on,” he yelled, scampering toward the corner where there was an opening in a pipe sticking out from the wall.

“Let’s go, Benjamin,” Cracker said

Before Benjamin ran after them, he checked to see where Theodore was. He smiled. Theodore had his back to him not paying any attention at all. He quickly leapt off the crate and made a mad dash.

Up the dirty pipe they went until they came out onto the back lawn. Wilson and Cracker holed up until Benjamin appeared. “Last one to the garage is a rotten egg,” Cracker shouted, turning and running through the high grass. Wilson looked at Benjamin. “Are you going to play that stupid game?” Benjamin shook his head. “Good,” Wilson chuckled, turning and running. “It looks like you’re the rotten egg,” he laughed, scampering through the grass after Cracker.

Benjamin shook his head. He looked up into the vast night sky. “You see what I have to put up with,” he said to the moon and stars above. With that, he took off after his friends.

Past the tall trees, over the cobble pavers, Cracker ran until he reached the garage’s wooden doors. When Wilson joined him, they turned to see Benjamin. “What took ya so long?” Cracker asked.

“You two,” Benjamin spewed. “Next time you’ll only see the dust off my feet.”

“That’ll be the day,” Cracker laughed.

“Alright, let’s get inside,” Wilson said, walking through the knothole at the bottom of the door.

As they walked in, they saw Wilfred sitting there bathed in the moonlight streaming down through the dilapidated roof.

“Wilfred!” Wilson excitedly said, extending his arms upward.

Wilfred opened his eyes. “Who’s there?” he asked, turning on his side kerosene lamps.

“We are,” Cracker replied, walking up alongside Wilson.

Wilfred looked down. His tin brow went up. "No… it can't be!" he gasped.

"Well count your blessings my old friend. It's us - we're back." Benjamin said to his startled expression.

"But how… It's been…" his voice trailed off.

"It's a long story. You mind if we climb aboard?" Wilson asked.

"Sure, I don't get many visitors."

"Well, those days are over," Wilson replied, walking around to Wilfred's wheel. He jumped onto one of the spokes, shimmied up to the top of the tire and then leaped across to Wilfred's hood.

Wilfred watched Benjamin and Cracker run around and do the same. They all sat down between his headlights.

"So," Wilfred said. "Are you going to tell me?"

Wilson glanced at his friends – they both nodded. "We used one of Baron Von Haussler's magic spells," he replied, lifting one little leg over the other and then folding his arms.

"Well… I'll be," Wilfred remarked, drifting back in time. He remembered Baron Von Haussler strolling out to the garage one afternoon madder than a hornet hitting the windshield. He was mumbling something about the mice getting into a mess again. Wilfred sighed with that thought. *Maybe that's when it happened. They were always getting into some sort of trouble when left all alone,* he mused. He shifted his eyes inward looking up at them sitting there. "Does Madam Rose know you're still here?"

"Yes," Cracker replied. "Well, it was Theodore who discovered us. You know that nose of his."

"Yes I do," Wilfred replied, thinking of Theodore. He could smell a bloodhound a half a mile away and that was always trouble. He couldn't remember how many dogs Theodore had chased off the property back then. If the town folk ever got wind of Theodore, it would have been curtains. Baron Von Haussler would have had a lot of explaining to do about keeping a male lion at the manor.

That thought brought him full circle. He could still recall the day Theodore arrived at the house. The Baron and Amelia had taken Abby to the Cloverdale County Fair. She was so excited to go. All those rides and games, and lots of sugar coated things to eat.

"Where's my gorgeous fraulein and that beautiful baby girl of mine?" Derek yelled up the stairs.

"We're coming, daddy," little Abby replied, holding onto her mother's hand as they walked down the huge circular staircase. *This was right before he had the elevator installed. Trips up and down became much easier then.*

"Well, you two are sure ready for the county fair today," Derek said with a beaming smile.

Amelia had picked out a yellow summer dress and had Abby in a pretty pink dress. Both were wearing hats with flowers attached to them. Derek opened the double doors and escorted them out to the car. Abby just loved Wilfred. She loved sitting up in the rumble seat alongside her mother, with the top down, when they all went out for a Sunday drive. Today, however, they were going to the county fair.

Wilfred sighed, thinking back to the good old days when he felt important chauffeuring the family around town. He remembered driving up to the Davenport farm where Mr. Davenport allowed the town to use the family's side acreage between planting seasons to put on the county fair. Derek pulled up and parked right by the gate that year. He watched them get out and walk into the fairgrounds with Abby holding each of their hands. Then suddenly, Abby stopped at one of the booths right near the entrance. She was pointing at something. He watched her father walk up, hand the man in the booth some coins, and the man gave Derek three balls to throw. Well, knowing the Baron, Wilfred knew he would hit the target every time, and bingo, top prize was a beautiful, white stuffed lion.

Abby was so excited with her present and she named him Theodore. He went everywhere with her. Then, on Abby's fifth birthday, her father gave her a huge surprise by tossing a magical spell over Theodore and he came to life.

Derek's lovely wife, Amelia, frowned on it at first. "How in Heaven's name are we going to manage having a full male lion roaming the house?" she scoffed. Abby's beaming smile melted her mother's worries away. "Don't worry, Mom," she said. "I'll look after Theodore. He'll be no problem at all, you'll see." Well, they could only wish that were true, but in the end, he was more trouble than they could swing a broomstick at. Her mother never once complained about Theodore when he'd get out of line. Amelia would just scream for Abby.

Wilfred smiled thinking of hearing Abby's name all the way out to the garage. "Abbbbbbbbbby!" When Abby showed up, good old Theodore would just roll over like a kitten for her.

"Hey, Wilfred," Cracker spoke up, bringing Wilfred out of his thoughts.

"Yes?"

"You by chance wouldn't know where the Baron hid his magic Potion and Spells book, would you?"

"No, and why do you ask?"

"Abby wants us to find it."

"Pray-tell."

"Yes. She put us on a mission to locate it."

"Hmm," Wilfred replied, pondering that. *These three on a mission was like sending kids in to mind a candy store.* "That, my little friend, I cannot help you with. All I know is this garage and I can tell you right now that it's not here."

"I suppose not," Wilson, yawned. "You mind if we sleep in your rumble seat tonight?"

"Not at all. Would you like my soft top up or down?"

"Down," Benjamin replied.

"OK, here we go," Wilfred replied, lowering the top.

They stood up and watched it go down. "There you are," Wilfred said.

Wilson took off across the hood, skirted around the windshield and then ran along the top of the door. There, he leaped down onto the rumble seat. Cracker looked at Benjamin and smiled. "You don't think I can do that?" Benjamin questioned the look in Cracker's eyes.

"Nope," Cracker replied, turning and running across the hood toward the windshield.

Benjamin stood there shaking his head. *One day I am going to run right over them to the finish line - then they'll see who's the best,* he thought, running across the hood. Ten minutes later, Wilfred heard the pleasant sounds of snoring. He closed his eyes and went to sleep himself.

Abby walked out of the wine cellar and headed over to the basement steps. She looked at the windowsill. The mice were gone. "Now where do you suppose they went?"

"Let's find out," Theodore replied, placing his nose to the ground. Abby watched him walk over to the pipe sticking out of the wall near the floor.

"They went up here," Theodore said, lifting his head and looking back at her.

Abby gave a pleasant smile. "I guess they're out visiting with Wilfred."

"Yes, I am sure they are," Theodore replied, flashing back to when he'd chased them out of the house. They were the best game in town, especially at night when he could scare the living daylights out of them.

After opening the basement door and walking into the kitchen, Madelyn, the red broom, spoke up. "Madame Rose, I think you forgot Hansel," she said, nodding toward the box on the counter that was rocking back and forth.

"Oh, my word," Abby replied, walking over and opening it. "I am so sorry, Hansel," she gushed, setting Hansel down on the counter.

Hansel stood up. "Well, as the day is long, so was sitting inside that box. When can I expect the rest of the utensils, pots and pans, glasses, and the likes to be set free?"

"Now, Hansel, it's been quite a day and I'm hoping by tomorrow we can start getting this kitchen in order," she replied, looking at the oversized box next to the wall. It was Simon, her fridge, and she hoped he was asleep. He was, most of the time anyway.

Hansel lowered her eyes to Theodore. Theodore gave her a look as if he were king, and rightly so, he was around here. "Well, I guess the best place to stand while this is all going on is over by the sink."

"Yes, Hansel my dear, that would be a good place for you to relax until we get everything back to normal," Abby replied, turning and walking out.

"Tonight, Theodore, I think after we gather my little tree from out of its box, I'll just lie down on my mattress. I'm sure we can find a rug for you to lie on, if you care to join me?" she said, walking down the corridor toward the staircase.

"It would be my pleasure, Madame Rose."

When they entered the master's chambers, Abby stopped in her tracks seeing Rebecca, her red broom, jumping up and down in the moonlight streaming through the window. "What is going on in here?" Abby gasped. Rebecca quickly stopped jumping and spun around. "Oh, I am so glad you're here, Madam Rose. Our duster is caught in the spider webs up there," she replied.

Abby sighed seeing the duster caught in a ray of old dirty webbing around the chandelier. She walked over to Rebecca. "If you don't mind," she said, reaching out and grabbing her handle and flipping Rebecca over.

"Madam Rose!" Rebecca gasped, upside down. Abby reached up using Rebecca's broom bristles to get the duster down. Bang… The duster hit the floor. "Oh, my head," the duster moaned.

"Sorry, I hope you're alright?" Abby asked, worried.

The duster got up still in a spin. "Yes, I think so, Madam Rose."

"Good. That will be all for tonight, cleaners. Please go down and dust-off Boris before you head to the closet. There will be lots to do in the days ahead."

After they drifted out the door, Abby frowned from the staleness in the air. She strolled over and opened the big windows. "Hmm… that's better," she quipped, turning and looking down at the small box. She waved her hand and watched the box open, exposing a gorgeous little tree sitting inside a pot. Abby sat down, set her candlestick on the floor and then began rubbing the tiny leaves and branches. "Now, if I can only find where my father hid that Potion and Spells book," she whispered.

Theodore walked over. He looked down at the tree and then cast his dazzling blue eyes upon Abby. "I am sure we'll find it, Madam Rose."

She turned her head and smiled at her majestic lion. Theodore was very special to her, and he looked so grand in the glow of the candlelight with his beautiful blue eyes, his immense white mane, his big powerful chest and his soft white coat. "I'm sure we will, Theodore. Let's just hope those little runts can find it first, before we have to tear this place apart looking for it," she replied, casting her eyes down upon her tree.

Theodore smiled. He liked calling them runts himself.

"Do you remember what my father whispered to me when he had me spin in a circle?"

Theodore could tell that she was drifting back in time now. "Yes, I remember."

"Let's say it together."

"Must we?" he asked, feeling silly.

"Oh now, Theodore, let's have some fun, shall we? Now on the count of three - one, two, three – go…. *Red belly frog legs jump over me, when you're in need of money, just sing to the tree*."

"Now wasn't that fun?"

He raised his lofty brow. “I’m just tingling all over, Madame Rose,” he replied, giggling.

“Oh, you,” she teased, reaching over scratching his chin. “Let’s go to bed. Tomorrow is almost here.

6
Spellbinding Charm

Abby awoke feeling her mouth so dry she could barely swallow when she sat up and opened her eyes. “Psst,” she whispered to Theodore lying there on the rug.

Theodore opened his eyes and yawned, showing his huge canines and his long, pink tongue. He looked over at her sitting there. “Morning already?” he asked.

“Yes, and I feel like I haven't slept a wink,” she replied.

Theodore stood up, shook his massive mane and walked over to her. “I am sorry to say, Madame Rose, the kitchen will not be making us breakfast this morning, and also your bath is out of the question. Brenda is probably pulling out all her porcelain feathers in the ballroom right now.”

Abby sighed at the notion, and she rightly could not remember the last time she found herself in such a predicament. Brenda was still inside a crate in the ballroom, Hansel was downstairs in the kitchen waiting for the rest of her kitchen staff freed from their boxes and then there was Theodore. *Not even a drop of water to put in his bowl. What am I going to do?*

That thought made her think of Claudia and her betting Claudia that she would be just fine up here all alone. *That woman,* Abby’s thoughts spun, *she’s such a pompous busybody.* It took no imagination to guess how Claudia ran things in town. She was the kind of woman who’d run right over you if you got in her way or disagreed with her. *She sure ran over the Mayor yesterday – made him look like a complete buffoon right in front of everyone.* She sighed with that thought, staring out the front windows. Turning her head, she stared at Theodore. “Well, how do I look? And please tell me the truth. I’m sure we don’t have much time before that windbag of a woman shows up.”

Theodore noticed Abby’s soft, facial features marred with dark rolls under each eye, and her hair looked more like a rat’s nest than a beauty queen’s hairdo. And, if that wasn’t enough, the wrinkled clothing she had slept in all night topped off the picture. “You’re a mess,” he sullenly replied.

“That good, am I? Well, I’m glad you’re honest, Theodore. Now let me get up and see what I can do to change that.”

Theodore sat up as Abby got off the mattress. She walked out into the center of the empty master’s chambers and looked down upon herself. “Hmm, let's see now," she whispered. "What rhyme shall I use?" she continued and then paused thinking. "I know…. *Galling winds and soaring tides,*" she started chanting, raising her hands in the air. Theodore covered his eyes with his enormous paws. "*Honey from a Bumble Beehive,*" she continued, turning in a circle. Theodore moaned as smoke started swirling around her. "*Teardrops welling up on a cliff – bring back the beauty of this fine witch,*" she finished, moving her hands upward, still in a spin. Small, colorful, firefly lights began swirling around her within the smoke. Theodore moaned again peeking out from his two front paws. Then WHAM, Abby stopped spinning. She looked down upon herself and smiled.

Theodore lifted one of his paws from off his eyes. There before him, Abby was wearing a beautiful, yellow sunflower dress. Her hair was done up in a bun and he noticed a light pink coloring on both cheeks that matched her lipstick. "Oh my, Madam Rose, you look stunning for sleeping in this run down shack," he laughed.

She smiled at him and then started to laugh remembering Claudia looking about the house as if only rats lived there. As the two made merriment over Claudia's ridiculous antics yesterday, two cars drove up the long driveway toward the manor.

Mayor Bumpkin was all alone in his car and in the other car was Claudia, Karen Bloom and Fanny Chamberlin, all from the Women's Club.

"I never thought I'd be coming up here," Fanny gasped from the back seat, looking at the manor's bell tower and rooftop coming into view. "Who in their right mind would want this place?"

"You're so right, Fanny," Claudia spewed, looking over at Karen in the passenger seat. "Just to let you know, Karen, what you're getting yourself into by allowing Mrs. Rose to come stay with you and Albert while this dump is being repaired, Mrs. Rose is a self-centered little woman who'll stop at nothing to get her way."

"Now really, Claudia," Fanny scolded from the backseat. "Using such words to describe an elderly woman like that. You should be ashamed of yourself."

Claudia took her eyes off the windshield and looked up into the rearview mirror at Fanny. "Trust me. Just wait until you meet her," she replied, focusing her attention back on the driveway.

Fanny sat back in a huff, shaking her head as Claudia continued toward the huge, twenty-acre plateau, which, in its day, was among one of the most spectacular properties in all of Pennsylvania. When they reached the plateau, Fanny gasped, "Will you look at that!" She was always afraid to come up here and check it out. The place looked as creepy as a gothic castle. Oh, she had driven by the Von Haussler Manor on numerous occasions, glimpsing up to see it through the trees, but now it sat right in front of her.

Stretching nearly two hundred feet across the front the manor was a haunting sight. The most impressive part was the entranceway, with its huge sandstone, circular pillars on each side - built straight up to the roof. Her eyes scanned along the decorative metal-framed windows running along both sides of the entranceway. She then cast her eyes upward toward the roof. *My God,* she thought, looking at the two large, cement gothic vultures resting on either side of the entranceway with one over the center, its wings stretched out looking down. And just above that, her eyes took in the rectangular sections of the roof, bell tower and eleven chimneys. The whole thing made her skin crawl right up her backside.

"Yeah, well, if you think the outside is a sight, just wait until you go in," Claudia remarked, bringing Fanny out of her harrowing stare. Karen looked back with big wide eyes. Her facial expression said it all - you did not want to go in. That put a lump in Fanny's throat.

As Abby was packing up her small suitcase, she turned toward the windows. "That sounds like cars coming up the drive."

Theodore looked back toward the windows. "Yes, it does. I think we better put the house to sleep."

Abby thought of Grandfather, Sir Henry, Boris and Hansel. "Yes, we better before they walk in," she replied, turning and walking out with her small suitcase in hand. As they made their way down the stairs, she asked Theodore, "I think I'll leave you here to oversee things while I'm away."

"As you request, Madam Rose."

At the bottom of the stairs, Abby saw three little figures standing in the parlor talking to Grandfather and Sir Henry. They turned around and greeted her. "Good morning, Abby," they said in unison. "Good morning, gentlemen," she replied, looking across at Grandfather.

"Morning, Madam Rose. I hear cars out front," he said.

"Yes, we heard them upstairs," she replied, stepping into the parlor. "Now," she continued, looking down at the mice, "have you three thought of your mission?"

"Yes," Wilson replied.

"Mission. These three on a mission, pray-tell?" Grandfather inquired. "What mission would that be, if I may ask?"

Cracker turned toward Grandfather. "It's a secret mission, so we can't tell you, right Abby?" he replied, looking back at her.

"That's right," she said, smiling.

Cracker then spun around looking up at Theodore. "Not one word out of you either," he warned Theodore. Theodore rolled his eyes toward Abby.

"As you know the mission they're on, Theodore, just remember - secret missions must remain secret," Abby said.

"That's right," Wilson stepped in.

Abby sighed, turned toward the den and greeted Boris. "Good morning, old timer."

"Good morning, Madam Rose. I'm guessing now - you've changed your surname?"

"Yes, Boris and that must remain a secret too. Well, for now at least."

Boris nodded. "My lips are sealed."

"Thank you."

"Hey, Sir Henry - did you hear the mice are on a secret mission?" Grandfather jealously whispered. Abby looked back at him and then at Sir Henry.

"Good morning, Madam Rose," Sir Henry greeted her. Abby nodded. He looked over at Grandfather. "Yes, I heard everything. Now in my day, I was the only one granted to stay in the room when King Louie the Third requested an audience with a man he was going to send out on a secret mission."

"Oh, my word," Grandfather fumed. "I just had to ask, didn't I?"

Sir Henry lifted his chin, and then turned his attention on the mice. "As a humble servant of King Louie the Third, you three can rely on me and hold my confidence in the highest regard. If there is anything I can do to help, just ask."

"Oh, please," Grandfather grumbled, rolling his large silver eyes.

Boris laughed from the den. "You two," he started to say. "I should be the one to guide these three if they need some assistance. I've guided whole herds through forests so thick not even a tic could pass through in my day."

"Not even a tic?" Grandfather snidely remarked. "I see you're wide awake now."

"This is not the time, gentlemen, we have guests out front," she said, turning and picking up the mice. "I'll be leaving for a while so the workmen can come in and do the work that needs to be done. Theodore will be in charge." The three looked over at Theodore as if he were king. "Can we come with you?" Wilson begged.

"You have nothing to fear. Theodore will look after you and the household. Now, I'm going to put the house to sleep before I greet my guests. When I do, you'll need to remember this," she replied, leaning over and whispering in their ears. "If, for any reason, you need to wake up the house, you need to say this: *Dreamtime dandies, wishes and bandies – wakeup, wakeup to the land of candy.* And if you need to put the house back to sleep, you must say this: *Lullaby blue, lullaby red, lullabies that's all that needs to be said, now.... sleep.*"

Cracker yawned. "Not you," she whispered, smiling. Cracker nodded.

"Did the Baron tell you those rhymes?" Wilson asked.

"Yes, when I was a little girl. My father said that I needed to know them just in case."

"In case of what?" Benjamin asked.

"Trouble," she whispered back.

"Oh no, not more trouble," Benjamin replied, placing his little paws up to his mouth.

"Now there's no need to worry. Just watch this," she said, setting them down and standing up. "*Lullaby blue, lullaby red, lullabies that's all that needs to be said, now sleep.*"

They turned and watched Grandfather and Sir Henry close their eyes. They looked at Theodore. He was still awake. "What about him?" Cracker asked, pointing at Theodore.

"Now, Madam Rose," Theodore interrupted.

"Shh, Theodore. I hear people getting out of their cars," Abby softly scolded, lifting her hand in the air, "*Moonlight, starlight - just say - goodnight.*" Theodore instantly transformed into a stuffed lion again. "Well, I'll be," Wilson, gasped. "I wish we would've known that a long time ago."

"I am sure you do," Abby laughed, setting them down. She picked up Theodore. The bell rang out front. "You three go hide now," she whispered, walking toward the door. "Good morning, won't you please come in," she greeted the ladies and Mayor Bumpkin.

The four stood there absolutely stunned staring at Abby's appearance.

"My, don't you look like a warm summer breeze?" Mayor Bumpkin gushed.

"Why thank you, Mayor," she replied, smiling at the women.

How in the dickens can she look that fabulous without running water, a shower or, Claudia thought, taking in Abby's dress, *electricity to iron that outfit?*

"Mrs. Rose," Mayor Bumpkin said. "I'd like to introduce you to Karen Bloom and Fanny Chamberlin from the Women's Club. Karen is the one you'll be staying with, that's if you've decided to leave while our contractors come in and get this place fixed up."

"It's nice to meet you all, and yes Mayor, I've decided to take you up on your offer."

"Mrs. Rose," Karen greeted her.

"Nice to meet you," Fanny added. "I just love your gorgeous white lion," she continued, looking at Theodore cradled in her arm.

"His name is Theodore. I've had him since I was a little girl."

"Really? Well you certainly have kept him in excellent condition. He looks brand new," Fanny replied.

"Thank you. Theodore and I look after each other. I take him everywhere I go. However, he won't be going with me this time. He'll be staying here and looking after the place while I'm away," she replied, petting Theodore's head.

Fanny contentedly smiled. *That's why old people are special,* she thought. *The older one gets, the younger their mind becomes.*

Abby liked Fanny right away. She had a delightful personality, was around fortyish, with a slender figure, long brown hair and was wearing square glasses on a perfectly straight nose. However, Fanny's hat, with its small plastic flowers woven into the meshing, did not sit well. Abby sighed under her breath knowing Fanny was probably as shy as a mouse; excluding Wilson, Benjamin and Cracker, that is. *They were a handful.* Nevertheless, Fanny looked like a bookworm type, and bookworm types to her were the kind of people who had no confidence in themselves. They were more contented with reading books and living in the world of make-believe instead of their own.

"Are you ready, Mrs. Rose?" Claudia asked, taking Abby out of her thoughts. She turned to see Claudia's glued on smile. "Morning, Claudia," she quipped, turning and walking back into the parlor.

That was a sharp reply, Claudia thought. *I guess Mrs. Rose wasn't happy with me barging in yesterday. Oh well, someone has to run this town because he sure can't,* her thoughts continued, looking over at Mayor Bumpkin.

After following Abby inside, Fanny immediately noticed the dirty foyer walls and the enormous, decorative, wooden archway covered in dust and cobwebs. She looked up at the twenty-foot high parlor ceiling and then stared at the gigantic, cobweb-covered chandelier. Looking down, she settled her eyes on the massive staircase with its large decorative wooden banisters covered in dust and cobwebs, as well. All Abby needed now to set the scene right was for Count Dracula to come up from the basement and say hello. That thought spun her around. *The basement... not in a million years would I ever venture down there.*

"What do you see?" Wilson whispered to Benjamin who was standing up on a support beam underneath the stairs and looking out from a small crack. When Abby told them to hide before opening the door, they scampered around the side of the staircase and ran through a small hole in the baseboard. "Lots of legs," Benjamin replied.

"Legs?" Wilson fumed.

"Yeah, that's all I can see."

"Here, get down from there and let me take a look," Wilson scolded.

Benjamin jumped down. Wilson got up on the beam and peeked out. "Well?" Benjamin asked.

"You're right. All I can see are legs."

Benjamin and Cracker climbed up. They gathered alongside one another trying to listen.

When Karen walked in, the first thing that hit her was the stale air. *That's awful,* she thought, bringing her hand up to her nose. She could not understand why anyone, especially someone at Abby's age, would subject herself to living in such squalor. She looked upon the old woman in the sunflower dress with her hair done up in a bun. That was another question she wanted to ask Abby, h*ow on earth, did Abby get all dressed up without running water?* That question could wait until later. Right now, all she could think about was Abby wanting to live here in the first place.

"So…" Mayor Bumpkin spoke up, taking the women out of their thoughts. "What are you bringing with you?"

"Just that small suitcase," Abby replied, walking over and setting Theodore down on the stairs. As she bent over to pick up her suitcase, Abby spotted three little heads peeking out from a crack between the bottom step and face board. She winked at her mice.

On the way out the door, Claudia grabbed Abby's ear. "Now, Mrs. Rose, once you're settled in at Karen's we'll bring you down to Flo's hair salon so you can meet all the ladies in the Women's Club. We always get our hair done together and it's a perfect time to sit and chat while Flo and her gals keep us looking prim and proper."

Abby stopped near the Mayor's car. "I would like that," she replied as Mayor Bumpkin opened her door.

"Great. Maybe with you there, we can all convince Fanny to stop wearing a picnic basket on her head," Claudia laughed. Abby sighed seeing Fanny utterly embarrassed over that comment. *The gall of saying that,* Abby thought. She looked down at Claudia's shoes. She was wearing high heels – possibly a size ten. *Hmm, let's see how you like melting, miss fancy pants. Dragon flames with soaring heat - make Claudia feel hot coals beneath her feet,* she thought with a nod.

Mayor Bumpkin looked at the ladies; one in particular - Fanny. *If she only knew how beautiful she was,* he thought, taking in Fanny's outfit. *If she stopped dressing like a 1920's librarian and put on something more revealing, she could have any man in town.* However, he knew most of the men folk thought she was – well, out there somewhere - maybe past Mars. He sighed and then stepped into the fray, "I kind of like Fanny's hat," he lied.

"Me too," Abby agreed. "Now, shall we?" she continued, getting in the front seat of Mayor Bumpkin's car.

The ladies got inside Claudia's car and waited for the Mayor to take off. Halfway down the driveway toward Daisy Lane, Claudia started feeling her feet getting warm. "You feel that?" she asked Karen, sitting next to her.

"Feel what?"

"My feet feel on fire."

"I don't feel a thing, how about you Fanny?" Karen asked.

"No," she said from the back seat.

"Well I certainly can feel it," Claudia scolded.

I wish your dress would catch fire, Fanny smugly thought.

Mayor Bumpkin stopped at the road, looked both ways and then up in the rearview mirror. His face went funny seeing Claudia stop her car, get out and start running around in a circle while trying to take off her shoes.

"Something wrong, Mayor?" Abby questioned, seeing his eyes glued to the rearview mirror.

"I think so. Claudia just pulled over and she's running around like a chicken with its feathers on fire."

Abby smiled with delight.

While Claudia was removing her shoes next to her car, Wilson, Benjamin and Cracker jumped down from the stairwell beam and raced out the small hole at the side of the stairs. They stood there looking at the doors. "Well, it looks like we're on our own, fellas," Wilson spouted.

"It sure does," Benjamin replied, turning and seeing Theodore sitting on the stairs as a stuffed toy.

"Now what are we going to do?" Cracker asked. "The whole house's asleep."

"Maybe it's better this way, Cracker," Wilson said. "This gives us plenty of time to try and find that Potion and Spells book."

"You really think we'll find it?" Benjamin asked.

"I sure hope so. Now, let's wake up Theodore."

"What! Are you nuts?" Cracker shouted.

"No, but I wish we had a whole bag of them right now. Hurry," he replied, turning and jumping up the staircase to Theodore.

"How do you do that, Wilson," Benjamin asked.

"I don't know. Just try."

Benjamin ran up and jumped. His little fingers barely grabbed on.

"Here," Wilson said, taking hold of Theodore's tail and lowering it. "Take hold of this and climb."

After Benjamin and Cracker climbed the stairs and stood next to Theodore, Cracker asked Wilson, "Are you sure we want to do this, Wilson?"

"Yes, now stop your worrying."

"But what if he does start chasing us again?" Benjamin questioned, fearing the worst.

Wilson shook his head. "You heard Abby – the game's over," he said and then paused, "if he starts any of his crap, we can use that magic spell to put him back to sleep."

Benjamin and Cracker both nodded.

"OK, now who can remember the spell?" Wilson asked. Benjamin and Cracker looked at one another then turned and looked at Wilson. "We thought you were supposed to remember," they replied.

Wilson folded his arms and pouted. "You know," he started to say. "I wish we did have a whole bag of nuts right now - I'd be pelting both of you with them," he continued, turning and looking up at Theodore. "Now let me see if I can remember. I know it had something to do with candy."

"Oh, I know," Benjamin said, walking up between Theodore's legs. "*Dreamtime dandies, wishes and...*" he said and then paused trying to remember the word.

"*Bandies,*" Cracker whispered.

"Yeah, that's it. *Dreamtime dandies, wishes and bandies - wakeup, wakeup to the land of candy.*" WHOOSH - Theodore instantly transformed into a real lion. They stood there terrified knowing Abby wasn't there to save them. He gave a big yawn, showing his large canines. They stepped back preparing to run. Theodore blinked then glanced down at them.

"Hello, Theodore," Wilson said, trembling inside.

"You three," he replied. "Has Madam Rose left?"

"Yes," Cracker answered, feeling brave enough to walk up to him.

"So, you know the spell to wake me up?"

"Yes, and the one to put you to sleep," Wilson remarked.

Theodore slowly nodded remembering Madam Rose's order - 'look after them.' He sighed in thought. *I gave my word, and that is that - no more games.*

"We woke you up so you can look after the house as we go about our mission," Benjamin said.

Theodore nodded stepping out of his thoughts. "Where are you going to start this mission of yours?"

"We're not really sure yet," Cracker replied.

"Have you spoken to Wilfred? He might know something about that book."

"We already asked him last night. He hasn't a clue, but I wouldn't mind some fresh air," Wilson replied, jumping up onto Theodore's enormous paw. "You mind taking us for a ride out to the garage?"

"I suppose I could. I wouldn't mind some fresh air myself."

"Come on, fellas," Wilson excitedly replied, leaping up and taking hold of Theodore's mane.

7

Magical Clippers

Mayor Bumpkin put his car in park and got out at the end of the driveway. Abby looked over at him walking back to Claudia's car. "*Sail away my dragons, sail away to the sea,*" she whispered. With that, Claudia's feet started to cool down.

"What are you doing?!" Mayor Bumpkin asked, walking up to Claudia who was leaning against her car with her shoes in her hands.

"My feet were on fire."

"Your feet!? Why, the way you were running around with your hands flailing in the air, I thought maybe your hair was on fire."

Claudia sighed, lifted her backside off the car and slipped on her shoes. Karen looked out her passenger side window at Mayor Bumpkin and smiled. He noticed Fanny sitting in the back seat, smiling as well. *Something's going on around here,* he thought, focusing on Claudia with beads of sweat running down her forehead. "Maybe it's…" he started to say then shut his mouth when Claudia glared at him.

"No, Mayor, I haven't crossed that threshold yet. It isn't hot flashes if that's what you were going to suggest."

"Well, it was only a thought. Now, are you ready?"

"Yes, I'm ready. I think I'll have the undercarriage of this heap checked out. Something was making my feet feel as if they were on fire."

"Maybe you should," he grumbled, turning and walking back to his car.

Claudia stood erect staring at the back of the Mayor's head. *How could the town folk vote him in as Mayor? The man can't even dress himself properly,* she thought, casting her eyes down his wrinkled blue suit coat and brown pants. *His wife must be as blind as a bat letting him leave the house that way,* her thoughts continued to spin. She let out a sigh walking back around and opening the car door.

When Mayor Bumpkin got back inside his car, Abby asked, "What was that all about?"

"Claudia was running around back there because her feet were burning for some odd reason. I was going to suggest menopause, but refrained."

That contented smiled appeared on Abby's face once again. "Maybe you're right about that. Women experience all kinds of things during menopause."

Mayor Bumpkin put the car in drive, looked over at her, and replied, "I didn't have the guts to tell her that."

Abby laughed. "With her attitude, I wouldn't either. She certainly can be a little obnoxious at times."

"A little!?" Mayor Bumpkin spat, turning onto Daisy Lane. "Claudia seems to think that she was the one voted in as Mayor," he continued, driving down the street.

"Well maybe Claudia needs to be reminded from time to time just who is in charge around here," Abby suggested.

"I've told her so many times already, but seeing as how her husband, Bart, manages the bank, she thinks she can run you right over. You saw Claudia tearing Fanny down. That's how she does it - one jab at a time, until you're all used up and you just start saying yes, Claudia – yes, Mrs. Hornsby."

"I've come across lots of people like that in my lifetime. It takes backbone to stand up to them. I am sure we can fix it," Abby calmly replied, looking at the houses as they drove down the street.

Mayor Bumpkin glanced over at her sitting there as if she did not have a care in the world. *How on earth could she fix it?* he thought. *Maybe the older you get you stop putting up with the bullies like Claudia.* Mayor Bumpkin dropped that thought pulling up to Karen's house.

Karen and Albert's home was a lovely three-bedroom cottage with manicured lawns and small shrubs along the front with flowerbeds running up the driveway. The beautiful maple tree in the center of the lawn gave the place a charming appeal. Abby could tell right away that Karen and Albert were meticulous in every way. Like two peas in the same pod, she knew they shared everything together. The multi-flowered cushion chairs under the front awning patio gave her that hint.

She also loved the color of the cottage: warm ocean blue with creamy white window frames and dark blue gutters. She could even see the tip of a weeping willow over the rooftop in the backyard protecting the yard with shade.

"This will be home sweet home for awhile, Abby," Mayor Bumpkin said, looking over at her.

"What a lovely little home," Abby sighed, coming out of her thoughts.

"I'm glad you like it and I am sure that you're going to fall in love with Karen and Albert. Their two children, Rick and Susan, have left the nest. Rick and his wife live up in Michigan and Susan and her husband live in Boston."

"My, my - you couldn't ask for a worse split than that; one living out east and one in the mid-west. They must get lonesome."

"Yes, I'm sure they do," he replied, opening his door.

For being such a spineless little man, Abby was getting to like the Mayor. She wondered what his wife was like. *Probably a tiny little thing herself,* she thought, opening her door and getting out.

"I'll get your suitcase," he said. Abby nodded. She turned and watched Claudia and the others pulling in right behind them.

Claudia looked upset opening her door. Karen and Fanny looked as if they needed fresh air getting out. Abby could tell by their facial expressions that Claudia probably cursed the whole way here.

"Mrs. Rose, I wish I could stay, but I must get back into town," Claudia said, walking up to her.

"That's no problem, and I do appreciate your coming out this morning."

"I wouldn't have missed it for the world," Claudia replied, glancing down at Abby's dress. *Impossible,* she thought. *No one can look that good after spending a night in that hellhole without even a shower or bath.*

Claudia stepped aside as Mayor Bumpkin maneuvered around the car with Abby's suitcase. "Are you staying or coming with me, Fanny?" Claudia asked her.

Fanny looked at Abby and smiled. "I think I'll stay if that's alright with you, Karen."

"Yes, please stay. I'll drive you home," Karen replied.

"OK," Claudia said. "I'll see you all down at Flo's in a few days," she continued, walking back to her car.

As the women watched her leave, Mayor Bumpkin cleared his throat on the porch. They turned to see that he wanted to go in. Karen walked up and opened the door. "Won't you all come in, please?" she said, stepping aside for Mayor Bumpkin.

After Mayor Bumpkin walked in carrying Abby's suitcase, he was ushered down the hallway to place it in one of the spare bedrooms. Fanny and Abby stood in the front room waiting. "OK, who would like something to drink?" Karen asked, walking back in.

"I wish I could stay ladies, but I must be getting back to my office," Mayor Bumpkin replied.

"Well, if you must," Karen said, walking him to the door. He turned and looked at Abby. "If there is anything I can do for you while our construction crew is getting the manor up and running again, please don't be afraid to ask."

"Thank you, Mayor, and thank you for coming," Abby replied.

After he had left, Karen said, "I have iced tea, soda, or a cool glass of lemonade. Which will it be?"

"Lemonade," Abby replied. "Me too," Fanny added.

"OK, how about we sit in here. Please have a seat, and I'll be right out."

Abby sat down on the sofa. Fanny took a seat beside her. They looked at one another and smiled. *She's a sweet old lady,* Fanny thought, *her eyes are so charming and full of life.* Abby's thoughts were much different. *If I could get Fanny to stay one night in the manor, I could change her whole world.*

"I really love your dress, Abby," Fanny said, still holding her smile.

"Oh, this silly thing, I've had it for so long now, I…" she started to say when Karen walked in with two glasses of lemonade. "Here you go," she said. "I love that dress too, Abby," she continued, turning and walking back into the kitchen.

"She has good ears," Abby whispered.

"I think so," Fanny agreed.

"I wear hearing aids, ladies." Karen spoke up from the kitchen. "The hearing specialist at the clinic said I'd be able to hear as good as a rabbit," she continued, walking back in and taking a seat.

Abby and Fanny laughed. Karen took a sip of her lemonade and set the glass down. The two stopped giggling looking at Karen, seeing that something was on her mind. "Now, Mrs. Rose," Karen said.

"Abby will do," she interrupted.

"Alright, now since we're on the subject of that dress, I'm wondering if you don't mind telling us how you got all done up today?"

Abby looked at her and then at Fanny. She could see a question mark in Fanny's eyes as well. She took a sip of her lemonade, set the glass down and simply replied, "Oh with just a little bit of magic, you'd be surprised what you can do."

"Magic… I'd say. I would need more than magic to look that good after a night in that old manor. Without running water and electrical outlets to plug in all my gadgets, why…" Fanny laughed, "I'd come out looking like Frankenstein."

The women laughed with that notion. “I could fix you up in a blink of an eye,” Abby then said.

“You don’t say?” Fanny gushed.

“Now, ladies,” Karen interrupted. “I was serious. How did you do it? I mean you must have slept somewhere in there and then got up this morning?”

Abby laughed. “Yes, I just pushed my mattress over and slept on that all night.”

“No…,” Fanny shockingly replied.

Abby nodded. Fanny glanced over at Karen. Karen raised her brow. With that, Abby sat back. *I just told them the truth, and they don’t believe me,* she thought. *Then again - who would?*

“The dress I’m wearing was dry cleaned and hanging up. My hair seems to fall into place after a good combing and,” she said and then paused, “putting it up in the bun, hides everything,” she lied with a wink.

Fanny laughed. Abby noticed the sides of Karen’s mouth slide upward.

“So that’s it?” Karen said.

“Yes, that’s it, but with you my dear,” Abby replied, turning and looking at Fanny. “I could do wonders with your hair.”

“Really?” Fanny excitedly replied.

“Yes, right now if you’d like, well… if that’s OK with you, Karen?” Abby said.

Karen pondered that. “The only thing I have is Albert’s hair trimming set. He cuts his own hair, well, not cuts it – he uses the number one and shaves it all off. Will that work?”

“A man’s hair trimming set? I was thinking more like maybe you showing me different styles,” Fanny replied, worried that Abby was thinking of actually cutting her hair.

“Men’s, women’s - it doesn’t matter. I could whip you into shape in no time.”

“Whip me into shape?” Fanny gasped.

“Now, Fanny,” Abby calmly added. “You have nothing to worry about,” she said then paused, looking down Fanny’s slender body. “You could be simply irresistible if you truly wanted to be. Right Karen?” she continued, hoping Karen would agree.

“Yes,” Karen agreed, nodding.

“You two really think so?” Fanny questioned, looking from one to the other. There wasn’t a hint of lying in their eyes.

"The first thing we need to do is for you to get rid of that hat," Abby said.

"My hat?" she replied stunned, glancing over at Karen. Karen slowly nodded. "You both think it looks like a picnic basket too?"

"No, Claudia just has a way of rubbing your nose. But if you like hats, I am sure we can find some that will make your new hair style stand out," Abby replied. "Now, before we start, where will we do this?" she continued, standing up.

"I think the small study will do. It used to be my daughter's bedroom," Karen replied, standing up too. "I'll go get Albert's hair trimmers and get a chair ready," she continued, walking out.

When Karen left the front room, Fanny sat up and folded her hands. "Have you cut hair before?"

Abby laughed, bending over and pulling her up out of her seat. She quickly ushered her toward the study. "Yes, I even cut my own hair. I've been doing it all my life."

"No, kidding?" she replied, being pushed along. "I don't think I've ever met a woman who cuts her own hair."

"Well, don't worry. Your hair will be easy – trust me."

Fanny felt a bit apprehensive as she walked into the study. She sat down in the chair while Karen placed a towel around her shoulders and then stepped back. "She's all yours," she said, walking out.

Abby looked at Karen, winked and then replied, "Shut the door, please. I want to surprise you after we're done."

Karen shut the door and sighed all the way to the kitchen. She turned on the faucet and began rinsing her hands under the water while thinking; *I sure hope Abby knows what she's doing. If Fanny comes out looking like a poodle - she'll be the laughing stock of Cloverdale.*

"OK now, I want you to close your eyes real tight while I work my magic," Abby whispered.

Fanny removed her glasses and closed her eyes, more worried than ever. *Why am I doing this?*she thought. *I like the way my hair looks. Well, the way it has always looked – straight and boring.*

Abby pulled out the comb and scissors. She closed her eyes and thought of a spell. *Quick snip and galloping brim - let the scissors do the trim.* The comb and scissors floated up in the air. She waved her hand around Fanny's head while humming softly as the scissors and comb went to work. A slight smile appeared on Fanny's face listening to Abby humming a tune. In just a short time, Abby had Fanny's hair cut just above the shoulders and neatly feathered around the sides. When she was finished, she waved her hand – the scissors and comb floated down inside the box. "There you go," she said, handing Fanny her glasses. As Fanny stood up, Abby took off the towel from around Fanny's shoulders - letting all the cut hair fall to the floor. "Now hurry into the bathroom and take a look while I clean up."

Fanny looked down on the floor. She almost fainted - seeing so much hair. She slowly reached up and ran her fingers through what remained. "It's really short," she gasped.

"That it is, but trust me, it fits your pretty face. Now go take a look."

Fanny walked out feeling apprehensive to look at herself. She stopped in the hallway when Karen stepped out from the kitchen to see her. She watched Karen reach up and clasp her hands to her cheeks. "Oh.... my... God," Karen sang out.

"Oh no," Fanny panicked, turning and racing toward the bathroom. "Fanny," Karen yelled after her. "It looks fantastic."

Karen then turned when Abby walked out from the study. "My, you really know how to cut hair," she said surprised. When the two ladies stepped up to the bathroom door, they saw Fanny looking at herself in the mirror - as if she were queen. "I love it," she excitedly yelled, turning and smiling at them.

"I thought you would," Abby replied. "Now maybe Karen and I could take you shopping."

Fanny's face went slack.

"You need new dresses and a hat." Abby added.

Fanny glanced down at herself then up at Karen. Karen slowly nodded in agreement.

"Alright, what seems to be going on in the bathroom?" Albert bellowed, walking down the hallway, startling the women. None heard him come in.

Karen quickly turned thinking of what to say. She didn't have to - Fanny walked out as if she were the princess of Egypt. "Well.... I'll be..." Albert shockingly gleamed.

"That sounded as if you approve, Mr. Bloom," Fanny asked, with an uplifted chin.

"Why... you look good enough to...," he started to say, stepping back to take her all in.

"Albert Bloom!" Karen scolded, slapping his arm. Albert frowned. "I was just going to say - to take out on a Sunday stroll," he replied, rubbing his arm. "What did you think I was going to say?" he continued, eyeing his wife.

"We ladies know oh so well what you men think. And besides, we have company, so mind your manners," Karen replied, glaring at him.

Albert turned toward Abby. *It's the old lady from the manor,* he thought.

"Albert, I want you to meet Mrs. Rose."

"It's nice to meet you, ma'am."

"Thank you," Abby replied, sensing Albert was not happy that she was going to be staying with them. *He was probably brow beaten into having me stay while my house was repaired,* she thought. The word *brow beaten* – gave her a clue. It was Claudia. *Oh - it just had to be her shoving her weight around until Albert agreed.* She could imagine seeing Claudia here demanding Albert and possibly Karen to take her in for a while. After seeing Claudia in full gear yesterday, softly demanding for her to leave the manor while the workers came in, she knew Claudia would move heaven and earth to get her way. And… she suspected that heaven and earth were Albert and Karen. If her assumptions were right, Claudia was, in fact, protecting her own backside. It had nothing to do with leaving an elderly woman up in that manor without running water and electricity. *If I could put that obnoxious, self-centered, little busybody in a cauldron and light a fire underneath – I certainly would,* she thought.

"Abby will be staying in Rick's old room," Karen said, bringing Abby out of her thoughts.

Albert nodded. "You look wonderful, Fanny," he then said, turning and walking down the hallway toward the kitchen.

Karen stood there for a second and then she got an idea. "Helena's Apparels is open until nine tonight. If you stay and have supper with us, Abby and I could take you shopping."

"I really would like that."

"Good," Karen replied, taking Fanny's hand and escorting her back to the front room.

8

Big Trouble

Theodore, Wilson, Benjamin and Cracker all sat inside the garage visiting with Wilfred - who, for all practical matters, might as well be sitting out in a field. There wasn't much left of the old structure. Most of the roof was gone and one side was practically collapsed. If it weren't for the wooden ceiling beams hanging down above his head, Wilfred would be completely exposed.

"So you can't remember ever seeing the Baron carrying a light-grey, covered book out to the garage?" Theodore asked him.

"No, and really – it's been so long that I can hardly remember anything anymore, except that I was parked in better conditions than this," he replied, rolling his eyes upward at the night sky showing through the gaping hole in the roof.

Theodore looked up. He shook his head with dismay. "Well, gentlemen," he said to the mice, "it appears we have the entire manor to search."

"Yes, but where to start in such a huge place?" Wilson asked.

"I thought we were going to start up in the bell tower and work our way down through each room," Benjamin spoke up.

Theodore lowered his head in front of the three mice. His eyes were almost as big as they were. "I think you three will have to check behind every wall, up in every ceiling cavity, underneath the flooring in every room, and while you're doing that, I'll look for any secret hiding places he may have hidden that book in."

Cracker walked up to him and leaned over against his paw. "Do you know how long that will take?"

Theodore pondered that. He knew a task like this would be no small undertaking. He then got an idea. "Alright, let's start with this. I want you to go back in time to when you three woke up from your stupor after you were done reading that longevity spell and the Baron was standing over you. Maybe then something will click."

Wilson walked up to Theodore, turned around, and leaned his back up against Theodore's paw. "I remember it was on a rainy spring day," he started his story. "We just got done performing a magic trick the Baron had put together for us to do at his next show." With that, Wilson drifted back to that terrible day when they found themselves in a terrible mess.

"Now you three look after the place and stay out of trouble while I drive into town. I'd take you with me, but it's raining outside," Baron Von Haussler said, standing up and rounding his desk in the study. They stood there watching him until he left, leaving the door ajar.

"Trouble," Cracker whispered. "Why, we're no trouble at all," he remarked, looking back at the door.

Wilson took his eye off the door and looked at Cracker. "That's right, when was the last time we got into trouble around here?"

"Try last week," Benjamin commented.

They raised their brows at him.

"Alright, don't you remember Hansel chasing us out of the kitchen with our hands full of walnuts; walnuts the kitchen was using in a vanilla swirl cake."

"Oh that. We weren't in trouble, Benjamin," Wilson spat. "And besides, the Baron enjoyed them just as much as we did when we ran into the parlor and then slammed right into his feet as he was walking out of the den."

Benjamin thought back. He remembered the Baron standing there looking down at them as if they had just robbed a bank and were carrying off with the loot. Then to their surprise, the Baron bent down, took a few walnuts from Wilson, smiled, and then continued on his way. He came out of his thoughts shaking his head.

"So what are we going to do today? We can't go outside," Cracker said, walking over and sitting down on the Baron's wooden pencil case.

"I don't know," Wilson replied, walking over and looking down at the drawing of the new flying mice act the Baron had just invented. Where the Baron came up with all these ideas was beyond him. If they weren't flying, disappearing, or simply floating down out of the air on stage during one of the Baron's performances, the Baron would have the audience believing that he just hypnotized them and then having them dancing on a stool. As he looked at the drawing, the thought of being hypnotized gave him an idea. "I know what we can do," he said, turning and facing his friends. "Let's go up in the bell tower and look through the Potion and Spells Book."

"Now you're talking big trouble," Benjamin replied.

"Oh, come on, Benjamin. You only get into trouble if you get caught. The Baron is gone and the rest of the house hasn't a clue. So what-cha say, fellas?"

Benjamin looked at Cracker. Cracker tilted his head and said, "He's right, there's no way we can get caught. No one ever goes up there."

Benjamin shook his head. *These two,* he thought, *will be the death of me yet.* "OK, but if we do get caught, I'm just going to tell the Baron that I was up there trying to talk you two out of it."

"Nice try," Wilson replied, turning around and jumping down onto the chair.

When the three hit the floor, they all looked back at the slightly opened door. "Maybe we should push it shut," Cracker whispered.

"Yeah," Wilson agreed, walking over to the door. "Now on the count of three – push. One, two three," he said. They pushed with all their might. The door slowly started to close.

"That's enough, you two. We'll leave it open a tad, so we can get out of here when we're done," Wilson said, turning and walking over to the bell tower door. "OK, let's pull it open a bit and slip through," he continued, putting his little paws on the door.

After opening the door enough to walk through, they stood there staring up at the winding staircase. The walls were made of small hardwood planks that went straight up and down. There was a wooden handrail connected to the left hand side. Up in the corners of the circular ceiling were old cobwebs that stretched across the walls. Some were hanging three feet down.

"It sure looks real creepy up there," Benjamin whispered.

"Yeah it sure does," Cracker agreed, taking in the dust and cobwebs.

"Oh - you two, there's nothing to be afraid of," Wilson said. "Besides, the only thing up there that might give you the creeps is seeing a spider, and they're more afraid of us than we are of them. Why, they'd probably just run back inside their holes."

"You think?" Benjamin asked, imagining seeing a spider bigger than him. *Benjamin may have been small, but his imagination was as big as an elephant.*

"Have you seen any in the basement?" Cracker asked.

"No," Benjamin remarked.

"OK then. These cobwebs all look as if they've been here for thousands of years."

"Thousands of years!!" Benjamin gasped.

"You know what I mean."

"Enough with the nonsense you two, let's climb," Wilson interrupted, walking up to the first set of steps. "Here, Benjamin, you lean over and Cracker and I will get up on your back and jump up, then we'll toss our tails down for you to climb."

Benjamin nodded, worried.

All the way up they went, one after another, until they got to the last set of steps and the bell tower floor. When Wilson and Cracker stood up, Wilson whispered into Cracker's ear. Cracker contently smiled hearing the prank that Wilson wanted to pull on Benjamin. "OK, grab onto our tails," Wilson said down to Benjamin.

"Wow, will you look at this place!" Benjamin gasped, standing there looking up at the small circular room with two large round windows on either side of the walls – covered in cobwebs and dust. There was a small wooden desk sitting in the middle with a large candle sitting on top of it.

In one of the rounded corners was a small bookshelf filled with old books. Next to that was a small table with a lamp on it and an old wooden chair with a dirty cushion. Overhead, Benjamin saw massive cobwebs hanging down like garland hanging off a Christmas tree. "This place gives me the spooks, fellas," he whispered.

"I'll give you the spooks. Come on - let's find a way to get up on the table," Wilson scolded, walking over to one of the table legs. "We certainly can't climb one of these legs. They're too smooth to hold onto," he continued.

"Hey, look here," Cracker said, walking over and looking up at one of the circular windows. "Maybe if we can somehow reach that string nailed to the wall, we can hoist ourselves up and jump from the windowsill."

"That might work," Wilson replied, walking over to the wall.

Benjamin stood there with his arms folded watching his buddies trying to find a way up to the table. He glanced back toward the open door and then noticed the lower door hinge. From there, he looked across at the wall and saw a gap in the slot boards. He walked over, jumped up onto the lower hinge, steadied himself and then leaped across and took hold of the edge of the slat board and started shimmying across toward the string.

"What in blazes are you doing?" Cracker shouted, seeing Benjamin shimmying across the wall toward the string hanging down.

"Come on, use the door hinge to climb and then jump over to the wall," he replied.

Wilson and Cracker looked back at the door's hinge and then let their eyes follow Benjamin's route. "Well, will you look at that? The kid does have a brain," Wilson beamed, walking over and jumping up onto the hinge.

A minute later, they were all standing on the small circular windowsill looking down at the table. "That's a big jump," Cracker said, eyeing up the situation.

"That it is," Wilson replied. "Who's going first?" he asked, looking at them.

"You are," they both said in unison. "You're always pushing us back and going first," Benjamin added. "So let's see ya do it, Big Guy."

Wilson shook his head. "I'll give you Big Guy. Watch this," he replied walking back to the window and using it as a springboard to push off. He ran three steps and then leaped into the air landing on the table. He rolled over twice and then stood up. "How's that?" he said half out of breath.

"OK, smarty pants," Cracker grumbled, stepping back and using the window as well. He rolled three times and stood up before going right off the table. "That was close," he sighed, looking down at the floor. "Alright, Benjamin. Let's see ya make it," Wilson shouted.

Benjamin felt his knees go weak. "Oh, I don't know about this," he said, walking back toward the window.

"Stop staring at the floor. We'll catch you if we have to," Cracker yelled back.

Benjamin swallowed, sucked in a ton of air and then ran three steps. The next thing he felt was flying through the air and landing on the table, hitting Wilson and Cracker. "Looook owwwt!!" Wilson screamed, tumbling over and over with Cracker and Benjamin. They all stopped rolling near the edge of the table. Three long sighs went out as they got up and looked down.

"That was close," Cracker whispered.

"You're telling me," Wilson said. "You almost killed us," he continued, looking at Benjamin.

"Oh, phooey, I knew you guys were going to catch me."

"I'll give you phooey - look how close we came to the edge! You ever thought of losing some weight?" Wilson fumed.

"Come on, fellas, I'm not that fat," he replied, rubbing his belly.

They both shook their heads. Wilson then noticed the book sitting there. "Come on, let's check this out," he said, walking over.

"How old do you think this book is?" Cracker asked, staring down at the old, worn-out cover.

"That's hard to tell, but you have to remember, his grandmother gave it to him, and who knows how long she had it or who gave it to her," Wilson replied.

"It probably goes back to the beginning of the earth," Benjamin remarked.

"Oh, will you shut up. The beginning of the earth," Wilson mumbled.

"It's called the beginning of time, lame brain, and I don't think it went back that far. Heck, no one was around back then except the dinosaurs and we all know they couldn't read or write."

Cracker started to laugh. Wilson and Benjamin looked at him.

"Dinosaurs reading and writing," Cracker giggled, "can you just imagine that? You're both lamebrains. Now, let's open the book and take a peek, shall we?"

The three looked down at the old dusty cover with its tattered binder. There was an eerie-looking eye in the center, encircled by snakes with their tails coiled together. On the bottom of the cover was a picture showing gale force winds pushing ocean waves across, and a woman who looked half-fish, half-human holding a lantern up out of the sea. Up at the top, there were two crossed swords and under them was the name: The Black Knight.

"Who could that be?" Benjamin asked.

"I don't know," Wilson whispered. "He may have been someone from the Barons' grandmother's side of the family."

"Kind of creepy, don't you think?" Cracker whispered.

Wilson and Benjamin looked at him. His eyes said more than that. They said, *maybe we shouldn't open the book.* They slowly turned their heads and looked down at the eerie eye. "It's almost as if the eye is staring up at us," Benjamin whispered.

"Yeah," Cracker sighed.

Wilson felt tiny shivers up his backside with Benjamin's thoughts while staring at the eye. He felt that it was beckoning him to open the book. He glanced over at Benjamin and then at Cracker. They too looked as if they were in a trance. *It's now or never,* he thought. *We certainly didn't come all the way up here just to stare at the darn thing.* "OK," he whispered. "I'm in to opening it. Anyone else?"

Benjamin and Cracker raised their brows.

"No guts – no glory," Wilson added to their worried look.

Cracker nodded to open the book.

"OK," Benjamin sighed. "I'm in."

"Alright you two. Cracker, go up and lift the top. Benjamin, take the middle, and I'll lift the bottom here."

When the three were in place, Wilson gave the count. "One, two, three – lift." Their little muscles strained lifting it up. "Keep lifting it and then we'll let it go," Wilson grunted. When the cover was straight up in the air, Wilson yelled, "Now." The cover fell back onto the desk with a thud creating a puff of dust.

Page after page, they turned each one, reading what it said. Wilson then winked at Cracker. Cracker nodded and then smiled, glancing at the side of Benjamin's face. When they came to a passage, not in English, Wilson started the prank. "Anyone know what that says?"

Benjamin shook his head.

"It looks German," Cracker replied.

"Well, can you read it?" Wilson asked.

"I don't know. The Baron only taught me a few words. Here, let me see," he replied, walking up onto the page and looking down. "It's a trance of some sort."

"A trance?" Benjamin questioned.

"Yeah, now let's see if I have the words right. Go stand over there, Wilson."

Benjamin watched Wilson walk over to the right of the book. Benjamin didn't like this at all. "Are you two nuts?" he scolded.

"No," Cracker replied. "If I say this right, I'm sure I can bring Wilson out of it," he continued and then paused, looking down at the foreign words on the page. He then stretched out his hands toward Wilson and made up some silly chant. "*Ooga Booga – Ooga Boo – flames from a dragon...*"

Benjamin looked over to see Wilson's head go down. He looked back at Cracker, "Ooga – Booga... that's not German," he questioned the chant.

"Yes it is, now hush," Cracker replied. "*Ooga Booga – Ooga Boo, flames from a dragon - who said who – storms in a teacup, storms in a pail - get on your belly and crawl like a snail.*"

Benjamin watched Wilson fall on the table and begin slithering across it. "What have you done?!" he yelled, racing over to Wilson. "Wilson, wakeup, wakeup. You're scaring me."

"Stand back," Cracker scolded.

Benjamin looked at him. He wanted to rip his little ears off. "Bring him back now!" he ordered.

"No, I'm not done with this little one," Cracker hideously said, trying not to laugh. "Stand up," he then ordered Wilson. Wilson stood up. "Stretch out your arms and walk toward me."

Benjamin watched in utter horror as Wilson walked over with his arms stretched out. "Now turn in a circle," Cracker ordered. Wilson began turning. "When you're face to face with Benjamin, open your eyes and look at him and then tell him what you think."

Benjamin stood there shaking like a leaf watching Wilson turning in a circle and then he stopped and opened his eyes. Wilson almost laughed before he could say it. "Gotcha," he laughed, leaning into Benjamin with a huge, beaming smile.

Benjamin's face went slack seeing it was all just a game – a dirty, little, lowdown, silly game played on him. He slowly shifted his eyes on Cracker and then back at Wilson. "You two," he started in on them. "I'll put you two in a spell," he continued, raising his little paws and turning them into fists. "I'm going to punch your lights out and send you both to the moon."

Wilson shook his head and then laughed. Cracker started to laugh as well. Benjamin had seen enough and swung at Wilson. Wilson slipped his punch and fell down. He rolled over still laughing. Benjamin jumped on top of him. Cracker raced over, jumped on Benjamin and then started tickling him. The whole mess ended with the three laughing so hard they could hardly breathe.

"Alright, alright," Wilson gasped between chuckles. "Let me go. We still have more pages to turn."

"I'm going to turn you," Benjamin replied, tickling Wilson as Cracker in turn was tickling him.

When they had enough of the nonsense, and their bellies ached from laughter, they lay there looking up at the ceiling.

"You know, fellas, even though you always have me believing half the crap you say and do, I still love ya," Benjamin confessed.

Wilson looked over at him lying there. "We love you too, Benjamin. That's why we like to tease you so much."

Benjamin turned his head and looked at Cracker. Cracker smiled at him while nodding his head.

"OK, let's check out some more spells," Wilson said.

"No more baloney," Benjamin said.

"No more baloney, I promise," Cracker replied.

They stood up and walked back over to the book. After turning some more pages, they came across one that said *Longevity*.

"What's that?" Cracker asked.

Benjamin walked up onto the page and tried to pronounce the word.

"*Long- ev - ity*." He looked back at his friends. "Beats me."

"You want to try it?" Wilson asked.

"I don't know, Wilson. If we can't even pronounce it something terrible could happen, don't cha think?" Cracker replied.

"It can't be too bad, fellas," Benjamin commented, looking down at the spell again. He noticed a symbol at the bottom of the page. It looked like two hands clasped together. *Hmm,* he thought. "Wait, I think I know what we have to do."

"What?" Wilson asked, walking up onto the page. "It looks as if we have to hold hands when we say it," he replied, pointing down at the symbol.

"Come on, Cracker," he said over his shoulder.

Cracker walked up onto the page. They all stood in a circle and held hands as Benjamin read the spell. "*Dribble drabble, dribble drum - a cork barrel full of rum. Now go to sleep, and dreams will come – the rainbow's promise will keep you young.*" WHAM – little lights went off inside their heads. They fell back upon the page. Out cold in dreamland, they were drifting inside a cloud. Strange lights then appeared and began swirling around them. The lights turned into a beautiful rainbow. They slid down the rainbow as if on a roller coaster toward the ground. Lying there still in dreamland, Wilson opened his eyes and saw the Baron looking down at him. He nudged his friends. They opened their eyes and looked up in horror.

"What on earth do you three think you're doing?" the Baron yelled.

Wilson tried to get up. His head felt as light as a feather. Cracker and Benjamin were feeling dizzy too.

"Get up!" the Baron ordered.

They got to their feet holding on to one another. Their little legs were shaking watching the Baron walk around the desk, pull up a chair and sit down in front of them. Wilson tried to speak, but his mouth was too dry. "I'm waiting," the Baron scolded.

Cracker looked into his stern eyes - he knew they were in trouble.

"Well," the Baron started to say. "Do you three have any idea what you've just done?"

They slowly shook their heads.

"So, you don't even know what the spell was you said?"

They shook their heads again.

Great, the Baron thought. *I'm not going to miss this opportunity of scaring them into never doing this again.* He looked at his mice standing there as if they were standing on pins "In twenty-four hours, you will all turn into pumpkins."

"Pumpkins!" Wilson gasped, looking at his friends. "You mean like Adolf and Tess?"

"That's right. Those two drunken fools deserved to be transformed into pumpkins at my Halloween party last year."

"Oh no... How could we be so stupid?" Benjamin sighed.

Cracker felt his stomach go into knots with worry. His little head began feeling as light as a feather - and then he simply passed out.

Wilson freaked seeing him lying there. Benjamin looked down at Cracker and then passed out himself. "Cracker, Benjamin!" Wilson screamed.

"Oh.... we're doomed," he continued, kneeling alongside his friends.

The Baron sat back with delight. Keeping his smile, he got up, fetched his small tin water jug and poured it out over his mice. Wilson screamed, not seeing it coming. Benjamin and Cracker woke up coughing and rolling over.

The Baron sat back down and waited for their little antics to stop.

"Now," he started to say. They stared up at him lying there soaking wet.

"Longevity means long life." He could see their little thoughts spinning. Wilson glanced over at his friends and then looked up at him again. "Long life – you mean as pumpkins?" he asked, standing up worried.

"No. Not as pumpkins, but I have a right mind to turn you all into pumpkins by coming up here and fooling around with spells you don't have a clue to what they mean."

"We're sorry," Benjamin wept.

"I'm sure you are."

Cracker stood up wiping his brow. “So what kind of life will we be living now?”

The Baron laughed. “Nothing will change except you’ll never get old for a time.”

They stared at each other with wondering eyes. Wilson then glanced up at him. “You mean we won’t grow old like our parents? No canes and grey whiskers?”

“Not for awhile.”

“How long do we have?” Benjamin asked.

“If you repeat that spell every twenty years, that’s if you can remember it, you’ll continue to be young,” the Baron replied.

“So...” Cracker said, questioning the pumpkin crap. “You said that we’d turned into pumpkins because you were mad?”

“That’s right, and I still am,” he sternly replied, picking up the Potion and Spells book and tucking it under his arm. He then stood up and headed for the stairs. “This time, I’ll hide this where you’ll never see it again,” he continued, walking down out of the bell tower.

“That’s the last we saw of the book,” Wilson said, ending his story.

“So that’s what happened?” Theodore asked.

“Yes,” Wilson replied

Theodore glanced over at Benjamin and Cracker. They nodded. He then looked at Wilfred. Wilfred lifted his eyes, pondering Wilson’s story. “Well, I guess we should get back now. It’s getting late,” Theodore said, lowering his head so the mice could climb and hitch a ride back to the manor.

“Goodnight, Wilfred,” they said.

“Goodnight. Thanks for coming out and visiting with me.”

When the four were gone, Wilfred drifted over Wilson’s story again. He closed his headlights thinking of the Potion and Spells book. *I hope when they do find that book they don’t open it.*

9

Blue Over You

The following day, three women gleefully strolled into Flo's Hair Salon like hummingbirds in a patch of wildflowers. One of them in particular stood out from the others, not because she was younger, but because it was Fanny, who in a blink of an eye had transformed into a sensational beauty. She waltzed in wearing a new hair style, feathered back on the sides and a brand new red pleated dress.

"Will you look at that!?" Harriett Bowman gasped, getting up from her salon chair.

Flo Zimmer turned around then froze. The hairspray bottle in her hand hit the floor. Claudia pushed the dryer over her head to the side and stood up. Her eyes went wide seeing Fanny walk in, spin in a circle in front of Flo and then charmingly do a curtsy. Flo looked down at Fanny's new haircut as Fanny bent over. When Fanny stood erect, Flo took in her new dress.

"What-cha think?" Fanny asked with a gleaming smile.

"It looks as if I am out of business," Flo drooled, "Who on earth, cut your hair?"

Fanny glanced back at Karen and Abby. Flo shifted her eyes on the two women standing near the entrance wearing bright smiles as well.

"You're kidding me?" Flo replied, focusing her attention back on Fanny.

"I wouldn't kid about a thing like that. It was Mrs. Rose's idea," Fanny replied. "She was the one who cut my hair. Now ladies," she continued, stepping away from Flo. "Let me introduce you to Mrs. Rose." She reached out her hand and beckoned Abby to come forward.

Abby walked up and smiled at Flo. "I don't know if I should say that it's nice to meet you, or just ask you if you want a job," Flo said, extending her hand.

Abby reached out and placed her hand in Flo's. It was as soft as velvet.

"It's nice to meet you, Flo, but I am not looking for a job."

"My name is Harriett Bowman," Harriett said, brushing past Flo and extending her hand.

"It's nice to meet you, Harriett. Please, just call me Abby."

Claudia almost swallowed her tongue hearing this crap. *It was Mrs. Rose's idea,* she thought. *This old bird could be a threat to my position. First, she brings in a suitcase full of money, plops it down on Sid's desk and purchases the manor without blinking an eye, and now this. I'd better do something quick.* "Fanny, I really liked the way your hair was before," she said, getting out of her chair and walking up to the group.

"Claudia, you need to get back underneath that hairdryer before your hair turns a color you won't want to be seen wearing outside this shop," Flo gently scolded, escorting her back to her chair.

"Now, Claudia," Fanny said, walking behind Flo. "That hair style I was wearing went out in high school, and when I look back, I see too many years between then and now. It was high time for a change. I'm so grateful to Abby for making me see the light of day."

The light of day, Claudia thought. *I'll show you the light of day,* her thoughts continued spinning, sitting back down.

Flo checked Claudia's hair then placed the hairdryer over her head. "You have fifteen more minutes under there then we'll wash the color out before we curl it," she said and then paused. "Harriett you're next. Please, have a seat over here."

Once Harriett sat down, Flo walked back over to Abby and Karen. "So, tell me, how long have you been cutting hair, Abby?"

"She cuts her own hair," Karen interjected.

"You do?" Flo replied shocked.

"Oh, it's nothing at all," Abby said, glancing at Karen. "I've been doing it since I was a little girl," she continued, casting her eyes back on Flo.

"Your mother allowed you to cut your own hair?" Flo questioned.

"Why yes," Abby replied, smiling. "She was the one who taught me."

"Well, I'll be," Flo said, pondering that. "Would you mind showing me how you'd cut Harriett's? Her hair is so curly it's hard to make it lie down."

Abby looked at Harriett. *This could be trouble,* she thought.

"Oh, go on, Abby," Fanny said, goading her. "Show us what you can do."

Yeah, I'd like to see this, Claudia thought, sitting there fuming.

"Well," she started to say, walking over to Harriett's chair. "Her hair would only need a touch of magic," she continued, running her fingers through it.

"I need all the magic I can get," Harriett whispered, looking up at her.

Abby smiled. *Everyone could use a touch of magic,* she thought.

"How long will it take for you to cut it?" Claudia interrupted the flock of birds all gathered around Harriett's chair.

Abby looked back at Claudia. Claudia smiled, lifting her brow as if to say – go ahead, show us how you do it. Abby slowly nodded looking up at the hairdryer over Claudia's head. *A hair color you don't want to be seen wearing outside this shop,* she thought of Flo's words. *Well, let's see what I can do. Boiling water from a cauldron's brew - make her hair turn the color of blue. Let it change back in a day or two - so Claudia has time to stew.* With that, she winked at Claudia, turned around and gave an excuse. "I'd love to cut your hair, but I am on my way to the grocery store right now. Tonight, I am making an apple strudel for dessert at Karen's."

"But what about our meeting?" Flo asked.

"Meeting?" Abby questioned.

"Yes, we always hold our club meetings here. And right now, we need all the help we can get with the county fair coming up next week."

County fair, Abby thought. *How grand.* "Well, you can count me in. How about we all get together at Karen's tomorrow night? That's if it's OK with you," she said, looking at Karen.

"That's a splendid idea," Karen beamed. "It would be nice to sit in a more comfortable setting, and I am sure I can kick Albert out of the house for a while. He's always looking for an excuse to slip out the back door. Tomorrow night, I'll give him that excuse. So, what do you all say?" she excitedly giggled.

Flo looked at Fanny. Fanny nodded. She looked at Harriett. Harriett nodded too. "Claudia?" she then said, turning and looking back at her.

Claudia opened her eyes hearing every word. She looked at all the faces looking back at her with big, bright smiles. She then shifted her eyes on Abby standing there in her pretty, blue dress and her little knit shawl. *She's a wolf in sheep's clothing,* she thought. *I can feel it in my bones.* She placed her fake smile back on and simply replied. "That is a splendid idea. What time?"

"After dinner, around seven o'clock," Karen replied.

"Sounds good." Claudia said.

"OK, I am off to the store now. I'll meet you back here, Karen," Abby said, walking toward the door.

"Alright," Karen replied, watching her leave.

"Isn't she just a hoot?" Fanny beamed, turning and facing the women.

"Yeah, a real hoot," Claudia remarked.

Fanny was shocked with that comment. "What-cha mean, Claudia? You seem to not like her for some reason," she questioned.

"Oh, I like her all right – I like her a bunch."

"Now, Claudia," Karen intervened. "Abby is a peach and you know it. Maybe that's why you dislike her."

"I never said I disliked her."

"Right," Flo butted in. "I saw it in your eyes, and now I can hear it in your tone. What's with you and Abby? I mean seriously. She's just arrived here in Cloverdale."

Claudia felt the claws coming out. She looked at Harriett who raised her brow for an answer too.

"OK, so you want my opinion," she said and then paused. "Well, first off, she made Mayor Bumpkin and I look like complete asses by staying up in that manor all alone. Can you just imagine the gossip buzzing around town right now by us allowing an elderly lady to stay up there without running water and/or having any electricity?"

"Really now," Flo commented, folding her arms and leaning her weight on one foot. "I just met the woman and she seems to handle herself alright. And besides," she said, walking back toward her, "maybe Abby got under your skin because she had the guts to stay up there in the first place. All alone no less, and I am sure if we wagered a bet right now you wouldn't stay up there for one night all alone. Would you?"

Claudia was feeling the heat and it wasn't coming from the hairdryer over her head. "You're right – because I have more upstairs than she does. Who in their right mind would want to stay in that dump of a place? We should have torn it down years ago."

"Well," Flo replied, pushing the hairdryer back and taking the plastic hood off Claudia's head. Her face contorted looking down at Claudia's hair. It was blue. Claudia looked up at her. She didn't like what she saw in Flo's eyes.

"What's wrong?" she gasped, standing and walking over to the mirror. "Oh… my God, what have you done?" she yelled, seeing the color.

All the ladies shrieked.

"I didn't do anything," Flo replied, picking up the dye bottle she used. She quickly read the color: light brown. She dabbed a little on her finger – light brown. She looked at Claudia who looked like a clown in the circus. "Look," Flo gasped, showing her the bottle.

Claudia looked at it then looked into Flo's eyes. They said more than she wanted to hear, *she looked like a fool.* "Now what am I going to do? I have to meet Bart at the bank around four today. He was going to take me out for dinner tonight."

Fanny stood there stoned-faced shaking her head. Then it just happened. Fanny started to laugh. Claudia turned and looked at her. "What's so funny?" That comment made Karen laugh. "You too, Karen," Claudia snarled. That comment made Harriett laugh. "Oh… in heaven's name," Claudia spewed, sitting back in the chair and folding her arms.

Flo was trying to hold her stomach and not laugh. She quickly placed her hands to her mouth and hurried out of the salon. When the women saw her bending over in front of the window to hide, they knew she was laughing as well.

When Abby opened the door to the grocery store, she walked over and grabbed a cart. Pulling out her little note pad, she went down the lists of items. *I need eggs, brown sugar, a piecrust, apples and some cinnamon spice,* she thought, glancing over at the fruit and vegetable stands. She picked out four large red apples, set them inside her cart and proceeded to the first aisle. From one aisle to the next, she picked up everything except the eggs and piecrust, which were near the back in the cold storage area. As Abby was heading up the last aisle, a young man came rushing around the corner and slammed right into her cart, almost knocking her over.

"Oh my God, I am so sorry," the young man panicked. "Here let me get those," he continued, bending over and picking up the apples. When he stood up, Abby looked into his savage blue eyes and handsome face. "You seem to be in a hurry, young man."

"Yes. I only get a half hour for lunch, and again I am truly sorry."

Abby noticed he was carrying a submarine sandwich in one hand and a bottle of Coke in the other. "That's lunch?" she questioned, looking up at him.

The young man glanced down at his lunch and then looked back up at her. He cocked his head finally realizing who she was. "Yes," he quickly replied. "You're the lady who purchased the manor."

"That I am. My name is Abigail Rose, but everyone just calls me Abby."

"Abigail," he remarked.

"That's right."

"What a beautiful name. You don't mind if I call you Abigail?"

"No, I don't mind at all," she blushed, feeling lighter than a feather. "So, what does everyone call you?" she asked.

"I'm sorry. My name is Shaun Stevenson. I work at Olson's service station in town."

"Olson's – that's right across from the real estate agency?"

"That's right. I saw you drive up in that nineteen o'seven Ford K."

"My, you know your cars, Shaun," she replied, stunned.

"That I do, Abigail. Henry Ford sure knew what he was doing when he designed that car. It was the best car on the road in her day. I just love the Ford K's rumble seat, convertible top and especially the air-piston crankshaft."

Abby stood there feeling as if she were twenty again staring at this handsome, young man - who knew more about Wilfred than she did. That thought made her think of Wilfred in his rusty old condition. It gave her an idea.

"Have you ever worked on a Ford K?"

"No, but I sure would like to."

"Well, Shaun, Wilfred needs at a lot of work. If you are up to it, stop by and see me when I get back up to the manor. Right now, I am staying with the Bloom's on Daisy Lane while the city workers restore the power and water."

"I see, and your car - you call him Wilfred?"

Abby laughed. "I named the car Wilfred after my father gave it to me on my twenty first birthday."

"Wilfred," he laughed. "I like that name. You have a deal, Abigail. When do you think you'll be going back?"

"Well, Mayor Bumpkin figures right after the county fair."

"Great. Look, I really have to be going. I'll come up and check out Wilfred right after the fair. You have a nice day, Abigail, and again – I am sorry for almost knocking you down."

"No problem. Just keep it in mind that there are older people still walking around," she replied with a smile.

Shaun nodded, tipped his head as if wearing a hat, and then strolled down the aisle toward the cash register. Abby stood there watching him leave. *Shaun Stevenson,* she thought with her head in the clouds. *I wonder how old he is. Eighteen, nineteen, maybe twenty,* her thoughts continued, turning and walking toward the cold storage area.

After Abby purchased her items, she exited the store. Sid and Don were driving along when Abby walked out. "Hey, there's Mrs. Rose," Sid said. Don spotted her pushing a grocery cart down the street. "I hear she's staying at the Bloom's place while the manor is being repaired," Don replied.

"That's right. Mayor Bumpkin said that it should be completed after the fair."

Don glanced over at him. "Have you talked to Willy Meyers yet?"

"No, but I saw Molly the other day. I told her that we wanted to talk to Willy and Bobby Ray."

"What about Willy's older brother, Ernie?" Don replied, worried.

Sid pondered that. Ernie had done time in Ohio for armed robbery. He just got back into town. "I don't know, Don. He might be more trouble than we need."

"Yeah, he might, but you better consider that once you tell Willy what you're planning, he might tell his big brother."

He could, Sid thought. He wondered if Ernie had learned his lesson. Sitting inside a cell for two years would sure give a person a lot of time to think. *If he did go straight – he just might talk his little brother out of helping us rob the old lady.* "I think we'll have to play this one by ear, Don. We need those three to sneak up there while the men are still working and try to get in somehow."

"Well, I hope your plan works. I don't know why you don't want us to go there and snoop around on our own. Letting these kids do it – hell, Sid, they could rip us off if they did find that suitcase."

"You might be right, but I don't want to get caught."

Don shook his head. "You know," he started to say. "We have the best excuse if we did get caught."

Sid rolled up and parked his car in front of the real estate agency. He shut off the engine and looked over at him.

"We sold her the place. So… we went up to check it out. What's wrong with that?"

"Nothing," Sid replied.

"Oh, I see," Don said, sitting back.

"See what?"

"You're chicken to go there at night."

"Yeah, right," he replied, getting out.

Don opened his door and looked across the hood. "Prove me wrong then. Let's go up there tonight."

"Tonight!? Are you crazy?"

Don nodded, rounding the car. "I thought so," he said, opening the agency door.

"Look, if we did decide to go up there tonight - what the hell am I going to say to Betsy to get out of the house?" Sid asked, following Don in.

Don turned around. "The same thing I'm telling Sue. We're going bowling."

"Bowling?"

"Yes, grab your ball on the way out," he replied, strolling over to his desk and picking up his briefcase. A sudden flash came to him. He turned around.

"I just got a thought," he said and then paused. Sid sat down at his desk. "What if we tell our wives what we're thinking about doing?" Don continued, raising his brow.

Sid tossed that around. *That might not be a bad idea,* he thought. *I could start by telling Betsy about the ten thousand we added into the sale, and our share was now sitting there inside the bank. If that sends a thrill up her leg, she just might want to take even more of the old lady's money.* "Alright," Sid said, coming out of his thoughts. "I've got an idea. Let's tell them about the money we took already." Don liked that idea as soon as it rolled off Sid's tongue. "You think we should sneak up there, or go home and tell our wives first?" he asked.

"I think we should open this can of worms first. I'd rather tell Betsy now than have her find out later. She can swing a mean bat."

Don laughed. "I'll pick you up around eight tonight. Be ready."

Sid watched him leave. He leaned back staring out the window. *I sure hope our wives go along with this,* he thought.

10

Two Snakes in the Grass

At seven that evening, Don pulled up at Sid's house. He honked the horn and waited.

"Don's here, honey," Betsy said, opening the door and stepping out onto the porch.

"I'm coming," Sid replied, putting on his coat.

Don watched her walk down the steps toward his car. *Here comes trouble,* he thought as she approached. He rolled down his window. "Hi, Betsy," he greeted her, seeing Sid walking out.

"Hello, Don. It certainly is a lovely night, isn't it?" she replied.

He looked up at her standing there. "Nice night?" he questioned, gazing into her eyes. *Nice night for what?* he thought - thinking her next set of words would blast him right out of his car for coming up with the stupid idea of wanting to rob the old lady.

Sid walked up and wrapped his arms around his wife from behind. She turned her head toward him and then glanced back down at Don. Sid winked at him. *She bought the idea,* Don thought with a sigh.

"You're in?" he simply asked.

"Damn right I am. How about Sue? What did she say?"

Don smiled. "She thinks it's a nice night too."

Betsy laughed. "You two be careful up there," she said, turning around. "I'll be waiting up, sweetheart," she continued, kissing her husband.

"We'll be back as soon as we can," Sid replied, letting her go and walking around the car.

Betsy stood there and waved as Don reversed out of the driveway. She walked back up the steps and opened the door. *I sure hope they find a way into that manor,* she thought, strolling in.

As Don headed down the street, he glanced over at Sid. "For a minute, there I thought she was going to come out and blast me."

Sid laughed. "I was going to call you as soon as I told her and she said yes, but she was like a kitten all day."

Don laughed. "I got the same thing from Sue. I am sure they're probably on the phone talking to one another right now."

"Yeah, I can just imagine. They're probably already planning on what to spend the money on."

Don laughed. "You know what?"

"What?"

"Well, not to change the subject, but do you think we can use flashlights up there?"

Sid let go of his smile. That was a good question. "I don't know," he said and then paused thinking. "There are lots of houses on Daisy Lane. Do you think we should?" he asked.

"Yes, do you really want to be stumbling around in the dark inside that castle?"

Sid laughed.

"What's so funny?"

"You calling it a castle."

"Well, it might as well be. That place is enormous inside."

Sid nodded. That was an understatement. It was more than enormous – *hell, a person could actually get lost in there if they weren't careful,* he thought.

"You're right. I guess I just like the term 'manor' instead of calling it a castle."

"If it helps settle your nerves, call it whatever you want. Now, how do you want to do this? We just can't roll up the driveway with the Blooms watching everything that goes on around there. Those two busybodies will certainly know. And remember, Mrs. Rose is living with them right now."

Sid tossed that around. "We'll drive around the back of the place. We can go up the hill off of Old Tiller Road."

"When did you think of that?"

"Just now, why?"

"Great. I wish we had thought of that earlier, I'm not wearing my boots," Don replied.

Sid shook his head.

"You got your boots on?" Don asked.

"Yep."

"Wonderful," he spat, focusing his attention back on the road.

They sat in silence for a while as Don drove along the winding backcountry roads to Old Tiller Road, which was just a country dirt road that traveled behind the manor up on Cherry Hill. The landscape behind the manor was a patchwork of rolling hills and farms that sat within the small valleys, along with some rustic homes that dotted the hillsides. As they turned onto Old Tiller, the forest came right up to the edge of the road.

"Just down a ways, do you remember that old barn still sitting there on the Klondike's farm?" Sid said.

"Yeah, the one with no doors?"

"That's the one."

"You think the Klondike's will ever come back?"

"No, and none of their kids want the farm either. I'm surprised they haven't put the place up for sale," Sid replied, and then quickly said, "OK, there's the driveway. Turn off your lights and roll up to the barn."

"You think we should just pull the car in?"

"It's your car," Sid replied. "You can risk it, but I wouldn't. These old structures can just fall over."

"You're right. I'll park it out here," Don replied, pulling up in front of the barn. They both got out. Don shifted his eyes down at his shoes and fumed. Sid rounded the car and looked at him.

"Forget about your shoes, will ya. Just watch your step as we climb the hill."

"Right," Don replied, handing him a flashlight and then started walking back up to Old Tiller Road. They looked both ways down the road. It was dark in both directions. Don looked back at the barn – he could barely make out his car sitting there.

"No one will see it, and besides, who the hell comes out here at night?" Sid whispered, walking across the road.

Don turned his flashlight on and followed Sid across. Right before the terrain started to rise, Sid stopped. Don walked up beside him. "You see those trees up there?" Sid asked.

"Yeah."

"Alright, we'll head up that way. Once we get to the trees just use them to hang onto as you climb."

"OK."

Once they made the ridge they holed up to catch their breath. "Sure is dark back here," Don said, scanning the area.

"It sure is. Now, do you see that old garage?" Sid asked, pointing his flashlight.

"Yeah."

"We'll head for that and slip up the side of it to check out the manor before we walk up."

"OK."

Wilfred opened his eyes inside the garage when he heard something moving nearby. He thought it was an animal at first until he heard whispering.

"Wow, will you look at that," Don gasped, standing next to the garage.

"Awesome, isn't it?"

"Awesome? You have to be kidding me – it looks creepy," Don replied, scanning the entire back.

"Don't get all choked up just yet. Wait until we're inside."

Don glanced at him in the glow of the flashlights. "Maybe I'll wait here and play lookout."

"You'll be looking out alright – looking out the side of your head right after I punch ya. Now let's get moving."

"Go ahead, I'll be right behind you, smart butt," Don grumbled, giving him a shove.

As the two slowly passed the open garage door and headed toward the manor, Wilfred's eyes beaded on them. *Who are they and what are they up to?* he thought. *They're sure playing with fire if Theodore gets one whiff of them. They'll be dinner for sure.*

Wilson sat up on Abby's mattress when he spotted strange lights below the balcony in the backyard. "Cracker, check this out," he whispered, nudging him awake.

"What, what?" Cracker replied, rubbing his eyes and sitting up.

"Look," he said, pointing toward the balcony.

Cracker's eyes went wide. "What do you think it is?"

"I don't know. Let's get up and take a look," he replied, hopping down to the floor.

Theodore, who was sleeping on the floor next to the mattress, opened his eyes. "What are you doing?" he asked. Before Wilson could answer, Cracker hopped down. Theodore looked at him. "We see lights out back," Cracker whispered.

"Lights?" Theodore gasped, standing up and looking back. He spotted them too. "Come on, let's check it out," he said, walking toward the balcony. He slowly pushed open one of the doors and walked out. The next thing he felt was Wilson and Cracker jumping up and grabbing his tail. Up they went, along his backside and stood there on top of his head. “What do you see?” Theodore asked, standing next to the balcony’s cement railing.

“Someone’s coming up from the rear of the garage with flashlights,” Wilson whispered in his ear.

“What!?” Theodore shockingly replied.

“Yes. I see two – they look like men,” Cracker whispered.

“Hey, what’s going on?” Benjamin said from behind them.

“Theodore turned around. “Shh… we’ve got company.”

“Company? At this time of night?” Benjamin questioned.

Theodore shook his head.

“They’re not company. Now get your little bottom up here,” Wilson whispered down to him.

Benjamin jumped up, grabbed Theodore’s tail, and ran along his back. Theodore turned around so the mice could see over the railing. “Well, I’ll be,” Benjamin gasped. “What do you think they’re up to?”

“No good if you ask me,” Theodore whispered. “Now all of you get down and let me handle this.”

Benjamin and Cracker jumped to the floor. Wilson stayed. Theodore cast his eyes upon him. Are you getting down?” he asked. Wilson slid down to Theodore’s nose and stared him right in the eyes. “If they see you - it’ll be game over.”

“What are you talking about? I’m Lord of this house and it’s my job to ensure everyone is safe.” Theodore grunted, tightening his brow.

“Yes, you are Lord of the house, but no one knows there’s a male lion living up here. If you go down there and scare them half to death, you can bet the authorities will be coming for you in the morning. You know people are not allowed to keep lions as pets.”

“Who said anything about scaring them,” Theodore replied, shaking his head making Wilson lose his balance. He fell on his bum holding onto Theodore’s whiskers. “I’m warning you, Theodore,” he said, sitting there.

Theodore lowered his nose to the floor. Wilson jumped off. “Theodore, come back here,” he scolded, watching Theodore trotting over to the master’s chambers door. He never turned to look back.

“Do something,” Benjamin yelled, “before he scares the life out of them.”

As soon as Theodore walked out of the room, he ran down the hall toward the staircase. Wilson panicked looking at Cracker. “Ooga booga,” Cracker said, giving him a hint.

Theodore made it down to the second landing. As he headed down to the first landing, he leaped into the air. Wilson looked at the door and said,

"*Moonlight – starlight, just say goodnight… Theodore.*"

In mid-air, Theodore instantly turned into a stuffed toy lion again. He landed upright on the staircase above the parlor.

"Shh.. listen. You hear anything, fellas?" Benjamin whispered.

"No, but we better find out if the spell worked," Wilson replied, scampering to the door.

Down the hallway the mice went. At the staircase, they hopped down.

"You want to check the windows or one of the doors?" Don asked, scanning the back of thc manor.

"Let's try the doors," Sid replied, walking up the large kitchen patio steps. The door was locked.

"Let's try the ballroom doors," Don whispered, turning and walking back down to the yard. Those doors too were locked. "Damn," Sid cursed.

"Now what?" Don asked.

"I don't know. Let's try one of the basement windows on the side."

When the mice made it down to the first landing, they were relieved to see Theodore sitting there as a stuffed toy. "My, that was close," Wilson gasped, walking up to Theodore.

"You know he's going to be really upset when we bring him back," Benjamin warned.

"He sure will," Cracker agreed.

"I'm not worried about him anymore. And remember, we now have the spell to put him to sleep."

"Hey, look at that," Don said, shining his light down on a basement window at the side of the manor. "You think it's open?"

"Well, I didn't come all the way out here to catch frogs," Sid replied, walking over and bending down. He pushed the window. It opened. He turned around and smiled at Don.

"OK, now what?"

"After you," Sid replied, waving his hand toward the window.

"Maybe we should check to see what's down there first before we go crawling in backwards. I really don't want anything grabbing me."

"Will you shut up and hold the window open for me?" Sid scolded, crouching down.

"Alright, just make sure you can reach the floor before dropping down," Don said.

"I will," Sid replied, tucking his flashlight inside his shirt. He lifted one leg in and then the other and started to crawl in backwards. His feet hit something, but it wasn't the floor.

"You feel anything below you?" Don whispered.

"Yeah," he moaned, stretching one foot further down. "It feels like a wooden crate of some sort. There, I got it," he said, placing his foot on the crate.

"Here, hold this," he continued, pulling out his flashlight and handing it to Don. Don watched him drop down and then heard a loud crash. "Ow… that hurt" Sid cursed, sitting on the floor and rubbing his backside. He looked up when Don shone his light down upon him sitting there on the filthy floor.

"What happened?"

"I knocked over some crates. OK, start in and I'll hold your legs steady," he replied, getting up.

"Hey, did you hear something?" Benjamin said, placing his little ear to the wind.

"Yeah," Cracker replied, walking toward the first set of stairs off the landing. He turned around. "Did you hear it too?" he asked Wilson.

"Yes, it sounded as if they're coming in, but where?"

Cracker's eyes lit up. "The basement," he said. "I'll bet-cha that they're coming in through the window."

"Boy, you have good ears. Let's go and see," Wilson replied, jumping down the stairs.

"Come on, Benjamin," Cracker yelled back, taking the stairs down.

Benjamin shook his head. *I'm always last,* he thought, hopping down.

"Man, will you get a load of this place," Don said, shining his light around the basement.

"Yeah, it looks like one hundred year's worth of cobwebs and dust," Sid replied, walking toward the wine cellar.

"You think her suitcase is down here?" Don asked, walking behind him.

"No," he replied, shining his light inside the cellar and then turned around. "I don't think anything is down here except rats and spiders. Let's go up," he continued, brushing the cobwebs out of his way. "You've never been in here, have you?" he asked, taking the steps up to the kitchen.

"No."

"You're in for a surprise," Sid replied, opening the door and shining his light about the kitchen.

"Will you look at this?" Don gasped, gazing up at the twelve-foot ceiling then across to the big windows over the sink. "This kitchen is bigger than my front room."

"It would have to be this big for the parties the Baron put on. However, you haven't seen anything yet," Sid said, walking out and down the long corridor toward the parlor. "We'll have to turn off our flashlights as we search the front," he continued over his shoulder.

As Don walked down the corridor, he stopped when he saw an elevator.

"You have to be kidding me," he gasped.

"What?" Sid replied, turning around.

"I never knew this place had an elevator."

Sid laughed. "You see, I told you. That goes up to the master's chambers. If I had his kind of money, I would've installed one too. Wait until you see the staircase, now come on," he replied, walking toward the parlor.

Wilson, Cracker and Benjamin had slipped into the kitchen and hid inside one of the bottom kitchen cupboards before Sid and Don came up from the basement.

"Who are these guys and what are they looking for?" Cracker whispered.

Wilson shook his head. Then his eyes grew wide. "They're after the tree."

"No, they can't be," Benjamin replied.

"No?" Wilson questioned.

Benjamin leaned into him and whispered, "They'd have to be spacemen to know about that tree."

"Spacemen?" Wilson fumed, wrinkling his brow. "Where do you come up with such nonsense? Spacemen…," he said, shaking his head. "If they're not after the tree, then what are they looking for?"

Benjamin looked at Cracker. A thought suddenly hit Benjamin square in the face to why they were here. "The suitcase… maybe they're here to steal Abby's suitcase full of money."

"Suitcase? How would they know about the suitcase? And if they did, they'll never find the money because Abby took the money out and hid it," Wilson said, looking at Cracker.

"I don't know you two, unless…" Cracker's voice trailed off. "Maybe they're after some of Abby's priceless items?" he continued, looking out into the dark kitchen.

"You know," Benjamin whispered and then paused, "they could be some of the workers who've come back to steal something." Benjamin continued.

"Maybe," Wilson replied.

With that, they all turned their heads toward the doorway leading out of the kitchen. "We won't find out standing here," Wilson said, walking out of the cupboard. When he got to the door leading into the corridor, he stopped in his tracks.

"Did you hear something?" Cracker whispered from behind him.

"Theodore," Wilson replied, looking back.

Their eyes grew wide. Theodore was sitting on the first landing.

"What if they take him?" Cracker remarked, panicking.

"Holy smoke, we better get moving," Benjamin gasped. He felt a paw on his shoulder. "Wait," Wilson whispered. Benjamin turned around. "We can't save him now," Wilson continued.

"What about the spell?" Benjamin replied.

Wilson shook his head thinking. "Well, maybe," he started to say. "If they try to take him, I'll use the spell, OK? Now let's go," he continued.

They peeked around the corner of the corridor. The men were gone.

"Come on," Wilson whispered.

"Will ya look at this?" Don gasped, walking into the parlor. "I wish we could turn on our flashlights. This place is enormous," he continued, glancing up at the winding staircase.

"Let's keep moving," Sid replied, walking past the stairs and into the stately den.

"How many fireplaces does this place have?" Don asked, looking back at the parlor fireplace and then the one in the den.

"Eight or nine, I think," Sid replied.

"Oh my God, will you look at that creepy thing?" Don gasped, pointing up at the giant moose head hanging over the den's fireplace.

"Awesome, isn't it?"

"Yeah. I'd hate to have that thing charging at me. By the size of its head it would be like running from a freight train. And look at those antlers – wow!"

"Come on, we don't have all night," Sid replied, looking up at Boris. He turned, walked through the den and opened the door to the billiard room. After searching the billiard room, they searched the pool area and then headed back out to the den.

"I don't think she left it down here, but we'll check the ballroom just in case," Sid whispered, heading for the corridor.

"Man, oh man, this place is unbelievable," Don gushed behind him.

"Well, check this out. On this side of the ballroom corridor, you have a large coatroom, and down there is the men and women's bathrooms. On the other side here," he continued, opening one of the doors, "is the ballroom."

Don stepped in and almost died looking up at four, large chandeliers hanging down from the thirty-foot ceiling. The walls were all made of glass. He then focused his attention on all the boxes sitting there in the middle.

"Alright, you take that side, and I'll start on this side," Sid said, walking toward the back doors.

They split up looking for the suitcase. After checking the entire ballroom, Don knew that the suitcase had to be upstairs.

"I thought that's where Mrs. Rose would have hidden it, but we had to check just to make sure," Sid replied. "We'll head up now."

"OK."

Wilson, Benjamin and Cracker slipped under the staircase and were now peeking out through a crack when Sid and Don headed up the stairs. At the first landing, they both suddenly stopped when they saw Theodore sitting there. Sid turned his flashlight on and shone it down on the stuffed toy. "Well… look who's minding the store," he said, bending over and picking Theodore up.

"You think she left that toy right here to watch the house?" Don asked, smiling.

"I wouldn't put it past the old bird. She's so far out there you'd need a telescope to see her."

Don laughed, glancing at Theodore in Sid's hands. "Yeah, well, set him down and let's keep moving. We've got wives at home waiting up for us."

Sid placed Theodore back on the landing and continued up the stairs. After they had left, the three mice scampered out from underneath the stairs and saw Theodore sitting there.

“What are we going to do now, fellas?” Benjamin asked.

“I don’t know,” Wilson replied.

“I’m not going up if that’s what you’re thinking, Wilson. You know there’s nothing we can do now except wait until they come down again,” Cracker said.

“Yeah, you’re right,” Wilson replied. “Let’s hide behind Grandfather and see what they do.”

Cracker and Benjamin nodded. They ran across the parlor floor and raced behind Grandfather. Three little heads then peeked out focusing on the stairs.

Sid and Don searched the second floor - nothing. They went up and searched the third-floor bedrooms. They too were empty. Up on the fourth floor they checked the study. It was empty. Before Sid turned to leave, he spotted a door leading up to the bell tower. “What do we have here?” he said, walking over and opening it up. Don stepped beside him. “Now that’s creepy,” he whispered, looking up the small, winding staircase. “It won’t be up there,” he continued, glancing at the side of Sid’s face.

Sid turned and looked at him. “You look scared.”

“You’re right. I am not going up there, and besides, you think that old lady could make it up these steps? I doubt it,” he continued, turning and heading for the door.

Sid gazed up the staircase. He felt shivers running down his neck.

“Yeah,” he replied. “I don’t think she could get up those stairs. It has to be in her bedroom,” he continued, shutting the door and following Don out into the hallway.

When they opened the master’s chambers door, Don walked in scanning the room. To his right were the walk-in closets. Past them were two large bathrooms, and across the chamber was an enormous fireplace and huge mantelpiece. To the left, he saw two large bay doors leading out to a balcony, and then there was the elevator. “I’m in the king’s chamber. Or, this must be what it felt like to be a king,” he said, turning in a circle.

“Well, Kingy Dingy, how about you go and search the bathrooms while I check the walk-in closet?”

“Yes, my faithful Queen,” Don quipped, walking over and opening the door to the women’s bathroom.

Sid shook his head opening the closet door. He smiled ear to ear when the beam of his flashlight shone on the suitcase. He quickly stepped out, opened the women's bathroom door and said, "I found it."

"No kidding," Don replied stunned, walking out.

"It's in the closet," he said, walking back to the closet door. "Here, take my flashlight," he continued, kneeling next to the suitcase. He set the suitcase on its side and opened it. His mind went blank. It was empty. "Somebody run me over with a bus," he cursed.

"Now what are we going to do?" Don asked, feeling sick.

Sid sat down and thought. *Forget about trying to find a needle in a haystack – there has to be a million places inside this manor to hide that money,* he thought. *We're screwed...*

"Well, oh wise one, now what?" Don smartly asked.

Sid looked up at him. "I think we better talk to them kids when we see them at the fair. It's going to take more than the two of us to find it now."

"It's your call, but you must consider Ernie."

"I know," he replied, standing up. "Let's get out of here."

When they got back to the car and slipped inside, Sid looked over at him. "We'd better come up with something to tell Betsy and Sue."

"Yeah, I sure hope they go along with this idea of asking those kids to get involved."

"Me too."

After they had left, Wilson, Cracker and Benjamin climbed the stairs as fast as they could. When they walked up to Theodore, Wilson whispered the spell to wake him up. WHOOSH... Theodore came to life. They quickly stepped back. Theodore looked down with fire in his eyes. "You three, how could you do that to me?"

Wilson stood there with his little knees shaking. "We had no other choice," he nervously replied.

"I wasn't going to eat them. And while we're on the subject, tell me, you little runts, just how many people have I eaten?" Theodore scolded.

"None," Cracker replied, shaking with fear.

Benjamin had had enough of Theodore's overbearing attitude, seeing his friends standing there trembling. It made him mad. He puffed out his little chest and pointed up at Theodore. "Listen here, you big brute. I've got a right mind to kick you square in the shins."

Theodore slowly lowered his head and glared at him. Benjamin stepped back. "Which one?" Theodore asked, tightening his brow

"All of them," Benjamin replied, "and then… I'm going to tell Abby," he continued, lifting up his chin and boldly folding his arms in defiance.

Theodore's eyes bore into him. Benjamin stared right back. Theodore glanced over seeing Wilson and Cracker now folding their arms too and glaring up at him as well. *Talk about having guts,* Theodore humorously thought. *I could take them in one bite, and yet here they are standing side by side as if they were the three musketeers.* That thought made him laugh. The three looked at one another confused. That made Theodore laugh even harder.

"What's so funny!?" Benjamin spat.

"You three," Theodore laughed.

"Oh, yeah?" Benjamin replied, stepping forward.

Theodore continued to laugh.

"Pick out a shin bone and start kicking, fellas," Benjamin ordered.

Theodore couldn't stop laughing. He hit the floor in a thud.

"Pull his ears," Cracker yelled.

Tears rolled down Theodore's cheeks from laughter as the three began kicking him and pulling on his ears. Then the laughing bug hit the three mice as well. They all started laughing while pounding on Theodore. "We'll show you," Wilson laughed, kicking and slugging him.

"Oh, please, somebody save me from the three musketeers," Theodore giggled.

Cracker stopped punching. "Did you hear that, fellas? He just called us the three musketeers."

"Yeah," Benjamin replied. "Let's show him what we can do," he continued, stomping one of Theodore's front paws.

In all that laughter and fun, the four never realized what was happening - they were bonding an everlasting friendship together.

In the morning, after waking up inside the master's chambers together, they all sat around and talked about the strangers. They concluded that whoever they were, they were after Abby's money. "We'll have to tell her when she gets home," Theodore said. "She won't be happy," Benjamin replied. Wilson shook his head. "You're right about that." *She'll be as mad as a hornet when she hears the news*, he thought.

11
Chemistry

On Friday morning, Fanny pulled in at the Bloom's house to pick up Karen and Abby and then drive them out to the Davenport farm. All the ladies in the Women's Club, the Cloverdale City workers, along with Mayor Bumpkin's volunteers, were to meet at the farm and assist in setting up the fair. It was going to be a day filled with activities. Gentlemen Jim's Big Top set up their tents and children's rides, along with soda, cotton candy and caramel apple booths, while Connie's Bakery, the IGA grocery store and Fletcher's Five & Dime set up the grills and bake sale tent.

Fanny stepped out of her VW Bug, fixed her dress and walked up to the door.

"Fanny is here," Albert yelled, walking over to the door. "Good morning, Fanny. My, don't you look fabulous today," he continued, casting his eyes down her dress.

"Good morning, Albert. I see your eyes approve of my outfit," she replied, stepping past him.

"Yes, I can still remember the day when Karen…" he started to say.

"When Karen - what?" Karen interrupted, walking into the front room.

Albert looked at his wife. He wasn't going to say it. Karen cocked her head and waited. Fanny looked from one to the other knowing Albert was about to dig his own grave. She thought she could save him. Well, maybe this one time, at least. "I think he was going to say something about the color of my dress. You like?" she asked, turning in a circle for Karen.

Karen looked at her then glanced over at Albert. He raised his brow.

"Yes, I love the color," Karen replied, eyeing up her husband. "I used to be able to fit into a dress like that once," she mildly continued.

Albert cringed. Before he could talk his way out of trouble, Abby strolled in. "Good morning, Fanny. Wow," she said, stepping back and looking at her dress.

"That's funny, that's what Albert just said," Karen spoke up.

"Coffee anyone?" Albert quickly asked, trying to excuse himself.

"Yes, please," Fanny replied, "just black for me, thank you."

"Black sounds good – right under both eyes," Karen humorously scolded. Albert smiled at Abby. "Did I miss something?" she asked, looking at Karen.

"Yes, you just missed the Fourth of July," Karen coldly replied, folding her arms.

Abby wrinkled her brow and then she smiled, knowing Albert must have stepped into another cow pie.

"Abby?" Albert said, sidestepping his wife's comment.

"Oh, iced tea for me, please. Thank you."

"Great," he replied, walking out of the room.

Karen watched him leave then looked at the women. "I just love placing him on a leash when I can," she whispered.

"I think you just did," Fanny giggled, sitting down.

After their tea and coffee, the women were off, allowing Albert time to relax in the comfort of his quiet home.

When they pulled up to the Davenport farm, the place was already swarming with busy little bees. Jim's Big Top was there and Mayor Bumpkin was running around with his volunteers.

"There's our group," Fanny said, pulling into the makeshift parking lot. Abby looked over from her passenger seat. She wasn't surprised to see Claudia standing in the center of the group wearing a head scarf. The women all looked over and waved at them as they got out of the car.

"Good morning, everyone," Karen greeted them.

"Good morning," the ladies replied in unison.

"What a day this will be," Flo said, walking up to Fanny. "My, my, are you here to work, or are you trying to catch the eye of one of those handsome devils over there?" she asked, nodding in the direction of the men from Jim's Big Top.

Fanny looked over. There were a few she thought she could see dancing with; however, today was a day of work. "No, I just like feeling beautiful, that's all," she teased, winking at Flo.

Beautiful, I'll make you beautiful, Claudia thought, walking over. "I'm glad you left your dancing shoes at home, Fanny. We were just discussing the assignments when you drove up. I'd like for you, Flo and Abby to take these boxes of bows and ribbons and place them around the trees. The rest of us gals will be covering the tables as Mayor Bumpkin's volunteers offload them from the truck. Once that's done, we'll be assisting Connie's Bakery in setting out the bake sale goods."

"Splendid," Fanny replied, walking over and picking up a box. "Let's go, you two," she continued, walking over to the nearest tree.

Abby and Flo picked up a box and headed over to her. "What do you mean by splendid?" Flo whispered.

"I didn't want to start a fight, that's all," Fanny replied, pulling out a ribbon. "Here, take hold of it while I wrap it around the tree."

"A fight!?" Flo whispered. "She's been downright irritable ever since her hair turned blue."

"Blue?" Abby questioned, hiding her joy.

"Yes. Somehow, after you left the salon, Claudia's hair turned blue. I was as shocked as she was and I even showed her the bottle of dye I used. But as you can see, she's still mad at me and I suspect that's why she's given us this assignment."

Abby looked at Fanny. Fanny raised her brow and said, "I think it was because we all laughed at her, Abby."

"I see," Abby replied, glancing back at Claudia. "So that's why she's wearing a scarf today."

"Yes," Flo replied, fixing the knot and letting go. "I am just glad that her hair color is almost back to normal."

"Hello, ladies," Mayor Bumpkin said, walking up.

"Good morning, Mayor," they all greeted him, standing back from the tree.

"Those are nice," he said, checking out the ribbons.

"Yes, I even like the colors," Abby replied, picking up a red bow to place over the pink ribbon.

"Mrs. Rose, I came over to tell you that Mitt Ryan, our foreman, just said that they're almost done inside the manor and that you may return on Monday around noon."

Abby smiled. She wanted to get home. That thought made her think of all her friends. *I sure hope they've been staying out of trouble while the workers have been there,* she thought. "That's great. Please thank your crew for doing the work. Oh, by the way, did they have any trouble with the elevator?"

"Mitt said that was the hardest part of the job. The whole thing needed new electrical wiring installed. However, the ten thousand dollars on top of the price for the manor was enough."

Ten thousand, Abby thought. *I paid Sid and Don twenty thousand for the work that needed to be done out there. Those two,* her thoughts continued spinning; *they've taken me for a ride - a ten thousand dollar ride at that.* She shifted her attention on Mayor Bumpkin. *This isn't the time nor the place to be discussing this*. "I am glad for that," she kindly replied. "I'll inform Karen and Albert that I'll be moving back in on Monday."

Mayor Bumpkin nodded, tipped his head toward the other ladies and left.

"Elevator?" Fanny gasped.

"Yes, my father, I mean the Baron had it installed. I guess, so he didn't have to climb the stairs every night," Abby replied, stumbling over her words.

Flo and Fanny froze for a moment with that comment. *Her mind must be slipping,* Fanny thought. *Did she just say her father?* Flo thought. *No, she couldn't have.* "It's amazing how much you know about the place, Abby," Flo said, wondering if Abby just made a mistake.

"I did a lot of research before I purchased the manor."

"You know," Fanny said and then paused, "I've been wondering why you actually want to live in such a big place like that, all on your own no less."

Abby sighed looking at the two. She could have kicked herself in the shins for making that slip up. She brought up a smile and then replied, "You only live once."

"I guess. But I would have never thought of doing something like buying a castle, Abby," Fanny remarked, "most elderly people find themselves a small cottage home to manage - like Albert and Karen."

"Well, maybe I am different, Fanny. I guess jumping out of planes would not be your style either," she replied.

"You're not thinking of taking up parachuting?" Flo asked, stunned.

No, Abby thought. *However, just the idea has led you both away from my stupid mistake.* "Why… certainly not. However, there are some at my age that do those kinds of crazy things."

"I suppose you're right," Fanny replied. "How about we get this done and then see what Connie has brought to sell. I'm getting a little hungry."

"Me too. What tree do you want to do next?" Flo asked, picking up her box.

"Let's just go in a circle and end up over by Connie's tent," Fanny replied, picking up her box.

As the women were going from tree to tree, a yellow city work truck pulled in. The three of them stopped to watch Mayor Bumpkin walk over and talk to the driver.

"He sure is a handsome man," Abby said, attaching a bow.

"That's Mitt Ryan," Flo replied. "Not married either," she teased, nudging Fanny.

"Oh, go on now. He could have his pick of any woman in town," Fanny replied, turning around and blushing.

"Hey, who's the dame in the pink dress?" Mitt asked Mayor Bumpkin.

He looked over then turned and smiled at Mitt. "Come on, Big Guy. You know who that is – it's Fanny."

"No…." his voice trailed off, looking over at her.

"Yes, I'm afraid so. You see that little lady in the light blue dress?" Mayor Bumpkin said.

"Yeah."

"That's Mrs. Rose, and what I've heard through the grapevine is that she has taken Fanny under her wing and transformed her into Miss Cloverdale U.S.A."

"Catch a cat by the tail," Mitt sighed, looking over at Fanny again.

Mayor Bumpkin kept his eyes on Fanny as she bent down, picked up a ribbon and then tied it to a tree. "Who would have suspected under all that nineteen twenty style clothing she used to wear was such a fine-looking woman?"

"I see she's not wearing those funny looking glasses anymore either," Mitt added.

Mayor Bumpkin looked at him. Mitt's eyes were still glued on Fanny. "Well, you just said – catch a cat by the tail. Why don't you go over and introduce yourself to Mrs. Rose?" he said with a wink.

Mitt looked at him then back at the ladies.

"And besides, Mitt, there's nothing better than strolling with a gorgeous woman at a fair. You haven't asked anyone yet, have you?"

Mitt looked at him again. "No, but I might," he replied, getting out of his truck.

"OK, boys, the Mayor here will show you where these generators go," he yelled to his crew. "I think I'll take your advice and go over and meet Mrs. Rose." he continued, walking over to the women.

Mayor Bumpkin stepped aside watching Mitt float over as if he were walking on clouds. He sighed and then turned his attention back on the work crew. "Come, I'll show you where we want these," he said to the men.

"Good morning, ladies," Mitt said. They all turned around. Flo suddenly felt her heart go weak. She glanced over at Fanny and then quickly looked back at him. “Why, good morning, Mitt,” she replied, stepping up with a bow in her hand.

Mitt looked at her then at Fanny. Their eyes met and settled on one another. “Good morning, Mitt,” Fanny said, feeling her heart skip a beat. Flo looked at them eyeing each other up and then she poured cold water over the moment. “Mitt, I’d like you to meet Mrs. Rose,” she said.

Mitt kept his eyes on Fanny for a split second longer then turned and looked at Abby. “Good morning. It’s nice to finally meet you. I came over to say hello and tell you that we’re almost done inside the manor.”

“It’s nice to meet you too, Mitt. Mayor Bumpkin just told me that you and your crew would be done sometime around noon on Monday.”

“Yes,” he replied, glancing over at Fanny again.

Abby and Flo caught the look. They both knew the chemistry was bubbling between the pair.

Abby hated to break the connection, but wanted to ask about some of her items. “Did the moving company come out and move the big items where they belong?”

Mitt glanced at her. “Yes, they did. I was amazed to see them hoisting that swan tub up into the master’s chambers. I’ve never seen anything like it. Where did you get it?”

“That was purchased by my great uncle in the 1700’s,” she replied, drifting back – all the way back to her great uncle, the Black Knight.

“It sure is a magnificent piece. It must be worth a fortune,” Mitt replied.

Abby stepped out of her thoughts. “It’s priceless. Well, to me it is.”

“I guess,” he replied.

“What about my refrigerator?”

“Yes, that too. We turned it on now that the electrical is up and running. They also unpacked the grand piano and set it up in the parlor.”

Abby shifted her eyes on Flo then at Fanny. Their facial expressions said heaps. They wanted answers to her slip up and she knew that once Mitt left, she’d be doing some explaining. "Look, if you wouldn't mind, Mitt," she said. “I’m getting a bit tired. You think you could help Fanny while Flo walks me over to Connie’s tent?”

Fanny almost fell over with that suggestion. Flo, on the other hand, just smiled. It would give her a chance to be alone with Abby and ask her a few questions.

"No, I wouldn't mind at all," Mitt replied, picking up Flo's box. "What tree are we doing next, Fanny?"

Fanny raised her brow at Flo and Abby. They gave her a sly wink in return. Fanny wrinkled her nose knowing what they were doing. "We've got three more trees left. Let's start with that one," she replied.

Before Fanny started over to the tree, she watched Flo take Abby's arm and escort her over to the tent. *Those two,* she thought, *those two wonderful ladies. They certainly know how to bait a man.* She stepped out of her thoughts, smiled at Mitt, and started walking over to the tree. He quickly turned around. "Mrs. Rose," he yelled after her. Abby stopped and turned. "We watered that plant in the master's chambers and then set it out on the balcony to get some sun. I hope that was OK."

"Thank you. I completely forgot all about it," she yelled back.

Mitt nodded and waved. Abby turned and continued walking alongside Flo.

"So," Mitt said, turning toward Fanny. His mouth suddenly went dry - feeling nervous.

Fanny gazed at him. Nothing more came out. "Sew a button," she teased.

He boyishly grinned then fumbled badly. "I didn't recognize you when I pulled up."

"You didn't recognize me?"

"Well, I did, but I…," he replied then laughed.

"Mitt Ryan, we grew up together," she humorously scolded.

"Yes, I know that, Fanny. I just…" his voice trailed off.

"It seems you've just lost your tongue because you've never seen me like this. Is that what's caught inside your throat?"

"Yes," he laughed with embarrassment.

"Well, I hope you can get used to it because I've left the 19th century, and I'll never be seen wearing clothing only worn on waxed figures again."

That was it. He was more than smitten - he was totally gone. Fanny was not only beautiful, she was gorgeous through-and-through. "Fanny," he said, mustering all his courage.

"Yes," she replied, stopping at the tree.

"Will you go to the fair with me this weekend?"

"Mitt Ryan," she gasped. "Are you really asking me to go?"

"Yes, that's if no one has asked you yet," he replied, hoping she was free.

"I would love to go with you, Mitt."

His heart melted. Her heart too was totally gone with all his boyish charm.

"Now, Abby," Flo started her questioning, walking slowly over to the tent. "You never mentioned that you played piano."

"Why, I never thought of it, Flo. Most children in my day were brought up to play an instrument," she replied confused. "It's terrible that today's children are not groomed to do so. I think they'd learn more than just to play an instrument, they'd learn discipline as well."

"I suppose you're right. Now tell me about that swan tub. It must be a magnificent piece."

Abby studied Flo's eyes. She could tell there was an underlining reasoning for all her questions. That thought made her think…. *I could just imagine her and Fanny wearing black hooded capes and chanting spells over a witch's cauldron.* She dropped those thoughts and answered her. "Yes, it's one of my favorite pieces. It's made of fine porcelain."

"Wow – purchased in the 1700s too," she cooed. "Now tell me, where do your ancestors come from? Mine are from Scotland."

If that weren't a baited line, Abby thought. *Tossing her ancestors out like that was surely a hint*. "My relatives come from Austria."

"Austria? You don't say." Flo quipped. *So was the Baron,* Flo thought. "How many relatives…" she started to say when a burly voice called over. "OK, you two, we don't have all day," Claudia yelled out from the tent.

Abby looked at Claudia standing there with her arms folded. "We're coming," she replied, turning and looking at Flo. "We'll have more time to talk later. Right now we have General Patton barking orders."

Flo sighed, *so close.* She gave her a slight smile then looked over at Claudia. *It's too bad the dye didn't make your face blue as well. You'd be home right now hiding under your bed.* "Let's go see what the General wants," she replied, escorting Abby over to the tent.

As all the women were setting out the baked goods onto the tables, Mitt and Fanny entered the tent. "Mmm…" Fanny purred, picking up a cookie and eating it.

"That's one of my new chocolate cookies," Connie said, picking one up and taking a bite.

"They're so good," Fanny purred, glancing over at Claudia.

"When you're done over there, you can help us with the last tables," Claudia barked.

Fanny looked at Mitt. Nothing had to be said. Everyone knew that Claudia thought she ran the town. "I'll be right back," she whispered to him.

"Take your time," he replied, glancing over at Mrs. Rose. He walked over. She stopped what she was doing and looked up at him. *His eyes are as dark as a moonless night,* Abby thought.

"I was just wondering, Mrs. Rose," he said and then paused. She cocked her head. "I noticed your car sitting out in that old garage, or what is left of it. Have you thought about tearing it down and building a new one?"

"Yes, poor Wilfred," she sighed. She instantly noticed a smile appear on Mitt's face. She leaned into him. "I have names for all my possessions, young man."

"You don't say," he quipped, feeling her warm sense of humor.

"Now that you have mentioned it, if you know any companies that do that sort of work, have them come out and give me an estimate."

"I do know a reputable company. Snider's Construction Company. They do garages as well."

"Then I'd love for them to come out, Mitt."

"Good. Now, do you have anyone to assist you in cleaning and painting?"

"She does now," Shaun interrupted, walking into the tent.

They both turned to see him standing there with his parents.

"Well, good day, Shaun," Abby said surprised, looking at the two adults right behind him.

"Hello, Mrs. Rose, I'd like you to meet my parents, Carl and Ruth. I've told them about your car and that I would be working on it."

Abby contently smiled, extending her hand and greeting Mr. Stevenson. "It's so nice to meet you."

"Likewise, Mrs. Rose," he greeted her back. Abby glanced over at Ruth. "You have a great son."

"Thank you. He's told us so much about you, Mrs. Rose," Ruth replied.

Abby looked at Shaun. *We've only just met. What could he have told his parents?* "Well I hope it was all good."

"It certainly was. All he talks about is working on your car," Ruth replied. "I'd love to see it, too," Carl added.

"You will, as soon as Shaun gets Wilfred looking new again. And now," she continued, looking at Shaun, "have you asked your parents if you could help me inside?"

"Yes, I told them how much work had to be done."

"Well, I pay a good price for a hard day's work," she said, focusing her attention on Carl and Ruth.

From what I've heard around town, she has to be a millionaire, Carl thought. "I'm sure you do, Mrs. Rose, and we'd love for Shaun to come work for you. That is, outside his normal working hours at Olson's."

Fanny walked over and took Mitt's hand. Everyone stopped and looked at her. "Mitt just invited me to the fair tomorrow," she beamed.

"Is that so?" Ruth replied, taking in Fanny's new looks. *Yesterday she looked like a duster and today she could sit on the throne,* she thought. Fanny saw the approving look. "Mrs. Rose cut my hair and then she took me shopping with Karen."

Ruth scanned down the front of Fanny's dress again and then looked up at her hair. "Mrs. Rose did that?" she questioned, looking over at Abby. Abby just smiled.

"That she did - with a little help from Karen."

"Well, Mrs. Rose did an outstanding job," Carl added.

"Look, I'd love to sit and chat all day, but I have to get over to the grills before Mayor Bumpkin has me arrested for not showing up. It was nice seeing you, Mrs. Rose," Shaun said, turning and walking away.

Abby gazed upon him as he departed. She knew in her heart that he was the one. She turned and looked at Carl and Ruth. "You must be very proud of him."

"Oh, we are. He's such a fine boy."

"Well," Mitt said, interrupting the group. "I'd better follow Shaun and get back to work myself," he continued, looking at Fanny. "I'll pick you up at..." his voice trailed off, thinking of a time.

"Around nine would be fine, Mitt."

"Nine it will be then," he said, letting go of her hand. "You all have a great day," he continued, walking after Shaun.

"I think we should be getting back ourselves, Carl," Ruth said.

"I am glad you two came out. It was a pleasure meeting you," Abby said. *I sure hope this all works out,* she thought, eyeing her possible future 'in-laws'.

Ruth stepped up to her. "After all the chatter from Shaun about you and Wilfred, we wanted to come out here and personally meet you."

"That was nice. I am staying at Karen and Albert's place until they bring the manor up to code. You are welcome to come up anytime once they finish."

"We'd like that," Carl replied. "Now let's go, honey. I can feel my stomach growling."

"You and food," Ruth spat, winking at Abby. They turned and headed for the entrance of the fair.

After they had departed, Abby turned toward Fanny. "You and Mitt? Gee that was quick."

"It sure was. I am so excited that I could just wet myself, Abby. And to think, Mitt having eyes for me?"

"Oh now, Fanny, lots of men would love to have a chance with you. That is, if you don't go wetting yourself," Abby laughed.

"You know what I mean!"

Abby again laughed. "Mitt seems like a real nice guy," she said.

"Oh, he is."

"Ladies!" Claudia yelped.

Abby and Fanny looked over at her. "She'd make a good drill sergeant," Fanny whispered.

"That she would," Abby replied, walking over to the group.

12

Suspicious Notions

That same evening, after all the work was done with setting up the county fair, Flo went home to enjoy the last of the day in her favorite chair on the backyard patio. Her eyes may have been watching the sun go down, but her thoughts were drifting on Abby. If it were not for Abby's slip up, by mentioning her father and then immediately trying to cover it, Flo would have noticed that the sun had already drifted below the horizon. When she finally stepped out of her thoughts, she looked around to realize that she was sitting outside in the dark. "I think I'll call Fanny," she said, getting up and entering the house.

"Hello?" Fanny said into the phone.

"Fanny, it's me."

"Hi, Flo."

"Do you have a minute?"

"Yes, what's on your mind?" Fanny asked, sitting down on her couch.

"I was wondering," Flo said and then paused, "did you hear Abby today mentioning her father and then say that it was the Baron when she was explaining the elevator to us?"

"Yes, I heard her say that, or I thought she did. But you know the elderly, they do get mixed up from time to time."

"Yes, I know that, but I think she actually meant it."

"You're not serious, are you?"

"Yes, I am serious."

"Wow," Fanny said, surprised.

"Look… as I was walking her back to the tent, I started probing."

"Probing?"

"Yes, in a roundabout way," Flo replied half out of breath from this conversation.

"Flo, how could you do a thing like that to Abby?"

"Do what?"

"Take advantage of that poor soul."

"Now, Fanny, I wasn't doing anything of the sort. I just wanted to know some things."

"Like what?"

"Like where her ancestors came from, that's all."

"What's that got to do with anything?"

"Everything… now listen."

"Alright, go on," Fanny sighed.

"Abby said that her ancestors came from Austria."

"So?"

"I thought you were going to listen?"

"OK, I'm listening," Fanny replied, sitting back.

"The Baron was also born and raised in Austria."

There was silence on the line.

"You there?" Flo asked.

"Yes, you told me to be quiet."

"OK – you can talk now."

"I thought the Baron was German?"

"Fanny, Austria has many German people living there. It became part of Germany during that awful war."

"It did?"

"Yes," she replied, rubbing her forehead. "Look," she continued, "how about we go down and do some research at the library on Monday morning?"

"Research? You mean snooping?"

Flo sighed. "Well, if you want to call it that. Researching, investigating and snooping are all the same thing."

"They are?"

"OK, maybe I should do this on my own. I'm sorry for calling."

"Wait one minute, Missy. You're not going to the library without me."

"Great. I thought you'd come. I'll pick you up around eight a.m. Don't forget."

"How can I forget something like that? I feel like a real poop for doing this, but I know you'd do it without me."

"You're right, I would do it alone. I'll see you at the fair tomorrow and good luck with Mitt. He's a great catch if you can land him in the boat."

"I'll land him, you'll see. Have a good night," Fanny replied and then hung up. She set the phone down and stared at the walls. *What if Abby's father actually was the Baron,* she thought. *The Von Hausslers did have a daughter, or was it a son? I can't remember now.* She leaned back in her seat then something hit her. "Wait a minute," she whispered. "I'm not going to sit here and wait until

Monday. I'm going to do some snooping on the computer right now," she continued, getting up walking toward her study.

She sat down, looked at her computer and then froze. "What was his name?" she said, thinking. "Don, Dan," she sighed. "I know," she said, typing in 'German male names' in the search box. Up came a list starting with 'A'. She scanned down the list. A smile appeared on her face. "Derek. It was Derek Von Haussler." She quickly typed the name *Derek*, sat back and waited. Derek Von Haussler, famous magician, appeared on the screen. She clicked on the name and waited. Up came the Baron's photo and his background history.

Derek Von Haussler:
Born in Austria in 1875; Married Amelia Eichmann in Germany. Moved to Boston in 1900 and then settled in Cloverdale, Pennsylvania. Derek had a daughter, Abigail Von Haussler.

"Well, I'll be," she whispered. "Abigail Von Haussler," she continued, sitting back staring at the computer screen. *Abby,* she thought. *I cannot believe this, Abby is short for Abigail.... Abigail Von Haussler.* "Abby Rose is undoubtedly Abigail Von Haussler. She has to be," she said, drifting. "So that's why she purchased the manor. But why is she using another name?" she continued, shutting off her computer.

Fanny sat there looking at the blank screen. "Something's not right," she said, getting up and walking into the bedroom. She took off her blouse to get ready for bed when a thought came to her, *Flo... oh my God... Once Flo finds out she'll spill the beans before we know why Abby's come back using a different surname. Wait... Maybe Abby was married. No, she would have said so, and besides – she's not wearing a wedding ring.*

Fanny quickly slipped on her blouse again. *I think I'd better find out what's going on before Monday comes and Flo knows everything.* She hurried into the front room, picked up the phone and then glanced up at the clock - nine p.m. *Not too late,* she thought, dialing Karen's number.

"Hello," Karen said into the phone

"Hi Karen. It's Fanny. Is Abby still up?"

"Yes, she's sitting right here," Karen replied, handing Abby the phone.

"Hello, Fanny," Abby said into her ear.

Fanny froze not knowing what to say.

"Fanny, are you there?"

"Yes."

Abby looked at Karen worried. She knew something was wrong with Fanny. She contentedly smiled at Karen waiting for Fanny to start speaking. Nothing… there was silence on the line.

"Yes, Fanny," Abby said into the phone as if answering Fanny.

"We need to talk, Abby."

"We do," she replied, glancing over at Karen.

"Tonight," Fanny said.

Abby could tell, by the tone in Fanny's voice, it was something serious.

"Alright, what's the reason?"

"Your past."

"I see," Abby replied, panicking. "Are you coming over now?"

"Yes, be out front in fifteen minutes."

"What's going on?" Karen mouthed.

Abby put the phone to her chest. "Fanny wants to go out with me for awhile tonight. I think she wants to talk about Mitt."

"She can do that here," Karen replied confused.

Abby raised her brow then put the phone back up to her ear. "Abby," she heard Fanny say.

"Yes, I'm still here."

"I'm coming over right now, so you think of a reason to get out of the house. I'll honk when I pull out front," she said and then hung up.

"Alright," Abby replied into a dead phone. She looked at Karen. "Well?" Karen asked.

"Fanny wants to go out for a coffee," she replied, getting up and walking over to her coat by the door.

"At this time of night? Why can't she just talk about Mitt right here?"

Abby slowly turned putting on her coat. "You know Fanny. She's shy talking about these things."

"I suppose you are right. I'll leave the front door unlocked."

Abby turned and walked out. Fanny pulled up three minutes later. She got out and opened the door for Abby. The two sat in silence until they were down the street. "Alright, I'm listening," Abby said, looking over at her.

Fanny kept her focus on the road. She didn't know what to say, or even for that matter, how to start this conversation. Then she just thought that she'd say it, "Abigail Von Haussler."

Abby sat back and sighed under her breath. *How stupid can I be calling the Baron my father.* "Does Flo know?"

"No, but she will. She wants to go to the library on Monday and look up your father's past. I wasn't going to wait, so I looked it up on the computer tonight."

"I see," Abby said, not knowing what to do or say next.

"Where would you like to go and talk?" Fanny asked, looking over at her.

Abby sat there and thought for a moment. *I've got no other choice now – Fanny must join the clan.* "Drive past the manor and then turn around and go up the driveway."

"What?" Fanny questioned.

"I think we better discuss this inside the manor. You'll have to turn off your headlights or Karen and Albert might see us from their window."

"The manor?" she questioned. "You honestly want to go there and talk?"

"Yes, it's my home."

Fanny sighed. *How stupid was that?* she thought, driving to the end of the street. She made a u-turn and then headed back toward the manor. "I guess we'll need a flashlight." Fanny asked, glancing over at her again.

"Do you have one?"

"Yes, it's in the glove box," she replied, shutting off her headlights before turning into the manor's driveway.

"Hey, I think I heard a car out front," Wilson said, from the staircase.

Cracker and Benjamin stood up.

Abby got out and shut her door.

"Yeah, somebody is here," Cracker whispered.

"Do you think it's those two men again?" Benjamin asked, worried.

"I hope not," Wilson replied. "We better go down and see," he continued, hopping down the stairs.

"Wait," Cracker yelled after him. Wilson stopped and looked up. "Maybe we should call Theodore."

"He's sleeping. We'll hide behind Grandfather if it's not Abby."

Cracker turned toward Benjamin. "Let's go," he said, hopping down the stairs.

Benjamin shook his head then started hopping down.

"Can you see the keyhole?" Abby said.

"Yes," Fanny replied.

"It's Abby," Wilson yelled, hearing her voice on the other side of the door.

Cracker and Benjamin were right behind him. They all stood there waiting until she opened the door then they'd surprise her by saying hello. When the door opened up, Abby walked in.

"Abby, you're home," the mice sang out.

Fanny was startled hearing little voices. Abby glanced down at the mice. Her facial expression told them to run.

"What was that?" Fanny said, walking up and stepping around Abby. Her eyes lit up seeing three mice standing there on the floor in front of Abby. She shrieked…

"Oh no," Benjamin gasped.

Fanny instantly froze hearing one of them speaking. Her legs started to give way and she grabbed hold of Abby's arm. Abby tried desperately to hold her upright. "Fanny, Fanny, please remain calm. I can explain everything."

"Be calm?" she replied, looking down at the mice. "I'm losing my mind."

"Madam Rose…." Theodore then yelled, leaping down onto the first landing. His face contorted seeing another person standing there.

Fanny looked up and screamed seeing a male lion coming down the stairs. Her scream was ear shattering as she turned around and ran right into Grandfather. She grabbed the clock trying desperately to keep it upright. Grandfather opened his eyes. "Pardon me," he said.

Fanny glanced up at him in utter terror. She screamed again letting go of Grandfather and raced toward the front door. Before Fanny could run outside, everything suddenly went black and she passed out on the floor.

"This is not what I wanted," Abby scolded herself, looking down at Fanny. She turned toward the mice.

"We're sorry. We thought you were alone," Wilson said worried.

She shifted her eyes on Theodore. If he wasn't pure white already, he should have been from the look on his face. "Now what are we going to do?" she asked.

"Hurry, get her inside," Grandfather said.

"What's going on?" Sir Henry asked, waking up.

"Go back to sleep," Grandfather replied.

"All of you – be quiet!" Abby yelled.

The room became dead silent.

"Alright…Theodore, pull her inside."

After Theodore gently took hold of Fanny's blouse, he dragged her over to the stairs. Abby quickly shut the door and then leaned against it. She sighed walking over and looking down at Fanny. "What on earth are we going to do now?" she asked.

"How about some water? That might wake her up." Benjamin suggested.

Abby looked into Benjamin's soft eyes. *If he weren't such a cutie pie, I'd be pulling out my hair.*

"Madam Rose," Sir Henry spoke up.

She turned and looked at him.

"Before you wake her up, do you have any idea what you're going to say?"

"We don't need any suggestions from you," Grandfather spat.

Abby fumed with that comment. She had no time for this. However, Sir Henry was right. She turned around in a minefield of thoughts. "Don't anyone move," she ordered, walking toward the corridor.

"What's going on out there?" Hansel asked, standing up near the kitchen sink.

"Nothing. We have a guest, that's all."

"Shall I serve up some tea, Madam Rose?"

"No, just a glass of water will do, thank you."

After getting the glass, Abby strolled back into the parlor and sat down on the staircase next to Fanny. She looked at the mice and then at Theodore. "I don't know what she'll do when she wakes up," she questioned.

"She just might pass out again seeing us," Cracker remarked.

"She might at that. But tonight, we're going to have to convince her to join the clan."

"Join the clan?" Benjamin asked confused.

"Yes, Benjamin. The clan of witches."

"Oh, will she be moving in then?" he asked, raising his little brow.

"No, Benjamin. But we cannot have her leaving this house without making her understand."

"What would you like *me* to do?" Theodore asked. "You know if Fanny sees me again…" his voice trailed off.

"You're right. But then again, maybe if she saw you all it just might be easier to explain," she replied, looking at all their faces. Without another word, without another thought, Abby splashed the water in Fanny's face.

Fanny quickly jerked. She gasped for air while wiping off her face. "Where am I?" she said, opening her eyes - still in a haze. Her vision was blurry as she looked up at something big and white, with lots of hair standing over her. She rubbed her eyes trying to see.

"Fanny," Abby said.

Fanny turned her head to see Abby sitting on the stairs. She turned her head back and looked up at the thing standing over her. Her vision started to clear. She then realized that it was a huge, white male lion with stunning blue eyes. Her mouth fell open. She was just about to scream when Abby softly spoke, "Theodore will not hurt you."

Theodore? Fanny's thoughts tumbled over, shifting her eyes up at the lion. *Theodore's a toy, a stuffed lion. What is she talking about?*

"My father," Abby started to say as Fanny's mind was desperately trying to engage. "My father, Baron Von Haussler, was a warlock. My great grandmother, Hilda, was a witch. And I am one too."

Wilson, Cracker and Benjamin walked up to the side of Fanny's face. "We're sorry if we scared you," Wilson said in his meek little voice.

Fanny turned her head toward the three grey mice. They all smiled at her. "So she is a witch?" she asked them.

They all nodded. "But she's a good witch," Benjamin whispered and then winked at her.

Fanny glanced up at Theodore again. "I suppose you can talk too?"

"Yes, Madam Chamberlin, I can," he replied in a husky voice.

"And the clock?" she asked, looking over at Abby.

"You can ask Grandfather yourself, Fanny," she replied.

Fanny sat up, still in a spin. "Grandfather?"

"Yes, Madam Chamberlin."

"I don't believe this," Fanny gasped. "It can't be true."

"Don't forget me," Sir Henry spoke up.

She turned her head toward the door. "Yes, my name is Sir Henry of Knotting Wood, a humble servant to King Louie the Third of England. I come from Royalty."

"Not the coat rack too?" Fanny gasped.

"Royalty," Grandfather spewed.

"Now, Grandfather, I will not entertain you in a quarrel while we have company," Sir Henry replied.

Abby sighed. Fanny looked over at her. "Is this what you have to deal with every day?"

"Yes, and sometimes it takes lots of aspirins just to make it through the day." she replied, standing up. "Here," she continued, extending her hand. Fanny took hold and stood up. "I would not have brought you here if I had known the house was up... Wilson?" she then said, glancing down at him.

"It gets lonely around here," he replied, lowering his eyes to the floor.

Fanny cast her eyes upon Wilson in the glow of the flashlight beam. Her eyes drifted over all three mice. *This is utter madness,* she thought, *animals and furniture magically talking.* As the word 'magically' drifted inside her head, she immediately thought back to Abby saying, "With a bit of magic, I could fix you right up." She turned her head toward Abby. Abby could see a question brewing. "So," Fanny said and then paused. "You've been cutting your own hair since you were a child."

Abby smiled knowing what she was talking about. She lifted her hands in the air, moved her fingers about, and made strands of Fanny's hair float upward in the air. A slight smile appeared on Fanny's face. She went to speak then a thought came to her. "Blue hair?" she asked without mentioning a name.

Abby kept her smile and nodded.

"Hot feet?" Fanny continued.

Abby raised her brow.

"No...!" Fanny gasped.

"Yes. And you my dear, can do it too."

"Me?" Fanny replied confused. "I have a hard time moving my own feet after getting out of bed in the morning."

"Excuse me," Boris said from the den.

"Who's that?" Fanny asked, jerking her head toward the den.

"That's Boris. You might as well walk in and say hello."

"Hello," Fanny mouthed. When she entered, she looked about the room.

"Up here," Boris said.

Fanny's eyes followed the voice. When she saw Boris, her world fell apart. "Oh my God..."

"Good evening, Madam Chamberlin, my name is Boris. I come from the forest region of Alberta, Canada."

Before Fanny could get her brain in gear, Abby walked up, wrapped her arm around her and said, "My family, along with five others, were a part of a witches clan that resided in the Austrian mountains. My father, as you know, was a famous magician."

"Yes, I read that, and now I see it," she replied, still looking up at Boris.

"It's nice to meet you," she said, feeling her mind unraveling.

"Well, it wasn't magic he used to thrill his audiences," Abby said, glancing up and smiling at Boris.

"No?" Fanny replied, turning and looking at her.

"No, it was magic spells. Just like the spells I used on Claudia."

"But I thought witches were evil."

Laughter filled the air. She looked at Theodore, then down at the mice in the parlor. She slowly turned her head toward Abby. "Theodore, would you please take the sheet off Steinbeck?" Abby said, escorting Fanny back into the parlor.

Fanny stood there watching Theodore stroll over and take the sheet within his mouth and then pull it off a beautiful grand piano.

"Now let me see," Abby said, placing a finger to her chin. "*Softly play sweet music to me along your piano keys. Like clouds drifting by, I would love to hear a sweet lullaby.*" Suddenly, Fanny heard the piano begin to play. She walked over, shone her light across the keys moving up and down, as if Mozart himself were sitting there. "Oh, my word," she sighed.

"Lovely, isn't it?" Abby said, walking over.

"It's that easy?" Fanny asked with her eyes still glued to the keys moving up and down.

"Yes, it's that easy, my dear."

"When, when can I join?" Fanny asked, glancing up at her.

"Hmm," Abby sighed, looking about the house. "I think as soon as this place is put back in order."

"Don't tell me. You can do that too?" Fanny asked not wanting to hear an answer.

Abby laughed. "Yes, I can. With just a snap of my fingers. However, to ensure no one gets suspicious, I'll call in some cleaners and painters."

"You've thought of everything, haven't you?" Fanny replied, shaking her head.

"Yes, and I rightly would have gotten away with it, that is if Wilson hadn't woken up the house," she replied, eyeing him up.

Fanny watched Wilson look at the floor alongside his friends. She knelt and whispered, "You three seem to get into a lot of trouble."

They slowly nodded. She sighed looking up at Theodore. "And you," she said and then paused, standing up and petting his head. "I suppose it's your job to keep them in line?"

Abby smiled listening to Fanny's charming little speech. She was delighted to see her step in and give some advice.

Theodore glanced down at the mice and then looked back up at her. "I try," he replied.

"I am sure you do," she whispered.

"If we're any trouble then we're the best trouble you'll ever find," Benjamin spoke up. Wilson gave him a nudge.

She knelt back down, rubbed Benjamin's little head, trying not to laugh. *No wonder they get away with murder around here,* she thought. *They're absolutely adorable.* "Well maybe, just maybe, you three could be more than the best trouble you'll ever find. You could become the jewels in this house."

"Jewels?" Cracker asked confused.

"Yes, like diamonds inlaid in a king's crown."

"Really?" Benjamin sang, wanting to hear more.

"Why certainly. But in order to become jewels, you'd have to give up getting into trouble."

"Well, there goes that idea," Wilson spewed.

"Whatcha mean?" Fanny asked.

"I can't watch these two all of the time," Wilson replied, looking at his friends.

"What do you mean – watching us? You're the one who's always getting us into trouble," Cracker spat, folding his arms.

"That's right," Benjamin weighed in.

Wilson looked up at her. "You see what I mean?"

Fanny laughed, standing up. She turned and smiled at Abby. Abby simply shrugged.

"Well," Fanny said over her shoulder, walking toward Abby. "I am sure the three of you will figure it out."

"I want to be a jewel," Benjamin said from behind her.

"Me too," Cracker added.

"Wilson?" Fanny inquired of his decision.

Wilson glanced at his friends and then slowly looked up at her. "Well, I'm not going to be left out in the rain. You can count me in too."

"Good," she replied, tossing a wink at Abby.

Abby hugged her. “I think it’s time you drove me back. Karen and Albert are probably getting worried.”

“Yes, it is getting late, and I have a big date tomorrow,” Fanny replied, heading toward the door. “Goodnight Grandfather, Sir Henry, Theodore, Boris, and my gorgeous gems,” she continued, turning and smiling.

“Goodnight, Madam Chamberlin,” they replied.

“I’ll see you all Monday afternoon,” Abby said, heading toward the door.

“Now behave yourselves while Mitt and his crew finish up,” Abby continued.

Wilson nudged Theodore’s paw. He looked down at him. “Are you going to tell her?”

“Oh, yes,” he replied, almost forgetting.

“Madam Rose.”

Abby turned before leaving. “Yes.”

“Tell Fanny that you’ll be there in a minute.”

Abby didn’t like the sound of that. Something was wrong. She turned and yelled after Fanny, “I’ll be with you in a second.” She closed the door and stood there with the flashlight shining down on the floor. “Yes, what is it?”

“We had strangers in the house the other night.”

“No…”

“Yes, two men.”

Abby’s mind flooded back. It stopped on two names.

“What did they look like?”

“One was short with black hair – the other was tall, thin and slightly bald,” Theodore replied.

Abby cringed. “What were they looking for?” she asked, not needing an answer. She already knew.

“We think they were looking for your suitcase,” Wilson spoke up.

She stood there studying their faces. “How did they get in?”

“Through the basement window,” Benjamin replied.

“I see,” she said, nodding her head.

“Do you know who they are?” Theodore asked.

“Yes. I know who they are. You leave this to me. We’ll talk more when I return,” she replied, turning toward the door.

“Goodnight, Madam Rose,” they said.

“Goodnight,” she replied opening and closing the door behind her.

After the car had gone, Grandfather spoke up. "Why wasn't I informed of this?"

Theodore turned his head. "That was the last thing we needed – having the whole house awake when they were here."

Sir Henry cleared his throat. Theodore turned toward him. "Sir Henry," he started to say, walking over. "You may be from Royalty, but I am Lord of this house. Wilson was given his instructions of putting the house to sleep whenever he chose to. I conveyed to him that the house would remain asleep while we investigated this matter," he slightly fibbed.

Sir Henry kept still.

"Now, do you have anything to say?"

"No," Sir Henry replied.

"Good," Theodore said, turning and walking back toward the mice standing there.

Wilson felt this overwhelming sense of pride welling up inside his little chest, as if Theodore just pronounced him king.

"Is there anything else?" Theodore then asked.

Grandfather cleared his throat. "Yes, I have one more thing to say," he replied, looking down at the mice. "Wilson, you may have been given the instructions, but I want you three to listen to me right now. I've been the time keeper here for over a hundred years. So, before you start thinking of something to do and getting yourselves into a mess, come and ask me first."

"Ask you?" Sir Henry spoke up. "If they're going to be the jewels in the king's crown, as Fanny so politely put it, I think you three should listen to me. I come from royalty and I've actually seen a king's crown."

Wilson sighed shifting his eyes on Cracker. Cracker shifted his eyes on Benjamin. They all looked up at Theodore. "Let's go to bed or we'll be here all night listening to this," Theodore said, bending down so the mice could climb aboard. He turned and headed up the stairs as Grandfather and Sir Henry continued their quarrel.

Before Abby got out of the car at Karen's, she asked Fanny, "What time did Flo want you two to be at the library on Monday?"

"Nine in the morning."

"I'll see you then," she replied, getting out. "I hope you and Mitt have a lovely day tomorrow."

"I'm sure we will, Abby. And thank you for everything. I am so excited."

"Well, I hope you can keep your excitement to yourself for now."

Fanny nodded. "I see a future as bright as the sun with you. Goodnight, Abby."

Abby smiled, shut the door and walked up to the front patio. She turned and waved before stepping inside.

13

Simply Magic

The following morning, the Cloverdale County Fair was officially open. It certainly looked like a weekend of fun was starting to brew. There were mothers and fathers pushing strollers, adults and teenagers, boys and girls all lining up at the entrance to get in.

"There's Flo next to the entrance waiting for us," Albert said, pulling into the parking lot.

Abby saw Flo waving as they got out. She waved back taking Albert's hand.

"Come this way," Flo yelled over the crowd and then turned toward one of the men attending the gate. "These two are in the Women's Club." The man looked over and nodded.

"We get in free?" Abby asked.

"Yes, all those who assisted in setting up the fair get in free," Flo replied.

As Abby entered the fairground, she inhaled the savory aroma from the open grills. She allowed her eyes to drift over the booths, tents and rides. It made her flood back in time when she was a little girl holding her parents' hands as they strolled through the fair. She could see that some things had changed. Jim's Big Top was new, the rides were much different and there seemed to be more booths strung along the pathways. Nevertheless, a county fair was just a fair wherever you went; cotton candy, caramel apples, booths enticing people to spend for prizes and those wonderful children's rides. It was all there before her once again while Flo gas-bagged in her ear as they made their way over to Connie's tent across from the grills.

"I've set up two folding chairs for you and Karen just outside the tent," Flo said.

"Thank you, Flo," the ladies replied.

Albert smiled at Flo seeing she had thought of Karen and Abby, so they had a place to sit during the day. As he seated his wife and Abby down, he looked over to see Sam Donaldson, owner of Donaldson's feed and fertilizer store, talking to some of the farmers. "You mind me talking to Sam? I heard Sam has as a new line of grass fertilizer," he said.

Karen sighed. "Leaving me already?"

"No, my dear," he replied, bending over and giving her a peck on the cheek.

She watched him walk off and then turned toward Abby. "I don't think I've met a man who has more excuses to run off on his wife than Albert."

Abby and Flo laughed.

"Hello, Ladies," Connie interrupted, walking toward her booth. "Did I miss something?" she asked, handing one of her staff a cloth money pouch.

"No, we're just talking about men," Karen replied.

"Now that's a deep subject, like a well that goes on and on and on," Flo remarked.

"It sure is," Karen replied, looking over at Albert talking to Sam. "That's why I keep him on a short leash, so he doesn't fall in."

The women laughed.

"Speaking of men, Flo," Abby said. "Where is your man?"

"Oh, I'm sorry. I never told you. I let him fall in years ago. After he had left, I married my salon."

The women laughed again.

Abby stopped laughing when she saw Sid and Don walking by with their wives. Seeing them made her mood rapidly change. *Those two have no clue to the trouble they're in,* she thought. She studied their wives as they walked by merrily swaying their hips and gleefully smiling as if they didn't have a care in the world. *Why wouldn't they be so happy,* her thoughts spun. *After stealing my money, their husbands have deeper pockets now.*

As Abby was about to turn and focus on the conversation inside the tent, she watched three young kids walk up to Sid and Don. She recognized them right away. They were the same youngsters she spoke to inside Fletcher's Five & Dime.

"Molly said that you wanted to talk to us?" Willy said.

"Not here, Sid," Betsy whispered, looking around.

"Why not?" Sue shot back, walking up with Don. "This might be the best place to talk."

"Talk about what?" Bobby Ray asked.

The four adults looked at the kids. "Let's go sit down over there by the grills," Don suggested, turning and prodding his wife to follow.

Willy, Molly, and Bobby Ray tagged along while eyeing each other up. They had no clue to what these bozos wanted.

Abby acted as if she were listening to the women all chattering like chicks in a hen house while her eyes stayed glued on what was happening over by the grills.

As Don sat down with his back toward the grills, he spotted Mrs. Rose sitting in a chair outside the baked good tent. He turned his head toward Sid and Betsy sitting next to him. Sid looked into his eyes. Don gave him a quick nod of his head toward the tent across the way. Sid slowly glanced over. *Caught before we even get started,* he thought, seeing Mrs. Rose sitting there chatting with the women. *There's nothing we can do now. Just act normal.* He focused his attention back on the kids sitting across from him.

Before he opened his mouth to speak, Betsy squeezed his hand. He knew what she was conveying. She too just noticed Mrs. Rose sitting there. He turned, smiled at her as if to say he knew, and then turned back and started the conversation. "How would you three like to make some money?" he asked, studying their faces.

"What do we have to do?" Willy asked, folding his hands on the picnic table.

Sid pondered his next choice of words. "You know Mrs. Rose?"

"Yeah," Molly quipped, chewing her gum. "She's sitting outside the doughnut tent right behind us."

"You don't miss a thing, do you?" Don said.

"Not much. We met her down at Fletcher's Five and Dime," Molly replied, blowing a bubble and letting it pop.

"You did?" Sid questioned.

"Yeah, so what's this have to do with her?" Bobby Ray asked.

Sid sat back looking at all the people walking by. When they departed, he leaned up toward Bobby Ray. "She's rich."

"Everyone knows that, Mr. Peterson," Willy replied. "Her wealth spread throughout the town like wild fire as soon as she dropped a cool half-million into the bank for that manor," he continued.

Sid slowly nodded. *They're as bright as light bulbs*, he thought. *I wonder if they're as sharp as tacks, too?* "Then I suppose you all know how she paid for the place?"

"Yeah, she had the cash inside a suitcase," Molly replied, shifting her eyes on Betsy and Sue. By the look on their faces, she knew where this conversation was leading. "So, you want to rip the old lady off, is that what you're thinking of doing?" she quickly added, chewing her gum.

"Not so fast, sweetheart," Sid replied. "Let me do the talking first and then you three can decide."

"OK, we're listening," Willy shot back.

"Molly's right," Don quickly said before Sid could continue.

Sid glared at him.

"Hey, she already guessed it so let's cut the crap, shall we?" Don spat.

"Alright," Sid whispered, looking from Don to the kids. "Yes, she dumped a cool half-million into the bank right out of her suitcase. Now here's something for you all to chew on, besides that gum," he continued, staring at Molly. Molly turned her head and spat her gum out. Sid figured she cleared her mouth, so she was ready to start chewing on his next set of words.

"There had to be over one hundred thousand dollars still sitting inside that suitcase when I carried it out to her car. Now… that money is somewhere inside that manor."

Willy, Molly and Bobby Ray all looked at one another. Sid could tell they were chewing on that bit of information.

"So, you're asking us to break in and help you steal it, is that it?" Willy asked.

"Yes, but we'll be there too," Sid replied.

"What about these two?" Molly asked, pointing at Sue and Betsy.

"Oh no, not us," Betsy quickly replied. "Someone has to play look-out."

Willy leaned up on the table. "I suppose you've heard the stories about that place?"

"That was years ago, Willy," Don shot across the table.

"I don't care if it happened years ago," Willy grunted. "After listening to B.B. Cooper tell his story about him and his friends going up there one Halloween night and what they saw - you wouldn't catch me dead in that place."

Sid laughed. "Don't tell me you believed old man Cooper's story. The man has been living out of a whisky bottle for most of his life."

"He may be," Molly fumed. "But I was there when he told that story. It lifted the hairs on my neck," she said and then paused, "pumpkins talking, witches flying around, heck you'd be half out of your mind to want to go there in the middle of the night."

Sid sat back catching Don's eyes. Don raised his brow. "Now look, you three," Sid started to say. "B.B. Cooper has been telling that Halloween story for over fifty years now. And besides, if it were true, it happened when old man

Cooper was just a boy and that famous magician, Baron Von Haussler, set Cooper and his friends up with one of his magic tricks."

"So, you believe B.B. Cooper actually saw those pumpkins talking on the ballroom patio steps when he was a kid?" Willy asked.

Laughter erupted from across the table. Willy tightened his jaw. He didn't care if they thought he was a fool for believing the story.

"Yeah," Sid replied, laughing. "B.B. Cooper also said that he and his buddies almost killed themselves while running down that thick, woody hill back to Old Tiller Road."

Don could see this conversation getting out of hand. He figured if he tossed a figure across the table, the kids would simply forget about old man Cooper's nonsense. "One thousand dollars each," he said.

Sid stopped laughing. He turned and glared at Don. "That's a fair price, Sid," Don replied to his look.

"OK," Sid grumbled. "We're willing to pay you one thousand each. I'm sure that's more money than you can comprehend right now, but just imagine riding mini-bikes tomorrow or having a big screen TV in your bedroom with enough computer games to last you a lifetime. How does that sound?"

Molly and Bobby Ray looked at Willy. Willy turned and faced Sid.

"We'll think about it Mr. Peterson," he replied, standing up.

"Alright, you three think it over, but don't take too long. I'm sure we could find other kids who'd jump at the chance," Sid remarked.

That felt like a jab, Willy thought. *However, I know there is no one else our age that would venture up there at nighttime.* "We'll stop by the real estate shop in a few days with our answer," Willy replied. "Come on, you two. I came here to have some fun," he continued, walking away.

Molly and Bobby Ray got up from the table. They smiled at the adults then turned and followed Willy over to the game booths.

"Whatcha think?" Sue whispered.

"They'll do it," Sid replied. "Didn't you see their little eyes light up when I mentioned the mini-bikes, big screen TVs and all those computer games?"

Don laughed, getting up. "Yeah, I wouldn't mind buying a big screen TV myself."

"Well, you can drop that thought, Don. Once we get our hands on all that money you're going to buy me a nice fur coat before any TV comes into our house," Sue teased, standing up.

"Fur coats - TVs," Betsy commented, getting up and taking Sid's arm.

"That can wait. Right now, let's go have some fun, shall we?"

As the four walked through the fairgrounds over to the game booths, Abby stood up.

"Would you like to take a stroll?" Flo asked, seeing Abby stretching her legs.

"That would be nice. Let's walk over to those booths over there," she replied, pointing to the games. As Abby and Flo started over, Karen decided to go too.

"Here comes, Mrs. Rose," Sid whispered from the side of his mouth. Sue and Betsy turned to see Abby walking up with two other women.

"Good morning, Mrs. Rose, Flo, Karen," Sid and Don greeted them.

"Morning everyone" they all replied.

"Mrs. Rose, this is my wife, Betsy," Sid said, turning toward her, "and this is Don's wife, Sue."

"Good morning, ladies. Are you having fun?" Abby asked.

"Oh, yes. I love the fair," Betsy replied, smiling at Flo and Karen. "How's the salon going?" she then asked Flo.

"Great," Flo replied, looking at Betsy's hair.

Betsy could see that Flo was checking out the color of her hair. It wasn't naturally blonde.

"Who does your hair?" Flo asked.

"I do it myself. Does it show?" Betsy replied, cringing.

"No. It looks great."

"Thank you," she replied, glancing over at Sue. Sue simply raised her brow. *After hearing about Claudia's hair turning blue down at your place, I'd do my own hair too,* she thought.

"How's the manor coming along, Mrs. Rose?" Don asked, changing the subject.

Abby took her eyes off Betsy and turned to face him. *I should be the one asking you that question, seeing you both have gone inside while I've been away,* she thought. "Mitt said it's coming along nicely and that I should be able to move back in on Monday," she replied, giving him a warm smile.

"Well, if there is anything we can do, Mrs. Rose," Sid spoke up. "Please give us a call."

"Thank you. You've both been very helpful."

"Have a good day," Don said, nodding his head to the women.

"We will," Flo replied, escorting Abby and Karen over to the gaming booths.

"You didn't say a word, Karen," Flo whispered.

"No, I didn't. There's something about those two that rubs me the wrong way."

"Is it because they're real estate men?"

"That's just a nice term for salesmen," Karen replied. "To me, salesmen are only out for what they can get."

As Abby stood there listening, she glanced back at Sid and Don walking alongside their wives. *It's not only real estate agents you have to worry about, you have to watch out for their wives, as well,* she thought. She pondered that notion while staring at Betsy in her fancy little dress. Her eyes homed-in on the buttons in the back and the tied lace around Betsy's waist. She quickly looked around at all the people and then cast her eyes back on Betsy again. *Why not?* she thought. Betsy said that she just loves going to the fair, so why not go in just your bra and panties.

Abby closed her eyes while thinking of a spell. *"Storms and winds of mighty souls – cast out your swords and cut the stitching - so Betsy feels somewhat - bewitching,"* she thought, opening her eyes. With that, Abby quickly turned her head and looked at the booth with the stuffed animals sitting on the back shelf. "Would you like to give that a go?" she asked Flo. Before Flo could answer, another voice spoke up. "I'll give that a go," Mitt said from behind the women.

The women all turned. "Fanny," Flo beamed. "Now don't you look nice," she continued, eyeing up her dress. "Good morning, you two," Abby greeted them.

"My, Fanny, you're the belle of the ball today," Karen gushed.

"She sure is," Mitt agreed, winking at Fanny.

"Oh now, stop it you all. It's just something I picked out yesterday," Fanny quipped, feeling embarrassed by all the flattery.

"Sid," Betsy said, reaching around her dress.

"Yes, what is it?"

"I think my buttons in the back are falling off."

"What?" he replied, stopping and checking the back of her dress.

"What's wrong?" Sue asked, turning around.

"My dress!" Betsy panicked. "It feels as if it's coming undone."

"No… Here, let me take a look," Sue replied. "Where did the buttons go?" she frantically asked, looking at Sid and then down on the ground. Sue's eyes lit up seeing another one fall off. As she bent down to pick it up, she noticed Betsy's seams coming apart. "You're dress, Betsy," she gasped, standing up, "it's falling apart."

The commotion around Betsy had everyone stopping and staring at her.

"Oh... Sid!" Betsy screamed.

"How long have you had this dress?" he asked, trying to cover her up.

Betsy turned and stared at him. "I bought it last year, why?" she scolded.

The wind suddenly picked up. Her shoulder seams started to unravel. "Sid!" she yelled. Sid took hold of her shoulder straps as Sue held the back of Betsy's dress together. Don noticed all the folks stopping and gawking at them. "You can move along now," he said, coaxing them to leave. As he looked back at Sid and Sue holding Betsy dress together, the seams to her waist let go. Betsy saw all the people standing there. "What are you looking at?" she yelled. "You heard the man, move on!"

Abby, Flo and Karen, along with Mitt and Fanny, looked over from the booth hearing the commotion in the middle of the fairgrounds. "What's going on over there?" Flo asked, stepping out from the group.

"I don't know," Fanny replied, tossing her head this way and that, trying to see.

Abby stood there smiling as if she were queen. In a matter of seconds, she knew what was about to happen - and it did. Betsy's entire dress came off. They heard a scream from the center of the crowd and then they saw Betsy running toward the fairground entrance trying desperately to cover herself with what remained of her dress.

"Hey, check this out," Willy laughed, seeing Betsy half dressed running toward the gate with Sid chasing after her.

"If that don't beat all," Molly replied, blowing a bubble and popping it.

"Do you two really want to go in with them clowns?" Bobby Ray asked.

They both turned and looked at him. "Why not, Bobby Ray, Mrs. Peterson looks pretty darn good."

"That's not funny!" Molly spat, slapping his shoulder.

"Ouch," Bobby Ray teased, smiling at Willy.

Willy rubbed his shoulder glaring at Molly. "That hurt!"

"Well, you're lucky I didn't slap your face," she shot back.

"Come on, you two love birds. Kiss and make up," Bobby Ray teased.

"I wouldn't kiss him after that comment," Molly replied, glancing over Willy's shoulder at Don and Sue leaving the fairgrounds too. "You know," she started to say. Both boys turned around to see what Molly was staring at. "I think we should take all the money," she continued.

"Are you crazy?" Bobby Ray said.

"Nope," she replied, blowing another bubble. Willy reached over and quickly popped it.

She slapped his hand. "Now that will cost you, Willy. The next time I give you a chance to kiss me will be in the Fall."

"Molly," he begged.

"Don't even try," she quipped, "let's go, Bobby Ray. I wouldn't mind a doughnut," she continued, walking off.

"Come on, Molly, I was only kidding about Mrs. Peterson," Willy pleaded.

She tossed her head in the air and kept walking.

"Of all the places," Betsy screamed, running toward their car.

"Hurry up and get in before we get laughed right out of town," Sid barked.

"OK," she fumed, opening her door.

"What the hell just happened?" Sid asked, getting in alongside her.

"I don't know! This dressed cost me forty dollars. Why would it just fall apart like that?"

Sid looked out to see Don and Sue running up. He rolled down the window. "You might as well have a good time. I'm taking Betsy home," he yelled.

"I don't believe this." Sue gasped, looking in at Betsy sitting there half-naked.

Betsy shook her head holding the last remains of her dress over her chest.

"I just want to go home," she cried.

"We're leaving," Sid angrily said, reversing back.

Don and Sue stood there like statues watching them leave. When Sid's car left the fairgrounds, Don slowly turned and looked at his wife. Sue caught his eyes and they both started laughing.

14

Mischief Brewing

After the fair closed for the day, Willy, Molly and Bobby Ray all got on their bikes and rode out of the makeshift parking lot onto Cross Ridge Road. It was just an old country road in the back hills of Cloverdale. On either side, past the Davenport farm, were fields and forest traveling all the way back into town. Not a streetlight in either direction or even the moon was going to show its face as daylight slowly turned into dusk and then total darkness.

"You know you guys, with that kind of money we could also have lights on our bikes," Molly said, riding up alongside Willy.

"I wish we had them now. It sure is getting dark out here," he replied.

"Cold too," Bobby Ray added. "When are your parents expecting you home, Willy?"

"I told 'em I'd be home after the fair closed. They said supper would be in the oven waiting. How about you, Molly?"

"My Pa is probably drunk on the couch and my mother said that she was going out with her friends for the night. So, I guess whenever I get home."

"Talk about not having parents," Bobby Ray remarked, pulling out in front of the two and doing figure eights across the dirt road.

"You keep that up and you'll be in lying in a ditch," Molly warned.

"Me? I'm too good," Bobby Ray bragged.

"Are you good enough to let go of your handlebars?" Willy shouted, letting go of his.

"You two better stop it. I can barely see ten feet in front of me," Molly scolded, riding along the side of the road staying out of their way.

As they came to the intersection of Cross Ridge Road and Old Tiller Road, Willy holed up and did a skid.

"Why are you stopping, Willy?" Molly asked, stepping on her brakes.

"We can take a short cut if you'd like."

"Short cut!? Old Tiller goes right along Cherry Hill. Not on your life, buddy boy. Let's stay on Cross Ridge then cut down Novi Street into town," Bobby Ray suggested, circling his friends.

"Molly?" Willy said, wanting to hear her decision.

"I don't know, Willy. Old Tiller Road is pretty spooky at night," she replied, looking down the dark, menacing road then up the hill to where the manor was.

"You know if we're going to help those two bozos steal the old lady's money, you can bet we'll be sneaking in from that hill over there." Willy replied. Molly said nothing. "You still want the money, don't-cha?" Willy goaded her for an answer.

"I don't even know about that anymore," she replied, eyeing up the hill.

Bobby Ray stopped his bike alongside her. "You just said we could have lights on our bikes, and today you said that we should take all the money, so what's it going to be, Molly?"

"Yeah, I know I did. But that was in broad daylight and a mile away from here."

Willy laughed. "Oh, so you had the guts then and now you don't?"

"I never said that!" Molly spewed.

"Then what is it, Molly? Either you're scared to go up there or you're not."

"How many questions are you going to ask me at one time? Just let me think, will ya?"

They both stood there holding up their bikes. She looked at Bobby Ray and then back at Willy. "I want the money as bad as you two do, but it's going to take a lot of courage."

"Sure, it is," Bobby Ray replied, glancing at Willy and giving him a wink. "We're both scared too, Molly."

"You are?"

"Yes," Willy added.

"OK, let's ride down Tiller. At least it's the back of the property," Molly nervously replied.

"That's my girl. And besides, we need to find a place to hide the money when we find it and take off," Willy said, already scheming a plan.

"You mean take off on Sid and Don?" Bobby Ray asked.

"Yes."

"You think that's wise?" Bobby Ray questioned.

"No, I didn't at first. But after Molly said it today, I've been kicking it around."

"You think we can pull this off?" she asked.

Willy nodded.

"What if Sid and Don go to the cops. Have you thought about that?" Bobby Ray asked.

Willy smiled. "And… what are those two bozos going to say… 'Sheriff Collins, while we were up at the manor stealing old lady Rose's money, these three came in and stole it from us."

Molly raised her brow at Bobby Ray. He grinned feeling stupid.

"OK, let's get moving. We'll ride down Old Tiller real slow and see if we can find a spot to hide the money," Willy said, pushing his bike and getting on.

They rode a few yards down the road then suddenly Bobby Ray thought of a place. He pulled alongside Willy and Molly. "I know a spot."

"Where?" Molly asked.

"You guys remember that old barn half falling over down here?"

"Yeah," Willy beamed.

"I think it's right behind the manor."

"You see how dark it is up that hill?" Molly said, slowing down. "If we use flashlights Sid and Don will see us for sure once we take off with the money."

"She's right," Bobby Ray replied. "We need to find a place now then we can come back and mark a trail leading from the top of the hill down to Old Tiller Road. I think we should use that old barn. I'm sure it lines up with the manor."

"Alright," Willy said.

As the three rode down Tiller Road, they spotted the barn sitting back from the road. They pulled up and looked down the dark path leading up to it. "It's sure dark back there," Molly whispered.

"It sure is," Willy agreed, turning and glancing across the road up the hill toward the manor. "Tomorrow we'll come back and make a trail from the barn across the road and then up that hill. Let's hightail it home. We have a lot of planning to do."

15

Romance in Bloom

After the weekend at the fair selling baked goods, walking the fairgrounds and watching the children enjoying themselves, Abby sighed knowing that she was finally going home.

"With the manor still needing to be cleaned and painted, you could stay longer with us," Karen said in the front passenger seat.

"I really appreciate that, but I'd just like to go home," Abby replied, thinking of all her wonderful friends.

Karen glanced over at Albert. Without turning his head, he raised his brow conveying his thoughts – *oh well, you tried.* He pulled up, shut off the engine and got out. Abby opened her car door and instantly inhaled the fresh morning air. It soothed her soul.

"When will you have a phone installed?" Karen asked, getting out.

"I have many things on the list and that one is at the top."

"Good, but if you need anything, Abby, please ask, OK?" Karen requested.

Abby nodded, turned and headed for the doors. Albert walked up carrying her small suitcase. "Where would you like this?" he asked, walking in behind her.

"Just set it over there, please," Abby replied, looking about the parlor still containing an assortment of boxes. She turned around, gave Karen a hug and then took Albert's hands. "Thank you two for such a lovely time."

"You're welcome," Albert said and then paused, "now we're only just down the street…"

"I know, I know," Abby interrupted. "If I need anything I'll certainly come down," she continued.

They said their goodbyes then Abby shut the door. She waited until the sound of their car was gone before walking over and sitting on the staircase. *Now where are those little runts and Theodore?* she thought, glancing at Grandfather and Sir Henry who were sound asleep. *They're probably up in the master's chambers sleeping as well,* her thoughts continued, shifting her eyes on Steinbeck, her beautiful piano. *Music, now that would be nice.* She raised her hand, waved her fingers in the air and Steinbeck started to play.

With a sweet lullaby playing in her ears, she wished that she could just snap her finger and put everything in order. She looked at the front doors thinking of all those who would surely come up to visit with her in the days to come. “It’s going to have to be done the normal way,” she said, getting up and walking back to the kitchen.

As Abby entered, she greeted Hansel who was lying there next to the sink staring up at the ceiling. Hansel stood up. “Madam Rose. I’m so glad you’re back.”

Abby sighed knowing what Hansel wanted to say. “We’ll have this kitchen put back into order as soon as possible,” Abby said. “Yes, Madam Rose. I wanted to tell you that the water is on.”

“Oh my, let’s check it out,” Abby replied, turning on the faucet. “Well, look at that,” she continued, picking up the bar of soap and washing her hands.

While Abby and Hansel chatted, a dirt bike rode up the driveway. Shaun Stevenson got off his bike, removed his helmet and stood there looking at the towering monstrosity Abigail called home. Glancing up the tall pillars on either side of the entranceway, his eyes glued onto the sandstone vulture with its wings spread wide open staring down at him. *I could not imagine living here,* he thought, walking up to the doors.

Just as he was about to knock, he thought he heard music playing from within. It sounded like a piano. He knocked and waited. Nothing… He knocked again and waited. *She can’t hear me over the music,* he thought, trying the door handle. The door opened. The music stopped as he entered the foyer.

He walked into the parlor and noticed the piano over in the corner next to the fireplace. He was stunned seeing no one sitting there. “Abigail?” he called out, turning and looking this way and that, up the staircase into the den and then noticed the corridor leading toward the back of the manor. “Abigail,” he yelled again, heading that way.

“Hey, wakeup, you two,” Wilson whispered to his comrades sleeping on the mattress in the master’s chambers.

Benjamin rubbed his little eyes. “Someone’s in the house,” Wilson whispered again. “Hurry, nudge Cracker, will ya,” he continued, hopping down from the mattress. Benjamin woke up Cracker and they hopped down to the floor. “Are you sure you heard someone, Wilson?” Benjamin asked.

“Abigail?” Shaun called out again, walking to the back of the manor.

“The three mice stared at one another. “Let’s wake up Theodore,”

Cracker whispered.

Wilson glanced over at the big brute sleeping on the rug. He walked over and tapped his paw. Theodore opened one eye. "We've got company," Wilson said to him. Theodore pulled up his lofty head still in dreamland. "Someone's downstairs," Wilson continued.

"It's Monday," Theodore replied. "Madam Rose is supposed to be coming home. Maybe she's here now," he continued.

"Abigail," Shaun called out again.

Theodore's ears shot up. "That sounds like a man," he said, standing up.

"Yeah, and whoever it is, is looking for Abby. She must be home," Benjamin whispered. "What are we going to do?"

Theodore thought for a moment. "If Madame Rose is home, I don't think she'll be coming up here. But we can't take that chance," he replied, walking toward the open door. He sat there a moment listening and then a thought came to him. He walked back over to the rug. "I think it's time for me to sleep."

"What…You've been sleeping all night," Benjamin replied, folding his arms.

Theodore cocked his head.

"Oh, that kind of sleep," Benjamin said to his expression.

Wilson stood back, recited the spell putting Theodore to sleep. Theodore instantly changed into a stuffed toy lion. "OK, let's go investigate," Wilson whispered, running toward the door.

"Abigail, there you are," Shaun greeted her, strolling into the kitchen.

"Shaun, well… this is a surprise," she said then suddenly froze. *Oh no,* she thought, *Flo and Fanny are going to the library this morning. There's no way I can go now. I sure hope Fanny can pull this off without me.*

"Is there something wrong?" Shaun asked, to her troubled look.

Abby placed a smile upon her face. "Why heavens no, Shaun. I was just thinking of all the things that have to be done around here," she replied, walking toward the kitchen door.

Shaun followed her back down the corridor to the parlor. As they entered the room, he glanced over to the piano and asked, "I thought I heard music playing when I came to the door."

Abby slowly turned giving her time to think. "That was me playing the piano," she fibbed.

"You were?" he asked, confused.

"Yes, then I got up and went to the kitchen."

Shaun pondered that. Something isn't right. *The kitchen was too far away for her to get up and go there before I walked in.* He slowly nodded not wanting to question her about it.

"Is this the first time you've been inside?" she asked, changing the subject.

"Yes," he replied, looking about the parlor and through the den. All he saw was dust and cobwebs everywhere. "It needs a lot of cleaning, Abigail," he sighed.

"That it does. I've been thinking about it for over a week now," she replied. "All these boxes here have to be opened and my bed needs to be put back together. I was also thinking that maybe I'd just concentrate on a few rooms at a time. I'll start with the den, kitchen and parlor and then move up the staircase and finish the master's chambers. That will make it feel so much more like home."

Shaun figured getting those rooms she mentioned done was at least a month's worth of work seeing the condition of the place. It gave him an idea.

"I've got some friends that would help out today if you like. We can at least start working on opening these items and getting rid of the boxes and put your bed back together."

Abby raised her brow to that idea. Shaun smiled then pulled out his mobile phone.

"Chuck, here."

"Chuck, it's Shaun."

"Hi, Shaun, what are you up to today?"

"I was going to ask you the same question. I've got a small project I'm working on today."

"You never have a small project. Are you tearing another engine down today?" Chuck asked, thinking Shaun wanted to work on cars. That's all Shaun did on his days off.

"No. I'm up here at the manor on Cherry Hill helping Mrs. Rose with some of her furniture," he replied, smiling at Abigail.

Abby winked and then walked over to the staircase and sat down.

"The manor up on Cherry Hill?" Chuck questioned, wrinkling his brow.

"I've never been inside that place."

"Well today is your lucky day. Before you come up, call the rest of the boys and see if they want to help. We could use a few more hands."

"Alright, give me a half an hour."

"Great… Oh one more thing. Bring your tool box too," Shaun replied.

"OK, I'll call the boys."

"Thanks. I'll see you when you get here," Shaun replied and then hung up. "OK, I've got a work crew coming." Abby stood up and walked over to him.

"You didn't have to do that," she said, gazing into his gorgeous blue eyes. They were as dazzling as Theodore's.

"I wouldn't have it any other way, Abigail. I came up here today to look Wilfred over, but seeing you living like this, I think we better start here."

She placed her arm through his and replied, "Well, while we're waiting, would you like a tour?"

"I'd love that. This place is absolutely amazing."

"That it is. Let's start in the den, shall we?" she said, escorting him into the room. "By the way, in my day furniture was called décor."

"Décor?" he mused. "I like that."

She smiled and continued walking him through the den. He looked at the magnificent fireplace and mantelpiece and then glanced up at the large moose head hanging above it. "My word that thing is huge."

"It sure is. But as you can see it needs to come down and be cleaned."

Shaun nodded. "So, does the fireplace," he replied. "Do you by chance know how many fireplaces there are inside this manor?" he asked.

"Oh, now let me think. There is one in each bedroom including the master's chambers. That's nine. Then there is one in the parlor and one here in the den. That makes eleven," she replied and then added, "by the way, do you think your friends would help us clean out the two down here and the one up in the master's chambers?"

"I don't see why not," Shaun replied, then mentioned the work it must have taken just keeping eleven fireplaces cleaned and stocked with wood.

"Oh, it was. I mean, it must have been," she replied, catching herself.

"Would you like to see the billiard room?" she quickly asked, walking over and opening the door.

Shaun heard the slip and figured it was just her age. "Wow… will you look at this," he gasped, walking in.

"Amazing, isn't it?" she replied, standing there remembering when it was the best room in the house. "There used to be two tables, one for straight pool and the other for billiards. On that wall over there," she continued, pointing, "you can see where the dartboard hung, and over there was a table and chairs to play checkers and chess."

Shaun stood back studying her eyes.

"Something wrong?" she asked.

"No. I was just thinking."

"Yes?" she questioned.

"Well, you seem to know a lot about this place. Do you know anything about the family that lived here?" he asked.

"You mean Baron Von Haussler and his wife Amelia?"

"Yes."

"I do, and I can't imagine anyone not knowing something about the Von Haussler's. The Baron was a very famous man. When I found out that the place was for sale, I did some research on the family and thought, why not purchase the place."

"So that's why you bought it? Because of the Baron being famous and all?"

"Yes," she replied, feeling sad that she was fibbing to him.

"I see," he said, glancing at the door to the adjoining room.

"That used to be the indoor swimming pool and sauna. Well… not like the sauna's we have today. Here, let me show you," she continued, opening the door.

Shaun's eyes lit up seeing the empty pool sitting there and a smaller pool connected to it over in the corner.

"Now you see that large metal cylinder next to the smaller pool?"

"Yes."

"Well, that was hooked up to the main water line and it was heated like your hot water heater at home. The tap on the side is like a faucet. They would turn it open allowing the hot water into the smaller pool."

"Well, I'll be," he replied. "The Baron must have been a really smart man."

"Oh, he was. Now let me show you the ballroom," she replied, turning and walking out.

As they re-entered the den, Abby turned left and walked down a long corridor. On the right-hand side of the corridor, Shaun noticed a large coatroom and just down from it were two bathrooms on the right. He then froze, seeing the tall ballroom glass wall and the immense double doors leading in. When he stepped inside, it reminded him of a basketball court – well not that it was used for basketball - it was the size of the room which blew him away.

"What do you think?" she asked, walking up alongside him.

"Unbelievable," he gasped, casting his eyes upward at the four large chandeliers hanging down from the decorative ceiling and then glancing back at the glassed-in wall leading out onto the backyard patio. "Wow, can you just imagine the parties he had in here?" he continued, walking around the boxes toward the patio doors.

"Oh, he just loved throwing parties, especially on Halloween night."

Shaun stopped in his tracks, hearing her say that. He slowly turned and looked at her. "Have you heard any stories about those parties he had on Halloween night?" he asked.

"No," she fibbed, feeling apprehensive of his next question.

"Have you ever heard of a man by the name of B.B Cooper?" he asked.

"No, that name doesn't strike a bell," she again fibbed.

"Well, B.B. Cooper grew up here in Cloverdale. For nearly half a century he has been telling this story about when he and a group of his buddies snuck up here one Halloween night to spy on the Baron's party." he said and then paused, hearing someone calling out.

"Hello. Is anyone here?" Chuck yelled from the foyer.

Shaun looked at Abby. He could see that she was still interested in hearing his story. "Your friends are here," she said.

He nodded. "If you'd like, I'll finish the story when we are through."

"I'd like that."

"Alright, let me run out and see 'em."

Abby followed Shaun, wondering about B. B. Cooper. *What did Cooper and his friends see that night?* she thought.

"Check this out?" Ed freaked, walking into the parlor.

"Yeah, talk about having a Halloween party. Can you just imagine having one in here this October?" Chris said, standing next to Grandfather.

"Not on your life! You wouldn't catch me dead in here on Halloween night." Randy gasped, staring up the cobwebbed chandelier.

"Get back, you two," Wilson whispered, standing on the second staircase landing.

Benjamin and Cracker hurried back to him. "I think we better hide," Wilson warned, jumping up the stairs. "Come on before they spot us and then crush us with their boots," he yelled down to them.

"Crush us?" Benjamin questioned, looking at Cracker.

"Can't you hear them down there? Those are all young boys and you know what boys like to do to mice?" Cracker replied, jumping up the steps.

Benjamin put his ears to the wind. They did sound like young boys. He quickly turned, jumped up and took hold of the step imagining being stuck to the bottom of one of their shoes.

"Hurry, let's get out of here," Wilson whispered.

"Hey guys," Shaun greeted his friends, walking through the den.

They all turned around.

"Wow, Shaun, you really know how to live," Randy teased.

"Yeah, right, like I could afford a place like this."

"I didn't mean it that way. I meant to be living in absolute squalor," Randy laughed.

Randy stopped laughing when he saw Mrs. Rose walking into the den. Shaun turned and smiled at her hoping she didn't hear that last comment. "Guys, I would like you to meet Mrs. Rose," he said, turning to face them.

They all stepped up and greeted her one at a time.

"Now I'm not good at remembering names, but I want to thank you all for coming and helping Shaun and I."

The four glanced at Shaun and then back at her.

"It's our pleasure, ma'am," Chuck replied.

"You can drop the formalities. Please, just call me Abby."

They all nodded.

"What would you like for us to do?" Ed asked.

"Well first off, did you bring your tools, Chuck?"

"Yes, I've got them in my truck."

"My bed needs to be put together."

Chuck shifted his eye on Shaun. "It's up in the master's chambers," Shaun said.

"Yes, you can take the elevator up," Abby added.

"Elevator?" Ed gasped, raising his brow.

"Yes, it's right down the corridor past the stairs. It only goes up to the master's chambers."

The boys all looked at one another.

"Is there something wrong?" she asked.

Shaun laughed seeing the expressions on their faces. "I don't think they've been in a home that has an elevator, Abigail."

Abby smiled. "Well, today you have. Now, Shaun if you'd be so kind to have two go up and put my bed together, the rest can help me start right here in the parlor," she continued and then paused, walking over to the boxes. "As you can see, some things are in crates and some things are in boxes. I think if you carefully take everything out of the crates and break up the boards, we can then toss the broken boards inside the empty boxes and carry them all out front on the lawn for the moving company to collect."

"Alright, we've got our orders," Shaun said. "Chuck and Randy take the bed, the rest of us can start unpacking this stuff and placing it where she wants it to go."

"Excuse me," Chris said.

Everyone turned to look at him. "I don't want to be nosy, but are you going to have this place cleaned up?"

Abby laughed. "Why certainly. You all know Mitt Ryan?"

They nodded.

"Well, Mitt, bless his heart, has contacted several companies. Snider's Construction will be tearing down the old garage out back and building a new one. Then Black Top Asphalt is coming in and will be laying a new asphalt driveway from the garage all the way down to Daisy Lane. Also, Mitt has contacted a cleaning and painting company."

"Wow," Chuck replied. "This place will look like a construction site soon."

"That it will. So, today I just want to make myself a little more comfortable."

"We'll see to that, Abigail," Shaun replied. "Let's do it, boys."

They nodded and went straight to work.

Three hours later, after everything she wanted done was finished, Abby walked over and picked up her purse. She handed each boy thirty dollars for their labor. They thanked her and then Shaun walked them out the door.

"Man, I didn't expect to get paid," Chris whispered, stashing his money in his pant pocket.

Shaun smiled at him. "She's a sweetheart, isn't she?"

The four looked at him. *She's a sweetheart all right - but what kind of sweetheart is he talking about?* Chuck thought. He quickly dropped that thought seeing Shaun was twenty, and she was, well, old.

"I heard you're going to come out here to work on her car," Ed asked.

"I was going to start today, but after seeing the condition she was living in, I decided to help her out."

Ed nodded, glancing over at Chuck. He could see it in Chuck's eyes. Shaun was acting as if he actually were calling her a sweetheart - the kind of sweetheart you dated.

"Well, I've got to get going," Randy spoke up, bringing everyone out of their thoughts. "Have a great day, Shaun - and thanks for calling me. I was hoping to go out tonight, and seeing that she paid us, maybe we could go down and bowl a few games."

"That's a great idea," Ed replied. "What cha say?" he continued, looking at the rest of them.

They nodded.

"OK, we're out of here," Chuck said.

When they left, Shaun walked back inside.

On the way down the driveway, Ed shifted his eyes on Chuck. "You don't think Shaun fell down and hit his head, do you?"

"I don't know, Ed," he replied. "I thought there for a minute that he was talking about Mrs. Rose as if she was his high school sweetheart."

"Me too. How crazy is that?"

"Too crazy to even think about," Ed laughed, sitting back.

Back inside the manor, Abby thanked Shaun. "That was quite nice of you to have them come up and help me out. Are you hungry?"

"No, but before I go, can I take a look at Wilfred?"

"Certainly, let me show you the way."

Through the corridor, past the dining area and into the kitchen they walked along together toward the kitchen patio. "My, what a wonderful day," she sighed, inhaling the fresh air opening the door.

Shaun stepped out and then froze. *Will you look at this?,* he thought, staring out and over the cement patio rail. "You could play a football game back here," he said.

"I'm sure you could, Shaun. Lots of games were played back here, but mostly Cricket."

"That was the sport back then," he replied, assisting her down the steps toward the cobbled pathway leading to the garage.

"However, as you can see now, the yard needs lots of work. Back when the Baron owned the place the tree line was closer to the ridge. Now it's almost right to the center of the yard."

He noticed the tree line thinking, *she must have seen old photos of how it used to look.*

"And over there," she continued, pointing at the dilapidated garage. "That has to go."

"Wilfred's in there?"

"Yes, poor thing. He might as well be sitting out in the weather."

Shaun laughed walking along side her. "The way you talk about your car, calling him Wilfred and all, it sounds as if he were alive."

"It may sound silly, but I've been like this my whole life. Everything I own has a name, even my stuffed toy lion. His name is Theodore."

Shaun laughed again. "I like that name," he replied, stepping up to the weather-beaten doors and pulling one side open. His eyes lit up seeing Wilfred sitting there. "Now that's worth some money," he gushed, walking in.

"I'd never sell Wilfred. We've been together forever – he's like family to me."

Wilfred opened his eyes and looked up at her standing in front of him. She wrinkled her brow while tossing a fleeting glance back toward Shaun. Wilfred quickly closed his eyes hearing the man walking around to the front.

"Even with the faded paint and dull brass work, I don't know how you kept him in such fine condition."

She didn't. I looked after myself. Well, sort of. Wilfred thought.

"I'm worried that he won't be if he stays out here much longer. So, what do you think?" she asked.

"Well," Shaun replied, placing his finger to his chin. "Let's look under the hood first. May I?"

"Certainly," Abby said, walking up to Wilfred's hood.

Watch it, cowboy, Wilfred thought. *I'm a well tuned machine.*

Shaun lifted both sides of the hood and locked them in place. "These little engines were amazing back then," he mused, fiddling with the wiring on top.

Little engine? Wilfred thought, *you better be careful. This little engine, as you call it, can go a million miles without stopping.*

Shaun lifted his head and looked out at her. "How does it run?"

"Purrs like a kitten," Abby beamed.

Better than that, Wilfred thought. *I'd beat anything on a racing track.*

"You don't say," Shaun replied, "it's pretty clean too."

Here, here, you're getting a little too personal now, Wilfred thought.

"I told you," Abby replied.

"I don't know how you've kept that engine running. But all in all, I think old Wilfred just needs a good sanding and a new paint job."

Old, Wilfred? Did you hear that? Wilfred thought. *Why, with a little soap and water I'd be looking like new.*

Abby stared at the faded paintwork. "He was a beautiful, fire engine red at one time. You think you could bring him back looking as new as the day he rolled off the assembly line?"

Now you're speaking my language, Wilfred thought. *I can still remember the day I rolled off the assembly line as everyone was cheering.*

"I think I could. I'll start taking him apart as soon as you're ready."

Take me apart!? Wilfred's thoughts spun. *What is this guy thinking?*

"How about we wait until the new garage is built and you have a cement floor to work on. Also, if you'd like, I could have them build some work benches and cupboards for your tools," she said.

New garage... Cement flooring... Tool benches... How wonderful. No more sitting out here in the mud, Wilfred's thoughts gleefully rolled over-and-over.

"That would be great. I'd even think Mr. Olson from Olson's service station would lend me the tools I'll need," he replied, setting the hood back down. "Do you have a phone, yet?"

"Not yet."

"Would you like me to stop over every day to see how you're doing? It wouldn't be a problem."

"I would like that, Shaun. You certainly are a gentleman."

Shaun blushed. "You're pretty nice yourself, Abigail," he warmly replied.

After he said that, she stood there for a second admiring his charm. He too was looking back at her soft, brown eyes. He could almost visualize what she looked like when she was a young woman. *She must have been a beauty in her day,* he thought. "I like your eyes, Abigail."

That flattering remark not only surprised her, it stunned her. The silence between them afterwards made Shaun feel stupid for saying it. He tried to turn it around. "I mean, they're so soft and honest."

There went the surprise. There went her fluttering heart. However, the look on his face made her laugh.

"Did I say something wrong?"

"No," she laughed. "It seems men have a way of saying something nice and then they blow it," she continued.

"Really?" he replied, feeling like a horse's behind.

"Yes, and then they wind up stumbling and bumbling while trying to talk their way out of giving such a compliment."

His brain tried to understand what she was saying. It went straight into his ears, but it ended up feeling as if someone poured glue in each one. "Is that good or bad?"

Abby laughed again. *He has a long way to go,* she thought, *and I have all the time in the world to get him there.* "Come, walk me back to the house and I'll try to explain it to you."

Wilfred waited until they had walked down the path. He slowly rolled forward to see the two of them walking back to the manor. *I think something is brewing between those two,* he thought, reversing back in.

While Abby and Shaun strolled back to the manor, Abby began explaining. "When you give a compliment," she started to say, "don't feel foolish if the person laughs. That's just their defense mechanism because truthfully, inside, they loved what you said and they just don't know how to respond to it. The best course for everyone is to just say thank you. However, when I saw you wrinkling your face and then trying to take it back, it made me laugh."

"Thank you, Abigail for giving me that advice. You're a very wise woman."

"Why, thank you, Shaun."

After entering the kitchen together, they walked down the corridor and into the parlor toward the front doors.

"You don't have to come out," he said, opening the door.

"But I want to. I've always liked motorcycles."

"Alright," he replied.

She stood there watching him putting on his helmet and get on his motorcycle. She smiled and waved. After he rode down the driveway, she walked in, shut the door behind her and sighed. *Now I have to find out about Fanny and Flo,* she thought, worrying.

16

The Black Knight

Abby had not heard from Fanny all day and it worried her. After supper, she walked into the den with the mice on her shoulder. She set them down on the arm of her brown leather recliner then with a wave of her hand she lit a fire in the fireplace.

"There," she said, sitting down. "It should be warm in here in a few minutes."

"It feels like old times, Abby," Benjamin said, sitting alongside his friends admiring the fire from across the room.

Abby looked down at her mice enjoying the evening. *Yes, it certainly feels like old times,* she thought.

"So, when is all the working going to start?" Wilson asked, gazing up at her.

"I believe in a few days."

Just then, Theodore walked in. "The house is secure, Madam Rose."

"Thank you, Theodore. Come lie down on the rug. We're just going to enjoy the evening together."

As they all sat in silence enjoying the fire, Abby closed her eyes. Wilson looked up at her and nudged Cracker. Cracker glanced back and nodded. *She must be tired,* he thought. With only the sound of the fire crackling and everyone in a slumber state, this little cozy setting was about to be interrupted as Fanny drove up the long winding driveway. She pulled up at the entrance and shut off her car.

"Did you hear that?" Benjamin asked.

"Yes, it sounded like a car out front," Theodore replied, getting up and walking toward the doors.

Abby slowly opened her eyes. "Is somebody here?" she asked, disgruntled.

"Yes, Madam Rose," Theodore said, hearing a car door shut.

"Who could it be at this time of the night?" she replied, getting up herself. She heard a knock and slightly opened the door.

"Abby!" Fanny excitedly bellowed.

"Fanny," Abby sang. "What happened this morning?"

"This morning?" Fanny, replied walking into the foyer.

"Yes, this morning down at the library?"

"Oh, that."

Oh that, Abby thought, *my whole world could be tossed right over the edge and all she says is 'oh that' like, oh that little thing.*

"When I met Flo down at the library I was hoping you'd walk in. When you didn't show up, I just pulled up different things about your father on the computer pertaining to his magic shows. I made sure she didn't see anything else about his wife and child."

"So, what did she say?"

"You have nothing to worry about. Flo may know how to cut hair, but she hasn't a clue to working a computer. She just figured there was no information on the subject and we left."

"You think that will stop her from snooping?" Abby replied, worried.

"I think so. As we were leaving I told her that you were, well…" her voice trailed off.

"Old," Abby finished her thought.

"Yes, you know how some old people start to lose it upstairs."

Abby laughed. "You are a gem, Fanny," she replied, giving her a peck on the cheek. When she stepped back, she noticed a large shopping bag in her hand. She looked up with a question in her eyes.

"I bought you a surprise," Fanny said to Abby's expression. "That was the other reason I came tonight. First, I wanted to tell you about Flo and then show you this," she beamed, stepping into the foyer. "Hello, handsome," Fanny greeted the big cat.

"Madam Chamberlin," Theodore replied, nodding.

"Good evening," Grandfather greeted her.

"Evening to you, and to you too, Sir Henry."

"Evening, me lady," Sir Henry replied.

"How charming," Fanny gleefully said.

Grandfather rolled his eyes to Fanny's comment as Abby shut the door and turned around.

"Now you're not going to believe this," Fanny started to say, waltzing into the parlor and turning around.

By Fanny's mannerisms, Abby thought that maybe Mitt had proposed to Fanny and she was going to show her a wedding dress. "Believe what?"

Before answering, Fanny looked about the house and then spotted the mice sitting on the arm of the recliner inside the den staring at her. "There you three are," she bellowed, walking over and rubbing their heads. "Hello Boris," she greeted him.

Boris opened his eyes. "Well good evening, Madam Chamberlin. It's a beautiful night to sit by the fire."

"It certainly is," she replied, gazing at the warm flames shooting up the chimney. She quickly turned and caught Abby's eyes. "Well," Fanny said and then paused, "I'm not sure how to start."

"The beginning is always a good place," Theodore commented.

"That it is," Fanny replied, walking back into the parlor and rubbing his head. "You have the most striking blue eyes I've ever seen, Theodore."

"Why, thank you," he replied, lifting his chin in admiration.

Abby stood there thinking she knew what Fanny was about to say – she was getting married. *If that's the case,* she thought, *I'll give her some womanly advice. "You've just met him, give it some time."* However, what Fanny was about to show her would change everything. Well, not right away, but it would in the future.

"After you left the fair last night with Albert and Karen, Mitt and I walked around the gaming booths one more time before we left. I was preaching in his ear all weekend to try to win me one prize. Now, he tried several times without success. He's not the best of pitchers, but last night I think he could have pitched for the Philadelphia Blue Jays."

Abby stood there listening to her long-winded story while glancing down every once in awhile at the large shopping bag in her hand. *So... she's not getting married,* she thought, *that's a relief.* "Would you like to sit down?" Abby asked, pointing toward the stairs.

"Maybe I should," she replied, walking over and placing the shopping bag in front of her. "Are you ready?" she continued, giving Theodore a wink.

Abby should have known from that sly wink what was about to happen.

"I hope you all like it," Fanny excitedly said, reaching in and pulling out a beautiful, light-brown stuffed lioness. She placed it on the floor in front of Theodore and then looked up at Abby with a big, bright smile.

Theodore sat back on his haunches. Wilson, Benjamin and Cracker jumped down and scampered across the floor. They stood there dumbstruck staring at the stuffed lioness. Abby, well, she almost fainted. Fanny, however, dismissed their startled reactions and continued delightfully talking. "I've even given her a name," she gushed, looking at Theodore. "I named her, Tasha.... You like it?"

Theodore looked at her then down at Tasha. His heart simply melted like butter.

"Well?" Fanny continued, staring at Theodore and then up at Abby.

"Are you...?" Abby said and then paused, shifting her eyes downward on the stuffed toy lioness.

"Am I what?" Fanny asked.

"Are you thinking that we should...?" Abby's voice trailed off again.

"Yes," Fanny sang out, standing up. "Oh... Abby, as soon as I saw her, I just knew Tasha belonged here and," she said and then paused, looking down at Theodore who was now lying there staring at Tasha. "Seeing that Theodore is Lord of this house," she continued, "I thought he'd love to have a mate, or at least a lady to stroll with."

As Benjamin stood there listening to all this, his little thoughts began imagining having two lions running around the place. He started feeling light headed and he simply passed out.

"Benjamin!" Wilson screamed.

"What's happening out there?" Boris asked.

"Nothing to be worrying about, Boris" Abby replied, looked down at Benjamin sprawled out like tenpins on the floor.

"Sometimes I hate hanging up here all alone," Boris grumbled.

"Benjamin!" Abby shrieked, kneeling and picking him up. She kissed his little nose. He opened his eyes. "What happened?"

"You fainted."

"I did?"

"Yes. Now what were you thinking?"

"Maybe he passed out from eating a whole bag of peanuts today," Grandfather spoke up.

"Grandfather," Abby scolded.

Sir Henry shook his head with his comment. Grandfather gave him a smug look back.

Benjamin sat in Abby's palm rubbing his head. "I was thinking," he said and then paused. "I was thinking we'd be lunch with Tasha in the house."

"He's right," Cracker agreed. "If you make her come alive, we could be lunch."

"Oh, now you two," Fanny coyly replied, walking up and looking at Benjamin in Abby's palm. "That will never happen. I am sure Theodore will teach her. Right, Theodore?" she asked him over her shoulder.

There was no response. Fanny and Abby slowly turned toward Theodore. Abby tapped Fanny on the shoulder. Fanny locked eyes with her. Not a word needed to be said. Theodore was lying there lovesick over a beautiful, brown lioness, regardless if she was just a stuffed toy.

"Well, there's your answer," Fanny quipped.

Wilson and Cracker were stunned seeing Theodore acting this way. Benjamin, on the other hand, was still worried. He wanted to know what Abby was going to say to all this.

"How about we wait?" Abby finally spoke up.

"You mean you'll do it?" Fanny gushed.

"Yes, on one condition."

"Anything!" Fanny excitedly beamed.

"We're looking for a book my father had."

Fanny wrinkled her brow. Abby sighed, turned and walked back into the den. She sat down on her elegant brown leather couch next to the fire. Fanny picked up Wilson and Cracker, walked in and sat down next to Abby.

"Now if I may ask - what happened out there?" Boris said.

"Benjamin passed out," Abby replied, rubbing his head.

"I heard that. Where is Theodore?" Boris asked.

Abby looked up at him. "He has company," she sighed.

"Company? Theodore has company?"

"Yes, she's a beautiful stuffed lioness, now shh…" Abby softly said.

"Hmm…" Boris mused.

Fanny waited until everyone was settled before she asked, "What kind of book are you looking for?"

"It's the Black Knight's Potion and Spells book," Benjamin whispered.

"Shh…" Wilson scolded. "Let Abby tell the story."

Abby smiled at Benjamin. "Why don't you tell Fanny what the cover looks like?"

Benjamin cast his eyes up at Fanny. "It was creepy looking. In the middle was an eerie eye staring at us. There were large snakes circling it. Up at the top was two crossed swords and under that was the name The Black Knight. On the bottom, it looked like waves rolling across the book and a woman who looked half-fish was holding a golden lantern out of the water."

"That would be a mermaid," Fanny whispered, leaning over to him.

"A mermaid?" Benjamin questioned with big wide eyes.

"Yes, they were mythical creatures that lived in the sea."

As Fanny was explaining mermaids to Benjamin, Abby closed her eyes and drifted back in time to her great uncle, Conrad Von Haussler. The name Conrad, or the German spelling of the name, Konrad, meant 'Bold Counsel'. It was a just and noble title for one who held court with the King of Austria, King Lenhard. And who, by his crown, gave Conrad a more prominent title. He christened Conrad the Black Knight. Conrad was also given the title of King's First Servant, and thus, no title was over him, not even the King's generals could order him about.

During one of Conrad's many journeys to foreign lands seeking trade for King Lenhard, Conrad's life would change. It was mid-July in the year 1735 while sailing back from England. He was on board a British naval frigate, The Iron Lady, under the command of Captain Sheldon.

This extraordinary adventure all started when Captain Sheldon's ship received orders via a letter from King Charles II to set sail to Whitefish Bay, Slovenia. There, he would pick up the Black Knight from the seaside port of Adrian and transport him back to England. The two countries now allied with each other. King Charles, now ruler of most of the world's oceans, had new ambitions wanting to explore the deep interior regions of Eastern Europe and thus was requesting the Austrian King in setting up trade routes. King Lenhard, on the other hand, ruling a landlocked nation and with no oceans to sail upon, needed a naval country such as England to assist him in gaining the seas for trade. The alliance was thus cemented.

After the Black Knight had held court with King Charles II, it was on his return that something magical, something mystical, something no human had ever experienced, had happened. However, seafarers and sailors for many centuries would bring back stories of seeing mermaids at sea. The villagers who heard such outlandish stories took them with a grain of salt, believing they were only stories woven together by seafarers and sailors pulling too many corks at sea. This is Conrad's story… One he never told a soul, with the exception of his family who lived in the small Austrian village of Nome.

It happened on an extremely foggy night just outside of Whitefish Bay. The Iron Lady was to make port that evening. Lieutenant Jon Longport, the captain's first mate, was standing near the helm observing the main sheet. It hung there like a curtain, begging for wind. "Captain Sheldon," he said, turning around. "I think we should stay out tonight and allow this fog to settle."

Captain Sheldon looked up at the main sheet. He then turned and glanced over at the jib. *Not even a flutter of wind,* he thought. Lifting his chin, he turned once again allowing his eyes to look through the fog rolling across his ship toward the stern. The fog was so thick he could barely see his stern lookout standing back there. Before he could respond to Lieutenant Longport, the crow's nest lookout hollered down, "Ship port side."

"How far?" Lieutenant Longport yelled up through his cupped hands.

"One hundred meters straight out from amidships, Sir. She's sailing south by southwest."

"She's on same course with us," Captain Sheldon said. "Boatswain Fox, bring up more lanterns and have them placed on the port side."

"Aye - aye, Captain."

Captain Sheldon watched Fox hurry down the ladder. He clasped his hands behind his back and turned on his heels toward the helm. "Helmsmen, remain steady on the same course," he ordered.

"Aye, Captain. Maintaining course south by southwest," the helmsman replied, steadying the wheel.

"Lieutenant Longport," Captain Sheldon then said, turning and looking at him. "Call up and ask the crow's nest if he sees their colors."

"Aye - Aye, Captain," he replied, casting his voice upward.

"Her colors are Slovenian, a fishing trawler I suspect. She looks as if she's changing course and sailing over, Sir," the crow's nest lookout shouted down.

"What is going on?" Conrad asked, coming out of his stateroom below deck.

"Me Lord, we have a ship coming alongside," Able Seaman, Jim Philips, the captain's steward, replied.

"I think I'll go up and see," Conrad mused, taking the wooden steps up to the main deck. After proceeding on deck and into the thick fog, he made his way up the starboard steps toward the helm. "Good evening, Captain Sheldon."

"Evening, Lord Haussler."

"I was told we have a ship coming alongside."

"Yes, we suspect it's a Slovenian fishing trawler," he replied, pointing toward the port side.

At the stern of the Iron Lady, Able Seaman Hornbeck, who was standing watch, began hearing a weird sound. He harkened his ear to the wind and listened. It was shrieks and shrills, sounds he had never heard before. Out there somewhere within the thick layers of fog he knew something was approaching. He turned his head toward the bow. He could barely make out the officers and the captain standing next to the helm. He quickly pulled out his pipe and blew the call 'Away the boats'.

Captain Sheldon quickly spun around hearing the call and then focused on his stern watch. He saw Able Seaman Hornbeck waving his arms.

"All hands stand by while the trawler comes alongside," Captain Sheldon ordered. "Boatswain Fox," he then said, "go back and see what has caught Able Seaman Hornbeck's attention."

"Aye - aye, Captain."

"Lieutenant Longport, have your men prepare all port side lines. Master Gunner – stand by at the ready with your men."

"Aye - aye, Captain," they both said, turning to carry out their orders.

"Busy night?" Conrad asked, stepping up alongside the captain.

Captain Sheldon turned and smiled. "I'd rather have a night like this than to be sailing around the Horn."

"I've never sailed those waters, but I've heard tales of those wicked seas down there," Conrad replied.

Captain Sheldon nodded and then cast his eyes on the two men coming up the port side steps. Conrad turned to see Boatswain Fox escorting the stern lookout to the helm.

"Why did you pipe the call 'Away the boats'?" Captain Sheldon sternly asked the young seaman.

Able Seaman Hornbeck looked at Fox. Fox knew, but he wasn't going to answer. Hornbeck turned toward the captain. "It's my best call, Sir, and I wanted to get your attention," he replied, glancing at Conrad. "There's something out there," he continued.

"Yes, we know that, lad. It's a Slovenian trawler," Captain Sheldon replied.

"No, Captain, there's something else out there besides the trawler," Hornbeck said.

"Ahoy there," Captain Finn, from the Slovenian trawler, The Tailspin, called over to the Iron Lady, as his ship came into view.

Captain Sheldon kept his eyes on Able Seaman Hornbeck for a second. There was fear within them, but right now it had to wait. He turned toward Lieutenant Longport. "Give the call, Lieutenant."

"Ahoy. This is the Iron Lady. We are an English frigate."

"Request your men to stand down, we're a fishing vessel," Captain Finn shouted back.

"Master Gunner, have your Marines stand down, but keep your muskets ready," Captain Sheldon ordered.

"Aye, Captain."

"Lieutenant, make ready all lines to toss over," Captain Sheldon then ordered.

Conrad stood back allowing the deckhands to move about as the two ships prepared to come alongside. With the ships secured, he walked up alongside Captain Sheldon as Sheldon greeted the trawler's captain coming onboard.

"Good evening, Captain," Captain Finn said, walking across the boarding plank.

"Good evening to you, Sir. I am Captain Sheldon," he replied, taking his hand and steadying him to the deck.

"Nice night to be out," Captain Finn remarked, looking over the British sailors standing there.

"That it is. Will you be making port tonight?" Captain Sheldon asked.

"Aye, we shall. I've been sailing these waters for ten years now, and no fog, even as thick as this, will keep me and my men from reaching shore," he replied, leaning over toward Captain Sheldon. "Our ladies are all waiting, and we've been out to sea for thirty-nine days now," he continued with a wink.

Captain Sheldon smiled thinking about his own wife that he had not seen for three months now.

"Pardon me, Captain Finn," Able Seaman Hornbeck spoke up. Captain Sheldon looked at him. By the expression on his captain's face, Hornbeck knew he was out of line. Captain Finn looked at the young seaman. "Yes, lad," he replied.

"Forgive me, Captain Sheldon, but I must ask," he said and then paused, taking his eyes off his own Captain and focusing on Captain Finn.

"Did you hear those eerie sounds out there?"

"Why yes, those are the sounds of the Oxbow whales."

"Oxbow whales," Captain Sheldon questioned. "I've never heard of them."

All the men gathered to listen. "Those are mysterious creatures. Seldom seen and seldom heard, but tonight, lad," he said and then paused, "for some odd reason, they're heading into Whitefish Bay."

"A pod of whales? Is that why you piped the call 'Away the boats'?" Lieutenant Longport asked Hornbeck.

"Yes, Sir. I've never heard such sounds before," he replied.

"What makes them so mysterious?" Conrad asked, stepping into the conversation.

"These are a pod of pure white whales."

"An entire pod?" Captain Sheldon questioned.

"Yes, I have not seen them, but I've heard their calls on several occasions. However, those who have seen them say that those whales follow an underwater light of some sort."

"Nonsense," Lieutenant Longport grumbled.

"Sir," Hornbeck interrupted. Lieutenant Longport looked at him.

"Those shrieks and shrills – they almost sounded like a chorus of singing."

Silence fell over the group standing there as an eerie sound could be heard on the wind. Captain Sheldon lifted his ears to listen. He looked at Captain Finn. Captain Finn smiled while nodding. "That be them, which leaves me to return to my ship. I don't want to be floating out here while they're about."

"How big are these whales?" Captain Sheldon asked.

"Hmm," Captain Finn replied, thinking. "Roughly forty tons - sixty meters long. My advice to you is to follow me into the harbor," he replied, turning and stepping up on the plank.

Captain Sheldon stood there as Captain Finn walked across, jumped down and started barking orders to his men to set sail.

"Captain," Lieutenant Longport spoke up.

Captain Sheldon focused at him. "We'll set sail, Lieutenant."

"Wait," Conrad intervened.

The two turned and faced him.

"How far is landfall?" Conrad asked.

"Two nautical miles," Lieutenant Longport replied.

"Lower a boat. I'm staying behind," Conrad requested.

Captain Sheldon tightened his brow. Conrad's request was out of the question. "You're not thinking of staying out here and having those whales approach you?" he asked.

"That I am, Sir."

"Lord Haussler," Captain Sheldon gruffly said. "I am under the king's orders to set your feet on dry land."

"Captain Sheldon, I am well aware of your orders," he replied and then turned toward the helm. "Quartermaster, what is the direction of the current?"

Quartermaster Higgins standing next to the helm looked at Captain Sheldon. Captain Sheldon nodded for him to answer. "Southwardly, Sir."

"And the port of Adrian?" Conrad asked.

Again, Quartermaster Higgins looked at his Captain. The captain nodded.

"Southwardly, Sir."

"So by boat, all I have to do is keep steady with the current, is that correct?"

"Yes, Lord Haussler," Quartermaster Higgins replied without looking at his captain.

Conrad turned toward Captain Sheldon.

"And what by chance, if you are taken by these whales, shall I tell your king what happened to you?" Captain Sheldon asked.

"Captain Sheldon, you know who I am. I am the Black Knight, First Servant to King Lenhard. You tell my king that you were given orders by me to lower a boat. But mark my word, on this very night I'll be in port toasting this voyage with you," he replied with a smile.

With that, Captain Sheldon turned and yelled out his next set of orders, "Cast off all lines." He then turned toward Boatswain Fox. "After we are set adrift, have your men lower the longboat, and then haul tight the main sheet."

"Aye – aye, Captain."

"You can't do this, Captain," Lieutenant Longport said.

"Lieutenant, you heard him. Tonight, we'll be toasting this voyage together," he replied, turning toward the helm. "Helmsmen, follow the Tailspin into port once Lord Haussler is lowered."

"Aye – aye, Captain."

After Conrad got into the boat and the boat lowered into the foggy seas, Conrad kept watch on the Iron Lady's stern light. When it disappeared within the fog, he lifted his collar around his neck to ward off the chill. He then pulled his ore handles across his waist and then sat there listening and waiting. As the boat swayed this way and that by the steady swells, Conrad could hear the eerie sounds coming up from behind him. He turned in his seat fearful yet excited, imagining having forty-ton creatures coming alongside him from up out of the deep.

As the sounds came closer, he spotted a luminous glow under the water. Then suddenly he spotted the large, white whales breaching the crests of the swells as they approached. Conrad counted two, three, four, and then something strange caught his eyes. There was something swimming in front of the whales carrying a light.

Whatever it was swam under his boat then around and around, pushing the longboat sideways. He looked this way and that, trying to keep his eyes focused on the light. Then suddenly, as he was looking down into the water on the port side of the boat, something came up out of the water on the starboard side. He quickly turned and was stunned at what he saw. It was a woman, wearing seaweed over her breasts. She had long, curly blonde hair and a pair of the most striking blue eyes he had ever seen before. She hauntingly stared at him while holding up a golden lantern. Conrad watched her cock her head from side to side and then she quickly disappeared under the water.

He quickly lurched to the starboard side of the boat looking down into the deep dark water. He could see with the lantern's glow the white whales swimming beneath him. Then – they were gone.

As he rowed his way back to port, keeping steady on the current, his thoughts stayed fixed on the woman who came up from the sea. When Conrad made landfall in Whitefish Bay, he rowed up to the pier where the Iron Lady had docked. "Ahoy," he yelled out, maneuvering his boat alongside the steps of the pier.

A seaman ran toward him. "Lord Haussler," he shouted.

"Hurry, lad, tie me off."

"Captain Sheldon is still onboard inside his cabin," he replied, taking the steps down to the water's edge. "The rest of the crew is inside the pub waiting for you," he continued, taking the lines and securing the boat to the stanchions.

Conrad made his way onboard the Iron Lady and went straight to the Captain's quarters. He knocked.

"Come in."

Captain Sheldon's eyes lit up seeing him standing there wet from the laden fog. He stood up, rounded his desk and extended his hand. "I was just about to write a letter to your king," he said, with a grin.

"That's foolish talk."

Captain Sheldon laughed. "That it is," he replied and then paused. "Tell me, what did you see?"

"I saw the whales."

"That's it?"

"As you can see, I am still alive."

"No mysterious lights?"

"No," he lied, keeping his secret. "I believe the sailors who came back with those haunting tails were fooling the villagers so they'd keep buying them drinks to listen to such stories. You know how that goes in these seaside ports."

"That I do," Captain Sheldon replied. "Are you up for a drink yourself?"

"Yes, rowing two nautical miles will make any man thirsty."

Captain Sheldon laughed again as he escorted Conrad up to the main deck and down to the pier.

The following day, Conrad bid farewell to Captain Sheldon and his crew then watched The Iron Lady set sail for England. As he walked along the pier, keeping his eyes on the Iron Lady's sails, he spotted a small boat secured to a stanchion below with two men sitting inside. He walked down the steps and greeted them.

They both glanced up to see a tall man coming down. "Good day to you too," they replied.

"I would like to rent your boat," Conrad said.

The two men looked at one another.

"Ten shillings each," Conrad added.

"When do you want it?" one asked.

"Tonight - and I promise it will be here in the morning."

"Alright, you have a deal."

Conrad, reached into his pocket, pulled out ten shillings and tossed it down. "I'll place another ten shillings under that cushion when I return." As he turned and headed up the steps, he stopped and turned around. "This could go on for a few nights, gentlemen."

"Same price?" one asked.

"Yes," he replied, turning and climbing the steps back to the pier.

After he had left, one man turned to the other and said, "We might not have to go fishing for a few days." His partner smiled.

Conrad spent two nights off the point of Whitefish Bay waiting and listening, without any luck. *Was it the fog that brought them in,* he thought, sitting inside the boat. *If so, when will the fog return?*

On the third night, as he sat there looking up at the stars waiting, he thought he heard something come up out of the calm seas and then disappear. He stood up looking out over the water. He could see fifty meters at best. There was nothing on either side. He sat back down, pulled his coat up around his neck and stared down into the hull.

Teal, goddess of the deep, slowly lifted her head up out of the water at the stern of the boat. She looked at the man with his back toward her. It was the same man. She slowly lowered herself into the water and swam underneath the boat. Conrad felt the boat slightly sway. He quickly glanced upward to see the bow moving to starboard. An eerie feeling washed over him. There were no shrieks or shrills from the whales. There was no glow within the depths of the sea. *Was it a shark,* he thought, *they are known to investigate things floating on top of the water.* He looked for the tell-tale sign of a fin. Nothing... He sat back - keeping alert.

"Psst," a voice came up from behind him. The voice made him jump He quickly turned around. It was her again, the mystical woman from the deep. Conrad was stunned by her ghostly beauty as he sat there watching her cocking her head this way and that - looking at him. "Do you have a name?" she asked.

He heard her speak. It made his chest tighten. *How could this be?* he thought. "My name is Conrad Von Haussler, the Black Knight of Austria," he replied, finding his courage to speak.

"The Black Knight?" she inquisitively questioned.

"Yes, I am servant to King Lenhard."

"You serve a king?"

"Yes," he replied, gazing into her stunning blue eyes. She looked like an angel with long hair cascading down past her shoulders and floating in the water. "And your name is?" he asked.

"I am Teal, goddess of the deep. The name means Gentle Seas."

"Are those your whales?" Conrad asked.

"They are free like the rest of us down here."

"The rest of you?" he asked confused. "There are more down there like you?"

"Yes, I come from the region of Noel, we are mermaids," she replied, snapping her finger.

With that, four mermaids came up from the deep and began swimming around the boat. When Conrad looked down into the water, he was startled at what he saw. From the waist down, they looked like fish, from the midsection up, they were beautiful women with flowing, long hair; some black, some brunette.

"Tell me about the land," Teal asked.

Conrad slowly looked up from the water and cast his eyes upon her. The question was like no other he'd been asked before. "The land?"

"Yes," Teal replied, pointing to the shoreline.

"I guess it's just like the oceans. I have no idea what's down there. Is that why you ask?"

"Yes, I am not able to leave the sea, but we can see the land and have always wondered.

"Where I come from it is surrounded by mountains like those," he replied, pointing at the high cliffs hugging the coastline.

She cast her eyes upon them. "Mountains," she said. "We have them too down here. We call them Biggonknots."

Conrad smiled and then continued. "I come from a small village that lies in the deep forest region of Austria."

"What's its name?"

"Nome."

She smiled cocking her head. "So, you are the Black Knight, who serves a king and you live in a little village called Nome?"

"Yes, and you?"

"In the region of Noel, there is a Shimmering Valley of Lights that we call home."

"Lights?"

"Yes, but they are like no lights that you have ever seen."

"Like your lantern?"

"Yes," Teal replied.

He nodded then sat there in silence for a moment, just looking at her.

"I'll be right back," she then said, sliding under the water. When she returned, in her hand was a book. When he reached out and took it from her, it was completely dry. It startled him when he looked at it, seeing his title, The Black Knight, at the top. Above his title were two crossed swords. In the center of the cover, was an eye encircled with snakes. At the bottom, there was a picture of ocean swells rolling across the cover from side to side and a mermaid coming out of the water carrying a lantern. He looked up with a question in his eyes.

"This is a gift to you and your people. Inside, you'll find secrets from the deep. But be warned, this book and the writings within can only be used for goodness," Teal said.

"Why are you giving me this?"

"You are a Knight, and you have come out here three long nights hoping to see me again."

"Yes..." his voice trailed off.

"That is enough to give you a gift."

He nodded and thought of her word, goodness. "So, what do you mean this book can only be used for goodness?"

"We are creatures who love all things and all things are free."

It sounded simple, and yet confusing. "All things are free?" he asked.

"Yes," she replied. "Nothing belongs to another and all things must be free to love."

He slowly nodded.

By the expression on his face, she could tell that where he came from things must be different. "Just use the book for goodness," she said and then paused. "Now, we'll be leaving you another gift. This gift will always remind you of what I've said tonight."

He nodded again.

"Her name is Brenda. She'll be waiting for you in a small inlet along the shoreline," Teal said, pointing.

He smiled still confused. "Will I ever see you again?" he asked.

"No. I must go back to my own. In your world, I think the appropriate thing to say now is goodbye."

"Goodbye, my lady of the deep," he replied.

She wrinkled her nose with his flattering expression then slipped under the water. Conrad sat there in a whirlwind of thoughts. *On the shoreline, there is a gift. Her name is Brenda. Was she a mermaid? No, she can't be.*

He picked up his oars and rowed back to Whitefish Bay. After tying up the boat, he placed the ten shillings he had promised the men underneath the cushion and walked up the steps. At the end of the pier, he walked along the shoreline for at least a half a mile outside the small port of Adrian. There, in a small inlet beach, was a beautiful porcelain swan that looked like a tub.

Conrad slowly walked around the swan and then cast his eyes upon the sea, hoping Teal would come up from the deep and tell him what to do with it. She never came.

Back in town, he ordered his men to slip under the cover of darkness and retrieve the gift from Teal. With the swan safely concealed within a wooden crate, Conrad, along with his men, returned to Nome.

"Abby," Benjamin whispered. "Are you going to tell Fanny the story?"

Abby opened her eyes and yawned. "Maybe tomorrow, Benjamin" she replied, turning and glancing over at Fanny. "It's getting late. Would you like to stay the night? My bed is large enough for four," she asked, giving her a soft, tired smile.

"I would like that."

"Good," she replied, picking up the mice and putting them on her shoulders. "I have a nightgown that may fit you," she continued, walking toward the elevator.

Fanny smiled getting up and following her out of the den.

"Come, Theodore," Abby called over her shoulder.

"Goodnight Boris," Fanny said.

"Goodnight, Madam Chamberlin - Madam Rose," he replied, yawning himself.

17

Brenda

Before the sun came up, Fanny opened her eyes seeing Abby still sound asleep. With that, she quietly slipped out of bed, walked down stairs and fixed two glasses of orange juice. On her return, Abby rolled over. "What time is it?" she asked, rubbing her eyes and sitting up.

"Good morning. It's five a.m. I brought you some orange juice," Fanny replied, handing her a glass and getting back in bed.

"Good morning," Benjamin greeted them jumping across the covers.

"Where are Wilson and Cracker?" Fanny asked.

"Wake up," he yelled back to the corner of the bed.

Wilson and Cracker sat up. "Isn't that the moon?" Cracker yawned.

"No, Dumbbell, it's the sun," Benjamin fumed.

"You're all up way too early for me," Abby yawned.

"Yes, it feels like Christmas," Benjamin sang out, holding his paws to his cheeks and smiling.

"Christmas? Why… it's only May," Abby yawned again.

"I think he's excited to hear the story of the Black Knight," Wilson said, scampering over and giving Benjamin a nudge.

Abby took a sip of her orange juice then set the glass down on the nightstand next to her.

"Are you up to telling the story?" Fanny asked.

Abby looked down at Benjamin. He raised his little brow and smiled. "I might as well, now that it feels like Christmas around here," she replied, propping up her pillow.

"Oh boy," Benjamin said, getting cozy next to Wilson and Cracker. Fanny snuggled up against Abby. They all lay there waiting for Abby to begin her story. Abby sighed, looking back toward the balcony bay doors and then started her story about her great uncle, Conrad Von Haussler, who was the Black Knight for King Lenhard. When she finished, she rested her head back on her pillow.

"That was the most incredible story I've ever heard," Fanny gushed.

"I think it was one of my favorites. But mind you, Conrad had a terrible time convincing the village of his tale while at sea," Abby said.

"Really?" Fanny questioned.

"Yes. You see, even though he brought Brenda, the swan, back with him, they believed he could have purchased it anywhere. Well, I would have never thought that. You saw her in my bathroom. She's absolutely magnificent."

"She sure is," Fanny agreed.

"It wasn't until my uncle brought Brenda inside his home that things began to change."

"Like what?" Fanny asked.

"Well, in the world outside these windows, I don't know many items coming alive and talking - do you?"

Fanny laughed. "I suppose you're right. I'm still having problems with all the things around here talking to me."

Abby laughed. "It wasn't until Brenda came alive that the little village of Nome finally believed my uncle. It was Brenda who taught them the rituals in the Potion and Spells book."

"So that's how it happened?" Fanny questioned

"Yes, and that is why my father gave her to me. She is a reminder for the generations to come that our lives, living as we do, is only for goodness, just like the beautiful mermaid, Teal, had mentioned.

"Can you actually imagine seeing and talking to a mermaid?" Fanny asked, staring into her eyes.

Abby shook her head. "So, what do you three think of that story?" she asked the mice.

"It was *better* than Christmas," Benjamin replied.

"Yeah," Cracker added. "I can almost imagine sitting in a small boat at sea, on a really foggy night and then seeing a mermaid coming up from the deep."

"Me too," Wilson said, "it sure would be spooky though."

Abby smiled. *Spooky,* she thought, thinking back to that part of the story. *I would have never asked Captain Sheldon to lower a boat,*" she continued thinking, *not with those forty-ton whales about.*

"So, that's why you want to find that book?" Fanny asked, taking her out of her thoughts. "Yes," she replied, turning and looking at her. "There are some spells that you must read from the book. Without it," she started to say, thinking of one spell she needed the most. "I won't be able to do what needs to be done."

"Like snapping your fingers and having this place going back to the way it used to be?" Fanny asked, raising her brow.

Oh... how I hate fibbing to her, even a little, Abby thought, glancing toward the balcony bay doors. *However, I have no other choice than to keep up this charade until Fanny becomes a witch.* "Yes, something like that, Fanny," she replied.

"It's our fault," Wilson spoke up.

"That doesn't matter now, Wilson," Abby replied.

"Yes, but that's why your father hid that book. If we hadn't gone up there and messed around with those spells..." Wilson's voice trailed off, looking down.

"Wilson," Abby kindly scolded.

He looked up at her.

"Just think - you three wouldn't be here right now if you hadn't gone up there and messed around, as you put it."

Wilson looked at his friends. *She's right,* he thought. *None of us would be here.*

"I'm awful glad you three are here," Fanny said, reaching down and rubbing their bellies. They rolled together laughing. "Stop it, stop it," Benjamin laughed. The scene made Abby laugh, which brought the giggles to Fanny too.

Time seemed to slip by so fast lying there in bed and having fun with the mice that Fanny almost forgot that she was supposed to meet Mitt today.

"What does your day look like?" Abby asked, watching her playing with the mice.

"Oh gosh, I almost forgot," letting go of the mice. "I have to get to the grocery store and restock my fridge. After that, I am meeting Mitt," she replied, tossing the covers off and getting out of bed.

Abby watched her walk into the bathroom and shut the door. She slowly looked down at the mice. "Don't you three worry, we'll find that book."

"We've already searched every nook and cranny, all the internal walls and ceilings while you were away," Wilson replied. Abby sighed, shifting her eyes on Theodore sleeping with Tasha by his side. "Well, it has to be here someplace," she said.

After Fanny walked in and closed the bathroom door, she stood there gazing at Brenda. Even with all the dust and cobwebs covering the room, Brenda was truly as magnificent as Abby described her. She stepped up to the mirror, wiped her hand across the tarnished glass and stared into it. *Should I become a witch like Abby?* That thought lingered while she washed her hands and then dried them off on a small hand towel. Before getting dressed, Fanny turned around to face Brenda once again. "You are so beautiful," she said, walking over and running her hand along Brenda's slender neck. *What an elegant gift*. That thought made her think of Conrad, the Black Knight. "Conrad," she whispered. I wish I had seen what you saw sitting in that boat."

Fanny sighed, thinking of Teal, goddess of the sea, while getting dressed. Before walking out of the bathroom, she glanced back at Brenda. "I will become a witch," she said, turning and walking out. When the door closed behind Fanny, Brenda opened her eyes. "You'll make a fine witch, Fanny," she whispered, reaching up and picking up some spice. She then sprinkled some into her tub and turned on her taps.

"OK, I am off," Fanny said, bending over and kissing Abby on the forehead.

"Would you like me to see you out?" Abby replied.

"No. You all stay here and keep warm," she replied, reaching down and tickling the mice. She looked over at Theodore. He was just stirring. "I'll come back tonight if you want," she continued, walking toward the elevator.

"You're welcome here anytime," Abby replied.

"Thank you, Abby."

"Goodbye, Madam Chamberlin," Theodore said, getting up. "And thank you for the gift."

"You're welcome my handsome prince. Please look after Tasha for me," she replied, looking back and giving Abby a wink. When the elevator door opened, she stepped inside and pressed the button.

Abby lay there for a while just snuggling with the mice. She smiled when Theodore walked over and nuzzled his head next to her on the bed. "You know, I don't think one could find better friends and companions than you four," she said, running her fingers through his thick white mane. Benjamin sighed. "We love you too, Abby," he said. She watched Wilson and Cracker nodding their heads and smiling up at her. In that moment, she felt a twitch of giddiness. She looked at Theodore and gave him a soft wink. Theodore smiled knowing that she was up for a prank. "Well, she started to say. The day is wasting," she continued, tossing her covers over the mice and getting out of bed.

"Hey, I can't see under here," Wilson muffled, fighting the covers off.

"Me either," Cracker fumed, rolling over Benjamin. "Will you get off me?" Benjamin scolded.

When the three finally fought their way out of the covers, they looked up at Theodore smiling at them. “Why didn’t you warn us?” Benjamin asked.

Theodore laughed. “Now why would I do a thing like that?”

“Oh… you’re something else,” Wilson grumbled.

Theodore kept his smile.

“Keep smiling and I’ll make sure you get *something.* Like maybe a fat lip,” Cracker spat, curling up his little paws into fists.

“Good morning, Brenda,” Abby said, walking into the bathroom.

“Good morning, Madam Rose. I thought you’d want a bath.”

“You’ve read my mind,” she replied, slipping out of her nightgown and stepping into the tub. After she lay back feeling the soothing warmth taking the chills away, three young kids walked into Meek’s real estate agency in Cloverdale.

18

Three Little Worms

"Well, look what the cat dragged in," Sid said, as Willy, Molly and Bobby Ray walked in.

"Funny," Molly replied, walking up to his desk. "Your wife seemed to be the one running like a cat on fire the other day at the fair."

"Hey, cut the crap. Don't be talking about my wife like that."

Molly gave him a smug, little grin back.

"Where're your bikes?" Don asked, changing the subject.

"We thought we'd walk into town today," Willy replied, taking a seat in front of Sid.

"Is that right?" Sid asked, sitting back. "Have a seat, Bobby Ray. We don't bite," he continued, looking up at Molly.

"Alright, let's get this over with," Molly said, taking a seat herself.

Sid glanced over at Don. Don raised his brow hoping the kids took the bait.

"Well, have you three thought it over?" Sid asked, picking up his pen and twirling it between his fingers.

"Yeah, we've thought about it," Molly replied, tossing her eyes on Willy.

Sid focused his attention on Willy, the leader of this small group of juveniles. He raised his brow for an answer.

"We're in," Willy said.

Sid smiled. "I am glad to hear that."

"So, what do we have to do?" Molly asked.

Sid looked at her and then shifted his attention on Bobby Ray. "Not talking today?"

"No, just listening. Pa always says you learn more by not moving your lips. I thought I'd give it a try."

"Is that so?" Sid laughed, glancing over at Don. Don smiled hearing the snot-nosed kid giving them advice.

"Well, in my business you have to move your lips or you won't make a sale," Sid countered his smart butt answer.

Bobby Ray shrugged.

"Alright, so what do we have to do?" Willy asked, staring at Bobby Ray.

Bobby Ray felt the stare. He shrugged his shoulders again.

"Just hold on, Willy," Sid replied, "one thing at a time."

Willy sat back and waited.

"Now," Sid started to say, leaning up on his desk. "First off, have you told anyone?"

"No, you think we're stupid or something?" Molly shot back.

"Maybe you should take some advice from Bobby Ray, Miss Fancy Pants," Sid remarked. "OK, now" he quickly continued, not wanting an answer from her. "So, you've told no one?"

"Nope," Willy replied.

"Good. Now here's what we're planning. Right now, Mitt Ryan is helping Mrs. Rose get that heap fixed up. There will be several companies up there this week. They'll be tearing down the garage, asphalting a new driveway and cleaning and painting inside."

"Are we going to wait until they're done?" Molly asked.

"Yes, we're going to wait until they're done before stealing the money. But while the workers are there, this gives us an opportunity to at least go up and snoop around."

"Snoop around?" Willy asked. "Like when?"

"After the workers leave for the day."

"Well, please tell us what you find out," Bobby Ray finally spoke up, "because I am not going up there to do any snooping around in the dark."

Don laughed. The three kids looked over at him.

"Are you going up there?" Molly asked Don.

Don laughed again.

"I'm serious," Bobby Ray added. "If Don isn't going, don't expect us to."

"I'm going up there," Don shot back.

"Good," Molly said. "Give us your report when you come back. That's if you come back."

"Now listen here, you three," Sid grunted, sitting back. "We're not going to get anywhere until you guys stop believing in ghosts and goblins running around up there."

"We've said nothing about ghosts and goblins, we're talking about witches and warlocks," Bobby Ray replied.

"Witches and warlocks?!" Sid spat, thinking of old man Cooper. "You three really believe that old buzzard was telling the truth about seeing pumpkins talking and witches flying around on broomsticks?"

"I do," Bobby Ray quickly shot back.

Sid shook his head. He needed to find a way of getting these kids to start thinking about the money instead of the things that go bump in the night. "OK," he said and then paused. "Let's look at the facts, shall we?"

"The facts?" Molly asked.

"Yes, the facts. If old man Cooper's story were true, it happened a very long time ago when Baron Von Haussler lived there. Do you honestly think that those witches and warlocks, as you call them, are still hanging around up there?" "And," he continued, not wanting to be interrupted, "right now we have a little old lady living up there all by herself. Alone. Don't you think we would have heard something by now if there were those kinds of creatures still there?"

"Like hearing what?" Molly asked.

"Like hearing what, you ask?" he replied. "Like hearing that Mrs. Rose was taken to a hospital and put on the doctor's juice because she saw those things you're describing, that's what."

Don laughed.

"What's so funny!?" Sid spat, looking over at him.

"You could have said it differently."

"OK, you tell 'em what I mean then."

Don sighed, sitting back. "If there were witches and warlocks up there, don't you think Mrs. Rose would have come down and reported seeing them? And that begs another question. If she did see them, they'd certainly have to be ghosts by now. Nothing can live that long."

Willy, Molly and Bobby Ray all sat there chewing on that.

"Maybe he's right, Willy," Molly said.

Willy glanced over at her for a moment and then turned and looked at Sid. "What night are you planning on going up there?"

"Tomorrow night. There will be no moon out."

"Great," Bobby Ray spewed.

"We're not going in, Bobby Ray," Sid replied to his fuming remark.

We're not?"

"No, not just yet at least. We're just going up there to check it out. You know, start getting a plan of attack together."

"Like how we're getting in and out," Molly asked.

"You're pretty smart, young lady. Yes, we need to get in, find that money and then get the hell out of there as fast as we can. That is without being seen."

"So," Willy said. "Where do you want to meet?"

"You know Old Tiller Road?" Don asked.

Three little minds lit up like streetlights going on at the same time. *If he says we'll meet near that old abandoned barn on the Klondike's place, I'll wet my pants,* Molly thought, keeping a straight face.

"Yeah we've been down it thousands of times. It's right behind the manor," Willy replied.

"Great, then you know where that old barn is sitting?"

"Yes," Willy replied, thinking about his own little plan.

"We'll meet you there - say around nine tomorrow night. Or, is that too late?"

"No, we'll be there," Willy replied, standing up and walking to the door.

Sid and Don watched them leave. "You really think this is a smart move getting these kids involved?" Don asked.

Sid took his eyes off the door and glanced over at him. "Now that you've been in that run-down shack and seeing how big it is, do you really want us to go back up there and search that entire place by ourselves?"

"No."

"Alright then. There's your answer."

After the three had left the real estate agency, they walked down Main Street toward the center of town. When they got to the corner of Dover Street, Willy looked left and spotted his older brother, Ernie, just as they had expected - sitting inside his car at the side of the road. He quickly glanced back at the real estate office. All clear. "OK, let's go," he said, running up and getting in the front passenger seat. Molly and Bobby Ray jumped into the back seat. "What's their game plan?" Ernie asked, rolling off the curb.

"They want to check the place out first. We're supposed to meet them tomorrow night at nine on Old Tiller Road next to that old barn on the Klondike's farm."

"You told 'em that you'd be there, right?" Ernie asked, shifting his eyes on him."

"Yes."

"Good," Ernie replied, taking the corner and heading up Main Street. He looked up into the rearview mirror at Molly and Bobby Ray.

"Does anyone know that you're back in town?" Bobby Ray asked, seeing Ernie in the mirror.

Ernie stopped at the light. He glanced over at his younger brother again. *Family business is family business, which means keeping your mouth shut,* Ernie thought.

"Yeah, I told 'em. They'd find out sooner or later anyway," Willy replied to his brother's stare.

Ernie slowly nodded. He looked up into the rearview mirror again. "Only a few people know that I'm back, Bobby Ray."

"What about the sheriff?" he asked.

"Yeah, I had to report into the police station as soon as I got back. But I'm not worried about those two bumbling idiots."

"You mean Roy Roger and Tonto?" Molly quipped, thinking of Sheriff, Roy Collins, and his sidekick, Deputy Larry Oxford.

Ernie laughed. "Yeah, those two clowns."

Bobby Ray sat back listening to Ernie. Ernie was around five-foot eight, as skinny as a rail and only wore jeans and white T-shirts with a black jean jacket. He was trouble from birth. Busted for petty larceny at the age of eight, caught joy riding in a stolen car at the age of ten, and then was charged with accidentally setting the church on fire at the age of fifteen. His last offense was for breaking and entering while trying to steal a bike at Wheel's Bike Shop. His parents finally packed him off to his uncle's place in Ohio. A year and a half later, he made the big leagues – armed robbery. It cost him two years in the Ohio State Pen.

"So, what's our plan?" Molly asked, taking Bobby Ray out of his thoughts.

"You three don't have to worry. I'll be inside that barn at eight-thirty watching everything when you ride up and meet those two." Ernie replied, turning onto Gantry Street toward Station Park. The three watched him enter the parking lot. He shut off the engine and then turned in his seat.

"You know, it gets pretty dark on that dirt road at night," Bobby Ray said.

"Yes, I know that, but don't worry. I'll be able to see you," Ernie replied and then paused. "What we need to find out is where their wives will be waiting outside in their car when you come out with the money."

"I sure hope it's not on Old Tiller Road," Willy said.

Ernie pondered that. *That would screw up everything,* he thought. Their game plan was Willy and his friends had to find the money first. That was the million-dollar bet on this whole swindle. If they did, they would then hightail it out the rear of the manor, run across the back yard, down the hill and then meet up with him inside that barn. He'd then take the loot, head across the old field, and hide it down by the river. *If Sid and Don's wives are going to hole up there waiting, I'll have to change our plans,* he thought.

Willy reached up and scratched his head while waiting for his brother to come down from the trees. "Alright," Ernie said. "That's what we need to know right now. You're going to have to ask them tomorrow night. We must know where their wives will be waiting."

Willy nodded.

"OK, I'll let you three get out here in the park. I've got to go and meet Arnold down at the pool hall."

That caught Molly off guard. Arnold was just as corrupted as Ernie was. She wondered if Ernie was going to get Arnold involved too. She opened her door and got out. Bobby Ray and Willy slid out. They stood there watching Ernie leave the parking lot before saying a word to one another.

"Arnold?" she questioned, looking suspiciously at Willy.

Willy shrugged. He hadn't a clue to why his brother was meeting up with Arnold Gilbert. Arnold and his brother went way back together, back to their foolish juvenile days as kids.

"I sure hope not," Bobby Ray said.

"Me too," Molly agreed.

"I don't know," Willy replied, watching his brother driving down the street. He turned and looked at his friends. "Don't worry. Ernie will make sure we get our share. Now, let's go back to my house."

19

A Romantic Dinner

That same day as Ernie was meeting Arnold down at the pool hall, Shaun rode up to the manor on his dirt bike. He pulled around two painting vans and parked. *She must be going crazy with all that noise and work going on,* he thought, walking up to the half-open doors.

As he walked in, he noticed five men wearing blue jumpsuits and ball caps. Over the breast pocket of the jumpsuit was the company name *Quick Fast Cleaners & Painters. I should hope it's quick fast - and then out of here,* he thought, walking in. "Where is Mrs. Rose?" he asked a worker.

"She's in the kitchen."

"Thank you," he replied, turning and walking toward the corridor.

"Hello, Abigail," he greeted her, walking in.

"Shaun," she sang out, turning at the sink. "Isn't this a pleasant surprise?"

"I told you that I'd stop by every day to see how you're doing," he said, glancing at the beautiful white stuffed lion sitting on the table in the middle of the kitchen.

"I'm glad you came," she replied, noticing him admiring Theodore. "This is Theodore," she continued, picking up her stuffed toy.

"Wow, he's awesome. I love his eyes. They look so real," Shaun replied, rubbing his hand down Theodore's mane.

I wonder what you're going to say when you do see him alive, she thought. "Thank you. I've had him since I was a child. My father won him at a county fair for me."

"Really," he replied. "You've had him that long. I mean…" he started to say.

"Yes, that long," she replied, interrupting him with a gleeful smile.

"Sorry, I wasn't insinuating that you were old."

She laughed. "Well, don't you go feeling bad that you had to break that awful news to me."

He looked into her eyes and laughed. She laughed, putting her hand on his shoulder. "Would you like something to drink?"

"Yes, thank you. Iced tea if you have any."

"I do," she replied, walking over and getting two glasses and then opening Simon, who was sound asleep. She handed him his glass.

"Thanks. How long will the cleaning and painting company be here?"

"A week I think. They're starting with the parlor, den, the entire staircase and the master's chambers. Would you like to walk out onto the patio? My ears need a break from all this noise."

"Sure."

As she escorted Shaun out the back door, he saw several trucks and a bulldozer next to the old garage. "That's Snider's Construction. They're getting ready to tear it down."

"Are they starting today?"

"No. Tomorrow," she replied and then remembered. "Oh, thank heavens you're here. I never thought of Wilfred. I have to move him before they can start. I was thinking of just parking him closer to the house. Would you mind moving him for me?"

Shaun cast his eyes on the men walking around the garage. He thought of another idea. "You know," he said and then paused, turning and looking at her.

"I could call Mr. Olson and see if he'd allow me to use the last stall at the service station to put Wilfred in while they're building you a new garage."

"You think he would?" Abby excitedly replied.

"I think so. We hardly use it, and besides, it would give me a chance to look Wilfred over."

Abby smiled at him. "I know he'd rather be out of the weather while they're working out there."

Shaun watched her facial expression as she spoke. *She talks about him as if he were a family member.* It was one of the most delightful things about her. It lent to her charm the way she talked about her possessions as if they were human. "Let me call him right now and find out. If he says yes, I could leave my dirt bike here and Chuck will drive me back."

She delightfully nodded.

Shaun pulled out his phone and made the call. The smile on his face and the nod of his head told her Mr. Olson said yes. "OK, Wilfred's going in today," Shaun said, closing his phone.

"Thank you, Shaun. Let me get you the keys," she replied, walking back in. She set her glass down, walked over to the last kitchen drawer and pulled out the keys. "Here you go," she continued, handing them to him.

"I promise I'll take good care of Wilfred," he replied, setting his glass down and walking toward the back door.

"Shaun," she said.

He turned around.

"If you'd like, you can stay for dinner when Chuck drops you off."

Shaun gave that a thought. "I'll let my folks know, thank you," he replied, heading out the door.

After Shaun left, she stepped up to the back window. "He's a fine young man," Hansel whispered, standing up at the sink.

Abby glanced down at her. "He sure is," she replied, lifting her head and focusing on Shaun walking up to the garage.

"Good afternoon, gentlemen. I'm here to move the car," Shaun said.

"Great," Dan Gilmore, Snider's supervisor replied. "She told us that she wanted it moved closer to the house."

"I'll be taking it to Olson's Service Station in town. That way it will be out of the weather."

Olson's Service Station, Wilfred thought. *What is Madam Rose thinking?*

"What do you think that baby's worth?" Dan asked, nodding his head toward Wilfred.

"It's priceless if you asked me," Shaun remarked.

Priceless? Did you hear that? Wilfred thought. *Now here's a kid that knows his cars.*

Dan nodded. "What year is it?"

"It's a nineteen o'seven Ford K," Shaun said.

"Wow. They don't make cars like that anymore."

You can say that again, Wilfred thought. *I'm a classic.*

"They sure don't. Check out all the brass work, the front windshield, the kerosene lantern headlights and side lamps," Shaun said, walking around Wilfred. "Get a load of the long gear shift and side break on the running board," Shaun continued, heading to the back of Wilfred. "Now, take a look at this," he said, "this is the gas tank and trunk, which looks more like a metal suitcase."

"Unbelievable," Dan quipped.

"The only thing I can see that was modified on this car was it used to be started with a hand crank in front. Now it starts up with a key. The vehicles back then operated like our tractors do today."

"So, you're saying," Dan said and then paused, walking over to the gearshift and brake on the running board, "that you push in the clutch, take the handbrake off and then shift it into gear forward or in reverse?"

"That's right," Shaun replied, stepping up and taking a seat behind the wheel. He pressed in the clutch, turned the key, released the brake and shifted the gear forward. "Well, I must get going. I'm looking forward to working on this."

"Drive slow," Dan replied.

"She can only do sixty miles per hour. That's down hill I think," Shaun laughed, rolling out of the garage.

Sixty miles per hour downhill? Wilfred thought. *I'll give you down hill, young man.*

Abby stood there watching Shaun waving to the men after he drove Wilfred out of the garage. *I sure hope Wilfred behaves himself,* she thought, turning and walking out of the kitchen.

Shaun stopped at the end of the driveway. He looked both ways and then turned left onto Daisy Lane. "OK, let's see what you got under that hood of yours," he said, stepping on the gas.

Wilfred took off. Fifty, sixty, seventy, and then he reached eighty miles per hour down Daisy Lane. "What the…?" Shaun freaked, letting off on the gas pedal.

How's that for speed? Wilfred thought, smiling to himself.

Fifteen minutes later, Kenny Wood, Olson's cashier, noticed Shaun pulling into the service station. "Shaun's here," he yelled.

"Open the last stall and let him in," Mr. Olson called out from his office.

"Hey, will you look at that," Sid said, standing up at his desk and looking across the street.

"What?" Don asked, looking toward the office windows.

"Shaun Stevenson is driving Mrs. Rose's car into Olson's."

"No kidding," he replied, standing up and walking toward the door.

"What do you think?" Sid asked, walking up alongside him.

"I don't know. Maybe Mitt arranged for her car to be moved before they started tearing down that old garage."

"Maybe," Sid replied. "I hope they haven't torn it down yet."

"I sure hope not, Sid. It would be a perfect place for cover tomorrow night."

"So, what do you think?" Shaun asked Mr. Olson, getting out of Wilfred.

"She sure is amazing," Mr. Olson replied, walking up to Wilfred.

She, who are you calling a she? Wilfred thought. *I'm all male. A classic, but all male through and through.*

"Mrs. Rose calls it Wilfred. She wants him fully restored," Shaun said, rubbing his hand down the hood.

"Wilfred? That's a strange name for a car," Kenny said.

Watch it, Sonny Boy, Wilfred thought.

"Are we going to be restoring it, Mr. Olson?" Kenny asked.

"No, I'm going to," Shaun spoke up.

Mr. Olson nodded as he walked around Wilfred. "It needs lots of work, Shaun," he said, looking up.

"Yes, I know, but I was thinking of just taking it apart and doing the brass work first and then the undercarriage and body."

"How does it run?" Kenny asked.

"Great. I was surprised how fast it goes."

"Really?" Mr. Olson questioned, looking at the front and seeing no crank. "I see it's been modified."

"Yes, it starts with a key."

"Did you prime it first?" Mr. Olson asked.

"No. That's funny," he replied confused - seeing that it started without being primed first.

"What?" Kenny questioned.

"I was telling the workers out there that it ran just like our tractors. How I forgot to prime it and it still turned over is beyond me," Shaun said, scratching his head.

"Well, let's take a look under the hood and I'll show you, Shaun," Mr. Olson said, opening both sides and locking them back. "You see this," he continued, pointing to a small bowl and lever. "You place a small amount of gas in here and then you pull this little lever. It acts like a primer on a lawnmower. As you pull it forward, the gas goes down onto the heads."

"Wow. I never even did that."

"Well, son," Mr. Olson replied. "Maybe there was enough gas inside already," he continued, putting the hood down.

"Maybe," Shaun replied, puzzled.

"So when are you going to start?" Kenny asked.

"I'd like to start today, however, Mrs. Rose invited me for dinner."

"Dinner?" Kenny questioned.

"Yes. I guess she wants to thank me for helping her out."

Mr. Olson smiled. "That would be the polite thing to do. She seems like a real nice lady."

"She sure is. And smart to boot," Shaun replied.

"A date with an older woman? How lucky can you get?" Kenny teased.

"That will be enough, Kenny," Mr. Olson lightly scolded. "I think the front office is calling you."

"Right, Mr. Olson," Kenny replied, looking at Shaun and smiling.

Shaun let it go. He didn't care what other people thought.

"Seeing that we're waiting for brake parts for that Buick, I think I'll let you go home and get cleaned up. Tell your parents I said hello."

"I will, Mr. Olson. Look after Wilfred for me," he replied, walking out the stall door.

Mr. Olson nodded. He turned around and looked at Wilfred. "You're the oldest car I've had in my shop," he said, turning and walking back into his office.

Oldest car in your shop, Wilfred thought. *You mean the most classic of cars you've had in your shop.*

After Mr. Olson had gone, Wilfred opened his eyes and glanced over at the Buick up on the hoist with its wheels removed. *I hope I'm not parked alongside this heap for very long. Rust could be contagious.*

At around six-thirty that evening, Abby heard Chuck's truck pulling up out front. Chuck said goodbye and drove back down the driveway.

"He's here," Abby said to the mice, walking over to the doors. Wilson, Benjamin and Cracker jumped down from off the arm of the recliner and made a mad dash under the staircase.

"Let me see," Benjamin said, squeezing between his friends."

"Shh… she's opening the door," Wilson whispered.

"Shaun, it's so nice to see you. Please come in."

"Hello, Abigail, I brought you this," he greeted her, pulling out one single rose from behind his back.

Abby was stunned and delighted all at the same time. "Why, isn't that beautiful," she replied, taking it from him and placing up to her nose. "Mmm the smell of roses," she gushed, "That was so nice of you."

"I thought it would look good on the kitchen windowsill."

"It sure will. Come on in and take off your jacket. I hope you like turkey."

"I love turkey," he replied, hanging up his jacket on Sir Henry and turning around.

She watched his eyes scanning the room. "You like it so far?"

"Somebody turn on the lights," he replied.

"They're on," she said, confused.

He laughed. "I meant, WOW," he replied, taking in the work already done. All the dirt, dust and cobwebs were gone from the foyer and parlor. The walls and ceiling were in primer, the white flooring looked new with protective paper to walk on. The dark grey stone fireplace looked new as well, along with the blacked marble mantelpiece. The staircase carpet was gone and the stairs and banisters had been sanded back to their original woodwork. He looked up at the huge chandelier, now clean and covered until the painters finished. His eyes then caught the decorative ceiling trim around the edges. He shook his head.

"Look in the den," Abby said.

Shaun walked in and shook his head. It was the same, plus the moose head looked as new as the day it was preserved by a taxidermist. "I can't believe it," he replied. Turning toward the parlor, his eyes drifted over the mantelpiece. "Do you have a small vase?" he asked.

"Yes, in the kitchen."

"I think that rose should be placed on that mantelpiece," Shaun said, pointing.

Abby smiled, casting her eyes on the mantle. She allowed her eyes to drift upward to where her father had hung the painting of her mother Amelia. She sighed remembering those sweet memories. "That would be a lovely place to put it, Shaun. Come, let's have dinner."

As they walked through the parlor and down the corridor, she asked,

"How are your parents?"

"They're good."

"Well, fellas, what cha think?" Benjamin asked.

"He seems really nice," Cracker replied.

"He sure does, but something smells funny," Wilson said.

Benjamin smelled himself then smelled Cracker. "Cut with the nonsense, will ya. I wasn't talking about you two. I'm talking about Shaun. I think Abby's up to something with him."

Benjamin pondered that. "Like what?" he asked.

"Well," Wilson started to say. "Do you remember what she said to Fanny in bed?"

They both wrinkled their brow.

"Abby said sometimes you need to have the Potion and Spells book for a spell to work."

Cracker's eyes lit up. "You don't think she wants to put a love spell on Shaun, do you?"

"That's what I was thinking," Wilson replied.

"What are you two talking about?" Benjamin said, folding his arms.

"Think about it, Benjamin," Cracker said.

Benjamin sat there and thought. "What about Theodore? He might know something we don't."

"Yeah…," Cracker replied.

"Well, we're not going to get to the bottom of this sitting here. Let's go up and talk to him," Wilson said, jumping down from the beam and walking out of the hole in the staircase baseboard.

After the mice had gone, Grandfather opened his eyes seeing no one in the room. He glanced over at Sir Henry with Shaun's jacket over his head.

"Psst," Grandfather whispered to him. Sir Henry muffled something under the jacket. Grandfather lightly laughed and then closed his eyes.

"You're not funny at all," Sir Henry muffled.

When Abby and Shaun entered the kitchen, she asked, "Did your parents question your invitation for dinner tonight?"

"Yes, they did. I told 'em you were thanking me for all the work I've done."

"I see," she replied, walking up to the sink. *That was only half of the reason I asked you to dinner,* she thought. "I hope you don't mind eating in here tonight. The dining room hasn't been done yet."

"No, I don't mind at all. Shall I get two chairs?"

"Silly me, I forgot. They're stacked in the corner of the dining room.

Shaun turned and walked out. She waited a few seconds then turned toward Hansel. "Is everything ready?" she whispered.

"Yes, Madam Rose. Everything is ready and the turkey is in the oven."

"Thank you, Hansel."

The evening with Shaun was everything she thought it would be as she sat and listened to him talk about his childhood growing up in Cloverdale, playing sports in high school, his passion for cars, which was the reason Mr. Olson asked him to work at his service station in the first place. When she finally had a chance to ask him about girls, his answer was simple. One, he was shy, and two, not many girls his age liked to play under the hood of a car. They'd rather be asked out to the movies, go bowling, hang out in the park, or just sit down by the river.

Her story, on the other hand, was somewhat made up. It had to be, and she hated fibbing to him. However, fibbing sounded much better than thinking that she was outright lying to Shaun. Although she knew that some would harbor such notions that she was, in fact, lying. Nevertheless, she was on a quest, a secret mission of sorts, and in her mind - one had to fib a little when on such a mission like this. Shaun had to fall in love with her all on his own. No potion or spell could be used to entice him to want her as his wife. That was the only way she could turn young again. *Nevertheless,* she thought, *I still need that book to cast the spell on our honeymoon. That's if he does fall in love with me and asks me to be his wife.* It was all that mattered to her now, sitting across from him while he enjoyed her succulent turkey, mashed potatoes, and homemade bread.

After their meal, Shaun stated that he had to go. His parents wanted to ensure he got home at a normal time. "I really enjoyed the meal, Abigail," he said, walking through the corridor.

"It was my pleasure, Shaun. Oh," she said and then paused.

He stopped and looked at her.

"We never discussed an hourly wage for you while you're working on Wilfred."

Shaun raised his brow. *No, we haven't,* he thought. Moreover, he had no idea of how much he should charge her. To him, he'd work on Wilfred for free, but he knew that she'd never accept that. "How about ten dollars an hour? That seems reasonable."

"Ten dollars an hour!? My word, you cut yourself short."

"I do? I mean, I'm worth more than that?"

"Yes, Shaun," she replied, escorting him to the foyer. "I think auto mechanics make much more than that these days."

"Yes, some do. I know some mechanics making at least forty an hour."

"Then forty it is then."

"Forty dollars an hour!?"

"Yes, and please keep a running log of your time," she said. "And," she continued, "I saw the blueprint for the new garage. There will be lights and electrical outlets and a drain put into the middle of the cement flooring. When it's finished, we can have the construction company build you some workbenches, cupboards and such for tools. How's that sound?"

"That would be awesome," he replied, taking his jacket off Sir Henry. Before opening the door, he asked, "Are you sure you want to pay me that much?"

"Yes, I want to pay you that much."

Shaun smiled with that thought, *forty dollars an hour - that's three times more than what Mr. Olson pays me.*

"By your smile I see you approve?"

"Yes, you have a deal," he replied, leaning over and kissing her cheek. "Thank you again for the evening," he continued, opening the door.

"Goodnight, Shaun," she said.

Shaun looked at her. A thought popped into his head.

"What is it?" she asked.

"You know that story I was telling you about B.B. Cooper?"

"Yes."

"Forget about it. It was silly anyway."

Abby coyly nodded.

"You're the kindest person I've ever met, Abigail. Don't worry about Wilfred. I'll take good care of him," he said walking out.

"I'm sure you will."

She stood there watching him until he rode down the driveway. After shutting the door, she leaned against it and sighed.

"Well now, Madam Rose," Grandfather said, opening his eyes.

"Yes, Grandfather," she replied waiting to hear what he was about to say, which she knew had to be about Shaun kissing her on the cheek.

"What did I miss?" Sir Henry asked now that he could see.

"Everything," Grandfather replied.

"Now, Grandfather," Abby scolded, standing between them. "I think Grandfather is trying to goad you. Shaun just gave me a lovely kiss on the cheek, that's all."

"I missed that, did I?" Sir Henry replied.

"Yes, and I don't want to talk about it. It's time for bed and I am shutting down the house," she said, turning for the elevator. "Lights," she continued, clapping her hands. The house fell into darkness. "Goodnight, you two."

They watched her walk down the corridor. Grandfather looked over at him. "It was the sweetest kiss I've ever seen."

"Really now," Sir Henry replied. "You should have seen King Louie the Third kissing Queen Anne goodnight."

"Oh, will you shut up and go to sleep," Grandfather spewed, closing his eyes.

He heard a huff from the other side of the foyer. It made him smile.

While Abby rode the elevator up, Wilson, Benjamin, and Cracker were sitting next to Theodore as he was telling them about Madam Rose's secret plan. A deal was struck between them that they'd never tell a soul. With that, they waited for Abby to come up to go to bed.

20

Whispering Schemes

The following night, Ernie and Arnold sat on the back steps at Ernie's house watching Willy retrieve his bike from the shed. "When will they be here?" Arnold asked.

"Molly and Bobby Ray should be here anytime," he replied, pushing his bike over and dropping his kickstand. "You two want to tell me your plans before they show up?" he asked, taking a seat.

Arnold tossed a glance over at Ernie. Ernie stood up and placed his hands in his front pockets. "We're going to take it all," he replied, without a waver in his eyes.

Willy slowly nodded thinking what Bobby Ray, Molly and his cut would be. Before he could ask, the back door opened. They all looked up.

"Your father and I are going out tonight."

"OK, Mom," Ernie replied.

"Look after your brother," she said.

"Don't worry, he'll be with me all night," Ernie replied.

She shifted her eyes down at Arnold sitting there. He was trouble. "No games in the house while we're gone, you hear me?"

"Yes, Mom. We're thinking about going bowling."

"Alright, we'll be home around midnight," she replied, closing the door.

After she shut the door, Willy whispered, "OK, so what's our cut?"

"I don't know, Willy," Ernie replied, picking up a stick and tossing it. "Let's just see how much the old lady has first."

"Sid and Don said we'd get a thousand each," Willy tossed back, hoping they'd get at least that much.

Arnold laughed.

"What's so funny?" Willy asked.

"You really think those clowns were going to pay you?" he replied, keeping his grin.

"Yes, and if they didn't, we'd go straight to the cops."

Arnold laughed again, tossing his eyes on Ernie. "You hear that?"

"Yeah, I heard it. Look, Willy, I think you three will get more than what those bozos promised you - that's if she has all that money stashed away as you said. But understand one thing…"

"What's that?" he interrupted.

"Once we get our hands on it, we're going to lay low for awhile."

"Lay low? You mean we can't leave the house?"

"No, stupid. We can't go out spending it right away. You know Mrs. Rose will report this to Sheriff Collins. Collins may be stupid about some things, but he'll know right away that we stole it if we go out and start buying up the town especially when we got no jobs."

"They'll never think we kids took it, Ernie."

"How about chewing on this for starters," Arnold jumped in. "Do you know any kids around here flashing money as if they've just won the lotto?"

"No."

"OK then. We can't be either," Ernie replied, sitting back on the steps.

Willy gave that a thought. Ernie was right. "OK, we'll play it cool. So what are you two going to do tonight?"

"Just like we said we would. We'll be out at the Klondike farm hiding inside that old barn," Arnold replied.

"Then what?" Willy asked.

"We'll be safeguarding your little butts when you meet up with Sid and Don out there, that's what," Arnold replied.

Suddenly, two bikes rounded the back of the house. Bobby Ray did a big skid in the dirt right before the shed. Molly rolled up and got off her bike at the steps.

"What took ya so long?" Ernie spat.

"I had to wait for Molly to sneak out of the house," Bobby Ray replied, riding over and getting off his bike.

Arnold stood up. "We have to go."

"Yeah," Ernie added. "We'll call out from the barn so you know we're there."

"How are you guys getting there?" Molly asked.

"We're going to walk," Arnold replied.

"Well, if you're walking, then you're probably crossing over Kessler's Dam, right?" Bobby Ray added.

"That's right. We're crossing over the dam and then heading through the woods to the Klondike farm," Arnold replied.

Bobby Ray glanced over at Willy. The numbers were finally adding up. Ernie and Arnold were going to hide the money inside the overflow pipe next to Kessler's Dam.

"OK, we'll see you both there," Willy said, standing up and walking over to his bike. "Let's go. We have a few miles to ride ourselves," he continued, getting on his bike and riding around the house.

Ernie and Arnold waited until they left. "You think they know?" Arnold asked, turning around and looking at him.

Ernie shook his head. "No, they'd never guess in a million years where we're going to stash the money once we steal it. Let's start walking," he replied, turning and heading toward the back gate.

Arnold followed him through the yard and out the gate. "What if Sid and Don find it first?" Arnold asked.

"If they do, then I'll introduce them to this," Ernie replied, pulling out a plastic, toy gun.

Arnold looked down and started to laugh.

"It looks real enough," Ernie said.

"Yes, it does. Where did you get it?"

"It's Willy's."

Arnold continued laughing as they made their way across an open field. When they came to the end of the field, they waded through an outcrop of trees and then headed down toward Kessler's Dam.

"I don't trust Arnold," Molly said, riding her bike between Willy and Bobby Ray.

"Neither do I, Willy," Bobby Ray agreed.

"You trust Ernie, don't cha?" Willy asked.

"Yes," Molly replied.

"Alright then."

Molly looked at Bobby Ray. He raised his brow then sped up out in front of them. She watched him clowning around on his bike - weaving back and forth across the road. *I don't like any of this,* she thought, shifting her eyes on Willy. He turned his head and smiled at her. She gave him a coy smile back.

When they reached the Klondike's barn, they pulled over next to the side of the road. "Ernie, are you guys there?" Willy yelled toward the barn, getting off his bike.

"Yeah, we're here," Ernie yelled back.

Willy tossed a glance at Bobby Ray and Molly in the dark. "Feel better?" he whispered.

"Yes," Molly replied, looking back at the barn. All she could see was the outline of the old structure sitting back there.

Five minutes later, they saw headlights coming down Old Tiller Road. The headlights went off as the car rolled up. "About time," Bobby Ray whispered, watching Sid driving past them and then turning down the path toward the barn.

"Get back," Ernie whispered, kneeling tighter against the barn's internal wall.

"It's nice to see you could all make it," Don said, walking back to the road.

"We're here, now tell us what we're going to do up there?" Willy asked.

"We're going up to show you the layout. I didn't want to explain this tomorrow night."

"Tomorrow night?" Molly questioned.

"Yes, tomorrow night," Sid replied, "now let's get moving. You three follow us up the hill."

Molly watched them walk across the road. She looked over at Bobby Ray. "Tomorrow night?" she mouthed.

Bobby Ray shrugged.

This is madness, she thought, crossing the road last. As she climbed through the brush, taking hold of tree trunks on the way up, she decided that she wasn't going through with it. *I'm not going to rip off an elderly lady,* she thought, steadying her hands-on Bobby Ray's back. That thought spun her in another direction. *Mrs. Rose was actually a charming old lady. She even helped me out at the store. This would be so cruel.*

"OK, we'll hole up here," Sid whispered, standing on level ground along the tree lined ridge.

"Darn it," Don cursed, coming up and looking over at the garage - it was gone. "I knew they were going to tear it down as soon as Shaun drove her car down to Olson's."

"Shaun Stevenson?" Willy asked.

"Yes, haven't you heard? He's been up here every day helping Mrs. Rose. He took her car to Olson's today while Mitt's construction buddies are rebuilding the garage.

Shaun Stevenson, Molly thought. *Is he after her money too?*

Bobby Ray stepped out of the tree line and looked at the back of the manor. "There," he whispered, pointing. "That's were B.B. Cooper said he saw those pumpkins talking and the witches flying around."

"Will you listen to yourself?" Sid grumbled.

"Well, that's what he said, and now that I am seeing the place up close, old man Cooper was back here all right."

"I am sure old man Cooper was back here when he was just a snot-nosed, delinquent. But that doesn't mean he saw pumpkins talking and witches flying around. That old buzzard made it all up to scare little kids like you," Sid replied, hoping the three wouldn't back out now.

"That's right," Don added, knowing Sid was getting worried. "Tell me, how in the world can anyone turn someone into a pumpkin? I mean, really now."

"Witchcraft," Molly replied.

"Witchcraft?" Sid shot back. "I think you all have been watching too many movies. No witch can turn someone into a pumpkin."

"No?" Molly questioned.

"No," Don replied. "It's all nonsense."

"Alright already," Sid interrupted. "Now the reason we came up here tonight is to tell you how we're going to do this."

Willy and Bobby Ray crept over to him. Don stepped up into the huddle. Molly held her ground, staying back by the trees.

"OK, you see all those rooms on the second and third floors?"

"Yeah," Willy and Bobby Ray whispered.

"Those are all bedrooms. The master's chamber is the large room on the fourth floor right over there," he said, pointing.

"That's where Mrs. Rose sleeps?" Bobby Ray asked.

"Yes. If we don't find it then we'll do that room last," Sid replied. "Now, what we want you three to do is go up the stairs and check out the bedrooms while Don and I search the main floor."

Willy nodded glancing back at Molly, who looked as if she wanted to be anywhere but there. He wrinkled his brow at her. She raised hers in response.

"So, how are we getting in?" Bobby Ray asked.

"Over there," Don whispered, pointing to the side of the manor. "There's a basement window open. That's how we got in the first time."

Willy looked at him. "How creepy is it inside?" he asked.

Sid gave that a thought. He'd have to keep his description light. "It's a bit dirty. There are lots of cobwebs, but it's like any old house that hasn't been lived in for a while."

Willy nodded, shifting his eyes on Bobby Ray. Their eyes locked on one another for a second. Both knew the other's thoughts. It had to be as creepy as Frankenstein's castle.

"Hey, you forgot one thing," Don said.

"What?" Sid questioned

"The bell tower?"

"I'm not going up in the bell tower," Bobby Ray sternly whispered.

Sid turned his head toward Bobby Ray and then he realized that Molly wasn't next to them. He glanced back to see her standing in the shadows of the trees. "Are you here or what?" he scolded.

"Yes, I am here. I can hear you just fine."

He didn't like the tone in her voice. He let it go focusing his attention on the boys. "Alright, the bell tower is not big. It has small circular steps leading up. If we don't find it in the master's chambers, that will be our last place to check, OK?"

"So, you two didn't go up in the bell tower when you snuck up here?" Willy asked.

"No," Don whispered.

"Oh, so you two wouldn't go up, but you want us to, is that it?" Bobby Ray asked, folding his arms.

"That's not the reason, Bobby Ray," Sid replied. "At the time, we thought the old lady wouldn't be able to climb those steps. But if we don't find it, we'll have to go up."

"OK, we'll all go up," Willy shot back. "So, tell us the layout."

"From the basement, the stairs lead up to the kitchen. From the kitchen, there is a corridor leading out into the parlor. The staircase will be to our right when we enter."

"Anything else?" Bobby Ray asked.

"No," Sid replied.

"What about your wives?" Willy asked remembering they needed that information.

"They'll be waiting down there by that barn."

Game over, Willy thought, *Ernie will have to come up with another plan.*

"Can we go now?" Molly finally spoke up from behind them.

They all turned and looked at her. "Yeah, we can go. We'll meet back here tomorrow night at ten," Sid replied.

"Ten o'clock? Are you crazy?" she said.

"No, Molly, we'll be here at ten o'clock. Or would you like to hit the place in broad daylight?"

"No. I didn't mean that. Ten is kind of late for me."

"It's ten right now," Don said.

"Yeah, I know that and I should be getting home."

Sid stepped up to her. "Can't you tell your parents that you'll be sleeping over at a friend's house tomorrow night?"

"Yeah, like who? Over at Willy's house? Gee, I can just hear my parents screaming as they're driving me to the hospital to have my head checked out."

"I didn't say over at Willy's house. Don't you have any girlfriends?"

"No." she fumed.

"That's wonderful," Don said and then sighed.

"That's enough," Willy stepped into the fray. "She'll be here one way or another. Right, Molly?"

Molly looked at him. He was the last person she'd tell that she wasn't coming. "Yes," she replied, hiding her thoughts.

"Alright, let's get back. We'll see you all tomorrow night," Sid said, turning and heading down the hill.

When Sid and Don drove off, Ernie and Arnold walked out from the barn. "What's the plan?" Ernie asked.

"We've got problems."

"What now," Ernie asked.

"They want to hit the place tomorrow night at ten. Their wives will be waiting down here for us."

"No…" Arnold's voice trailed off, glancing over at Ernie.

Ernie pulled his hands out of his pockets. He looked down and saw a rock. He kicked it to the center of the road then walked over and kicked it again. When he turned around, Willy could see his wheels spinning. "I have no idea what we're going to do now," Ernie said, walking back to the group.

"I've got an idea," Bobby Ray spoke up.

Everyone looked at him.

"How about when we ride our bikes out here tomorrow night we ditch them in the field behind the barn. You two park Arnold's car on Cross Ridge Road just past the intersection of Old Tiller. When we come out with the money, we'll hightail down the hill toward Cross Ridge and meet you there. Their wives will never see us. And…" he said and then paused, "we can come back the next day and get our bikes."

Arnold nodded looking at Ernie.

That could work, Ernie thought. His plan was to stash the money in the overflow pipe at Kessler's Dam, which meant walking to the barn as they did tonight. *However,* he thought, *I could take the money from Willy and Bobby Ray and then run to Kessler's dam when everyone jumps into Arnold's car and takes off.*

"What do you think?" Arnold asked him.

"I like the plan," he replied, and then told them his thoughts about taking off with the money.

"You're going on foot?" Bobby Ray asked.

"Yes, we don't want to get caught having it inside the car."

"Are we done now?" Molly said.

They all looked at her. She's right, it's getting late," Willy said.

"OK, I'll see you back at the house, Willy," Ernie replied, focusing his attention on Bobby Ray and Molly. "I want to see you both on the back steps tomorrow night at nine."

They nodded and got on their bikes.

The long ride home for the kids was made mostly in silence. They all had a lot on their minds. Bobby Ray and Willy worried about getting caught and Molly, well… she was thinking of all kinds of excuses as to why she wasn't going to show up.

When Molly got home, she noticed all the lights in the house were off. She got off her bike at the side of the house and pushed it around the back. After parking it near the steps at the door, Molly found it unlocked. To her surprise, when she entered the house, her parents were not up. She hurried down the hall, opened her bedroom door and quietly shut it behind her. She deeply sighed removing her clothes and slipping into her nightgown. She got under the covers, glad to finally be home. However, sleep evaded her as she tossed and turned with worry.

What am I going to do? she thought. *Tell 'em I am sick? Yeah, they'll believe that alright.* She rolled over onto her back and stared up at the ceiling. *What about Mrs. Rose? I'll have to warn her,* her thoughts continued. *Wait a minute, how about I start feeling sick right after dinner. I could tell Willy and*

Bobby Ray that I am sick with food poisoning. They know my Mother is the worst cook in the world. They'd believe that. I could then slip out of the house around eight, ride over to the manor and warn Mrs. Rose. After she knows, I could be home before the cops show up. That might work. The last thing Molly remembered before falling asleep was using food poisoning as her excuse.

When Ernie finally arrived home, Willy ushered him into his bedroom. They sat down on the bed.

"I don't think Molly will be showing up tomorrow night," Willy whispered.

"Why?"

"I think she's scared."

"Did she tell you that?"

"No, but I got this funny feeling when we were up there."

"Like what?"

"Well, she stayed back along the tree line as we all crept out to look over the manor and talk about how we were going to sneak in. When Sid tried to get her to move up and join the conversation, I heard something in her voice."

Ernie looked into his brother's eyes. "You think she'd tell anyone?"

"No, she's not stupid."

"Alright. If she doesn't show up, she gets nothing. You tell her that if she calls and gives an excuse."

"OK."

"Good," Ernie replied, getting up. "Get some sleep," he continued, walking out.

After Ernie closed the door behind him, Willy sat there thinking about Molly. He suspected that she was bailing out because of Arnold. He stripped out of his clothing and crawled into bed. His last worrying thoughts were about Molly. *Would Molly leave me if my brother's plans fell apart and we all ended up in the big house - the house with bars on every window and guards walking the perimeter?* It was the last thought Willy had before he closed his eyes and fell asleep.

21

A Splash of Affection

In the morning, Abby awoke feeling as fresh as a daisy. She softly sighed hearing the slumbering sounds of snoring. It was her mice all curled up together next to her pillow. Without disturbing them, she quietly got up. Before entering the bathroom, she smiled seeing Theodore lying there on the rug next to Tasha. *Hmm, love. What a wonderful thing,* she thought.

Inside the bathroom, Abby found Brenda still asleep as well. She freshened up, grabbed a glass, filled it with water, then quietly walked out. Tippy toeing out onto the balcony, she bent over and poured the glass of water into the money tree planter. Its little limbs reached up to her. She sat down, gently running her fingers over its leaves and then softly started to sing. "*Blue birds... sitting by my window... on a warm summer's day... Lilacs swaying on a hill top... all in the month of May,*" to the tune of 'Somewhere Over the Rainbow.' The little tree began swaying. Tiny buds appeared on the leaf stems. Then magically, one hundred-dollar bills unfolded from the buds and started falling all around the patio floor.

Wilson awoke hearing someone singing. He sat up, rubbing the sleep away from his eyes. When he saw Abby sitting out there singing to the tree, he nudged Cracker and Benjamin. They opened their eyes. "Shh..." Wilson whispered, nodding his head toward the balcony.

They stood up still in a fog. Their little eyes lit up seeing Abby singing to the little tree. The tree was gleefully swaying back and forth as buds appeared sprouting money. Theodore awoke to the sounds of singing too. He spotted the mice standing on Abby's bed staring out toward the balcony. He turned and sighed, looking out at Abby singing to the tree.

Wilson, Cracker and Benjamin ran across the bed and slid down the covers hanging down to the floor. Walking over to the rug, they sat down next to Theodore.

After Abby finished her second song, she kissed the little tree then gathered the money around her. When she stood up and turned, she froze. "I'm sorry if I woke you all up," she said, walking back into the room.

"I'm not," Benjamin replied. "That was wonderful."

"Why thank you, Benjamin," she replied, walking toward the fireplace next to them. She reached out, took hold of one of the fireplace corner bricks and pulled the whole brickwork out as if it were on hinges. Inside was a large metal safe. She opened the safe and neatly stacked the money on a shelf. "There," she said, closing the brickwork. None of them said a word as she turned and looked at them. "It's high time you all knew anyway," she said to their surprised expression. Abby then rubbed Theodore's head, picked up Tasha and strolled back to bed. "Now," she said and then paused, "we must find that book to bring this one to life," she continued, petting Tasha cradled in her arms.

Theodore walked over. "You think we'll ever find it, Madam Rose?"

"Madam Rose," she slowly repeated his words. "You know," she continued, "I'm getting tired of that name.

Benjamin put two and two together fast. He knew what she was saying. He wanted to speak his mind on the subject now knowing Abby's secret little plan - trying to make Shaun fall in love with her. Before Benjamin remembered the deal they had struck with Theodore, to not say a word about Shaun, he opened his mouth. "I like the name, Madam Stevenson," he said, then instantly felt eight eyes staring at him: Abby, Theodore, Wilson and Cracker - four people with two eyes each - makes eight. Yes, Benjamin could count, and he didn't like the look they were giving him.

Without a word, Abby slowly locked eyes with Theodore. "Madam Stevenson?" she said.

"I… um," Theodore dribbled, knowing he was in trouble for telling.

Wilson and Cracker shook their heads at Benjamin. "I'm sorry, I forgot the deal," he whimpered.

"You forgot what deal?" she asked already knowing Theodore let the cat out of the bag.

"Abby we…" Wilson started to explain.

"Hush," Abby interrupted him. "Benjamin," she said, trying to keep a straight face while watching him hesitantly walking over to the side of the bed with his eyes glued to the floor. He didn't want to look up at her or at Theodore. He knew he'd be lunch for sure, knowing Theodore was mad as well.

Abby nodded to Theodore to pick Benjamin up. He lowered his head to the floor in front of Benjamin. Benjamin slowly climbed up on his snout knowing he was in big trouble. Abby almost laughed when Theodore lifted him up to her bed with his little head down. She reached over and lifted his chin with her finger. "So you like the name Madam Stevenson?"

Benjamin simply nodded with a pout.

She leaned over, looked him straight in the eyes, and said, “So do I,” then began tickling him. Theodore, Wilson and Cracker were stunned. They all thought they were next to get a good scolding.

“Abbbbby… stop it,” Benjamin laughed, falling off Theodore’s snout and onto the bed.

Wilson and Cracker raced over to the corner of the bed and climbed the covers. She smiled at them while tickling Benjamin. “You’re not mad?” Wilson asked.

She stopped playing with Benjamin.

“Mad,” she said and then paused. “Theodore is Lord of this house. I’ve had him since I was a child. He knows everything,” she continued, turning and looking at him. His eyes melted into hers. He knew he made a big mistake by telling the mice. Before he could speak and convey his apology, she let him off the hook. “But seeing now that I have the three musketeers to defend me, they too must know the plan.”

A sigh of relief filled the room. Benjamin stood up. “I’m sorry,” he said to his friends.

“You,” Wilson grumbled, walking over to him. “As Captain of the three musketeers, I find you guilty of treason.”

“Now wait a minute, fellas,” Benjamin replied, backing up.

“Let’s get him, boys,” Wilson shouted, running across the bed toward him. Theodore pushed Benjamin over with his snout as Wilson and Cracker pounced on Benjamin and started tickling him again. Abby shook her head seeing this display of affection. She lay there petting Tasha as the rumbling continued.

When the rumble stopped, and the mice were gasping for air, Abby said, “You all act like children sometimes.”

“Children?” Wilson replied still out of breath. “He’s the child around here,” he continued, pointing at Benjamin.

“Not so fast,” Benjamin scolded.

“Now, fellas,” Abby said. “You’re all my children. Even Tasha.”

“Madam Rose,” Theodore said, “I would prefer the title Lord instead of being called a child.”

“Will you get a load of this fellas?” Cracker spewed, staring up at Theodore. “You want another sock in the eye?”

Abby laughed. “Am I missing something here?” she asked, smiling.

Benjamin tapped her hand. She looked down at him. "We had to teach him a lesson of whose boss around here when you were gone."

"You did?" she asked, glancing over at Theodore. She gave him a wink to allow this little conversation to go on. "So… what happened?" she asked.

Wilson stepped forward. Abby wasn't surprised because Wilson always thought that he was in charge. She lay there listening to his story about when the two men broke into the house and he finished by telling her that the three of them had to beat Theodore up because Theodore was getting out of control. She laughed looking over at Theodore. "You're a doll," she sighed, knowing he let them get away with something like that. She then giggled to herself remembering when she heard Theodore telling the little runts down in the basement that together they wouldn't even be a morsel. Yes, Theodore might have thought that she was out of earshot when he said that to them, but she heard every word.

"You know, Abby," Benjamin said.

"What?" she replied, stepping out of her thoughts.

"I think Theodore liked getting beat up."

"Is that right, Theodore?" she laughed, reaching over and pulling him closer to her.

"I learned my lesson - you can't mess with the three musketeers," Theodore laughed.

She laughed shaking her head.

"Hey," Cracker spoke up.

"What?" she replied, raising her brow, seeing by his expression that he had a brilliant idea which would probably make her laugh even more.

"You think you can make us musketeer's outfits? You know… pants, shirts and boots, along with hats with long feathers and swords?"

"Oh, please," Theodore gasped. "Don't you think you're carrying this a bit too far?"

"No," Benjamin replied. "You won't be messing with us again if we had all that gear."

Theodore laughed. *I just had to call them the three musketeers - now they think they are,* he thought.

"You know, I just might have some material." Abby beamed.

"Really?" Wilson excitedly said.

"Yes, down in the sewing room."

"No," Theodore sounded off.

Abby laughed looking at him. She then sat back, cuddling Tasha while drifting on the wind. They waited to see what she was thinking. Theodore had a guess. She was probably thinking about those men Wilson had mentioned. "You think they'll be back?" he asked.

Theodore was right, the two men did enter her thoughts. "I'm sure they will," she replied, staring into space.

"You said that you know who those men are?" Cracker asked.

She glanced down at her mice and sighed. "You four," she said and then paused. "When did you all start reading minds?"

"It's the look on your face. You always look like that when you're worried," Benjamin said.

"I do?"

"Yes," Wilson replied.

"Well, I am not worried, gentlemen. Those two are snakes in the grass and you know what happens to snakes, don't you?"

"Are you going to cut their heads off?" Benjamin asked, worried.

She smiled. "No, Benjamin. However," she said, thinking, "they might find themselves inside a pickle jar if they do return."

A pickle jar? Benjamin thought, glancing at his friends. *How could she fit them inside a pickle jar?*

"By the look on your face, Benjamin, you don't think I can do it?"

"I know you can. You think I can watch?"

"Oh, will you stop with the nonsense," Wilson said, giving him a nudge.

They all laughed.

"Well, gentlemen," she replied, setting Tasha down and getting out of bed. "We're just going to have to prepare ourselves for unwanted visitors in the future," she continued, walking toward the bathroom.

"I'll see to that," Theodore spoke up.

"I'm sure you will, Theodore," she replied, turning around. "Right now, however, I want a quick bath. Please go down and tell the kitchen that I'm up. Have them fix you something to eat as well. We don't have much time now before the workers show up, so hurry," she continued, opening and closing the door behind her.

Benjamin turned toward his friends. "You know, fellas, if she makes us those outfits, we can take care of those two snakes."

Wilson shook his head. "Theodore," he said, waving his hand for him to lean over the bed. After Theodore placed his head on the bed, Wilson and

Cracker climbed on his snout. He turned and said, "Come on, Benjamin. Let's go have some breakfast."

As they were heading for the stairs, Wilson looked into Theodore's eyes.

"Can you just imagine Benjamin whacking them two bums in the shoes with a sword?" Theodore shook his head. *No,* he thought, *I rightly can't see Benjamin taking them on. However, I can see those two men climbing the curtains as I'm ripping their pants off if they ever come back again.*

22

A Morning of Mayhem

After Abby's quick bath and breakfast, she put the house to sleep along with Theodore. Twenty minutes later, the cleaning crew and painters arrived. "Good morning, Mrs. Rose," John Towers, Quick Fast's cleaning and painting supervisor, greeted her, walking through the door.

"Good Morning, John."

"I think you'll like the news thus far. Today, we'll finish touching up the parlor and den. Afterward, we'll continue up the stairs past the first landing. While my team is doing that, I'll be cutting in the trim inside the master's chambers."

"Great. Does that include putting up all the curtains and the remaining decor for each room?"

"Yes, ma'am."

Abby smiled. "Then you'll start on both corridors, the coat room and bathrooms, and then on to the ballroom?"

"Yes. I'll have two teams in tomorrow. That will give me around twenty-five men to start those projects. Plus, we'll be finishing the billiard room, kitchen and dining area. The main floor should be completely done in three days."

Abby sighed.

"Have you thought about the pool?" John asked.

"No, I'll wait until everything else is done."

"OK then what about the eight bedrooms on the second and third floors? How soon would you like those completed?" he asked.

"Well, let's see. Today is Monday. You should have all this done by Wednesday. How about the following Monday, which gives me several days of peace?" she replied and then paused. "Will you be using those fans and blowers to take away the fumes today?"

"Yes, all the windows will be opened too."

"Wonderful," Abby replied, turning her head hearing more trucks pulling in. She stepped out the front door and saw Snider's Construction along with two cement trucks. They were going to start laying the cement flooring for the new garage. "My, wouldn't this be a nice day to sit on the beach listening to nothing but the waves coming ashore, instead of this racket?" she whispered.

John laughed alongside her.

"Are there any beaches close by?" she asked, raising her brow and smiling.

"No ma'am. The nearest one is five hundred miles away."

"Well, that takes care of that idea. I'll not keep you any longer," she replied, walking in and heading toward the corridor to the kitchen.

John watched her leave. He shook his head wondering where she got all the money to purchase and restore this place. *If her last name were Ford,* he thought, *that would have been an easy guess.* However, her surname is Rose. *I've never heard of any wealthy family by that name.* He bent over, picked up his ladder and carried it inside.

Fifteen minutes later, Butch Denver, a cleaner, walked into the kitchen. "Mrs. Rose, you have visitors getting out of their cars out front."

"I do?" she replied, turning at the sink. "Who'd want to come up here with all this going on?" she continued, drying her hands and walking out.

"Will you look at this?" Claudia said, getting out of her car.

"Unbelievable," Flo replied, sliding out. "What did she do, call in the National Guard?" she quipped, turning and waiting for Fanny and Karen to get out of Fanny's car.

"Oh no. Look who's here," Claudia grunted, looking back to see Mayor Bumpkin driving up.

"Morning, ladies," he said, opening his car door.

"Mayor Bumpkin, how'd you find out that we were coming up here this morning?" Claudia asked.

"Your husband Bart told me when I went to the bank this morning."

"Well, remind me to whack him when I get back. Come, ladies, let's see what's going on inside," Claudia said in a furious tone, turning and walking up to the door.

Flo looked at Fanny. "I know someone I'd like to whack," she whispered, leaning into Fanny. Fanny giggled taking Karen's hand as they walked through the doors.

John looked down from his ladder when they came in. "May I help you?" he asked.

Claudia said nothing, nor did the rest as they stood there with their mouths gaping open and their eyes glued to all the work that was finished.

John started down the ladder. Abby walked in. "It's OK, John," she said. He nodded and headed back up.

"Abby," Fanny beamed. "My, my, you have been busy out here, haven't you? Your home looks so wonderful," she continued.

Wonderful, Claudia thought. *It's fabulous,* her thoughts continued, watching Fanny hugging Abby. *I hate rich people. All they have to do is snap their little fingers, purchase a place like this and then they sit around and drink tea while the work is done.*

Wilson, Cracker and Benjamin were all peeking out from a small hole in the wall, right behind Boris's head in the den. "Hey, will you two move over?" Benjamin whispered, nudging them out of the way. "I can't see a thing."

"Now I can't see," Cracker fumed.

"Oh, for Pete's sake, you two," Wilson scolded.

Back in the days of wine and roses when Baron Von Haussler was still alive, the mice had a million places to run and hide from trouble. One of those places was in the den. There was a small hole on the right-hand side of the fireplace between the wall and brickwork. They used this many times to escape trouble, or when Theodore chased them at night when everyone was asleep.

Before the workers walked in this morning, Abby had the mice go and hide. They quickly scampered across the parlor floor, ran into the den and up through the hole next to the fireplace. There, they climbed the internal wood framing through the holes for the electrical wiring to where Boris was hanging over the mantelpiece.

"Alright, can you two see now?" Wilson whispered.

"Yeah," they both replied.

"OK, just be quiet, will ya? Abby has company," Wilson said, looking down at the people.

Abby let go of Fanny and then turned to the rest of her visitors standing there admiring the work. "Good morning. This certainly is a surprise."

"Good morning, Mrs. Rose," Mayor Bumpkin greeted her, studying the room.

"Good morning, Mayor," she replied.

"What's a Mayor?" Benjamin whispered.

"I think he's the boss of the city," Wilson whispered.

"Well I must say…" Mayor Bumpkin's voice trailed off admiring the parlor. *I cannot believe that under all that grime, dust and cobwebs the place could look this good,* he thought, glancing down at the beautiful white floor now cleaned and polished, the wooden banisters and stairs sanded back and sealed, the pearl white walls and the outstanding work done on the chandelier.

He cast his eyes upward at John who was painstakingly painting the sculpted ceiling moulding. He shook his head. "It's truly amazing. I'm surprised to see this much work already done," he continued, turning and looking at Abby.

"Well, you'll have to check out the den, too" she replied, ushering them in. "As you can see it's done as well, along with the staircase. They have started the master's chambers and in the next few days the billiard room, corridor and the ballroom will be completed also."

Billiard and ballroom, Claudia thought, drooling. *All I have is a back-yard patio with a small table and chairs.*

"Get back," Wilson whispered, pulling on Cracker and Benjamin when the people were looking about the den.

"Now what about the electrical and plumbing? Is everything working properly?" Mayor Bumpkin asked.

"Yes, everything seems to be working just fine," Abby replied.

"What about the pipes? No leaks?" he asked.

"No, Mayor, and if there were, I would've called Mitt. He's been a real blessing getting all these companies out here to assist me."

"He sure is something, isn't he?" he replied. "The man has more connections than a washing machine," he continued and then laughed.

Claudia rolled her eyes. *More connections than a washing machine,* she mused. *I'll connect you to a fan and watch you spin around when I throw the switch.*

With a pause in the conversation, Karen stepped up and said, "Oh, Abby, I am so happy for you."

"Me too," Flo beamed.

Abby looked over at Claudia standing there looking up at Boris. *Not a word out of her mouth. How charming,* she thought. *Well, Miss Fancy Pants, you called it a heap. I wonder what you think of it now.* "You like that?" she asked, walking over to her.

Claudia stared at her for a second then slowly glanced up at the large moose head again. “That thing gives me the creeps,” she replied.

Everyone laughed.

Claudia turned and mockingly smiled back at them.

“Who’s that big fat lady?” Benjamin whispered.

“Look who’s talking,” Cracker replied.

“Who, me? I’m not fat. Well, not as fat as she is.”

“Shh…” Wilson scolded.

“Oh, I don’t know, Claudia,” Abby said. “I think Boris adds a wonderful richness to the den.”

“So, you’re keeping it?” Claudia snidely remarked.

“Why certainly. I imagine it’s probably been hanging up there since the place was built.”

“Wonderful,” Claudia fumed, turning and looking over at Mayor Bumpkin who was checking the windows in the den which were now all sparkling clean.

“Excuse me, Mrs. Rose,” Ted Turner, one of the cleaners said, entering the den from the ballroom.

“Yes, what is it?”

“We’re ready to complete the parlor once John comes down. Where would you like your furnishings?

Abby looked into the parlor. “Place the sofa straight out from the left side of the fireplace there. The recliner, small table and lamp next to the door facing the fireplace, and please remove that sheet off Steinbeck.”

“We certainly will,” he replied, turning and walking back down the corridor.

“Steinbeck?” Flo questioned.

“Yes, that’s my grand piano.”

Fanny laughed. They all looked at her. *If you only knew,* she thought, smiling at Abby. That thought made her think of the mice. *I wonder where they could be hiding.* Little did she know that they were right above her looking down at them.

“Well,” Mayor Bumpkin spoke up, walking toward the parlor. “I just wanted to stop by and see how you were doing. And now that I’ve seen the place, you certainly must be happy.”

"I am at that, Mayor Bumpkin, and thank you for coming," she replied, walking him to the door.

"You're welcome," he replied and then asked the ladies if they were staying.

Karen looked at Claudia. She could tell she wanted to leave. *Why she came up in the first place is beyond me,* she thought. "I'll stay if Flo is. We can ride back with Fanny."

"I'm staying," Flo replied, raising her brow at Claudia.

"Suit, yourselves. I've got things to do today," Claudia said, walking toward the door. *You can stay up here with Miss Rich Britches,* she thought. *I can't stand the lady.*

"Thank you for coming, Claudia," Abby said.

"It was my pleasure, and besides, I wouldn't have missed it for the world," Claudia replied, walking out with Mayor Bumpkin.

Abby shut the door. "I wouldn't have missed it for the world," she quipped, looking back at the women.

They all laughed.

"You know, Abby," Flo said and then paused, "I think she wanted to come up here and see you in a terrible mess. I guess she got the shock of her life seeing the place looking like this."

"I'll give her a shock," Karen laughed.

They all giggled.

"No, I mean it. That woman has some gall at times," Flo said.

"That she does," Fanny replied.

"OK, ladies, please move out of the way," a worker said, hauling in the furniture.

"My word, those are beautiful," Fanny beamed, looking at the lavender sofa and recliner.

They all moved aside as the men walked past. John came down from the ladder to assist them. Then the doorbell suddenly rang.

"Who could that be?" Abby said, walking over. When she opened the door, she was surprised to see two men standing there.

"Good day, ma'am. You ordered some carpet?"

"Yes," Abby replied, eyeing them up.

"I'm Stan Cummings and this is Joe Rollins, we're from Carpet Land. We're here to install the carpet you ordered for the stairs."

"Well, you're just in time. I'm having a party in here."

Stan wrinkled his brow.

"I'm kidding. Please, come in."

"Carpet," Karen said, walking up. "What color?"

"Red. Deep red," Abby replied.

Flo placed her hands to her face seeing the men carrying the first roll in. "That's going on the stairs?"

"Yes," Abby replied. "You like the color?"

"Like the color?" she gasped. "I love the color. How about you two?" she continued, glancing over at Karen and Fanny.

They both nodded. "It's a magnificent color for this room," Fanny delightfully replied.

"Who's in charge of the work going on here?" Stan asked the men moving furniture.

"I am," John spoke up.

"Can we install this now?"

John looked over at Abby. "The staircase is done. It's up to you, but we still have to do all the bedrooms upstairs."

Abby pondered that. "I guess it'll be OK. Go ahead and install it. We'll just cover it for now."

John nodded.

"Abby," Fanny said.

She turned around.

"Would you like to go out to lunch?" she asked, raising her brow.

Abby smiled. *One minute away from all this would be like heaven.* "Yes. How about you two?" she asked Karen and Flo.

"That would be nice," they both replied.

"Let me get my coat," Abby said, walking toward the corridor.

Benjamin taps his friends. "It looks like we are on our own, fellas," he whispered. Wilson and Cracker devilishly smiled.

23

Oh My… Out of Gas

As Abby was heading into town with the ladies for an early lunch, Shaun was just putting the wheels back on the Buick at Olson's service station. He lowered the car, glanced up at the clock and then turned and looked at Wilfred. *It's eleven thirty. Mr. Olson isn't showing up until one this afternoon,* he thought. *This gives me an excellent opportunity to look underneath Wilfred and see how to take him apart.*

He walked over, adjusted the hoist underneath Wilfred and then aligned the four long metal arms outward locking them in place.

What's he up to? Wilfred thought.

Shaun reached up and hit the button to the hoist, lifting Wilfred into the air.

Whaaaat are you doing?! Wilfred thought, panicking. *I'm afraid of heights.*

"Now let's see how easy this will be," Shaun said, walking underneath the car.

See how easy what will be? Wilfred thought.

"It looks like these six bolts hold the undercarriage in place and these outer bolts here attach the body to the chassis," Shaun said, walking toward the rear of the car.

You're seriously thinking about taking me apart, aren't you? Wilfred thought. *Where is Madam Rose when I need her?*

As Shaun moved back to the gas tank to see how it came off, he looked up and noticed a small, dark, rust spot in the tank. "Hmm," he whispered, reaching up and gently pushing on the spot. To his surprise, his finger went right through the gas tank. "Well, I'll be," he mused, looking down at the floor for any signs of a leak. There was none.

Oh, oh, Wilfred thought, feeling Shaun sticking his finger inside his tank. *I'm busted. Now how are we going to get out of this mess?*

Shaun stood back, rubbing his forehead. *I didn't prime it before starting the car and then I drove it all the way here. That's impossible,* he thought, glancing down at the floor once again. *Abigail hardly uses the car. So….* his thoughts continued, *even if it had a full tank of gas, that gas would have leaked out by now.*

Shaun turned and began pacing back and forth behind Wilfred. *I didn't smell any gas when I went out to drive the car here. Wait...* he thought. *It could have soaked into the ground out there. But even if it had leaked out, how did the darn thing start in the first place? And how the heck did I drive it this far without any gas?*

He pushed the button to lower the car then got in behind the wheel. "OK let's see if it will start," he said, pushing the clutch and turning the key. The engine cranked over, but it would not start. He pushed down on the gas pedal, lifted his foot and tried it again. Nothing... "There's something funny going on," he grumbled.

There's nothing funny going on, Mr. Know-It-All, Wilfred thought. *I'm simply out of gas.*

Just then, Kenny walked into the service stalls. "Hey, you want something for lunch?" he asked.

Shaun looked over. The question gave him an idea. "No. Go ahead and have lunch then I'll split for twenty minutes."

"Alright, I'll take off."

When Kenny returned, Shaun walked out, got on his dirt bike and rode up Main Street. He never saw Abby sitting inside the restaurant on the corner as he made the turn onto Fifth Street and headed out into the country. When he rode up the long driveway to the manor, he saw tons of vehicles out front. He pulled up and parked.

"Where is Mrs. Rose?" he asked John, who was hanging the curtains in the parlor.

"She went out to lunch with a few ladies that came to visit."

Shaun shook his head. "Can I borrow your pen?"

"Sure," he replied, pulling it out of his top pocket.

Shaun walked through the corridor to the kitchen. When he entered, he saw a pad of paper sitting by the sink.

Dear Abigail,

I'm sorry I missed you... I just wanted you to know that Wilfred has a hole in his gas tank - he wouldn't start. Also, I am going shopping with my parents tonight so I'll not be able to see you until tomorrow. Have a lovely day. Shaun. P.S. The place looks fantastic.

After writing his message, he left it on the kitchen table. On his way out the door, he handed John his pen and left. When he returned to the service station, Mr. Olson was standing out front. *I don't think I'll tell him,* Shaun thought, pulling in.

"Howdy, Shaun," Mr. Olson said, walking over to him.

"Hi, Mr. Olson, did Kenny tell ya that I was going out for a minute?"

"Yes. Have you had lunch yet?"

"No, I went to tell Mrs. Rose that I will not be over after work. I have to go shopping with my parents tonight."

"How is Mrs. Rose doing? I've heard word the place is coming along real nice."

"She wasn't there, but you'rc right, thc placc looks fantastic. You'll have to go up and see it for yourself."

"I just might do that," Mr. Olson replied, checking his watch. "Look, we still have some time before that Oldsmobile comes in. How about you take off for lunch, seeing you didn't have it yet?"

"Thanks, Mr. Olson. I think I will," Shaun replied, turning and walking down toward the grocery store.

24

A Spoonful of Trouble

After Shaun had left, Don pulled up and parked in front of Meek's real estate agency. He got out, opened his passenger side door and retrieved a box. As he walked in, Sid asked, "Whatcha got?"

"I thought we might need a few things," he replied, setting the box down on his desk.

Sid got up from his chair to see what he brought.

"I went to the store and purchased two ski masks, two sets of gloves and two new flashlights. I thought the ones I had were bad. Oh, and a pair of miniature bolt cutters…"

"Miniature bolt cutters?" Sid questioned, interrupting him.

"Yeah, why?"

"That's what I was going to ask. Why the bolt cutters?"

"I don't know. I thought all burglars carried them."

Sid ran his fingers through his hair, shaking his head. *What a bumbling idiot,* he thought. "Look, stop watching those stupid movies. We're not breaking into Fort Knox."

"Alright then, I also picked up two sub-machine guns, one shoulder rocket launcher, two bazookas and I am hoping Sears drives up this afternoon with the tank I ordered from their catalog," he smartly replied.

"You know what?" Sid sarcastically replied.

"What?"

"You're simply useless."

"Come on, Sid, you're the one who started this."

Sid walked back and sat down behind his desk.

"Alright, I'll stop with the crap," Don replied.

"Good, because if this all goes south, you and I will be wishing we had all that stuff to break out of jail."

"Now look who's chasing their tail. This will be like taking candy from a baby. Heck that old bird will probably just sleep right through the night, Sid."

"I sure hope so."

Don walked over, placed a ski mask, one pair of black gloves and one flashlight on Sid's desk. Sid looked up at him. "Don't forget to wear your boots this time."

"I brought them with me," Don, replied. "So, what did Betsy say when you told her that we're going to hit the manor tonight?"

"She's scared, but excited too."

"Yeah, same goes for Sue. She's about half out of her mind with worry and then she starts telling me what she wants to spend the money on."

"Women," Sid replied, shaking his head.

"Have you heard from the kids today?" Don asked.

"No… but their little butts better be there tonight or we're on our own."

"They'll show up. I saw dollar signs in Willy and Bobby Ray's eyes last night," Don laughed.

"Yeah, well I certainly didn't see any in Molly's eyes," Sid replied. "You saw her. She was as cold as a dead fish last night."

"Maybe she's scared. Tonight, she'll be OK, you'll see."

"Let's hope so."

Well… they could only hope, because as Sid and Don were making their plans, back at Molly's house, it was a whole different story. Molly had firmly made her mind up - she wasn't going through with it.

Why hasn't Willy or Bobby Ray come over today? Molly thought, walking over and looking out her bedroom window. She turned and sat down on the bed. *If they're not coming, maybe I should just call Willy and tell 'em?* She glanced at her clock sitting there on the nightstand. *I am getting so worried now that I don't think I'll even have to try and fake having food poisoning. I'm feeling absolutely sick to my stomach*, her thoughts continued while sitting there biting her nails. She spit one out and stood up. *I'd better call and find out what's going on*. With that, she got up and walked out of her room.

"Hello," Ernie said.

Great, Molly thought, walking into the front room with the phone to her ear. "Hi, Ernie, it's Molly. Is Willy there?"

"Yeah, he's right here. By the way, what are you wearing tonight?"

Molly panicked. She hadn't thought of that. "Black," she quickly replied.

"Good. I didn't want you showing up wearing anything white. Let me get Willy for ya."

"Thanks," she replied. *How stupid can one person be?* she thought, *wearing white clothing to a robbery?*

"Hey, Molly," Willy said.

"Hi, Willy. Where have you been all day?"

"I've been here with Ernie and Arnold. We've been preparing for tonight. How do you feel?"

His question was like a pitch right over the batter's plate. All she had to do now was to keep her eye on the ball and swing. "I've been feeling sick all day."

"You have? From what?"

"Mom's corn beef and hash," she replied, closing her eyes.

Willy put the phone to his chest. "I don't think she's coming," he whispered.

"What?" Arnold mouthed.

"Are you there, Willy," she asked.

Willy shook his head at Arnold then placed the phone up to his ear.

"Yeah, I'm here. Look, we're not leaving for a few hours, maybe your stomach will feel better by then. Do you want Bobby Ray and me to come over and get you? We can head out to Old Tiller Road from there tonight," Willy replied, winking at Ernie and Arnold.

They both smiled.

"No, I'll call you around seven if that's OK?"

"Seven?"

"Yes, I'm skipping dinner tonight. I just want to lie down for a while. I'll call you then."

"Alright," he replied, shaking his head. "I hope you're feeling better by seven. Talk to you soon," he continued and then hung up.

Molly put the phone in her lap. She looked out the window. *He doesn't believe me,* she thought.

After Willy hung the phone up, he locked eyes with his brother. "She's not coming, is she?" Ernie asked.

"No. Molly said that she has food poisoning. Said it was her mother's corn beef and hash."

"That would make anyone sick," Arnold replied. "I hate that crap."

"Will you shut up?" Ernie scolded. "She's faking it."

"You think?" Arnold asked.

Ernie looked at Willy. "You think she's faking it?"

"Yes, I think she's scared."

Ernie stood up and started to pace. He quickly turned and faced Willy.

"You think she'd tell anyone?"

Willy gave that a thought. "No."

"Really?" Arnold countered.

"Even if she is trying to back out now, she's not stupid, Arnold," Willy scolded.

"Alright then, we'll play this by the book. With her or without her, I want you and Bobby Ray there by nine-thirty," Ernie said. "Arnold and I will drive up and park the car just past the intersection on Cross Ridge and Old Tiller Road."

Willy nodded.

"Now call Bobby Ray. I want no screw ups."

"Alright already," Willy replied, walking out of the room.

Ernie looked at Arnold. "We need to make new plans," he whispered.

"New plans?"

"Yeah, I think that little brat is going to tell that old lady."

"What? You heard Willy," Arnold replied.

"I don't care what Willy thinks. My gut instinct is telling me that she's going to blow this wide open."

"OK, what are we going to do?"

"Not here. Let's go for a ride."

In the car, Ernie reversed out and drove down the street. He weaved through the side streets toward Station Park. When they rolled up and parked, Arnold watched Ernie get out and walk over to one of the picnic tables. He got out, walked over and sat down across from him.

"Now this is what we're going to do," Ernie said and then paused.

"We'll drive your car past the intersection and hide it in the field. That way, if Sid and Don choose that route they won't see the car sitting there when they turn onto Old Tiller Road."

"OK, then what?" Arnold asked.

"We're going up to the manor."

"We are?"

"Yes, just shut up and listen, will ya. It's the only way to catch Molly if she shows up. We can sneak up and hide on the ballroom side of the manor so we can watch the front and the back at the same time."

Arnold wrinkled his brow.

"Do I have to draw you a map? If that brat comes up the front, we'll be able to see her. We'll also need to watch for Sid and Don coming up the hill in the back," he said and then paused, glancing over Arnold's shoulder at a group of boys playing touch football. He trained his eyes back on Arnold. "Now I'm thinking if Willy and Bobby Ray come out first with the money, we'll hightail it after them. If Sid and Don come out with the money, we'll walk up and introduce them to Willy's toy gun and take the money."

Arnold nodded. "What are we going to do if we see Miss Fancy Pants, whose stomach's too full of her mother's corn beef and hash?"

"We'll have no choice but to try and grab her before she can knock on the doors."

"That's a long run, Ernie."

"Yes, I know that. That's why I want you to keep your eyes peeled on the front while I'm watching the back of the manor. Now, if you can remember, there has to be a good forty yards of clearing from the trees along the driveway up to the front doors. You'll see Molly for sure before she can even reach them."

Arnold nodded.

"Good, now let's get back. I want to eat something before we go."

25

A Slumbering Afternoon

After their lunch, Fanny drove Karen and Abby home. She dropped Karen off first and then drove down Daisy Lane toward the manor. "It's nice to finally be alone, Abby," she said, turning into the driveway.

"Yes, I wish we had the whole day to be alone together."

Fanny looked over seeing her sitting there wearing that warm, pleasant smile like the afternoon sun. It made her wonder what she was thinking. *Was it seeing her father's estate restored to its former glory? Or, was it Shaun Stevenson?* She had heard that Shaun had kept his promise by coming up and seeing how she was doing every day. She also heard that Wilfred was now sitting down at Olson's while the new garage was going up. "I'm really impressed with the manor," she said.

"I am too. They're doing a great job," Abby replied, glancing back at her. "Please tell Mitt how grateful I am for all that he's done."

"He already knows that, Abby. I tell Mitt all the time how you feel about him."

"Good."

"I heard Shaun has been coming up to visit with you?" she asked, snooping.

Abby waited until Fanny had pulled up and parked before she answered. "Yes, he's such a charming young man. He and his friends came up and helped me with some of my furniture and then Shaun took Wilfred down to Olson's service station. I sure hope Wilfred's behaving himself."

Fanny laughed getting out. She rounded the car and opened Abby's door. "I really can't wait to meet Wilfred."

"I'm sure he'll like you just like the rest of my misfit friends," Abby replied, laughing.

"Misfits? I wouldn't call 'em that. They're the most charming bunch I've ever seen. Mind you," she replied and then paused, "even though they can cause more havoc than a wind storm over Kansas, I just love being around them."

Abby laughed patting Fanny's shoulder. Together, they stepped around the plastic blower tube lying there sucking out the fumes from inside.

"Would you like me to come back tonight?" Fanny asked, hugging her at the door.

"You're always welcome here, Fanny."

"Then I'll try, that's if Mitt doesn't carry me away tonight," she replied with a teasing grin.

Abby raised her brow. "I am so happy for the two of you. And if he does carry you away, don't fight too hard," she replied, kissing her cheek.

Fanny watched her walk in. "Maybe just a little," she said. Abby waved over her shoulder. Fanny turned and danced back to her car. *I just love that woman,* she thought, getting in.

After Abby had walked in, she froze looking about the parlor. It was completely finished. When she turned toward the fireplace, her eyes lit up seeing her mother's decoratively gold-leaf framed portrait hanging over the mantelpiece.

"I wasn't sure if it went there," John said, walking into the parlor.

Abby slowly turned and looked at him. "I'm surprised. That's actually where I thought of hanging it once I found that crate."

"Who is she?"

"She's my mother."

"Well, we found another portrait of her standing alongside a man inside one of the crates in the ballroom. Where would you like that one to go?"

She glanced up at the wall over the first landing where that portrait used to hang. *That one,* she thought, *will have to stay hidden for now.* "Yes, that is my father, but for now I think I'll leave that one down until you're finished with all the rooms upstairs."

"Alright, we're about to pack up for the day. If you turn around, you'll see that we have completed the den along with your bedroom. I have two of my crew looking over the kitchen right now. We'll be starting there in the morning."

"Great," Abby replied, walking toward the corridor.

"By the way," John said behind her.

She turned around. "There was a young man here asking for you. I think he left you a note in the kitchen."

"Shaun."

"Yes, I think that's his name," John replied, turning and walking outside.

When Abby entered the kitchen, one of the painters turned and said,

"Hello, Mrs. Rose, we should be done in a minute."

"Take your time, gentlemen," she replied, walking over and picking up Shaun's note. As she read his simple words, she placed her hand to her mouth. *Oh no, Wilfred,* she thought. *You never mentioned anything about having a hole in your gas tank.* She looked up at the men checking the walls and cupboards while still in thought. *I hope Shaun doesn't ask too many questions.* She folded the note, slipped it inside her hip pocket and walked over to wash her hands.

"I think that's it, Mrs. Rose. The kitchen shouldn't be all that complicated to sand back and paint," the man said. "You have a goodnight and we'll see you in the morning."

"Thank you," she replied, watching them leave. *I think I'll go and lie down for awhile,* she thought, turning and walking out behind them.

After John and his crew had left, she closed the front doors. "Now to sit and rest a bit," she sighed, walking back into the parlor. Before she sat down on the sofa, she looked up at her mother's portrait again. "The house is finally coming back to life, Mother," she said, taking a seat.

As she sat there admiring the portrait, she smiled, feeling a warm and tender love for her mother. *Not only were you a gorgeous woman, you were beautiful through and through,* she thought, gazing at her mother's soft, caring eyes, her fine complexion and those long, stylish curls they wore back then. She rested her head back against the sofa and closed her eyes. When she awoke several hours later, she was surprised to see herself sitting there in the dark. "My, I must have been tired. I wonder what time it is?" "Lights," she ordered. The room lit up. She snapped her fingers - waking the house.

Wilson woke up when the lights came on. He stretched his little arms and yawned. When Boris awoke, he felt something on the top of his head. He turned and looked up to see what it was. "Waaait…" Wilson screamed, rolling. He quickly grabbed Boris's antler and hung on for dear life. Benjamin woke up thinking the floor beneath him was turning sideways. "What's going on?" he panicked, rolling off Boris's head. He grabbed onto Wilson and hung to him, looking down. Cracker suddenly awoke feeling his body sliding. He quickly grabbed Boris's ear.

"What is going on up there?" Boris asked.

"We fell asleep on top of your head," Wilson grunted, trying to pull himself up with Benjamin hanging off his back.

"It sounds as if there's trouble in the den," Grandfather said.

"Hello, Grandfather. It certainly does," Abby replied, getting up and walking into the den. When she looked up at Boris, she started to laugh, seeing her mice hanging off one antler and his ear. “You three,” she said and then paused, placing her hands on her hips. “I see you’ve found yourself in another pickle.”

“Abby!” Wilson shouted, pulling himself up. Benjamin started climbing over him. “Will you get off me?” Wilson scolded.

“I’m trying - I’m trying,” Benjamin huffed, climbing over him. “Wow, that was close,” he said, standing on top of Boris’s antler and looking down.

Abby stood there amused as the mice got back on top of Boris’s head.

“I am sorry, Madam Rose, I didn’t know they were up there,” Boris said, raising his brow.

“That’s quite alright, Boris. They shouldn’t have fallen asleep up there.” “Now,” she continued, “if you three can find your way down, let’s go and have some dinner, shall we?”

When the mice made their way to the floor, Abby bent over and said,

“So… that’s where you were hiding all day.”

“Yes,” Cracker replied. “Wilson said that it would be a great place to watch all the commotion.”

“Commotion?” she quipped, laughing. *It was more than commotion today,* she thought. *It was absolutely nerve racking with those generators playing in my ears.* She looked down at Wilson - her little angel. “Now, how long have you been using Boris as a lookout post?”

“Since you were a little girl,” he replied with a boyish grin. “We used to sit up there and giggle while watching Theodore sniffing around the house trying to find us.”

“I see,” she laughed, standing up. “Well, let’s go have some dinner. I’m sure you three would like nothing more than a bowl of peanuts.”

“Peanuts! Did you hear that, fellas?” Benjamin beamed.

Wilson rolled his eyes toward him. “Like you need another peanut,” he replied, patting Benjamin’s stomach.

“Cut it out,” Benjamin scolded. “Tonight, we’re having peanuts, right Abby?”

“That we are,” she replied, turning and walking toward the corridor.

As they strolled past the staircase, Theodore leaped down onto the landing. “Did I hear something about dinner?”

Abby laughed. “My word, you have good ears. Yes, I have something special for you too.”

After they had left the parlor, Grandfather looked over at Sir Henry. “It’s like having kids running around, isn’t it?”

“It is at that. Maybe I should school them in mannerisms.”

Grandfather raised his brow with that comment. “School them in mannerisms?”

“Yes, English children were taught good manners by learning to properly walk, properly speak and to properly curtsy before the Queen.”

“Properly walk, speak and curtsying? You don’t say?” Grandfather humorously repeated. “Well, good luck with that. You’d be better off trying to teach Huck Finn all that nonsense than those three hooligans.”

Sir Henry gave him a smug look. “You know,” he started to say. “Maybe I should start with you.”

“Me?”

“Yes, you could use a good tutoring in how to properly speak.”

“Not on your life. Even though I was finely crafted in Switzerland, I’m an American through and through. And we Americans, well....”

“You Americans.” Sir Henry interrupted.

“That’s right; we Americans don’t take kindly to having others telling us what to do.”

“I am certainly aware of that. You are the most obnoxious brew of scallywags I’ve ever had to deal with.”

“Scallywags, you say? Well, you British are nothing but overzealous, pompous windbags,” Grandfather replied, closing his eyes.

“You see what I mean?” Sir Henry replied.

26

Lies & Betrayal

At seven o'clock that same evening, Molly sat down in the front room next to the phone. She felt like she was actually going to be sick, knowing when she called and talked to Willy - Bobby Ray, Ernie and Arnold would be sitting there listening in on their conversation.

As she reached for the phone, her father yelled from the kitchen, "Molly!"

Startled, she jumped back jerking her head sideways. "Yes, Dad?"

"Your mother and I will be going over to the Almond's house to play cards tonight."

"OK," she replied. She looked up at the clock. *Great,* she thought, *I won't have to lie to get out of the house tonight.* "When will you be home, Pa?"

"Around midnight, honey."

That gives me plenty of time. "Alright," she replied, staring down at the phone. *Now to get this over with,* she thought, picking it up.

"Hello," Willy said.

"It's me."

"It's about time you called. We were getting worried about you."

She heard the word *we* and knew they were all sitting there in Ernie's bedroom down in the basement. "I'm sorry. I just got out of the bathroom."

"The bathroom?" he questioned, looking over at his brother. Ernie raised his brow. Willy shook his head. Ernie, Arnold and Bobby Ray all sat back looking at one another. They knew the little weasel wasn't coming.

"Yes, I've been throwing up," she lied.

Willy slumped back in his seat. "I guess that means you're not coming tonight?"

"I can't. I just want to go to bed. I'm sorry, but you guys really don't need me anyway, Willy."

"Tell her that she'll get zip if she doesn't come," Ernie whispered.

Willy wrinkled his brow. "I mean it, Willy," he replied to his expression.

"Look," Willy said and then paused, "if you don't come, you won't get a dime."

There was silence on the line.

"Molly?"

"I'm still here."

"Did you hear what I said?"

"Yeah, I heard you. That's OK. I knew you never cared about me."

"What are you talking about?"

Molly smiled. *I got you now,* she thought. "Here I am, sicker than a dog and all you can think about is will I be there tonight."

"Now wait a minute."

"No, I am not going to wait another second, but you can bet your sweet bottom that you'll be waiting for me for the rest of your life, Willy Myers," she replied and then hung up.

"Molly… Molly…"

Willy put the phone in his lap. He stared at the three disgruntled faces looking back at him. "She hung up."

"She what?" Arnold scolded.

"She hung up on me."

"That little toad," Arnold spat.

"She's not a little toad - she's my girlfriend."

"Your girlfriend?" Arnold spewed. "Did you hear that?" he continued, looking at Ernie.

"I heard it," Ernie said. "Some terrific girlfriend you got, Willy."

"No kidding," he replied, placing the phone on the table. *What am I going to do now?* he thought.

"We don't need her anyway," Bobby Ray spoke up.

They all looked at him.

"She's just a girl. She doesn't have the guts to do this," Bobby Ray continued, standing up.

"You look pretty nervous yourself, Bobby Ray," Ernie said, sitting back on his bed.

Bobby Ray felt that jab. Sure, he was nervous, but he wasn't playing sick like Molly was. "You three can sit there acting like you're not scared, but I know…"

"So you think we're scared?" Ernie interrupted him, standing up.

Bobby Ray stepped back. "Well…" Bobby Ray started to say, feeling his knees shaking. "If you're not, then you might as well be dead."

"We'll all be dead if we get caught," Arnold shot back, standing up.

"Alright," Willy interrupted. "Enough with the crap."

Ernie and Arnold turned and faced him.

"We're not getting caught," Willy said, standing. "Come on, Bobby Ray. Let's go get our stuff ready," he continued walking toward the door. He turned around. "You two better be there."

"Did you hear that crap?" Arnold whispered.

Ernie turned toward Arnold. "You know, Arnold, the next time you say 'did you hear that' when I am standing right next to you, I'm going to punch your lights out." Arnold raised his brow. Ernie sighed looking at his brother again.

"We'll be there," he said.

Willy nodded, shifted his eyes on Arnold, and then walked out with Bobby Ray.

After they left, Arnold sat down on the old couch. Ernie stood there for a moment, thinking.

"Punch my lights out," Arnold spat.

"Arnold," Ernie sighed. "You say that a million times a day."

"I do?"

"Yes, and now I know that you haven't a clue."

"Clue about what?"

"You see what I mean," he replied. "Look, just forget about it. It's almost eight. Let's get going," he continued, walking out.

"What do you think about Molly?" Arnold asked, getting up and following him.

"I don't know. Maybe she'll just stay home tonight. That would be the smart thing to do," he replied, taking the steps up to the back door.

"But what if your gut instinct is right about her going up and telling old lady Rose, or worse - she goes to the cops?"

Ernie turned around at the door. "She's not that stupid, Arnold," he replied, walking out the door. "Besides," he continued, taking the steps down and walking over to Arnold's car parked next to the shed. "If she does decide to go up there tonight, we'll see her for sure."

"I hope she stays home," Arnold replied, unlocking Ernie's door.

"Me too," Ernie said. "You know where we're going to hide this car?"

"Yep. Down in that gully within the high grass," he replied, rounding the car and getting in.

Ernie got in and shut his door. Arnold put the car into reverse and started backing out of the driveway.

As the two of them took off for Old Tiller Road, Molly got up from the couch and strolled into the kitchen. "What are you going to do tonight, honey?" her mother, Megan, asked.

She glanced over at her father sitting there eating left over stew. She shifted her eyes back on her mother. "I'll probably just stay home and watch a movie tonight."

"What are Willy and Bobby Ray up to?" her father, Larry, asked.

"They're going bowling with Ernie and Arnold," she lied.

"Why don't you go? I'm sure your father would give you a few dollars to go bowling tonight?" Megan said, looking over at Larry.

"No, that's OK. I don't mind if the boys go out together."

Larry laughed. Megan locked eyes with him. He stopped laughing, knowing her thoughts. *He drank too much, spent too much time at the bar and when he was home, he occupied the couch.*

Molly caught the look between her parents. She turned and walked out of the kitchen. Larry sat there knowing he upset his little girl. He slowly glanced over at Megan. "Larry, you could spend a little time with her," she whispered.

"You could have taken her to the county fair this year." Megan's whisper might have been soft, but her words were like a knife. "I know, I should have," was all he said.

"Well?" Megan pushed, leaning up on the table.

"How about next weekend we all go fishing down on the river?"

Megan smiled. They hadn't done that since Molly was a baby. "I'd really like that."

"OK, then we'll do it. Are you ready to go now?"

"Yes," she replied, pushing her chair out and standing up.

Molly saw them out the door and then waved goodbye as they backed out of the driveway. After they had gone, she closed the door behind her, walked into the front room and looked up at the clock. It was a quarter to eight.

"If I leave at eight, it should only take me around twenty minutes to ride up to Cherry Hill," she said, walking toward the closet in the hallway. As she put on her coat, she thought about Mrs. Rose. *I sure hope when I tell her, she doesn't call Sheriff Collins until I'm gone.* That thought made her think of Willy and Bobby Ray. "I sure hope those two don't get into trouble," she sighed, walking toward the back door. *This is worse than stabbing them in the back. They may never speak to me again, but I honestly have no choice,* she thought opening the door.

It wasn't until she walked up to her bike in the backyard that she had an idea. *What if I just tell Mrs. Rose that it's Sid, Don, and their fancy little wives who are going to break in? She'll have to believe me when I tell her about the suitcase.* She got on her bike and started pedaling down the driveway.

27

Two Bad Apples

As Ernie and Arnold drove down Cross Ridge Road toward Old Tiller, Ernie requested Arnold to turn off his headlights.

"Are you crazy?"

"No. The moonlight should be bright enough for us to see."

"Alright," Arnold replied, bringing his car to a crawl and turning them off. Whcn hc camc to thc intersection, he glanced down Old Tiller Road.

"You're right. I can see the path to the barn," he whispered.

"I told ya. Now pull over to the side of the road while I check where we can head down into the gully," Ernie said, sticking his head out the window. Forty feet down the road, he said, "OK, that's far enough. Go into the high grass right here."

"What if the gully is a mud pit and we get stuck?"

"It hasn't rained in months. The ground has to be solid."

Arnold sighed, leaning up over his steering wheel. He carefully watched the front end of the car rolling through the high grass. As the car went further in, he saw the grass sweeping past his door, and then suddenly, he felt the car rolling down into the gully. "Man, this better be cool," he whispered.

"Stop worrying, will ya," Ernie replied, with his head still out the window. "We're in! Turn the wheel now!" he yelled.

Arnold quickly pulled the steering wheel over, put on the brakes and shut off the engine. He sat back and sighed.

"See, I told you," Ernie said, opening his car door and stepping out. The ground was as hard as a rock.

Arnold looked at him standing there. He reached over, opened the glove box and took out two ski masks and two pairs of gloves. "Here, take these," he said, tossing them across the front seat.

"Wow, I almost forgot about these," Ernie replied. He shoved them in his coat pocket and closed his door. Arnold got out and leaned on the roof. "This is a great place to hide the car. No one will ever see it down here."

"No, they won't. But I sure hope we can find it once we come back with the money," Ernie replied, rounding the back end and heading up the small incline. At the top of the gully, he turned to see Arnold right behind him. "Can you believe how high this stuff grows?" he said, walking through the grass.

"No, kidding," Arnold replied.

When they made it to the road, they brushed off their clothing and started walking up toward the intersection.

"Let's get moving," Ernie said, picking up his pace.

As they came upon the barn on Old Tiller Road, they headed up the hill right behind the manor. After reaching the top, they stopped and caught their breath. "Wow, will you look at that?" Arnold said, bending over and gasping for air.

"Yeah, frightening isn't it. Thank God there are no lights on back here. Let's hurry over to the far side," Ernie replied, walking out from under the trees and then running across the back property.

When they reached the side of the manor, they holed up to catch their breath. "Man, can you believe this ballroom?" Arnold whispered, looking through the glass wall.

"I can't even imagine being that rich," Ernie replied. It was so dark he could hardly make out the boxes stacked inside. "Let's check the front and see what kind of view we have," he whispered, walking to the corner and heading up toward the front. When he got there, he holed up tight against the wall and peered out in front.

"What can you see?" Arnold whispered.

Ernie stepped back. "I can see the entire driveway all the way back to the trees. Like I said, I thought it was at least forty or fifty yards."

"Great. There's no way we'll miss anything from here."

"That's right. Now, what time is it?"

Arnold looked at his watch. "It's eight-thirty. We have lots of time before Sid and Don show up."

"Yeah, it's plenty of time to watch for Molly too."

"You really think she'd be that brazen?"

Ernie looked at him. "Where'd you learn that word?"

"From a TV show."

"Really… a TV show?" he replied, wrinkling his brow.

"Cut the crap. We've got more important things to worry about right now," Arnold spat, stepping around him and peeking out. "I'll take first watch if you want to sit a spell," he said, glancing back at Ernie.

"Not a bad idea," Ernie replied, sitting down and resting his back against the wall.

As the two started their vigil at the side of the manor, Abby strolled into the den carrying her three little mice. She set them down on the arm of the recliner, then walked over and lit a fire. "How is that?" she said.

"That's wonderful," Wilson replied.

"I thought you'd like it. Now we can sit and enjoy the evening together."

Benjamin gazed up at her. She could see a question in his eyes. "Yes?" she said.

"Abby, I've been wondering."

"Yes?"

"Do you think we'll ever find that Potion and Spells book?"

She glanced over at the fire and thought for a moment. "I'm sure we will one day," she replied. "Sometimes when you stop looking for something you've lost, it seems to just magically appear. I've had it happen so many times."

"You think you could use your magic to make it come out of its hiding place?" Cracker asked.

She smiled at him. "Hmm… I honestly never thought of that, Cracker. However, now that you mentioned calling out for something to appear, I can call my cape and broom from upstairs."

"You can?" Wilson beamed.

"I sure can," she replied, looking over at Theodore lying there by the fire. "Let me see now," she said and then paused. She cupped her hands to her face, "Oh… Gertrude - Isabella, come down here, please."

Wilson, Cracker and Benjamin excitedly turned and stared out toward the parlor. Theodore opened his eyes and lifted his head. Boris turned toward the parlor as Grandfather and Sir Henry stood there looking up the winding staircase.

Inside the master's chambers, the closet doors opened. Isabella, Abby's broom, floated out. Gertrude slipped off her hanger. She floated out of the closet and straddled Isabella. The chamber's door suddenly opened. Isabella turned in midair and flew out the door with Gertrude. Together, they flew down the hallway toward the staircase. When they came whizzing down, Isabella stopped in midair inside the parlor.

Grandfather lifted his brow. Sir Henry stood there startled seeing the broom and Abby's cape floating there.

"Will you look at that!" Benjamin yelled.

"I can't see a thing," Boris fumed.

"Come in, you two," Abby ordered, smiling up at Boris.

Theodore stood up. Boris's eyes went wide seeing Abby's black hooded cape riding the broom into the den.

"Be careful of the small chandeliers, Isabella," Abby said as Isabella made a full circle of the room. She stopped right in front of Boris. Gertrude turned her hood as if to look at him. Abby laughed. "Come down here," she said.

"Wow," Benjamin excitedly gasped, standing up and looking at Isabella. He cast his eyes up at Gertrude. "Can she talk?" he asked, turning toward Abby.

"No, Gertrude cannot talk, but she knows what you're saying."

"Really?" Wilson said. "Do you think we can ride Isabella?"

Abby sighed sitting back. *Now that would be interesting,* she thought, *mischief on a broom.* Before she could answer, there was a knock at the door.

"That might be Fanny," Abby said, getting up. "She thought about stopping by."

"It could be someone else," Wilson questioned, raising his little brow.

"You're right," she replied, thinking of Shaun. *Oh, I wish it were he,* she thought. "Alright, before I go and open the door, Isabella, take Gertrude to the ballroom. You three run up the chimney to Boris," she said. She quickly turned and extended her arms toward Theodore. "OK, jump up."

As Theodore leaped into the air, he magically turned into a stuffed toy lion within her arms. With everyone now hiding, Abby sighed heading toward the foyer. "The rest of the house - be silent," she ordered, walking up to the doors. Before opening them, she thought of Shaun. *It can't be him. He went out with his parents tonight,* she thought, pulling the handles. To her surprise, a young girl was standing there.

"Hello, Mrs. Rose."

"Molly," she said, cocking her head to see behind her. "Where are your friends?"

"They're not with me. I'm alone," Molly replied, looking up at the beautiful stuffed white lion in her arms.

"I see," Abby said. "What brings you up here at this time of night… on your bicycle, no less?"

"I've come to warn you."

"Warn me!? Warn me about what?"

Molly shuffled on her feet, and started fidgeting with her fingers.

"Please, please, come in, dear."

Molly shyly walked in and stood there motionless in the foyer.

"Now, what's this all about, young lady?" Abby asked.

"You're going to be robbed tonight."

"Robbed!? You mean someone is going to try and break in?"

"Yes."

Two names immediately flashed before her. Molly confirmed her suspicions. "It's Sid and Don and their wives."

Abby stood there shocked. *I think I'll let her tell me what they're after,* she thought, already knowing. "Why would they want to break in?" she asked.

"They're after your money."

"My money!?"

"Yes, Mrs. Rose, they pulled me, Willy and Bobby Ray over at the fair and told us about your suitcase. We told 'em that we wanted no part of it," she lied.

As Abby stood there listening, she could feel her blood begin to boil. "I think you and I had better sit down and have a little chat," she sternly said, walking around Molly and shutting the doors. Before she could close them, two men ran up from out of nowhere wearing ski masks over their heads.

"Hold it right there," Ernie said, barging in.

Abby stepped back and froze. Molly quickly turned around. Terror filled her eyes hearing Ernie's voice.

"Get back inside," Ernie ordered, looking down at Molly standing there as if she were going to pee her pants.

"You little weasel," Arnold added.

"You know these two?" Abby asked alarmed.

"You'd be smart to keep quiet, Molly," Ernie shouted. "That's if you want to go home tonight."

Abby spun on her heels. "Now you listen here, young man!" she yelled.

"No, you listen, Grandma!" Ernie shouted back.

"That's right, you old bat," Arnold added.

Ernie shot Arnold a glance. "What?" Arnold said.

"Just shut up. I'll do the talking here," Ernie replied, turning his attention on Abby. He reached into his pocket and pulled out Willy's toy gun. "Now where's the suitcase with the money?" he ordered.

Molly scooted over and held onto Abby's waist. Abby reached down and gathered her to her side.

"I'm not going to ask you again. Where is the suitcase?" Ernie yelled, pointing the gun at Abby.

Abby glanced down at it. She cast her eyes up to meet the man's face hidden behind the ski mask. Molly started shaking looking at the gun. Her heart stopped, recognizing it immediately. "That's not real. That's Willy's soft air pistol," she said.

"Shut up, you little toad," Ernie spat.

"Well…." Abby gasped, clutching Theodore in her arm.

"Alright, so it's not real," Ernie interrupted her. "You still can't get past us, so just tell us where it is."

Abby looked down at Molly. She squeezed her shoulder. "I think it's time for you to sleep, my dear child," she said, bringing her hand up and waving it over Molly's head. Molly instantly slid down her side and crumbled to the floor.

Ernie and Arnold froze seeing Molly go out like a light. They slowly looked up at Abby.

"You two aren't going anywhere," Abby yelled, extending her hand and waving it at the doors. They slammed shut and then locked behind them. The sound of the doors slamming made Ernie and Arnold jump. They quickly turned and looked back.

"You bring a toy gun to rob me, do you?" Abby fumed.

They slowly turned their heads back toward her. Their eyes instantly filled with fear seeing her face turning green and then her nose and chin started growing longer. She bent over and set Theodore down on the floor beside her. "Well," she hissed, standing up pointing at them. Her index fingernail started to grow. It stretched out far enough to touch Ernie's nose. He stepped back shaking.

"As you see," she said, casting her eyes downward on Theodore, "I have a toy too, but this one gives me all the advantages, you low down scoundrels," she continued, looking up and staring into their eyes.

They glanced down at the little stuffed toy. If they weren't shaking so much, they might have laughed at her.

"Theodore!" she yelled, waving her hand over him. WHOOSH…. Theodore suddenly came alive as a giant male lion. His eyes were like daggers staring at the men standing there. He snarled and growled at them, shaking his massive head.

Arnold screamed seeing Theodore's large canines. Ernie turned and bolted for the doors. He yanked on the handles, but they would not open. "Going somewhere?" Abby wickedly hissed.

Ernie slowly turned keeping his back tight against the doors. Grandfather opened his eyes. Ernie looked up to see him. “If you want to know the time, it’s time for Theodore to have his dinner, you misfit heathen,” Grandfather scolded.

“No, no, please!” Arnold begged, falling to his knees.

Theodore lurched forward, growling and swiping his massive paw at him.

“Not so fast, Theodore. I think they need a little tenderizing first in a large cauldron of boiling water,” she said, taunting her quarry.

“You’re a witch!” Ernie gasped.

“Why, I most certainly am,” Abby replied, leaning toward him. “I’m far more evil than the wicked witch of the west.”

Ernie looked at Theodore. His blues eyes were on fire. “Please,” Ernie begged.

“Pleading for mercy will do you no good, now,” Sir Henry spoke up from behind.

Ernie jumped back realizing that the whole house was alive.

“Oh… this is awful,” Benjamin said worried, standing on top of Boris’s head.

“Shh...” Wilson whispered. “Theodore isn’t going to eat ‘em.”

“No?” Benjamin replied.

“Well, if he doesn’t eat them, he sure is going to scare them to death,” Cracker spoke up.

“Shh...” Boris whispered.

“Now, take off your masks,” Abby ordered.

They did as she asked.

“Step forward,” she ordered.

They came forward shaking like leaves on a tree.

“Now, where are Sid and Don and their fancy little wives?” she asked, shifting her eyes from one to the other.

“They’re not coming until ten tonight,” Arnold replied, shivering in his boots.

“Who else is with them?”

“My brother Willy and his friend Bobby Ray,” Ernie replied.

“Your little brother, Willy and his friend Bobby Ray? Well, well,” Abby replied, glancing down at Molly lying there sleeping like a kitten. “How are they going to break in?” she asked, looking up.

"They're going to come through the basement window at the side of the manor. That's how they came in before," Arnold replied, shivering.

"I'm well aware of those two breaking in when I wasn't here. But before I can take care of them, I must do something with you," she hissed.

"Please, please… we'll do whatever you want, just let us go!" Arnold begged.

"I have all the intentions of letting you go, but how you go, is what concerns me," she wickedly replied.

"We'll leave right out this door. We'll never come back, I swear," Ernie said.

"Oh… I am sure you'll never come back, but we have one very small problem."

"What's that?" Arnold asked, looking down at Theodore next to her.

"You two know that I'm a witch."

"We won't tell a soul, I swear on my mother's grave, we won't," Arnold begged.

"Swear on your mother's grave? How dare you say a thing like that!" she angrily replied, thinking of what to do. Her thoughts landed on Arnold calling Molly a little toad. The thought made her smile. They did not like the smile that suddenly appeared on her hideous green face.

"Little toads," Abby whispered. "You like little toads?" she asked, clutching her hands together.

Neither said a word.

"I think being little toads for two days just might change your whole outlook on life."

Ernie's thoughts began racing. They landed smack dab on old man Cooper's story about him seeing pumpkins talking and witches flying around out back. "Now look...," he started to say.

Theodore stepped forward and snarled. Ernie quickly stepped back.

Abby cocked her head from side to side as if studying them. Her eyes started to change into shimmering black marbles as she raised her hands and began hissing a spell, "*Whispering winds from a den of fools - slithering through a slimy pool - up from a muddy river's bog - you two will now change into frogs.*" WHOOSH… Ernie and Arnold instantly disappeared. Their clothing fell to the floor around their boots. Abby walked up noticing movement underneath them. Ernie and Arnold hopped out of their pants and looked at each other in utter terror. "She did it, Ernie. Look at us! We're frogs now!" Arnold gasped.

"You both have two days to think about what you have done," Abby scolded.

They looked up in terror. "Two whole days? How shall we eat?" Ernie asked.

"Hmm… well I don't think you'll be eating too many hamburgers. Maybe try finding some flies."

"Flies?" Arnold moaned, feeling his stomach roll.

Abby leaned over. "However, I wouldn't be so worried about what you'll eat. I'd be more concerned about what may eat you."

Arnold looked at Ernie with fear in his eyes.

"Snakes perhaps, or maybe a barn owl," Abby continued, taunting them.

"Snakes, barn owls? We're dead, Ernie," Arnold cried out.

"Please, if we have two whole days, couldn't we just stay here?"

"No," she snapped, waving her hand at the doors. They unlocked and slowly opened. "You two heathens like to frighten others and take what is not yours. I think it's high time you both felt what it's like to be scared," she said and then paused. "Now try to make it home without ending up in the belly of a snake or a large barn owl tonight," she continued, bending over. "My advice would be to stay out of sight until you return to normal. Now leave my house before I put a spell on you that will keep you being frogs forever!"

Ernie and Arnold leaped out of the front doors as fast as they could. The doors slowly closed behind them. "What are we going to do to now?" Arnold gasped.

Ernie frantically glanced around the area then looked at him. His mind was on fire seeing Arnold sitting there as a big, fat bullfrog. "I'm feeling sick," he spewed.

"You're feeling sick? I'm feeling sick just looking at you, Ernie. Why did I listen to you, I…"

"I, what?" Ernie interrupted. "You wanted the money as bad as me."

"Yeah, you're right, but never again. I'm through with this crap. I'll never steal another thing."

Ernie shifted his eyes back at the doors. *This conversation can wait,* he thought. "We better leave before she opens those doors and crushes us with a broom," he said.

That thought scared Arnold. "Let's hurry and get back to the car."

"No. We're not going there."

"Why?"

"Too many snakes live in that gully and besides, you think you can drive in your condition?"

"Then where are we going to hide?"

Ernie quickly looked down the driveway. He shook his head. "Well, I'm not hopping down to the road."

Arnold glanced in that direction. *Getting run over by a car is out of the question.* "You're right, so where do you want to hide for two days, then?" he asked.

"We'll go around the back and head across the Klondike farm to the river. We can hide inside that overflow pipe down by the dam."

"The Klondike farm…? The river…? Are you crazy, or what? You know where snakes like to hunt for a meal?" he said then paused. "In a field or near a river."

Ernie sighed, "OK, so it's risky, but we'd have a better chance of leaping into the river and floating down to the dam than trying to make it home tonight. That's unless you have a better idea?"

"No."

"OK then," Ernie replied, hopping away. "We'd have a better chance of finding something to eat down there anyway," he said over his back.

Arnold sat there for a second. *Run across the Klondike farm to the river,* he thought, watching Ernie, hopping toward the side of the manor. *Oh... we'll find plenty to eat, alright - like slimy little mud worms, flies, and maybe some big, fat, juicy grasshoppers. Gee... I can already taste 'em,* his thoughts tumbled. "Ernie, wait up," he yelled, hopping after him.

"Abby!" Wilson yelled, scampering across the floor.

Abby took her eyes off the doors and looked down at him.

"Your skin!" he gasped, frightened.

She lifted her arms up. They started to change. "I never told you," she said and then paused. "That mermaid my great uncle met, she warned him if the magic was used for evil that you'd turn into evil as well."

"You're not evil," Benjamin said, walking up to her.

She smiled at him then caught Theodore's eyes. She reached out and rubbed his head. "No, I am not evil. They were," she replied.

"Well, they got what they deserved," Sir Henry spoke up.

Abby turned to face him. "You did the right thing, Madam Rose. Right now, however, we'd better start preparing for what's coming," Grandfather suggested.

"You're right," she replied, walking over and picking up Ernie and Arnold's clothing and boots. She turned and stood there looking down at Molly.

"Poor child," she whispered.

"What shall we do with her?" Theodore asked.

"We'll leave her for now. I need to bag up these clothes to give to Willy when he and the others show up," she replied, walking toward the kitchen.

They all stood there watching her leave. Theodore glanced down at the mice. "We need to devise a plan," he said.

"That's right, we do," Wilson replied, scratching his chin thinking.

"Why, I just want to stomp on their toes and kick them all in the shins," Benjamin grumbled.

Theodore laughed. "I mean it," Benjamin replied to his laughter.

"I know you do. We'll wait for Madam Rose and see what she has in mind," he replied.

When Abby returned with the clothes and boots inside two bags, she set them down on the sofa in the parlor and then she walked over to Molly. "You three hide," she said to the mice. They looked at Molly knowing what Abby was about to do. They quickly scampered toward the hole leading under the staircase. Abby then looked at Theodore. He knew he had to go to sleep. With a simple wave of her hand, Theodore changed into a stuffed lion again. With that taken care of, she bent down and waved her hand over Molly's head. "It's time to wake up, Molly," she whispered.

Molly awoke opening her eyes. "Where am I?" she asked, sitting up.

"You're here with me, Molly. You do remember coming over tonight?"

Molly rubbed her eyes sitting there. "Yes," she replied. Abby reached down and took her hand, bringing her to her feet.

"Where are Ernie and Arnold?" she asked, looking about the room.

"They went home, and you need to go home too."

"But what happened?"

Abby put her arm around her. "I convinced them to leave, and they did," she said and then paused. "Now," she continued, "why did you lie to me?"

Molly knew right away that Ernie and Arnold must have told her the whole story. She glanced down at the floor. "Molly," Abby said. Molly looked up at her. "When young children start to lie, they will lie to people their whole life. It's the worst habit to get into."

"I'm sorry, Mrs. Rose," she sniffled.

"You should be. Now, it's getting late. I am sure your parents must be worried."

"Yes, I should be getting home. I'm truly sorry that I lied. I was just scared, that's all."

"Forget about it," Abby replied, ushering her to the door. Before she opened it, she placed her hand on Molly's shoulder. Molly glanced up at her.

"How would you like to come up here when everything is finished and I'll give you a grand tour of the place?"

Molly smiled, wiping her tears. "I'd really like that, Mrs. Rose," she replied and then paused. "Can I ask you one thing?"

"Yes?"

"Are you going to call the police?"

"No, I am not."

"No?"

"No, Molly, I will handle this. Now you run along and get home safely. And please, do not worry. I've been taking care of myself for an awfully long time now."

Molly nodded as Abby opened the doors. She walked out and got on her bike. Before pedaling off, she looked back at Mrs. Rose standing there. "Don't worry about Willy and Bobby Ray. I'll have a nice long chat with them and then send them on their way too, Molly."

Molly again smiled. She had one more question. She wanted to know what was going to happen to Sid and Don and their wives. She decided to keep that question to herself. "Goodnight, Mrs. Rose."

"Goodnight, and thank you, Molly."

Molly pushed her bike around and then started pedaling down the driveway. When she disappeared in the shadows of the trees, Abby closed the door. Grandfather and Sir Henry opened their eyes. She looked from one to the other. "Now to take care of the rest of these heathens," she said, walking into the parlor toward the corridor.

When she was gone, they both sighed knowing the night was just getting started.

28

Plan of Attack

When Abby returned to the parlor, Theodore and the mice stood there waiting for their orders.

"Alright, gentlemen," she said, taking a seat.

"We're ready, Abby," Benjamin spoke up, puffing out his chest.

She stared at his cute little face. "You are?"

"Yes, I've got a plan."

"You've got a plan?" Wilson spat. "Please, by all means, entertain us with it," he continued, folding his arms.

"I'll do more than that," Benjamin replied. "Now look," he said and then paused, stepping out from the group. "Wilson, Cracker and I will go hide downstairs in the basement rafters. When those four come through the window, we'll jump on Sid and Don's head and start punching their lights out," he continued, showing off his shadow boxing skills.

"Really now?" Abby replied, smiling with delight at his little antics and bravery.

"Will you look at him thinking he can box?" Cracker fumed.

"I can. Just ask Theodore. I gave him a good thumping when he got out of line, Abby," Benjamin replied, showing her his fancy footwork and jabs.

Abby rolled her eyes toward Theodore. He slightly shook his head to Benjamin's foolishness.

"Yes, I do recall hearing that story and I suppose I'll be hearing it for some time to come," Abby sighed.

Benjamin paid no mind to the stares and looks thinking he was inside a boxing ring. "We certainly showed him, didn't we fellas? And now, we'll take care of those two heathens as you called them," he replied, dancing in a circle tossing punches left and right.

Grandfather and Sir Henry laughed under their breath. They too were enjoying this little display of bravery. Wilson and Cracker, on the other hand, were not at all amused; leaning on one foot with their arms folded, while staring at Benjamin.

"Benjamin," Abby softly said, getting his attention.

"Yes?" he replied, stopping his boxing and gleefully looking up at her.

"You're a brave little soul, and I am sure you three musketeers could handle any situation. However, tonight I am going to show those two they should never taunt a witch."

"You sure you don't need me? I've got a great upper cut too."

"I'm going to give you an upper cut if you don't stop with the nonsense," Wilson scolded.

"Gentlemen, we don't have time for this," Abby intervened, sitting up.

"Gertrude and Isabella, come out here, please." Isabella flew down the ballroom corridor, through the den and into the parlor with Gertrude. "Alright now," Abby continued, focusing on her team. "This could get a little messy. However, I'm not concerned about that right now. I want those low-down hooligans, Sid and Don, on their knees. As for Willy and Bobby Ray, we'll just scare them really good and hopefully they'll think twice about getting involved in any criminal activities again."

Abby's team nodded.

"OK now, this is my plan," she said, casting her eyes down on her mice. *What on earth, can I have them do?* she thought. *Oh, I know.* "You three, I want you to be our lookouts."

"Lookouts?" Cracker questioned.

"Like spies?" Benjamin excitedly whispered.

"Yes, like spies," Abby replied. "I want you, Benjamin, since you're the bravest, please go down to the basement and hide near the steps…."

"Benjamin… the bravest?" Wilson interrupted. "He can hardly climb the stairs around here. And since I'm the captain of the three musketeers, it should be me who should go down the basement and wait for those hooligans coming though the window."

"Captain," Cracker laughed, shaking his head.

Wilson tossed him a cold stare. Theodore smiled. *We'd get nothing done if they were in charge,* he thought.

"Alright, alright, now listen," Abby interrupted, getting everyone's attention again. "Wilson, you can go down in the basement. When you see them coming in, I want you to signal up to Benjamin, who'll be standing at the top of the stairs inside the kitchen. Wilson nodded. "Now, Benjamin, I want you to wave at Cracker who'll be standing at the kitchen corridor door. Cracker, once Benjamin gives you the signal, you run down the corridor and tell us, OK?" she continued, looking into each of their eyes. "Now go," she said, shooing them away.

Wilson quickly turned and bolted for the basement. Cracker and Benjamin took off after him. "And stay out of sight when your assignment is done," she yelled. She then gazed at Isabella and Gertrude for a moment.

"Isabella, I want you to stay with me. Gertrude, I want you to hide in the pantry. When they come up, wait until they've passed the pantry door, and then sneak out and float above their heads. Your job will be to go after Willy and Bobby Ray if they decide to run."

Gertrude's hood went up and down and then she flew toward the parlor corridor. Isabella walked over and settled her bristles on the floor next to Abby.

"Now, Theodore," Abby said, "You're staying with me too."

He nodded and then asked, "Where are we going to trap them?"

Abby scratched her chin thinking. "That all depends on where those fools go when they do come up."

Theodore again nodded. "Seeing that you're letting the boys go, what are you going to do to Sid and Don?"

Abby smiled. "I think they'll be leaving the same way Ernie and Arnold had left - hopping out the door. What do you think?"

Theodore pondered that. "Have you thought about when all four return to normal?"

Abby tilted her head.

"They could report this to the authorities, you know."

"They may," Abby replied, "but who's going to believe them?"

"What about their wives?" Theodore asked.

Abby stared into his eyes while thinking. "Now that's a good question," she replied. "I don't think they'll be coming in, which leads me to believe, they'll be parked somewhere near the manor. My guess would be Old Tiller Road," she continued, wishing she could give them a good fright.

"Is there anything you want Sir Henry and I to do?" Grandfather asked.

She turned and walked over to them. "I know you both would like to get involved, however, you cannot move."

"I wish we could, Madam Rose," Grandfather replied, looking over at Sir Henry.

"Madam Rose, since we cannot move, we'll stand here as sentries. And be reassured they'll not get past us, right, Grandfather?" Sir Henry said.

"That's right, we'll hold the fort here together," he replied.

Abby smiled. *Finally, after tonight, they just might become friends again,* she thought, turning toward Isabella and Theodore.

"Madam Rose," Boris spoke up from the den.

"Yes?" she replied, walking in and looking up.

"I'm a bit stuck myself."

"Yes, Boris, but you can still give them a good fright," she replied, raising her brow.

Boris smiled. "That I can do," he replied, tilting his antlers and winking at her.

"Alright then," she said, turning and walking back into the parlor.

"Lights," she continued, snapping her fingers. All the lights in the manor went off. She strolled down the corridor toward the kitchen. "Are you ready, Cracker?" she asked, looking down at him standing next to the kitchen door.

"I'm ready, Abby."

"Good. How about you, Benjamin?" she asked, walking into the kitchen.

"I'm ready to start punching their lights out," he replied, holding up his little fist next to the basement door.

"You just do what I ask, and then we'll see if we need you to start punching someone's lights out, OK?" He nodded. She turned around and called out to Hansel.

"Yes, Madam Rose," she replied, at the kitchen sink.

Abby walked over and gave her instructions. Her only request was… "I want none of them to try and escape out the kitchen patio door and… no knives, just toss the pots and pans if you must."

"Yes, Madam Rose," she replied, turning toward the cupboards storing those items. Abby watched the doors open. "Aim for their legs and feet. I want no one hurt if they try and leave this house," Abby ordered, walking out.

Hansel stood there watching her leave. "You heard the order?" she said.

All the pots and pans started to rattle.

"Good," Hansel replied.

29

Escape to the River

"Ernie, wait up," Arnold yelled, hopping across the backyard toward the hill.

Ernie stopped before heading down. "Come on, hurry up, will ya?" he yelled.

Arnold hopped up alongside him. They sat there staring at one another. "You look awful," Arnold said.

"So, do you."

"I can't believe this is happening," Arnold spewed, glancing back at the manor. "I wish we had known she was a witch."

"Yeah, me too" Ernie sighed, looking back. "It's hard to imagine that everything in that place is alive," he continued. "That lion she called Theodore, can you believe that? He scared the living daylights out of me!"

"He did more than that. I thought my knees would never stop shaking. You think we should tell the sheriff when we turn back to normal?"

"I don't know," he replied, thinking of old man Cooper. *He's been telling the truth the whole time,* he thought. That thought led him to another. *The Von Haussler's were witches - every single one of them. Now Mrs. Rose comes along, and she's a witch too. Something's not right here.*

"Whatcha thinking, Ernie?"

"I'm thinking of the Von Haussler's. The Baron was a warlock. I'm sure of it now."

"So, you do believe that old man Cooper has been telling the truth all this time?"

"Yeah, that whiskey drinking fool has been telling the truth, alright."

"That was a long time ago, Ernie."

"I know, and now this lady purchases the place and she's a witch too?" he replied, shifting his eyes on the manor again. He glanced over at Arnold. "Don't you find that strange?"

Arnold pondered that. "You think she's a relative?"

"I'm thinking she is, but we can't prove that, not with her last name being Rose."

"What if she changed it?"

Ernie spun that thought, “She may have,” he replied, taking one more look back at the manor. “Come on,” he continued, “we’d better get going. They’ll be coming soon.”

“Yeah… we’d better get down there and warn them.”

“Yeah right,” Ernie laughed

“What’s so funny?”

“Can you imagine two frogs going down there and telling them not to go?”

Arnold tilted his little green head.

“Come on, Arnold, think about it.”

“I am. I’m thinking about your little brother and Bobby Ray.”

Ernie cringed. “Alright, we’ll try and warn them before Sid and Don show up,” he replied, turning and hopping down the hill.

When they got to the road, they looked both ways. The coast was clear.

“Come on, let’s get across and hide in the grass,” Ernie said.

Ten minutes later, they heard the sound of bikes coming. “That’s got to be them,” Arnold whispered.

“It sure is,” Ernie replied, hopping closer to the road.

“I beat you again,” Willy said, rolling up and putting on his brakes, tossing gravel everywhere.

“I just let you win,” Bobby Ray replied, pulling up and skidding alongside him.

“Right, that’ll be the day. What time is it?”

Bobby Ray looked down at his watch. “It’s nine forty-five.”

“They should be here soon,” Willy replied, getting off his bike.

“Willy,” Ernie said within the high grass.

Willy turned his head toward the old barn. He looked at Bobby Ray. “Did you hear something?”

“No.”

Willy shrugged focusing his attention on the road. “Come on, where are you guys,” he sighed, waiting for Don’s car to pull up.

“Willy,” Ernie said again.

Willy jerked his head back staring into the field toward the barn. “Did you hear that?”

Bobby Ray glanced back and then focused on where Willy was staring. “Hear what?”

“I thought I heard something.”

Bobby Ray laughed. "Maybe it was just a barn owl."

"No, it sounded like someone calling my name."

"Please, don't start that crap with me. I hate being out here at night, especially having to go into the spooky looking place."

"I'm serious."

Before Bobby Ray could speak, they spotted headlights coming. The lights went off. "That's them," Willy said, pushing his bike to the side of the road.

Ernie heard the car. *It's too late now,* he thought, hunkering down in the grass. When Don drove up, he turned his vehicle onto the dirt path toward the barn. Ernie quickly hopped back to where Arnold was. They sat there watching the four get out and walk back up to the road.

"How long have you been waiting?" Don asked, strolling up with his wife.

"Not long. Ten minutes, maybe," Willy replied, checking out the ladies. He smiled remembering seeing Betsy running out of the fairgrounds half-naked.

"OK, we brought you these," Sue, said, stepping up handing them each a ski mask.

They slipped them in their jacket pockets.

"We also have these," Sid said, handing them each a small flashlight.

"Now, don't turn them on until we're down into the basement."

They nodded, looking up into the moonlight at the four adults.

"Now, you know what you're going to do, right?" Don asked.

"Yes," Willy replied. "The two of us are going up the stairs to search the bedrooms."

"Right," Don replied.

"Where do you want to meet after we get done?" Bobby Ray asked.

Willy shifted his eyes on Bobby Ray. *Smart boy,* he thought. They needed to know where these two bozos wanted to meet afterward so they could take off with the money.

"After Sid and I search the main floor, we'll meet you two up on the third floor."

They nodded without looking at each other.

"What if we find the suitcase with the money? You still want us to wait up there?" Willy asked.

"Yes," Don replied. "It might be too heavy for you to carry."

Willy nodded.

"Alright, let's get moving," Sid said, turning toward his wife. "We should be back within the hour, I hope. You two just hang tight," he continued, leaning in and giving her a kiss.

Don kissed Sue and the two started across the road. Bobby Ray stood there a second eyeing up the women. *I wouldn't mind a kiss myself,* he thought, smiling up at them. They smiled back. He winked and headed across the road with Willy. The women wrinkled their brow at one another. Betsy shrugged then headed back to the car.

Ernie and Arnold waited until the women were inside the car before heading across the Klondike farm toward the river. Through the high grass, hopping around old brush piles and deadfall, the two made it to the small forest before the hill and the river below.

"Wow," Arnold gasped. "That was a hike."

"It sure was. I always hated getting my shoes wet walking through the grass like this. Now my whole belly is wet."

Arnold laughed.

"What's so funny?"

"You… you're more than wet. There's grass stuck all over you."

Ernie rolled his large eyes. "We don't have time for this. And besides, maybe the snakes won't see me in my grass camouflage."

Arnold's little brain lit up. "Yeah, maybe you're right," he replied, rolling over on the wet grass. "There, how do I look now," he asked.

"Gee, where did you go?" Ernie replied, faking as if he couldn't see him.

"Cut the crap, will ya?"

"Alright, just keep quiet," he scolded. "Hopefully this camouflage works until we leap into the river," he continued, hopping toward a tree right before the hill.

"Do you think we'll run into any snakes down there?" Arnold replied, following him.

Ernie stopped at the tree and turned around. "Did you notice there were no snakes in the field we just crossed?"

"How lucky was that?"

"Where do you think they are right now, lame brain?" Ernie sighed.

Arnold pondered that. "The river?" he said, feeling stupid.

"That's right. They're probably down there looking for a big, fat juicy meal, like us."

"Wonderful, you just had to say that, didn't you?" Arnold spewed.

"Shh," Ernie whispered, peeking out from the side of the tree toward the river. "Just stay close to me as we hop down," he continued, glancing back at Arnold. "We'll use the trees for cover. Once we get to the riverbank, jump in as fast as you can. The current should take us to the dam."

Arnold sighed. "Alright. Let's go."

Ernie focused on the incline as he started down. From tree to tree, they slowly hopped over small rocks and logs. At the last tree just before the river, they stopped and searched the bank knowing snakes would lie and wait for a meal to come by. They had caught hundreds knowing where to look for them at night.

"You see anything?" Arnold whispered behind him.

"No," Ernie replied, scanning the area. "Wait, look over there," he whispered, nodding his head.

Arnold peered out over him. "Oh, that's one, alright. It's a large garden snake."

"Yeah, a big female at that, too," Ernie whispered.

"She certainly looks hungry."

"Yep, but she's not getting me. On the count of three, hop into the water and swim like crazy toward the center where the current is fast."

"Wait a minute."

"What?" Ernie whispered, looking back.

"She can swim too, you know."

"Yes, I know that. You have any better ideas?"

"Yes, we could call a cab," Arnold replied, with a slight grin.

Ernie shook his head. He had no time for games. "Are you ready? One, two, three - JUMP!" Ernie said, leaping out and hitting the water.

Arnold watched him go under and then come back to the surface. He glanced over at Mrs. Garden Snake. She turned her head, darting her tongue in and out. Their eyes met. "Jump, Arnold," Ernie yelled.

The snake lifted its head, eyeing up Arnold. Arnold jumped. The snake struck at him, missing him by an inch. *Splash…* Arnold hit the water.

"Swim, Arnold… swim!" Ernie yelled, catching the current and going under. He rolled and flipped several times and then came back up to the surface. Looking back, he saw Arnold go under and then pop up beside him.

"That was close," Arnold gasped, spitting out water.

"You're telling me."

Fifty yards down the river they swam until they spotted the dam up ahead. Ernie made his way to the muddy bank and hopped out. Arnold hopped out after him. “Hurry, let’s get down the bank and inside that pipe.”

When they leaped into the pipe, they both sat there staring out into the night.

“Wow, I never want to do that again,” Arnold said out of breath.

Ernie closed his eyes, fuming. He never wanted to be a frog ever again.

30

The Witching Hour

After Abby gave her orders to the kitchen, she walked down the corridor thinking of Shaun and Fanny. *I wish they were here right now,* she thought, *well, maybe Fanny. If Shaun saw this, he'd never come back.* When she entered the parlor, she stood there for a second looking about the room. "Everyone is in place. Now all we have to do is sit here and wait for those fools to enter," she said, taking a seat on the sofa.

"Alright, just watch your footing going up. There are lots of broken limbs and rocks on the ground." Sid said, climbing the hill.

"It sure is dark out here," Don whispered, catching his breath next to a tree.

"Dark ain't the word for it," Bobby Ray, whispered, climbing behind Willy. "More like scary."

"Shh," Willy whispered back.

At the top of the ridge they all hunkered down under the shadows of the trees.

"Wow, not a light on," Don whispered.

"Yeah," Bobby Ray replied, feeling his knees twitching. "You think she's home?"

"It'd be nice if she had gone out for the night, but I'm not betting on it. Let's just hope the old bat is already asleep," Sid whispered. "If she is, you two better be quiet when you're searching the third floor."

Willy and Bobby Ray nodded.

"OK, now remember, keep your flashlights off until we're down in the basement," Don whispered.

"What about our ski masks?" Willy asked.

"We'll put them on down there," Sid answered. "Now," he continued, "we'll walk this ridge toward the back of the new garage and then make our way around to the side of the manor."

Everyone nodded. Sid stood up and headed that way. The three followed like Boy Scouts on parade. When Sid raced across to the garage, he holed up and looked back at three wide-eyed faces. They looked like three tree stumps kneeling in the grass. He waved them on.

When they reached the garage, Willy looked in through the unfinished, rear doorframe. "Do you believe this garage?" he whispered.

"Yeah," Bobby Ray replied, peeking in at the two car bays. "It's bigger than my house. She must be loaded."

"Trust me, she is," Don quipped.

"I guess that's why we're taking some off her hands," Bobby Ray jibed, smiling and raising his brow.

Willy shook his head. Bobby Ray dropped his smile.

"OK, are you all ready?" Sid asked, peeking out from the corner of the garage.

"Yes," they replied from behind him.

"Let's do it then," he said, running toward the side of the manor. Don took off next. Before the boys headed after them, Willy felt a tug on his arm. He turned back to see Bobby Ray's expression; he was scared.

"Don't give me that look now. Just think of all that money we're going to split with Ernie and Arnold," he whispered.

Bobby Ray heard every word. He nodded to hide his fear. *I wish I had called and told 'em I was sick too,* he thought. Willy turned and started running to catch up. Bobby Ray sighed staring at the manor. He watched Willy race up to Sid and Don. He shook his head. *Tomorrow, we could be rich, or we'll be making phone calls down at the jailhouse,* he thought, running.

When he caught up to them, they were kneeling by the basement window.

"I'll go in first. Once I drop to the floor, I want you guys to follow me," Sid whispered, looking at Willy and Bobby Ray. They nodded, feeling nervous.

"Now hold the window, Don," Sid continued.

Don held it up as Sid crawled in backward. He hung there a moment then dropped to the floor below. Willy and Bobby Ray went in next. Sid grabbed their legs and steadied them to the floor.

"Willy, get up on that crate and keep the window open for Don," Sid ordered.

While Don was making his way in, Bobby Ray slowly turned around staring into the pitch-black basement. He felt tiny prickles on the back of his neck. The moment made him flood back to all those scary movies; the ones he laughed at, trying to look cool in front of his friends. He wasn't laughing now.

Wilson was standing on the bottom step when the four slipped in through the window. He quickly turned and waved up the stairs to Benjamin. Benjamin turned and waved at Cracker. Cracker nodded and took off down the corridor.

"They're in the basement," he said, running into the parlor.

"Good," Abby replied, standing up. "Now, I want you to go hide under those stairs and don't come out until I tell you."

"What about Benjamin and Wilson?" Cracker asked, worried.

"Wilson can take care of himself. Theodore, go down and get Benjamin, quick," Abby said.

Theodore got up and headed toward the kitchen. He came back with Benjamin riding on top of his head. Abby reached down, took Benjamin off Theodore and set him on the floor. "Hurry, Benjamin, go hide under the stairs with Cracker."

"But what if you need me? I'm as mean as a Ninja Warrior," he replied, showing her a karate chop.

Abby held back her smile. "I'll yell out if I need you, now go."

Benjamin shrugged, turned and bolted for the stairs.

Abby stood up catching Theodore's eyes. "Don't even say a word," she whispered between her tight lips. Theodore kept his laughter. "Now, let's hide," she continued, looking about the parlor and then through the den.

"How about we hide inside the cleaning closet," Theodore suggested.

"That might be a good place, Madam Rose," Grandfather agreed.

Abby nodded. "You may be right," she replied. "Let's go," she continued, turning and walking toward the corridor.

Wilson jumped down from the stairs and bolted underneath them. *You just wait,* he thought, peeking out. *Tonight, you're all going to meet a witch. One very mean witch.* That angry thought made him think of Abby's great uncle the Black Knight and the warning he received from Teal, Goddess of the Sea. He quickly flashed back to seeing Abby's face change and her skin turn green. It made him worry. *Would she change completely when she had these four in her clutches?*

Sid pulled out his flashlight, turned it on and shone the light down onto the floor. The rest followed, shining their lights about the room. Willy and Bobby Ray noticed all the dust and cobwebs hanging everywhere. Bobby Ray thought back to those movies once again. His heart started pounding thinking about the movie that scared him the most. It was *'The Man with no Legs'.* His name was Michael Edison. He lived on top of a haunted hill inside a manor - just like this one. His mother was a wicked woman who would lure unsuspecting travelers up to the manor and have them stay for the night. When everyone was asleep, she would help Michael down from his bed and he would crawl to those poor souls and do all kinds of horrible things to them. That thought lingered as he stood there waiting for Sid to give the next order. He wished Sid would change his mind and head for the hills. He was wrong.

"Alright, we've already searched the basement," Sid said, putting on his ski mask. "Now when we go up, we'll be entering the kitchen. The corridor leading to the parlor and staircase is to the right."

"Are you sure you want us to use these flashlights when we get up there?" Willy asked, putting on his ski mask.

"He has a good point," Don said, slipping his ski mask on too.

"OK, we'll shut 'em off until we know she's not downstairs. Just follow me and be very quiet," Sid replied, walking toward the steps.

Bobby Ray pulled out his ski mask and looked at it. "Hurry, put it on," Willy whispered, giving him a nudge. *Oh, this is great… What about the man with no legs, the Werewolf, Frankenstein, and all those other scary creatures? I won't be able to see a damn thing with this over my face,* he thought, slowly pulling the ski mask over his head.

Wilson backed up against the wall under the steps. He cringed, feeling old cobwebs stuck to his back. When the four were heading up, he frantically began wiping them off.

Hansel slightly turned when she heard the basement door creak open. She could see dark figures walking into the kitchen. She hoped the pots and pans would remain quiet as they entered.

Sid raised a finger to his lips and then pointed toward the corridor. Willy and Bobby Ray nodded. When they walked to the door, Sid raised his hand and then peeked down the corridor into the parlor. No lights were on. He waved his hand and started down. Bobby Ray turned and looked at the enormous kitchen one more time. He was amazed at how big it was. Willy reached back and tugged on Bobby Ray's jacket making Bobby Ray jump, place a hand to his chest and sigh. Willy shook his head. Bobby Ray rolled his eyes and then prodded Willy to keep moving.

Sid held up at the parlor entrance. Don walked up alongside him and looked in. "She must be in bed," he whispered. Sid nodded, glancing back at Willy and Bobby Ray. As they walked up Sid pulled out his flashlight and aimed it at the staircase. "Turn your flashlights on as you go up, but keep them pointed down on the stairs. They both nodded. "Everyone ready?" he asked.

"Let's do it," Don whispered.

Wilson crept out from underneath the basement stairs and started jumping up to the kitchen door. When he entered the kitchen, he tippy toed over to the corridor door and peeked around the corner. All clear… He quickly headed for the hole in the staircase.

Cracker and Benjamin were staring out from under the stairs when the four entered the parlor. Grandfather slightly opened one eye. He watched the two boys head up the stairs. Sid and Don headed into the den. Grandfather looked over at Sir Henry. He had one eye open as well.

Boris glanced down when Sid and Don entered the den with their flashlights pointing toward the floor. When Don lifted his flashlight up toward him, Boris quickly raised his eyes as if he were just a head mounted on the wall.

Back in the corridor, the pantry door slowly opened. Gertrude floated out and swooped down the corridor toward the parlor. Wilson looked up to see her. He made a mad dash to the staircase. Cracker and Benjamin jumped when he entered. Wilson quickly got up on the beam and stood there alongside his friends.

Inside the cleaning room, Abby and Theodore stood there listening by the door. "We'll give them a little more time before we walk out," she whispered. Theodore looked up at her in the dark. He felt her hand come down and rub the top of his head.

"Is there anything we can do?" Rebecca asked from behind them.

Abby turned around. *I completely forgot about my cleaning crew.* "We'll see, Rebecca. I'll leave the door slightly ajar. If you hear me call out, I want you and Madelyn to block the corridor. Give them no way to escape."

"We'll have the buckets, scrub brushes and mops ready, Madam Rose," Madelyn replied.

"Good," Abby said, turning and placing her ear to the door.

Sid and Don walked through the den then entered the billiard room. Grandfather saw Gertrude hovering in the corridor. "The boys went upstairs," he whispered. She looked down at him, nodded her hood and quickly swooped into the parlor and flew up the stairs.

"I'm not liking this one bit," Bobby Ray said, taking the last steps up to the second floor.

Willy put a finger to his lips and pointed his flashlight down the hallway. There were two doors on the right and two on the left. "Come on," he said, walking toward the bedrooms.

Gertrude stopped in mid-air when she heard Willy and Bobby Ray talking.

"Let's check the two on the right first," Willy suggested.

When Gertrude heard them walking again, she floated up the last remaining steps near the ceiling and peeked around the corner. Bobby Ray was right up against Willy shining his light toward the end of the hallway. She watched Willy stop at the first bedroom door and turn the handle.

"It's open," Willy said, pushing the door inward. When they entered, Gertrude flew down the hall and hovered above the door.

"Do you believe how big these bedrooms are?" Willy gasped, shining his light about.

"Unbelievable," Bobby Ray replied, seeing the fireplace. He cast his eyes upon the closet. "Let's check in there," he continued walking over. Willy stood there watching him opening the door and shining his light inside. "It's empty," Bobby Ray said, turning around.

"I'll bet cha they're all empty on this floor."

Bobby Ray nodded looking at him in the glow of the flashlight. "Tell me, where would you hide all that money?"

"If I had that kind of money, Bobby Ray, I'd hide it under my bed. Wouldn't you?"

"Yep, that's what I'm thinking. You still want to check the rest of the rooms on this floor?"

"We might as well. We'll make it quick and head up to the third floor," he replied, walking out.

Gertrude floated up to the ceiling when the boys came out. Bobby Ray turned and shone his light back toward the stairs. "Did you hear something?" he whispered.

Willy stopped and turned around. "No."

"I thought I heard something."

"It was probably your heart pounding. I can hear it from here."

"Cut the crap, Willy. This place gives me the creeps."

"You think I like being in this dungeon? Come on, I want to get this over with," Willy spewed, turning and heading for the next room.

Bobby Ray stood there for a second listening. *Maybe it was my heart pounding,* he thought.

Back downstairs, Abby and Theodore crept out of the cleaning closet and quietly walked into the parlor. She bent over looking at the hole where Cracker and Benjamin were hiding. "Psst," she whispered. Wilson jumped down from the beam and looked out. "The men went into the den and the boys went upstairs."

"OK. I'm glad you made it back. We'll wait right here then," she whispered, standing up and stepping back inside the corridor.

Sid and Don searched the pool and billiard rooms without any luck. When they walked back into the den, Sid shone his light on the bookcases across the room. Don watched Sid's light scan down the books on both sides of the fireplace. "You thinking what I'm thinking?" Sid asked, raising his brow.

"Yeah, it's funny we didn't think of it before," Don replied. "There just might be a hidden safe behind those books," he continued. Sid thought so too. They walked over to the fireplace. "You check that side and I'll check this side," Sid whispered, shining his light on the shelves starting at the bottom.

Boris lowered his eyes watching them pulling out books as if searching for something behind them. *Maybe it's time to get this party started,* he thought.

"Excuse me," he said.

Sid and Don quickly stood up and looked at one another. "Did you say something?" Sid asked alarmed. "No," Don replied, startled. They slowly turned and shone their lights around the room. No one was there. "You did hear it, didn't you?" Sid whispered again.

"Yes, I heard someone say something," Don whispered back, feeling tingles.

Abby and Theodore heard Boris too. She devilishly smiled. *Leave it to Boris,* she thought. "You stay here when I walk out, Theodore. I'll call you when the time is right," she said. Theodore nodded.

Don slowly turned toward the fireplace. He shone his light up the bookcase and it landed on the massive moose head over the large wooden mantelpiece. Sid's eyes followed Don's light up. They both stood there for a moment staring at Boris. When they looked across at one another, Boris saw his chance.

"Is there a book I can help you with?" he asked, not looking down.

Sid and Don jumped back. They quickly shone their flashlights up at Boris again. "Did you say something?" Don asked, quivering.

Boris lowered his eyes on them. "That I did. But the question is - why are you here?" he replied, turning his head looking from one to the other.

Sid freaked seeing the enormous moose head moving and talking. Don's heart stopped, or he thought it did.

"LET'S GET OUT OF HERE!!" Sid screamed, turning and running toward the parlor.

Don's legs would not move. He stood there frozen as if his feet were nailed to the floor.

"Going somewhere?" Abby hissed, walking into the parlor alone.

Sid screamed again, shining his light on her. His eyes bugged out seeing this wretched old woman. Her face was green with a long, crooked nose and her eyes shimmered like two black marbles staring back at him. "Mrs. Rose," he gasped. "Is that you?"

"Why of course it's me, Sid," she hideously replied. I've been expecting you to come back," she continued, rubbing her hands together like a fly preparing for its meal.

Don spun around hearing Mrs. Rose's voice or what sounded like Mrs. Rose.

Upstairs, Willy and Bobby Ray walked out of the last bedroom. "Let's hurry and check the third floor. If we don't find it up there, we'll have to wait for Sid and Don before going up to the forth floor and searching the old bat's room," Willy said.

"This sucks, Willy."

"I know it does. Ernie and Arnold aren't going to be happy either," he replied, turning and heading for the stairs.

Gertrude saw her chance as the two boys made their way down the hallway toward the stairs. She quickly swooped down right behind Bobby Ray as if walking right behind him. Bobby Ray suddenly felt a rush of wind on his back. He turned his head and looked. His eyes went wide seeing a dark shadow right behind him. "RUN FOR YOUR LIFE!" he yelled, turning and slamming straight into Willy. Willy flew up against the wall and fell. Bobby Ray tripped over Willy's legs and hit the floor. Gertrude opened her cape and flew right over them and down the hallway. She quickly turned in mid-air and flew straight back at them. Willy's mind melted. He covered his head. After the thing had flown past - he screamed, "It's a ghost! The place is haunted. Run, Bobby Ray!"

Bobby Ray scrambled to his feet. He wanted to scream, but his tongue was stuck to the roof of his mouth. Gertrude caught up to them leaping down the stairs. When they came to the last landing before the parlor, they instantly froze, seeing Abby standing there with Sid and Don. The two looked like absolute fools wearing ski masks.

"It's about time you two showed up. Did you find what you were looking for?" Abby hissed, turning and glaring up at them.

Neither said a word. They just stood trembling. "Come, little ones. Come and join the party," she continued. As the boys slowly gathered their nerves, they walked down the stairs. Gertrude swooped right over their heads and hovered in the parlor. Sid and Don ducked when she flew above them.

"Isabella and Gertrude," Abby said, raising her hand beckoning them to come to her.

Isabella, her broom walked over on her bristles. Gertrude floated down and then slipped herself around Abby's body. When Abby's cape was on, she turned her attention back to Sid and Don. She could see fear in each of their eyes.

In that silent moment, Willy glanced at the front doors thinking it was now or never. "Run, Bobby Ray!" he shouted, racing between everyone. Bobby Ray took off after him.

Willy's quick reaction caught Abby off guard. She stepped back as the two raced past her. She hissed at the men then turned her head toward the foyer. Before she could speak, Grandfather spoke up. "Going somewhere?" he asked the boys trying to escape.

Willy let go of the door handles and turned around. Bobby Ray screamed looking up at the grandfather clock talking. "It's not time to leave yet," Grandfather said, wrinkling his silvery brows and staring at the boys. Bobby Ray immediately backed up. He slammed right into Sir Henry, knocking Sir Henry to the floor. "Oh, my head," Sir Henry moaned, lying there.

"Enough of this nonsense," Abby yelled. "Theodore!" she bellowed.

Sid and Don slowly turned and locked eyes in fear hearing her calling Theodore. *No...,* Sid frantically thought, seeing a large white male lion entering the parlor. Theodore growled shaking his white mane back and forth. Willy and Bobby Ray ran out of the foyer and stood next to the men. They were all shaking out of their pants as Theodore approached.

"Nice little kitty," Don quivered.

Theodore growled, showing his canines. Don stepped back with his hands raised in the air. Abby smiled seeing she had them all in a noose. "Theodore," she said. He sat down on his haunches glaring at the four.

"You two pick up Sir Henry," Abby ordered Willy and Bobby Ray. They walked over and bent down. "Careful," Sir Henry said as they lifted him upright and settled his stand.

"Are you alright?" Grandfather asked.

"Yes, just a little bruised, that's all."

Willy and Bobby Ray were utterly mystified. The whole house was alive.

"What time is it, Grandfather?" Abby asked, taking her focus off the boys.

"It's time for Theodore's dinner, Madam Rose."

Abby slowly turned and stared at Sid and Don.

"Now look…" Sid bravely started to say.

"I am looking right at you, Sid," she interrupted. "Now take off those silly looking ski masks."

After they had taken them off, Sid cast his eyes down on Theodore. His thoughts flooded back to seeing the stuffed white lion in the car, then on the staircase when they were here last. He was amused with her ridiculous antics and now he knew why she carried him everywhere she went. *She's a witch,* he thought, looking up at her hideous green face.

"Let's go out there, fellas and start kicking their shoes," Benjamin grumbled.

"Are you crazy?" Wilson scolded. "Can't you see? Abby is no longer Abby."

Benjamin turned and peeked out through the hole. He looked up at Abby all shriveled over inside her cape. It made him cringe seeing her face. It was as green as a green tomato. "Maybe you're right," he said, glancing back at Cracker. Cracker shook his head.

"I've seen all kinds of evil in my life," Abby started in on them. "But you two," she hissed, eyeing up Sid and Don, "you two are the most evil men I've ever encountered."

"Now, Mrs. Rose," Don replied, shaking. "We're sorry. We…"

"You're sorry?" she yelled, interrupting him. "You're going to stand here and tell me that you're sorry, after you two took advantage of me by stealing ten thousand dollars on the sale of this place, and now getting children to help you in your stupid little scheme of taking even more. It wouldn't be by chance that you're sorry now because you've gotten yourselves in a pickle, is it?"

Sid and Don were stunned hearing that she knew they had lied to her about the price in restoring the manor. But one thing was for certain, they also knew by her demeanor - they were in serious trouble now.

"And you two," Abby continued, walking over to Willy and Bobby Ray. She reached down and pinched Willy's cheeks together. "You're both heading down the same road as your brother, Ernie."

Willy wrinkled his brow confused. *How does she know my brother?*

"Mrs. Rose," Bobby Ray spoke up, trembling.

"Stop shaking in your pants and speak up, young man," she replied, letting go of Willy's cheeks.

"We'd just like to go home," his voice quivered.

"Go home?" she laughed.

"Yes, it's getting late."

Again, she laughed. "Why, my dear child, the fun is just about to start."

"Fun?" Willy asked, glancing over at Theodore.

"Why, of course. Now," she replied, pacing back and forth. She turned on her heels and stared at the boys. "Willy, I want you to go into the kitchen and fetch the large glass jar from off the counter. Bobby Ray, I want you to go down in the basement. Grab a box in the corner and then gather as much sawdust as you can from the carpenter's workroom. You'll see some cloth bags on the workbench. Bring one up with you."

Willy and Bobby Ray locked eyes on one another.

Abby smiled knowing their little scheming thoughts. She bent over close enough to rub noses with them. "If you're thinking of running, I'd get rid of that notion, quick."

They both stepped back. "What do you mean?" Willy asked. "Why, we weren't thinking of running Mrs. Rose, were we Bobby Ray?" he continued, worried.

"No ma'am." Bobby Ray stammered. "We weren't thinking of running."

"Really now," she hissed, standing erect. "Well, let me tell ya, I cannot only see it in your eyes, but I can also smell a plot brewing," she said and then paused. "Have you ever heard the story about B.B. Cooper?" she continued, remembering Shaun trying to tell her the story, one she already knew.

Sid and Don slowly turned their heads toward one another. Don raised his brow. *How does she know about B.B. Cooper?* he thought.

"B.B Cooper? What stories?" Bobby Ray lied, scared stiff at what she was about to say.

Abby bent over. "Come now, Bobby Ray. Don't lie to me now. You know all about B.B. Cooper and his wild story about seeing and hearing pumpkins talking up here."

Sid and Don locked eyes again. The numbers were adding up quicker than they could count. *If she knows old man Cooper and the story he's been telling, then she must have been there during that Halloween Party, put on by none other than Derek Von Haussler himself.*

"Yes, we know," Willy confessed.

"Well, let me say this only once. If you two try to leave this house, you'll both turn into pumpkins too. NOW, do as I say!" she shouted, pointing toward the corridor.

The two stepped around her, walked past Theodore and then scurried down the corridor. After they had gone, Abby stood erect and focused her attention on Sid and Don. "Now gentlemen, I have plans for you as well."

"Plans?" Don asked, worried.

"Theodore," she said. He stood up on all fours. "Now you two kneel down."

They slowly got down upon their knees looking at Theodore.

"I think it's high time you both felt what it's like to be humbled. You'll have four days to think about what you have done. Once you return to normal, you'll take the ten thousand dollars you stole from me and you'll give it to the Children's Relief Organization in town."

"We'll give it to them tomorrow, as soon as they're open," Sid pleaded.

Abby hideously laughed and then stopped when Willy and Bobby Ray came back into the parlor.

"I see you found what I asked for."

"Yes, we did," Willy replied, holding out the glass jar.

"Set the jar on the stairs and take the cloth bag from Bobby Ray."

Bobby Ray handed Willy the bag.

"Bring me the sawdust, young man."

"Is this enough?" he asked, holding out the box.

"Why of course. That should be enough for four days," she replied, turning and eyeing up the two kneeling in front of her. "Now, Willy, open that bag," she continued, reaching into the box and pulling out a handful of sawdust.

"To show you that I am a kind old woman, I will prepare your meals for the days to come."

Sid and Don were beyond words staring at the sawdust in her hand. They had no clue to what she was about to do.

As Abby poured the sawdust from her hand into the cloth bag, she started her spell. *"Up from the depth after a thousand years, slimy maggots slithered out from their lairs. One day juicy - one day not - you have four days before they all rot."*

Willy's eyes glued onto her hand as the sawdust spilled into the bag. He screamed seeing the sawdust changing into maggots. "Don't move," she said, reaching in and gathering up more and pouring it into the bag. "How does the weight feel now?"

Willy's face went flush. "I think that's enough," he gasped, feeling sick.

"Good," she replied, turning and looking at Sid and Don.

"I'm not eating them," Sid gruffly remarked.

"Oh, now, Sid, what kind of woman do you take me for? I would never force a human to eat such vulgar food. However," she said, lifting one long finger and tapping it on her chin, "I know just the creature who would love such a meal like this," she continued.

Don stared at Sid. "You care to guess," she asked, seeing the horror on Don's face. "No," he replied, not wanting to look up at her.

She walked over and bent over Don with his head down. "Frogs just love a juicy mouthful of maggots," she whispered, standing back up.

"Frogs!?" Don gasped, feeling his stomach tighten.

"That's right. I think you two would look rather nice as big, fat bullfrogs."

"Now wait a minute," Sid yelled, getting up.

Theodore snarled stepping closer to him. Sid fell back onto his knees shaking.

Abby raised her hand and then pointed at them. *"Whispering winds from a den of fools - slithering through a slimy pool,"* she wickedly hissed. *"Up from a muddy river bog - you two will now become big fat bullfrogs." WHOOSH...* Sid and Don disappeared.

Willy screamed. The lights in Bobby Ray's head went out. He hit the floor with a thud. "Bobby Ray!" Willy shouted, kneeling by his side.

"Theodore," Abby said.

Theodore walked over and licked Bobby Ray's face. Willy jumped back with fear of the big cat. Bobby Ray came to.

"What have you done to Sid and Don?" Willy asked, sitting on the floor.

"You'll see," Abby replied, turning and focusing at the clothes lying there.

"Hey, where am I?" Sid muffled from underneath his pants.

"I don't know. I can't see a thing," Don muffled back, fighting the clothing off and jumping out.

Willy's eyes went from dime size to silver dollars staring at Don and then seeing something moving inside Sid's pants. Bobby Ray sat up wiping his forehead. "What happened?"

"You passed out," Willy replied, keeping his eyes glued on Sid's clothes as Sid leaped out.

"What in the world?" Bobby Ray gasped, looking at the frogs sitting there.

"Sid?" Don gasped.

Sid looked at him and screamed.

"You two get up," Abby ordered Willy and Bobby Ray. She turned toward Sid and Don. "You two will remain frogs for four days," she said. "Now, Willy," she continued, "Pick them up and put them inside that jar."

"Four days?" Sid yelled, panicking.

"That's right. I'm giving you four days to think about what you have done," she replied, glaring at them.

"What are we going to do, Sid?" Don asked

"You'll do as I say, or you'll remain frogs forever," Abby snapped.

"What about our wives?" Sid asked.

"Well," Abby replied, "as far as your wives are concerned, you've both dug your own holes. My only advice to you is to stay inside your bathtubs. It'll be safe there and the maggots won't be able to get out."

Don's head felt light. Sid felt even worse with that thought - *eating maggots.*

"Now pick them up and place them inside the jar, Willy."

Willy did as she asked. Abby walked over and looked down into the jar.

"Remember, gentlemen, those maggots will start rotting in four days so eat as many as you can. On the fourth day, you'll turn back to normal. When you do, you'll follow my instructions and turn over that money you stole. You understand me?"

They both looked up and nodded.

"Good. Now," she said, looking at Willy, "hand Bobby Ray the jar and come over here."

Willy followed her to the sofa. "Take this back along with Sid and Don's clothing and shoes," she said, picking up the bags.

"What is it?"

Abby leaned over close to his face. Willy cringed looking at her. "These are your brother's and Arnold's clothing and boots."

Willy wrinkled his brow. *My brother and Arnold are waiting for us on the road out back.* She saw the confusion in his eyes. "Your brother and Arnold paid me a visit before you all came tonight. It seems those two were in a much bigger hurry in getting their hands on my money than you four imbeciles. But don't you worry none, I am sure they'll find their way home sooner or later."

"Did you..?" his voice trailed off.

"Yes, they have two days to think about their criminal behavior. As for you two," she continued, standing up and looking back at Bobby Ray. "Let this be a lesson to you both. No good comes from evil. Now, take this warning: if you say one word to anyone, just one word, you'll both turn into pumpkins every Halloween night for as long as you live."

Willy swallowed. Bobby Ray's mind went blank.

"I mean it, boys," she snapped.

"Yes, Mrs. Rose," they replied in unison.

"Now leave my house," she said, pointing toward the corridor.

Willy quickly gathered the clothing and shoes on the floor. "Theodore, see them out," she ordered.

The two hurried down the corridor. Bobby Ray set the bags down and opened the door for Willy. As they left, neither one of them looked at Theodore.

"Good riddance to you too," Theodore huffed, turning and walking back through the corridor.

"Come on, Bobby Ray," Willy said, taking the cement steps down to the yard. "Let's get out of here before she changes her mind."

"Hey, be careful. You're tossing us around like ping-pong balls in here," Sid yelled from within the jar.

"Sorry," Willy replied, stopping and waiting for Bobby Ray - who looked like he had just finished doing a week's worth of grocery shopping carrying those bags.

"This is madness - absolute madness!" Don spewed.

"You're telling me," Sid croaked.

"Are you going to make it down the hill carrying all that?" Willy asked Bobby Ray.

"I hope so. If not, I'll toss 'em. I just want to go home."

"No, you're not tossing my clothes," Sid yelled.

"What are you going to do about it?" Bobby Ray spat.

"Now, you wait one minute, smart butt," Don said.

"Willy, dump the jar and let's walk home. Their wives can sit back there all night for all I care," Bobby Ray snapped.

Willy looked down inside the jar.

"Don't do it, Willy. In four days, I'll have your little hide," Sid swore.

Willy laughed. "You're finished, Sid. Your days of screwing people are over. So just shut up."

Sid swallowed hard. He wanted to protest, but refrained. He knew these kids would dump them out on the grass and leave.

"Just get us to the car," Don pleaded.

"OK," Willy replied, looking up at Bobby Ray. "Let's go. I want to get home too," he said, turning and walking toward the ridge.

It was rough going down. Bobby Ray slipped twice and Willy almost dropped the jar. When they got to the road, they looked across to see Sue and Betsy nervously standing there.

"Let's go ladies," Willy shouted, running across.

Betsy looked back toward the hill. "Where's Sid and Don?" she asked.

"They're inside the jar."

"WHAT!?" Betsy yelled. "Stop playing foolish games with us!"

"I'm not kidding. Mrs. Rose is a witch," Bobby Ray replied.

"Cut the crap, Bobby Ray. We don't have time for jokes right now. Where are Sid and Don?" Sue scolded.

Willy looked down inside the jar. "You two want to tell 'em?"

Betsy and Sue locked eyes on the jar. They froze seeing two fat bullfrogs sitting inside. They screamed watching one turn its head and start talking. "He's telling you the truth."

Betsy's face went three shades whiter. Sue stepped back. "Oh my God!" she gasped, clutching her face.

"These are their clothes along with Ernie and Arnold's."

Sid and Don glanced at one another. They slowly looked up at the bags.

"You little weasel!" Sid fumed.

"It doesn't matter now, Sid," Willy replied. "My brother and Arnold are now out here somewhere hopping around."

"Them too?" Betsy gasped alarmed. "You're telling us that Mrs. Rose is a witch?"

"Yes," Willy and Bobby Ray replied.

Betsy glanced up and stared at the hill.

"Come on - let's get out of here!" Sid yelled. "We'll tell you everything when we get home."

Betsy looked down. Her reality was slipping.

"Hurry!" Sid yelled.

Betsy snapped out of her thoughts, turned and opened the rear passenger door. "Place the bags in the back seat and give me that jar," she said, turning and staring at Sue, who for all practical matters was not there anymore. She was somewhere over the rainbow.

"Sue," Betsy scolded.

Sue blinked and looked at her. "You can lose your mind at home. Right now, we have to get the hell out of here."

Sue gathered herself. She quickly raced around to the other side of the car. When they were in, Betsy reversed out and then punched the gas. Gravel and dust flew up from her tires as she fishtailed down Old Tiller Road.

Willy and Bobby Ray stood there with blank expressions watching Betsy drive away. When they were finally out of sight, Willy looked over at Bobby Ray. "You remember me saying that I thought I heard my name being called?"

Bobby Ray took his eyes off the road and glanced over at him. "Yeah," he replied.

"I'll bet-cha that was my brother."

Bobby Ray pondered that. "You think they're still out here?"

"I don't know," he replied, turning toward the barn. "Ernie," he yelled. Nothing… "Ernie, are you there?" Nothing…

"Where do you think they went?" Bobby Ray asked, casting his eyes out over the field.

Willy thought for a moment. “The dam. I betcha they’re at the dam. That’s where I’d go.”

“With all those snakes down there?” Bobby Ray questioned.

“Maybe you’re right,” he replied, walking over to his bike. “Let’s go to my house and sit out back on the steps. They could have made it back by now. If not, we’ll check the dam tomorrow.”

Bobby Ray nodded. He walked over and picked up his bike. “You know we can never tell a soul,” Willy said, getting on his bike.

Bobby Ray gazed into his eyes for a second. Nothing had to be said between them as they stood there straddling their bikes on that old dirt road - in the middle of the night - contemplating their dilemma.

31

Good and Evil

After they were gone, Abby stood there in utter dismay. No one dared to speak, not even Benjamin who had jumped down from the beam with Wilson and Cracker and walked out from underneath the staircase.

In all my years of being a witch, I have never used the gift of magic to perform evil, Abby thought. *My father never did either, except when he turned two drunken warlocks into pumpkins until they became sober enough to fly home.*

She glanced down at her green hands and long spindly fingernails. After reaching up and slowly pulling back her hood, Benjamin swallowed seeing her face. Theodore cast his eyes down to the floor.

"Madame Rose," Sir Henry said from behind her.

As Abby turned still in deep thought, Grandfather glared at him for speaking out. Sir Henry lifted his chin as if he were royalty. The mice, Theodore and Isabella waited to hear what he had to say.

"Yes?" Abby said.

"There are times when one has to take a stand regardless of the outcome. You were right in what you did."

Abby sighed. Her shoulders went slack, like air escaping from a balloon. Grandfather pondered Sir Henry's advice. He could tell by Abby's posture that she accepted his reasoning. In that despairing moment, it felt like all the bad air in the room was gone. Grandfather no longer despised Sir Henry for being a highly educated buffoon. Sir Henry felt the same way about Grandfather. Even though Grandfather was a simple-minded, old windbag, he was still a dear friend.

As the room remained silent, Benjamin got up the nerve and walked over to Steinbeck. He tapped on one of the music bench legs. "Play something for us," he softly asked, looking up at the piano. Everyone turned toward Benjamin. He stood there with an uplifted brow. Abby smiled as sweet music filled the air. Theodore walked over and noticed her color start to change as she knelt down and hugged him. Wilson and Cracker walked over, climbed on Theodore's head and smiled at her. She kissed the top of each of their heads.

"Hold it right there!" Benjamin spewed. "What about me!?" he continued, walking over. Abby picked him up and laughed. "Who could ever forget you?"

"Like maybe the whole world," Wilson quipped.

"Now, Wilson," Abby half-heartedly scolded.

"I was just kidding," he replied, holding out his hand so Benjamin could climb up onto Theodore's head. "What am I around here, a bus that you can hop on and ride?" Theodore said, rolling his big blue eyes.

Abby laughed. They all laughed as well. Boris, however, wasn't amused. He was stuck on the wall in the other room. "Excuse me," he said.

Abby turned her head. *Oh dear,* she thought. *We almost forgot Boris.* She strolled over and stood under the archway. "I'm sorry Boris. You are a big part of this family too. You did a terrific job."

"Thank you, Madam Rose. You should have seen the look on their faces."

Theodore walked into the den and stood right underneath Boris with the mice on his head. Boris looked down into his blue eyes. "We were all impressed with you Boris for starting this party," Theodore said. Boris smiled. *Yesterday, I would have been lunch to him. Today, however, Theodore is a very kind and wonderful protector,* he thought. "Thank you, Theodore."

"I wish you could have come down from that wall and booted them out of the house with those big antlers of yours," Benjamin added.

Everyone laughed.

Abby stopped laughing, feeling this overwhelming sensation. The power of her magic felt stronger than ever. *They all changed into frogs,* she thought. *Is it possible without my father's Potion and Spells book that I could change one more thing without it?* She spun on her heels looking up toward the staircase while thinking of Tasha. "Come, gather around. I have one more spell to give tonight," she said, walking back toward the staircase.

Theodore turned around confused. Grandfather and Sir Henry were confused as well. As Theodore walked back into the parlor with the mice, Abby closed her eyes while raising her hands in the air. *"Clouds of darkness, clouds of light, bring me the power that will ignite. Cast these words up on the wind and let life begin,"* she chanted, turning in a circle. After Abby stopped turning, she called out to Tasha.

Up in the master's chambers, Tasha, the stuffed female lion, was lying there on the rug in front of the fireplace. The wind outside began to howl. The bay windows blew open. A shimmering green fog rushed into the chamber. Three little fairies appeared within the mist. They flew down around Tasha sprinkling stardust on her head. Tasha's little body began to stretch. Her legs started to grow. The fairies then tapped their wands upon Tasha's head. A million little starbursts shot out from their wands like a miniature Fourth of July over Tasha. WHOOSH.... Tasha instantly came alive. She opened her eyes. The fairies smiled with delight and then disappeared.

Tasha stood there watching the mist swooping out of the chamber through the rear bay doors. When the mist disappeared into the night, the bay doors slowly closed. Tasha cocked her head confused. Taking a step forward, she fell like a newborn. She tried again. Her legs felt weak standing up.

"Tasha," she heard someone calling. She stared at the door leading out to the hallway. "Tasha, come down here," Abby called out again.

As everyone stood there anxiously waiting. Theodore felt his heart pounding. He could not even imagine seeing Tasha walking down the stairs as a real lioness.

Tasha blinked her big brown eyes, listening. *Who are they calling?* she thought, staring at the chamber's door. *Is it me? Am I Tasha?* She took a step forward. Her legs felt stronger. She walked toward the door and peered down the dark hallway. "Tasha, my dear child, come down here please," Abby again shouted.

Tasha's eyes lit up. *It's me. I must be Tasha,* she thought, walking into the hall. Every step she took her strength grew stronger. She stopped at the stairs looking down.

Abby lowered her hands and turned. "On the count of three I want everyone to call out her name. One, two, three… T A S H A!" they all yelled.

The beautiful lioness raised her ears. She smiled with delight heading down. When she came to the last landing, everyone sighed. She was as beautiful as a princess. Tasha immediately glued onto Theodore. He was truly handsome and breathtaking to look at.

"Tasha," Abby whispered.

Tasha slowly peeled her eyes off him and looked at Abby. Wilson, Cracker and Benjamin glanced down at Theodore from atop of his head. Hearts were fluttering out of his eyes. They could tell that Theodore was gone to never-never land. Wilson nudged his friends to climb down to the floor before Theodore melted like butter on a hot spoon.

Tasha opened her mouth to speak.

"Come now," Abby said. "You have the power to talk."

"I'm confused," Tasha softly replied.

Abby nodded. "You will be for awhile, my dear," she said, shifting her attention back on her friends. "Let me introduce you to your family," she continued. As she went to introduce Theodore, Theodore's eyes were glued onto Tasha. "This is Theodore. He is lord of the house."

Lord, Tasha thought, *he looks so enchanting.*

"Good evening, Tasha," Theodore greeted her in a big husky voice, while bowing his head.

She slowly bowed hers, not knowing what else to do.

"These three here are Wilson, Cracker and Benjamin," Abby said, pointing down to the floor.

The three all stood there in a row smiling up at her. "And you are called?" Tasha asked.

"We are called mice," Benjamin replied, stepping out of the group. He cupped his little hands together. "However, you can call us the three musketeers if you like," he whispered.

"Will you cut with the nonsense?" Wilson scolded, pulling him back into line.

Abby laughed. Theodore rolled his eyes with embarrassment.

"We are all so pleased to meet you, Tasha," Wilson said with a beaming smile.

"Likewise," she replied, taking the stairs down.

Theodore melted watching her stroll down to the floor. His eyes caught her long tail going this way and that. It made his heart race.

Abby turned in a circle as Tasha walked around the group. Tasha stopped in front of Isabella. Isabella curtsied before her. It scared Tasha making her jump back. "Her name is Isabella. She means you no harm," Abby said, smiling.

Tasha raised her head to Abby. "And she is?"

"She is my magical broom."

Tasha slowly nodded.

"Now there are several more you must meet," Abby said, walking over and standing in front of Grandfather. "This is Grandfather. He's the time keeper and supervisor.

"Good evening, Madam Tasha. It is so nice to meet you."

"Good evening to you too," Tasha replied. "Tell me, Grandfather. What is time?" she asked.

Grandfather looked at Abby. Abby nodded for him to answer. "Well, it may be confusing at first, but let me try and explain it this way to you, Madam

Tasha. Time is a number, which we place on each moment. We call them seconds, minutes, hours and days. There are sixty seconds in one minute - sixty minutes in one hour - and twenty-four hours in one full day. There are three hundred and sixty-five days in a year."

Tasha's mind tried to gather it all in. It went in OK, but it all became a jumbled-up mess.

Abby reached down and rubbed her head. Tasha looked up at her more confused than ever.

"All in good time, all in good time, my dear. Now, let me introduce you to Sir Henry," she said, turning toward the elegant wooden coat rack.

Tasha gazed at the tall thin object.

"Good evening, Madam Tasha," Sir Henry greeted her.

Tasha jumped back again not expecting it to talk.

"Forgive me if I startled you," Sir Henry said. "I am Sir Henry, a humble servant of King Louie the Third of England."

"King Louie the Third?" Tasha repeated, cocking her head.

"Yes, my dear. I come from royalty."

"My, my," Tasha replied, turning in a circle seeing all the faces looking back at her. "I must say, this is a bit of a surprise to me."

Theodore saw his chance. He stepped up alongside Madam Rose.

"Madam Rose," he said.

"Yes, Theodore?"

"It is getting late. I am sure we can continue this tomorrow. Right now, if I may, I'd like to escort Tasha outside onto the ballroom patio and allow her to get some fresh air."

Abby gazed into his eyes. She slowly smiled, knowing Theodore's thoughts. "I suppose you're right, Theodore. It is getting late. Tasha if you wouldn't mind going with Theodore while the rest of us go to bed?" she said.

"I wouldn't mind that at all," Tasha replied, eyeing up the handsome big cat.

Abby saw the look. There was love in the air. "Alright then," she said, turning. "The rest of us are going to bed now."

Wilson, Cracker and Benjamin stood there watching Theodore and Tasha strolling through the den toward the ballroom outer doors. Benjamin's eyes were fixed on their tails swinging back and forth in unison. "You know, fellas," he started to say, keeping his eyes on their tails, "I think Theodore's in love."

"You don't say," Wilson jibed, watching the two exiting the den. "I knew the minute Tasha came down those stairs."

"Well," Cracker spoke up, turning toward his comrades. "We'll never be chased by *him* again. Not in his condition."

"What condition?" Benjamin asked.

Cracker raised his brow. "Love sick. Yes, I've seen it many times."

Abby looked down and smiled hearing this little conversation.

"You have? When was this?" Wilson asked, folding his hands.

"You remember that beautiful lady that sang for Max the piano player in New York?"

"Yeah."

"Well, as you know, he was marvelous on stage, but I noticed that he always turned into a bumbling idiot after the show while strolling with that woman back to their dressing rooms."

Wilson glanced at Benjamin. They both turned and looked into the den where Theodore just escorted Tasha through. "I'll sock him in the eye if Theodore starts walking around here like a bumbling idiot now that Tasha is here," Benjamin scolded, cupping his little paw into a fist.

Abby laughed. "It's time for bed, gentlemen" she whispered.

"Abby?" Benjamin said.

"Yes, what is it?"

"Can we ride Isabella up to the master's chambers?"

Abby again laughed.

"On one condition."

"What's that?" Wilson asked.

"No horse playing."

"Horse playing? Why, I would never play with a horse. Those things could crush us in a second," Benjamin replied.

"Cut the crap," Wilson spewed, slapping his arm. "Horse playing means fooling around. Right Abby?"

"That is correct," she replied. "Isabella," she said, "take these three to the master's chambers."

Isabella lifted off the ground and then floated down toward the floor. When the three climbed on top of her bristles, she glided up the stairs.

"Wow, this is fun!" Benjamin shouted.

"Yeah," Cracker added.

Abby contently stood there until Isabella had gone. She turned and bid goodnight to Grandfather, Sir Henry and Boris and then strolled down the corridor toward the elevator. When she stepped inside, four names popped into her thoughts: Arnold, Ernie, Sid and Don. *Maybe Sir Henry was right,* she thought. *Regardless of the outcome, those four needed a lesson.* She leaned back and sighed. *Tonight, I used my magic for evil and then for goodness,* she thought, thinking of Theodore and Tasha. When the door opened to the master's chambers, her heart felt lighter. *Love sick,* she thought, remembering Benjamin's remark. *His condition was much worse than that. Theodore was dancing on the moon, over her.*

32

A Startling Discovery

The following morning, Abby awoke in a ray of sunshine. She quietly slipped out of bed not wanting to wake the mice who once again had nestled together on the pillow next to her. When she opened the bathroom door, Brenda turned and greeted her. "Good morning, Madam Rose. Will you be taking a bath this morning?"

"Good morning, Brenda. Yes, a nice warm bath sounds refreshing.

"Shall I add your favorite spice?"

"You ask me that all the time, Brenda and I always say by all means," she replied, smiling and taking off her nightgown. Brenda sighed. The water felt warm as Abby stepped inside the tub. "We had company last night," she said, sitting and lying back.

"You did?" Brenda replied. "Was it Shaun?" she hoped.

"No, it was the same men who came the first time."

Startled, Brenda straightened her long neck looking down at Abby.

"What happened?"

"I turned them into frogs."

"In the world beneath the sea…" Brenda started to say.

"I know, I know. I saw my own skin turn green and I am well aware if Teal were here right now she'd be highly upset with me."

Brenda nodded.

"You know," Abby continued and then paused. "After I did it, I felt this overwhelming sensation last night."

Brenda knew why. When the gift of magic was used for evil, evil always comes knocking.

"However," Abby said, taking Brenda out of her thoughts. "I turned it around."

"You did?"

"Yes. I used it for goodness."

"How?"

"I made Tasha come alive."

Brenda lifted her eyes.

"You should have seen Theodore," Abby beamed. "He looked like a schoolboy when Tasha came down."

"Can she speak?" Brenda asked.

"Yes."

"My, my. Your power is much stronger than I realized, Madam Rose."

"I was taken aback a bit myself. Oh, you should see Tasha though. She's the most beautiful lioness on the planet."

"And the mice?"

Abby turned and glanced up at her. "I think they're smitten with her too."

"You don't say?"

"Yes. They even think Theodore's days of chasing them are finally over."

Brenda smiled knowing Madam Rose was probably right, now that Theodore had a companion, one that would keep him in line. As Brenda was thinking, she thought she heard a noise coming from outside. "Do you hear that?"

"Yes, that sounds like a truck. The workers must be here to finish the garage. They only have the side and back doors to install and the two roller doors in the front."

"When do you expect Shaun?"

"I don't know, Brenda. I am hoping he comes out today. I sure miss him."

Brenda contentedly smiled. She wanted to ask how it was going between the two of them without sticking her beak in. A thought popped into her head.

"I'm sure he misses you as well."

There was a moment of silence and then Brenda heard Madam Rose sigh.

"I sure hope so," she finally said, picking up the bar of soap and washcloth.

"I am sure he does. You'll see. Everything will work out just fine," Brenda added.

"I wish I had your confidence, Brenda. Our times together are only short and sweet."

"Then you'll see only sweeter days ahead."

Abby laughed as she finished washing and then allowed Brenda to rinse her off. Stepping out of the tub, Abby grabbed her towel and then looked back at her beautiful swan. "Do you honestly think he'll ask me to marry him?" she said, drying off.

"Why of course. You are too irresistible," Brenda replied with a sly wink.

"Oh, you go on now with that talk. I'm a very old lady, Brenda my dear."

Brenda cocked her head. "Not forever. Your day is coming, Madam Rose."

Abby sighed placing the towel on the rack and slipping into her robe.

"Have a good day, Brenda," she said, opening the door and walking out.

Brenda watched the door slowly close. She sighed wishing she had the power to turn into a real swan. *If I could only get up the nerve to ask her,* she thought, turning her long neck and looking out the window. The sun was out and the air smelled fresh. *To be out there instead of being cooped up in this bathroom would be heaven sent.* She turned toward the door. *Madam Rose,* she thought, pondering the name. *I sure wish she'd let the house call her by her real name - Madam Von Haussler. But then again,* her thoughts twirled, *Shaun could change everything. Madam Von Haussler could rightfully become Madam Stevenson.*

After getting dressed, Abby walked over to the chamber bay doors. Her heart leaped right out of her chest seeing Shaun unhooking Wilfred from the service station's tow truck. She stepped out the doors and walked up to the cement balcony stanchion. Shaun looked up to see her standing there. He waved. She waved back. "I'll come down," she called. Shaun nodded, taking off the chains. He walked back and released the hoist lowering the car.

"Hurry, get up," Abby said panicking. "Shaun is here," she continued, looking over at the rug where Theodore and Tasha should be sleeping. "Oh, dear," she gasped.

"Good morning Abby," Wilson said, standing up and yawning.

"Good morning. I need you three to go downstairs and have your breakfast."

Benjamin opened his eyes. "Did someone say breakfast?" he yawned.

"Yes, dummy, now wake up Cracker and let's go," Wilson replied, jumping down from the pillow.

Abby sighed watching the three hightailing it off the bed and run down the hallway. She raised her hands in the air. "Sleep children sleep," she said, clapping her hands together.

Downstairs on the rug in the den, Theodore and Tasha instantly turned into stuffed toys. Grandfather, Sir Henry and Boris closed their eyes. Abby then hurried toward the elevator and stepped inside. When the door opened to the main floor, she rushed down the corridor and entered the kitchen. Hansel was sleeping next to the sink. She quickly walked over, opened one of the cupboards, and pulled out a box of oatmeal cookies for her mice. She crumbled them up in a bowl and set it on the floor. With that, she opened the kitchen door and walked out onto the patio.

Shaun had already pushed Wilfred inside the garage when she entered.

"Good morning, Shaun," she greeted him with a big bright smile.

"Good morning, Abigail," he replied. "I brought Wilfred back along with some tools."

She looked over his shoulder at Wilfred and then gazed into Shaun's eyes. "You found a hole in the gas tank?"

"Yes. I was amazed I got all the way back into town before he ran out of gas. Here, let me show you," he replied, walking back to the rear of Wilfred.

"Boy, this place is something else, Abigail."

"It sure is," she beamed, looking about the interior. "Now, let's take a look, shall we?" she continued. She stood there watching Shaun stick his finger into a little rusty hole underneath the gas tank. "It's about the size of a dime."

"I see," she replied, allowing her eyes to roam across Wilfred. *All these years of driving without a drop of gas,* she thought.

"I brought some tools to remove the tank," he said, taking her out of her thoughts.

"That's great."

"I was going to do it at the station, but I wanted your permission first," he continued.

"Well you could have done it there, however, thinking of me was kind of you."

Shaun blushed. *I've been thinking about you more than you know*. That thought made him feel an odd sensation, one he had never felt before. Abby noticed the longing look. "Is there something else wrong with Wilfred?" she asked, worried.

"Oh no, I was just thinking."

"About what?"

He laughed to hide his embarrassment.

"Go on, tell me now. Let's have no secrets between us."

That caught him off guard. "Well," he replied and then paused, slipping his hands inside his front pockets.

"Well - now that's a deep subject," she said, smiling.

Shaun cocked his head and sighed, "Abigail?"

She raised her brow. "Yes, Shaun," she retorted.

"I missed you yesterday."

Abby stepped back catching her breath. "I missed you too, Shaun," she replied, looking into his beautiful blue eyes.

Shaun glanced down at the floor. Abby could tell by his boyish reactions that there was more to this. "I don't know how to say this," he said, looking up.

She tilted her head and waited.

"I really like you a lot," he continued, shoving his hands deeper inside his pockets and leaning his weight on one foot.

Abby caught the nervous two-step, well, that's what she called it when men clammed up and began fidgeting in front of a woman. *If they only knew that their body language spoke louder than their words,* she thought. "Well, Shaun, as I said, let's have no secrets between us, and with that, I must admit I like you a bunch too. You're a very sweet young man," she replied. "One day you're going to make a beautiful lady very happy."

Oh, dear, Wilfred thought behind them. *This boy's in love and doesn't know how to say it.*

As her words fluttered inside Shaun's head, he didn't know what to say next. *I could date many girls right now. Pretty ones too,* he thought. *However, none of them has the wisdom of Abigail.*

"You seem to be somewhere over the rainbow," she said, taking him out of his thoughts.

"I was just thinking."

"I noticed you do a lot of that, Shaun" she replied. "So, tell me, what's really on your mind today?"

Shaun removed his hands from his pockets. He reached up and ran his fingers through his jet-black hair. "Has anyone ever told you that you are as clever as a fox?"

Abby laughed. "Yes, lots of people. It comes with age. One day you'll be as clever as one too."

Shaun nodded. *How stupid was that?* "Well, I better start working on that gas tank. I sure hope I can repair it down at the station. If not, we'll have to order a new one."

"Do what you can. By the way," she replied. "The contractors will be out to install the doors."

Shaun turned and looked back. "They did a great job, Abigail. Plenty of room and the work benches look fantastic," he said, facing her.

"I am glad you like it. Now, I won't keep you any longer. Please come up for lunch or if you want something to drink. You know where the refrigerator is," she replied, turning and walking back toward the manor.

Shaun stood there watching her leave. He looked down and felt his sweaty palms with his fingers. He sighed knowing something inside of him just changed. Something he had never experienced or felt before. It made no sense. *How can I be smitten with an older woman - one that is old enough to be my grandmother?* He dropped those thoughts, turned around and headed into the garage.

"Now, let's see if I can remove this tank," he said, walking alongside Wilfred. He reached underneath and placed his fingers on one of the nuts. "That's a nine sixteenth," he said, walking over to his toolbox. With the wrench in hand, he crawled underneath the car and removed four nuts. "OK, that should do it," he said, crawling back out and setting the wrench down. As he tried to pull the tank off - it would not budge.

Wilfred sat there amused. *You thought you could simply take me apart,* he thought.

"Hmm," Shaun said, letting go and walking around the side of the car. He tried pulling the tank away from the rumble seat. "You have to be kidding me," he fumed. "The rumble seat has to come out."

Wilfred sighed.

Ten minutes later, Shaun finally had the rumble seat bolts removed. He lifted out the back portion and set it on the workbench. He then climbed up on the outside running board and lifted the seat portion. To his surprise, he saw an old cloth pouch. "Well, what do we have here?" he questioned, lifting the seat out and placing it on the workbench.

Oh my, Wilfred thought thinking back in time. He remembered the Baron coming out one day and speaking with his mechanic about his rumble seat. The next thing he knew the mechanic was removing the seat. He did not know why then, but he had an awful feeling now. *It has to be the Potion and Spells book,* he thought, listening to Shaun.

Shaun turned around, picked up the old cloth pouch and opened it. There was an old book inside. He pulled it out. "The Black Knight," he whispered, looking at the eerie eye in the middle surrounded by snakes and what appeared to be a mermaid swimming in the ocean at the bottom of the book. "What is this?" he questioned, opening it and flipping the pages. "They're all rhymes or riddles," he said.

Oh no, we're in trouble, Wilfred panicked.

"*Howling winds from across the sea - slithering creatures roaming free, come up from the depths and out of the dark...* " Shaun began reading one of the spells aloud.

Wilfred cringed. He knew something awful was about to happen. *Do something before it's too late,* he thought. He quickly opened his eyes and sounded his horn. Shaun jumped backward startled, looking at Wilfred. "What in the blazes?" he gasped, holding the book to his chest. After catching his breath, he walked over, set the book on the workbench and stared at Wilfred. *What made the horn go off?*

Abby heard Wilfred's horn too. She looked out the kitchen window. Shaun was nowhere in sight. *He must be still fiddling around in there,* she thought, turning and walking out of the kitchen.

Shaun walked over to the horn. He shook his head. *That's odd,* he thought, *I've never seen that happen before.* He walked back, removed the gas tank and then secured it on the tow truck. When he came back inside, he picked up the book, placed it inside the cloth pouch and then headed up to the manor. As Shaun walked into the kitchen, he called out, "Abigail."

"I'm in the parlor, Shaun," Abby replied, raising her brow to the mice.

"Be quick. Hide underneath the sofa," she whispered.

She heard Shaun whistling down the corridor. It made her smile. Her smile disappeared when he walked in with something in his hands. "I found this underneath the rumble seat," he said, sitting down next to her.

Abby glanced down at the cloth pouch and then up at him. "It's a book filled with all kinds of rhymes or riddles," Shaun said, pulling it out.

Abby almost lost her breath staring down at the eerie eye. *It's the Potion and Spells book,* she thought, completely stunned. "Well, I'll be," she replied, keeping her composure. "Let me see that."

Shaun placed it in her hands and then watched her slowly open the cover.

"Have you ever seen this before?" he asked.

She hated to fib. "No. Maybe my father placed it there before he gave me the car for my birthday," she replied, turning the pages.

Shaun nodded. "Well then, maybe it was meant to be a surprise. You know, something you'd discover years later, perhaps. Was he that kind of a father, surprising you with things like this?"

Abby raised her brow. "He did give me all kinds of surprises. One of them was Theodore," she replied, thinking. *Of all the places to hide it father, you had to hide it there.*

"I can remember when my dad gave me my first pocket knife. He hid it inside the back pocket of my jeans. It wasn't until I put them on that I discovered it."

Abby closed the book looking at him. "That's a creepy cover, don't you think?" he said, glancing down at the book.

Abby lifted it up in front of them.

"Who is the Black Knight?" he asked.

Abby laughed. It was all she could do to hide her fear of answering his questions. A thought quickly popped into her head. "Wow," she replied and then paused, gazing at him. "I didn't even look at that when I opened the book. The Black Knight was someone my father made up. It was one of his favorite characters when he told me bedtime stories."

"The Black Knight? I suppose your father liked telling you stories about princesses too. What little girl doesn't like those types of stories?"

"Well actually," she replied, thinking back. "The Black Knight was a legendary Knight who was first servant to the King of Austria. He would sail across the oceans on wild sea adventures seeking trade with other countries."

Shaun laughed. "Your father sounds as if he had an awesome imagination."

"That he did, and I loved all his bedtime stories."

"I guess he also liked telling you rhymes?"

"Yes, he was really good at it too. After he had left this world, I wished I had written them all down. And now," she said and then paused looking down at the book, "it looks like my father did it for me."

"I wish I had met him, Abigail. He sounds like a wonderful man."

"He was at that," she said, "are you hungry?"

"Now that you ask, yes," he replied with that boyish smile.

"Come then," she said, setting the book down beside her and getting up.

"Let's go and have some lunch, shall we?" she continued.

After they had walked out of the parlor, Wilson, Cracker and Benjamin stuck their heads out from underneath the sofa. They slowly turned their heads gazing into one another's eyes. "Our mission is over, fellas," Wilson said. Cracker smiled thinking of his prank on Benjamin. He turned toward him and started his made-up chant. "Ooga booga - Ooga boo..."

"Go on with that nonsense," Benjamin spewed, folding his arms. "I'll never fall for one of your pranks ever again."

33

A Whirlwind of Activities

That same morning, Molly awoke still in a haze. She spent the whole night lying in bed worrying about Willy and Bobby Ray and then imagining seeing the whole town ignite like the Fourth of July once they discovered Sid and Don's evil plot to steal Mrs. Rose's money. She rolled over and looked at her clock - 7:00 a.m. "Oh no," she said, sitting up. "Willy!" she shouted, getting out of bed. After getting dressed, she crept out of her bedroom to see if her parents were up. They were still in bed. She quietly walked into the front room and picked up the phone. "Good morning. Is Willy there?" she asked his father, Ted.

"No, Molly, Willy and Bobby Ray went fishing this morning."

"Fishing?" she replied, stunned. *After last night,* she thought. *I thought they'd all be in jail by now.*

"Yes. I'm sure if you hurry you'll catch them down by the river."

"Are Ernie and Arnold with them?"

"No, I suspect Ernie stayed the night over at Arnold's house."

Something's wrong, unless, she thought, *Mrs. Rose did not call the Sheriff on them.* "Where did they say they were going fishing?" she hastily asked.

"Down by the dam."

"Thank you, Mr. Myers," she replied and then hung up. She walked into the kitchen and wrote a note stating that she had gone fishing with Willy. On the way out the door, she grabbed an apple from off the counter, placed the apple inside her mouth and ran down the back-door steps.

At six thirty that morning, Willy and Bobby Ray went fishing alright, but not for fish. They went down to the dam looking for two frogs. When they came to the small path leading to the dam, they got off their bikes. The only sounds they could hear were the morning birds and the river rushing over the dam.

"Do you really think they're down there?" Bobby Ray asked, pushing his bike behind Willy.

"Like I said," he replied, turning his head, "that's where I'd have gone."

Bobby Ray shrugged. When they got to the dam, they laid their bikes down in the tall grass. Willy walked out and stood on a large boulder overlooking the dam.

"Be careful, Willy," Bobby Ray said.

"I'll be fine," Willy replied, looking down at the water and slippery rocks. The dam below was a ten-foot drop. He slowly waded into the water. It was cold and filling his shoes fast. When he got to the middle of the dam, he shouted, "Ernie!" Nothing came back but the sounds of the birds. "Ernie, it's me, Willy," he shouted again.

Ernie opened his eyes inside the overflow pipe. "Psst," he whispered, nudging Arnold. Arnold opened his eyes. "What?"

"I thought I heard something."

"It was probably your stomach growling. I'm starving, aren't you?"

"Shh... listen."

Arnold looked toward the opening. All he could see was the morning sunlight streaming through the tree branches on the opposite bank.

"Ernie!" Willy shouted.

"I told you they weren't here, Willy," Bobby Ray yelled, taking a seat on an old tree stump.

"It's Willy," Ernie excitedly said, hopping toward the opening.

"Wait for me," Arnold yelled, hopping after him.

When they got there, they spotted Willy standing in the middle of the dam. The water was rushing over his shoes.

"We're down here, Willy," Ernie yelled.

Willy's ear picked up the little voice. He started scanning the area below. His eyes bugged out seeing two large bullfrogs sitting just inside the pipe.

"Ernie, is that you?"

"No, it's little red riding hood, stupid. Get us out of here."

Bobby Ray quickly stood up. He almost slipped into the water from the shock of seeing one of the bullfrogs talking. *It's Ernie and Arnold,* he thought, wading across the dam.

Willy ran across, jumped down on a small bluff and then jumped again down to the riverbank. His shoes sank deep into the mud as he made his way toward the overflow pipe. He stared at his brother and Arnold in shock. "What happened last night? I thought you two were going to stay at the car?" he asked.

"Your clever brother had a gut feeling Molly was lying about her being sick and was going to tell that wicked witch," Arnold spewed.

"Will you shut up! She did go up there to warn that witch," Ernie scolded.

"She did?" Willy asked, confused.

"Yes," Ernie replied. "She squealed like a pig. We caught her right as that wretched witch opened the door for her. So, what happened to you guys?"

"Molly wasn't inside the manor when we showed up," Willy replied, wrinkling his brow.

"Trust me, she was there. So what happened?" Ernie pushed.

"That witch turned Sid and Don into frogs," Willy answered. "She then told us that she did the same to you and Arnold. That's why we're down here this morning. I thought you'd pick this spot to hide."

Ernie shook his little green head. "Didn't you hear me calling you last night near the barn?"

Willy froze. "I knew it, I knew it…"

"You knew what?" Arnold interrupted.

"I knew someone was calling my name. I thought it was just a barn owl or something."

Ernie rolled his large green eyes. "So why didn't she turn you two into frogs?"

"I'll tell ya why," Bobby Ray said, walking up.

Ernie and Arnold glanced at him. "She warned us that if we ever told anyone she'd turn us into pumpkins every Halloween night for the rest of our lives."

Arnold and Ernie stared at one another. Old man Cooper popped into their thoughts.

"That's not the only thing. We watched her change sawdust into maggots for Sid and Don to eat," Willy gasped.

Arnold's stomach turned over. "You're kidding me?"

"No, she did," Bobby Ray replied.

"So, tell us what happened with you two?" Willy asked.

After Ernie had told them what had happened, Willy sighed. "So, you took my soft air pistol. How stupid was that?"

"Listen here, bird brain," Arnold spat.

"No, you listen here, frog breath," Willy shot back. "It seems Molly was the only one smart enough to back out of this whole stinking mess."

Ernie and Arnold sat there listening. They were more than in a stinking mess, they were going to be frogs for one more day.

As the four were talking, none of them heard Molly walking up with her bike on the other side of the dam. "Willy!" she shouted.

Willy and Bobby Ray quickly spun around. They looked at her with scorn. "I think you have a lot of explaining to do," Willy shouted back.

Molly felt the anger in his voice. It startled her at first. *How do they know?* she thought. "I'm sorry, Willy. I just couldn't go through with it. So, who told you?" she asked, thinking it was Mrs. Rose.

Willy and Bobby Ray stepped away from the pipe. Willy then pointed at the two frogs sitting there. "They told us," he shouted.

Molly looked at the frogs. "You hit your head or something this morning?" she laughed.

"That's my brother and that's Arnold," Willy shouted.

Molly again laughed. "You two are really funny."

"They're not joking, Molly," Ernie yelled.

Molly let go of her bike in shock. The bike fell over in the tall grass.

"That's right you little squealer!" Arnold yelled. "See what you've done?!"

Molly gasped reaching up and holding her hands over her mouth. The color in her face washed out. Everything then went dark and she crumbled into the tall grass alongside her bike.

"Oh, that's great," Willy spat, looking back at his brother. "You made her pass out. Now what are we going to do?"

"You're going to take us home, that's what," Ernie spat, shifting his green eyes on Bobby Ray. "Bobby Ray, go over there and wake her up. When she's feeling better take her home."

"Take her home? Are you crazy?" Willy spewed. "She'll tell her parents."

"Willy might be right, Ernie," Arnold said, worried.

Ernie sat there fuming. "Alright… Bobby Ray, go over there and wake her up. We'll have her come with us. Now, let's get out of here. I need something to eat."

As Bobby Ray took off along the riverbank, Willy picked up his brother and Arnold and followed Bobby Ray. After making their way across, Willy placed his brother and Arnold inside a bucket next to his bike. "Wait here," he said, looking down.

"We're not going anywhere with all them snakes out there. Just hurry up," Ernie scolded.

Willy shook his head. He walked over to where Molly was lying in the grass. Bobby Ray was kneeling beside her. “Molly, Molly - wake up,” Bobby Ray said, gently slapping her face. Her eyes slowly opened. “What happened?” she mumbled.

“You passed out.”

“I did?”

“Yes.”

She quickly sat up. Her head was still spinning. “Did I really hear those frogs talking?”

“Yes,” Willy replied, standing there. “You know that nice old lady you went and squealed to,” he started to say. Molly looked up at him. “She’s a witch,” he continued.

Molly shook her head in disbelief. “She, she, she can’t be, I was there,” Molly stammered.

“You were there. We know you were there. So, what happened?” Bobby Ray asked, sitting beside her.

She looked at him and then squinted up at Willy. After she told them everything that had happened, she cupped her chin and stared at the ground still puzzled.

“So, you simply fell asleep?” Willy asked, not wanting an answer. “Have you given it any thought that maybe she put you to sleep so you wouldn’t see what she was going to do to my brother and Arnold?”

Molly sat there staring at the ground. She slowly shook her head trying to grasp it all. She turned her head and glanced over at the bucket. “Maybe,” she said and then paused, “All I can remember is standing alongside Mrs. Rose while your brother was pointing that stupid toy gun at her. The next thing I knew I was waking up,” she replied.

Willy tossed his eyes on Bobby Ray. “Should we tell her?”

Bobby Ray wrinkled his brow confused. “You know,” Willy said and then he paused, nodding at Molly, “what Mrs. Rose said she’d do to us if we told anyone?”

Bobby Ray raised his brow. He turned and stared at Molly. “She said that if we told anyone, Willy and I would become pumpkins on Halloween night for the rest of our lives.”

Molly sat back. Her thoughts landed on old man Cooper. “Did she mention B.B. Cooper?”

“Yes, she knows all about him,” Willy spat.

"Oh dear," Molly gasped. "You think Fanny told her about him?"

"I don't know. Maybe she did," Willy said.

"Oh, dear is right," Ernie yelled. They all turned and looked at the bucket.

"We'd better get going," Willy said, walking over to his bike.

"Are you three enjoying yourselves?" Arnold asked.

"We're going home now," Willy replied. "Come on you two, we can talk back at the house," he continued, picking up the bucket and securing it to his handlebars.

Bobby Ray and Molly slowly got up. "What are we going to do?" she asked.

"Nothing."

"What do you mean nothing, Bobby Ray? How are we going to get Ernie and Arnold back?"

"The spell is only to last two days. They've been frogs for one so far. But Sid and Don, well, they're going to be frogs for four days."

Molly's mouth dropped open. "Sid and Don?" she gasped.

"Quit the gas bagging," Willy interrupted, getting on his bike. "We'll tell you back at the house."

"Come on, let's get out of here," Bobby Ray added, walking over and picking up his bike.

As they rode their bikes back to Willy's house on the other side of town, two women were sitting in a front room pulling out their hair.

"What are we going to do?" Betsy grumbled underneath her breath, sitting on Sue's couch.

"I don't know," Sue replied, pacing back and forth in front of her. She walked up to the front windows and stared out.

Betsy sat there waiting. *One second longer and I'll scream,* she thought, looking at Sue staring blindly out the windows. "We have to do something," she said.

Sue just stood there.

"Did you hear me?"

"Wait a minute," Sue replied, placing her hands to her hips. "Wait one cotton picking minute," she continued, spinning on her heels.

"I'm waiting."

"Claudia."

"Claudia? What does that overweight pompous woman have to do with this?"

Sue looked down at her. "Blue hair, that's what," she replied, walking over to the couch.

Betsy laughed. "That's why I don't let Flo come within an inch of my hair."

"I'm not talking about Flo," Sue replied, sitting down next to her.

"What do you mean?" Betsy asked, searching her eyes.

"Who else was there?"

Betsy's face went flush. She sat back and sighed. "Are you thinking…" her voice trailed off.

"Yes, we know those two never liked each other from day one. I seriously think Mrs. Rose did it," Sue replied.

Betsy closed her eyes. A haunting vision came back to her. "My dress," she whispered.

Sue's mouth hung open. "Oh my, I never thought of that," she replied and then paused, thinking back to that awful day.

"Those two bozos up in the tub said that witch knew they stole her money. I betcha she knew before the county fair," she continued.

"Oh, sweet lilies," Sue replied, sitting back and placing her hand to her mouth.

"Sweet lilies my backside!" Betsy gasped. "How about dried up old lilies? That vile creature made my dress fall apart right in front of the whole town."

"We have to report this," Sue said.

"Yeah right," Betsy laughed.

"No, I mean it. We have to go to the Sheriff."

"Are you serious? You want to go and report this to Sheriff Bumble and his sidekick Deputy Stumble?"

"I don't think we have any choice, regardless what you think of Sheriff Collins and Deputy Oxford. That woman is evil!"

Betsy stood up. She turned around and looked down at Sue. "You heard our husbands," she snapped, pointing up the stairs. We can't tell anyone. That evil witch will cast a spell on all of us."

Sue laid her head back on the sofa and rolled her eyes. *My poor husband,* she thought. *He's up in our tub eating maggots. I don't think I'll ever want to kiss him again.*

Betsy could tell by the expression on Sue's face that she was somewhere out in space. "What has crawled inside your head?" she asked.

Sue blinked and looked up at her. "I was thinking of kissing Don."

Here we are, up to our necks in trouble, and she's thinking about kissing Don. Betsy's thoughts unraveled.

Sue saw the expression on Betsy's face. "I can already taste those maggots," she said, wrinkling her nose.

Betsy glanced over at the staircase thinking of Sid up there in that bathroom and eating those maggots too. *I don't think I'll kiss him for a year after this.* That thought made her angry. She slowly turned toward Sue. "You know what could happen to us if we do tell someone?"

Sue gave that some thought. "Are you asking me what I think the town will do, or what Mrs. Rose will do if we tell someone?"

"Well, now that you put it that way - both."

"Well," she started to say, fiddling with her fingers. "I really don't know. The whole idea scares me now."

"You just said that you wanted to go to the Sheriff."

"Yes, I know."

"Well? You do or you don't. Which is it?" Betsy asked, walking up to the front windows and staring out. "I don't know," she heard Sue reply from behind her. She tightened her lips thinking. Then suddenly a light went off inside her head. She spun around. "Where is your computer?"

"My computer? Why?"

"I think we should do some research."

"What do you want to do research on, nutritional frog recipes?"

"Don't be stupid. I want to look up the law on witchcraft. I am sure we'll find something."

Sue's eyes lit up. "Come on. It's in the study," she replied, getting up and racing toward the room.

Ten minutes later, they found what they were searching for. "Will you look at that?" Betsy beamed, pointing at the computer screen. Sue stared at the heading - Pennsylvania Ordnance 33; Section Ten - Witchcraft - dated 1812. It read:

> *The use of witchcraft, black magic, casting spells - and any other form of mid-evil rituals is/are prohibited in the state*

of Pennsylvania. All violators caught will receive a maximum penalty of five years in jail and a one thousand dollar fine.

"Well I'll be," Sue gasped, thinking back in time. "Hey wait a minute."

"What?"

"You remember B.B. Cooper telling that story about when he was a kid?"

A question mark appeared on Betsy's forehead.

"Come on, you remember," Sue pushed.

"Are you talking about the story of him and his friends seeing pumpkins talking during one of Derek Von Haussler's Halloween parties?"

"Yes."

"Oh, come on now," Betsy replied. "Everyone knows that B.B. Cooper was just spinning a yarn. You don't believe…" she said and then froze.

Sue smiled seeing Betsy adding it up. "If that were true, then Baron Von Haussler was a warlock, which means… No...!" Betsy gasped. "This can't be happening again?"

Sue glared at her. "Just imagine if B.B Cooper's story were true? Don't you think it's a bit odd that we have another witch living in that old manor up there?"

Betsy peered into Sue's eyes. She could tell that Sue was steering toward the unimaginable idea that the two were somehow connected. "Are you thinking that maybe Mrs. Rose is one of Derek's relatives?" she asked.

"I don't know, but something has me spinning."

"I can see that. You're biting your nails again."

Sue looked down at her fingers inside her mouth. She never even realized she was chewing on them. "So, what should we do?" she asked, checking her nails.

Betsy sat there studying Sue's face. Sue looked like a child not wanting to go to her first day of kindergarten. "Well… we're not going to just sit here biting our nails. I think we should go over and talk to Claudia."

Sue's eyes grew wide. It was the last thing she wanted to do. "Are you crazy? You seriously want to get that oversized bus involved?"

"Look, if we're going to do this, we'll need all the ammo we can get, and Claudia is a whole box of ammo if you ask me."

"What about Don and Sid?" Sue asked, worried.

"Just leave that to me. Come on," she replied, getting up. "Let's go see how those two bozos are doing. They probably need a little more water to keep them moist."

"Oh, you're something else," Sue replied, getting up.

"Yoo whoo..." Betsy said, opening the bathroom door and looking down at Sid. "How's my prince charming doing?" she asked, smiling.

"Oh, you're real funny my sweet lily pad. I am just fine sitting here watching these maggots crawling all over the place."

Sue stepped around Betsy and glanced down at Don. "Don't say a word," he said, looking up.

"Alright, we need to go out for awhile," Betsy said, sitting down on the side of the tub.

"Where are you two going?" Don asked.

"Shopping," Sue replied.

Betsy quickly glanced up at her. Sue smiled back and then focused her attention on Don. "Would you like us to get something while we're out?"

"Yes, that would be great. How about a large pepperoni pizza?"

"Yeah. Like you two need that," Betsy scolded, standing. "I'd imagine the pepperonis alone would bloat you two even more," she continued, turning for the door.

"Gee, no kiss?" Sid asked.

Betsy turned around. *No way,* she thought, thinking of Sue's comment downstairs. She placed her hand to her mouth and blew him a kiss. "When you're back to normal you'll get a real one. Now let's go, Sue," she replied, walking out.

Sue looked down at Don. She blew him a kiss, as well.

"That's it?" he fumed.

"That's all you're getting from me," she replied, waltzing out the door like a summer breeze.

"Do you believe this?" Don moaned.

"I wouldn't kiss you either," Sid replied, shaking his head.

"Look who's talking, fatso."

As the women pulled into Claudia's driveway, Sue gushed all over the dashboard. "So, this is how a banker's wife lives."

"You haven't seen anything yet. Just wait until you step inside."

"I don't have to. Just look at that lawn, the flowerbeds and that pretty gabled awning before the garage. What kind of flowers are those?"

"They're called creeping roses," Betsy sarcastically replied, pulling up and parking. "OK, now remember, I'll do the talking," she said, opening her door.

Sue got out and shut her door. She stood there a second, admiring the beautiful creamy yellow house with the long veranda and decorative window trimming.

"Are you coming or are you just going to stand out here with your mouth wide open?" Betsy scolded, walking up to the door. "The mailman just might mistake you for the mailbox and shove the letters inside that gaping maw of yours."

"Funny, that's really funny. Now are you sure we're doing the right thing?" Sue retorted, walking up behind her.

"You started this and now we're going to finish it," Betsy replied, knocking.

The door opened. They both smiled at the big woman.

"Hello, you two. This is a surprise," Claudia greeted them.

"Morning, Claudia. We're sorry for coming over without calling," Betsy replied.

"Oh, that's alright," she said, looking at Sue.

"Hi, Claudia," she greeted her still holding her smile.

"Hello, Sue," she replied, shifting her eyes from one to the other. She noticed the restrained expression on their faces as if they had some gossip to unleash. Her ears were already burning to hear what they had to say. "Well, won't you come in?" she said, opening the door and stepping aside.

"Thank you," Betsy said, walking past her.

"Let's go sit in the lounge. I have a nice sofa and couch," Claudia said, escorting them through the front room.

"Wow," Sue beamed, looking at the beautiful fireplace.

"You like?" Claudia asked over her shoulder.

"Do I like? I lovvvvve ittt!" Sue gleamed.

Betsy turned and looked at her. Sue zipped her lips and proceeded on.

"Now, would you two like something to drink?" Claudia asked, walking into the lounge at the back of the house.

"Tea would be great," Betsy replied, checking out the backyard through the bay windows.

"Please take a seat. I'll just be a moment."

They quickly sat down on the sofa and stared at one another. "Relax," Betsy whispered. "I'm sure she'll believe us."

"I hope so, or we'll be laughed right out of Cloverdale."

"Here you go," Claudia said, walking in and handing them each a cold glass of iced tea. "So, what brings you here, or should I guess?" she continued, sitting down on the couch opposite them.

Sue slowly turned toward Betsy. With that, Claudia knew Betsy was going to be the one to tell her.

"Well," Betsy said and then paused, "I really don't know how to say this, but it's something that will blow your mind."

"I knew it! I just knew it!" Claudia replied, slapping her leg. She sat back with a big bright smile. "Isn't it funny how you can tell when someone has gossip brewing inside their head and they can't wait to spit it out? Well, I saw it in both your eyes before letting you in. Go ahead, tell me now. What happened?"

Claudia drooled. *There was nothing better than good county gossip,* she reckoned.

"It's about Mrs. Rose," Betsy sighed, setting her iced tea down and crossing her legs.

"Mrs. Rose?" Claudia said thinking of all the people that she thought it could be. She was over the moon to hear that name roll off Betsy's tongue, but she held back her delight. "What could that little lilac be up to these days?" she continued, barely containing herself.

Betsy turned and looked at Sue for a moment. Claudia shifted her eyes to Sue. *She certainly looks nervous,* she thought. "I don't know how to tell you this," Betsy repeated her words.

Claudia sat up folding her hands on her lap. *This better be good,* she thought. "I'm listening."

"She's a witch," Betsy quickly said.

Claudia's face contorted. That statement caught her off guard. Before she could compose herself, Sue confirmed Betsy's statement. "She is," Sue added. In a flash, Claudia watched Betsy twist in her seat and slap Sue's leg.

"Ouch," Sue scolded, turning toward Betsy.

"Shh," Betsy replied.

Claudia looked at the two women sitting across from her now staring at one another. "Ladies," she said, getting their attention. "You came all the way over here this morning to tell me that Mrs. Rose is a witch. I mean a real witch?"

They both nodded. Claudia glanced from one to the other and then started to laugh. The women just sat there stone-faced; no smile, no laughter… nothing. "You must be pulling my leg," Claudia continued, laughing.

"We're not," Sue boldly stated, sitting up.

Claudia stopped laughing seeing the look in her eyes. She shifted her eyes on Betsy. S*he's not kidding either,* she thought.

"Maybe I should say this next before we go on," Betsy said and then paused, "blue hair."

Claudia's facial expression suddenly changed as if she were actually pondering that notion. However, a moment later Claudia just sighed. "Are you two telling me that it was Mrs. Rose who turned my hair blue? Because if you are, I know Flo did it on purpose, or I suspect she did."

Sue frowned. "Maybe we should just tell her, Betsy."

"Tell me what?" Claudia quickly asked.

That sharp remark, 'tell me what', sent Betsy scrambling. *There's no way out of this now,* she thought, feeling Claudia's beady little stare. She quickly picked up her iced tea, took a sip and set the glass back down. "Can you keep a secret?" she asked.

"You know I can."

"No. I mean a real big secret."

"Betsy, how long have you known me?"

Betsy sighed.

"Whenever you're ready," Claudia pushed, sitting back.

Of all the lame brained ideas, Betsy thought, fixing her eyes on Claudia. *If she goes shooting her mouth off, we'll all be heading to jail.* "OK, now what I am about to tell you could land us in some very hot water and what I mean by hot water is jail."

"Jail?" Claudia gasped.

"Yes, now please."

"What have you two gotten yourselves into?" Claudia sarcastically asked.

Betsy sat back and sighed. "Let me say this as politely as I can," she said and then paused. Claudia knew she was about to be slapped before Betsy struck her. "Claudia, for once in your life I want you to shut up and listen for a minute."

Sue almost fell out of her seat with that comment. Claudia released the air from her lungs. That slap almost knocked her right to the floor. Betsy sat there mad, not caring how Claudia felt. "Now let me say this while you sit there and compose yourself, Claudia. What I am about to say is true and you must swear that you'll not tell a soul."

Claudia slowly nodded thinking, *you little twit.* The only reason she did not get up and order them out of her house was the look in Betsy's eyes. *OK, I'll take that slap,* she thought, *but this better be good.* "You have my word, Betsy. I'll tell no one."

Betsy sat back and started her story. At the end, she mentioned Claudia's blue hair again and her own dress falling apart at the county fair and that she suspected it was Mrs. Rose who did it.

Claudia just sat there looking at the two. *Not a twitch, not even a slight smile,* she thought. *The house came alive... Sid and Don are now frogs and they suspect Ernie and Arnold left the manor the same way.* "I don't know what to say," she finally replied, dumbfounded.

"It's all true," Sue replied. "Sid and Don are in my bathtub right now. Also, Willy and Bobby Ray said that they were going to go down to the river this morning to try and find Ernie and Arnold."

Claudia's mind unraveled. The whole thing sounded so surreal to her. She looked at Betsy. "Theodore, that stuffed lion…" her voice trailed off. "You're telling me he came alive?"

"Yes," Betsy replied. "Sid and Don said that they melted into their shoes when they saw Theodore walk out into the parlor."

Claudia shook her head. "The Grandfather clock, the coat rack and the moose head?" she questioned, raising her brow.

"Look, Claudia. If your husband was sitting inside your bath tub right now as a frog and telling you this, wouldn't you believe him?" Betsy sternly replied, folding her arms.

Claudia went to speak. Sue raised her hand. Claudia closed her mouth. "I would love to take you over to my house right now and show you our husbands, but we can't. They have no idea we're here. Besides that, they'd never forgive us, right Betsy?" Sue said. Betsy slowly nodded.

Claudia sat there for a moment feeling her whole world spinning out of control with the notion that Mrs. Rose was a real witch. She stood up and walked over to the window.

Sue glanced over at Betsy. Betsy rolled her eyes. A thought then popped into Betsy's head. She looked over at Claudia. "Do you remember B.B Cooper's story about seeing those pumpkins talking?"

Claudia turned around. “Yes, I’ve heard his story. He’s nothing but an old windbag. He probably smells even worse.”

“What if it were true?” Sue questioned.

Claudia placed her hands on her hips. “What’s that got to do with this?”

“Everything, maybe,” Betsy replied.

Claudia walked over and sat back down. “Go on,” she replied, still spinning inside.

“As Sue and I were discussing our dilemma...,” she started to say.

“Dilemma?” Claudia laughed, interrupting her. She immediately stopped laughing seeing the anger in Betsy’s eyes. “OK, go on.”

“Anyway, while Sue and I were talking we remembered B.B. Cooper’s story. If B.B. Cooper is telling the truth, that would mean Derek Von Haussler would have been a warlock. With that idea, we did some research on witchcraft.”

“I’m not seeing the picture,” Claudia replied, confused.

“Alright, let’s see if I can paint one for you,” Sue stepped in. “As we all know, Derek Von Haussler was a famous magician, right?” Claudia nodded. “OK, now let’s pretend that B.B Cooper is telling the truth, which would mean Derek wasn’t a magician at all. He was a warlock and he was using his magic spells to thrill his audience.” Claudia went to speak. Sue raised her hand. “I’m not finished, Claudia. Let’s keep pretending, shall we? If Derek was a warlock, don’t you find it a bit strange that another witch just happens to come along and purchase the manor?”

Claudia started seeing the picture. Her thoughts quickly cycled back to Derek and then spun forward when Sue mentioned another witch purchasing the manor. “Are you suggesting to me that Mrs. Rose…?” her voice trailed off trying to imagine it.

“Yes,” Betsy replied. “We think Mrs. Rose is one of Derek Von Haussler’s relatives.”

Claudia closed her eyes. The bottle of rum sitting inside her kitchen cupboard popped into her head. *It would take the whole bottle to believe this,* she thought, opening her eyes and looking at them. *There is only one way to believe this nonsense,* she thought, standing up. “Alright, let’s go.”

“Go where? You’re not thinking of going to the Sheriff, are you?” Sue asked, worried.

“No, my dear. You’re taking me over to your house right now. It’s the only way I’m going to believe this story.”

“What?! You must be joking?” Sue gasped. “We can’t. Right, Betsy?”

Before Betsy could agree, Claudia placed her hands on her hips and glared at them. "Did you honestly think that you could come over here and tell me something like that without showing me proof?"

Betsy and Sue looked at one another. It was written all over their faces - *how stupid can we be?* Betsy thought. Claudia caught the look between them. She knew she had them in a jam. "You two better take me over there right now, or I'll go over there myself and bust down the door if I have to," she warned.

The two sat there numb, not knowing what to say. "Let's go, ladies. The day is wasting," Claudia ordered, walking out of the room. They slowly stood up and followed Claudia through the lounge.

Claudia opened her front door for them to walk out. "Take in some air girls. It's not the end of the world you know," she said to their frowns.

"It will be as soon as Don sees you," Sue moaned, walking toward her car.

Claudia grabbed her coat, walked out and shut the door behind her.

After getting into the back seat, she sensed the somber mood between the women up front. She tossed her eyes on Betsy and then glanced over at Sue. In that moment, she felt a strange feeling wash over her. *This could be a prank,* she thought, *a cruel prank. Why... the whole town could be there waiting to see us driving up.* She could even imagine them all laughing knowing she fell for it.

That thought made her worry. *I could be the laughing stock of Cloverdale as soon as we pull in.* She beaded her eyes on Sue and Betsy thinking - *these four clowns are setting me up. How simple would it be to place two frogs inside the tub and start talking to them and then Sid and Don walk out from one of the bedrooms upstairs and start laughing.* She wanted to say something then realized Sue was turning onto her street. She looked down the road. There were no cars and no people out front. She sat back and sighed.

After Sue had pulled into her driveway, she said, "Alright now, Betsy and I will go up and talk to them before you see for yourself."

"Not on your life, Sue. The three of us are going up together," Claudia replied, thinking it was a prank.

Sue glanced over at Betsy. Betsy rolled her eyes. The all got out and walked up to the front door. Claudia took off her coat as she entered and hung it on a hook. "Follow me," Sue said, heading toward the stairs.

As Claudia proceeded up, her thoughts were dead set that it was a prank. *If they think they can get away with this,* she thought, *they have another thing coming.*

"We're back," Sue said, opening the door to the bathroom.

"What took ya so long?" Don replied.

Claudia immediately stopped in the hall when she heard the little voice. Betsy turned around. The two stared into one another's eyes. "You said you wanted to see this for yourself, Claudia," Betsy whispered. Claudia just stood there, hesitant to move. Betsy sighed, turned and walked in. "We've got company, gentlemen," she said, looking down inside the tub.

"What do you mean we have company?" Sid barked.

Sue glanced at the open door waiting for Claudia. "You might as well come in," she said. A puzzled expression appeared on Sid and Don's faces. "I thought we told you two not to say a word to anyone," Sid fumed, staring up at as his wife.

"I'm sorry, dear," Betsy replied. "But we had to do something," she continued, turning and waiting for Claudia to walk in.

"Who is it?" Don asked.

"It better not be Molly," Sid grumbled.

Sue sighed. She walked back out. "You said that you wanted to see this, so you'd better come in and take a look."

Claudia gazed into Sue's eyes. She knew that what she was about to see would shock her to the core. Taking a deep breath, Claudia walked up to the door and looked down inside the tub. The color in her face washed out seeing two frogs looking up at her. Her mind completely melted. She staggered back, placed her hands over her mouth and then slowly slid down the opposite wall toward the floor. "Oh jeepers, will you look at this?" Sue spat, placing her hands on her hips.

Betsy walked out. "Get some water, will ya, Sue?" she sighed, looking down at Claudia as white as a bed sheet.

Sue walked in, grabbed a glass and filled it. "Here you go," she said, handing it to Betsy. Betsy knelt and placed the glass to Claudia's lips.

"Here, take a sip and relax."

Sid and Don sat there looking at one another. "Of all the people, they had to tell her," Sid grumbled.

"Well it doesn't matter now, Sid," Don replied. "I hope you like being a frog because once that witch finds out that our lovely wives went and shot their mouths off…"

"Will you two shut up?" Sue interrupted him.

"Well, go ahead and get mad. I'm just telling you the truth. If Mrs. Rose finds out that you told someone, we'll all be sitting inside this tub for the rest of our lives," Don yelled back.

Sue shook her head in disgust. She turned around and looked down at Claudia sprawled out in the hallway. "Claudia," she started in on her, "I think you said something about coming over here and busting my door down to see this. Now stop acting like a child and get in here."

Claudia drank the water, handed the glass back to Betsy and slowly got up. "Are you feeling any better now?" Betsy asked, looking into her eyes.

"No," she replied, taking a step toward the door. She placed her hands on the doorframe and glanced down inside the tub again.

"You like what you see?" Sid asked her.

Claudia felt faint seeing two fat bullfrogs and maggots crawling everywhere. "Cat got your tongue?" Don snidely asked.

"I'm, I'm...," she stammered.

"We're freaking out too, Claudia," Betsy spoke over her.

"Now do you believe us?" Sue asked.

"Yes, but give me a moment, will ya?" Claudia replied, feeling her head in a cloud.

"Come on you two," Betsy said, leaning over and picking up Sid. "Grab Don and we'll go downstairs and talk. I think Claudia would prefer a couch instead of hugging the doorframe," she continued, carrying Sid out.

Sue leaned over and picked up Don. "Let's go," she said to Claudia, walking past her.

Claudia placed her hand over her mouth while staring inside the tub. She felt her stomach lurch looking at all those nasty maggots. She quickly turned and proceeded down the hallway toward the staircase.

After everyone sat down inside the front room, Claudia asked for something to drink. "What would you like?" Sue asked, setting Don down on the arm of the couch. Claudia looked over at him and then shifted her eyes on Sid.

"Something stronger than iced tea," she replied.

"We have a bottle of whiskey," Sue suggested, walking toward the kitchen.

"Great, add some color to it, thanks," Claudia replied.

"I wouldn't mind a shot myself," Don said. "How about you, Sid?"

Sid glanced over at him. "I think it would be best if you just shut up," he replied, turning and staring at Claudia.

"Now boys," Betsy spoke up, looking down at Sid in her lap.

"Forget the coloring - I'll take it straight up," Claudia firmly requested, trying to hold onto reality.

"Suit yourself," Sue replied.

"A tall glass, please," Claudia added.

Sue turned and nodded. "How about you, Betsy?"

"Water for me, thanks."

When Sue returned, she handed Claudia and Betsy their drinks, and then sat down next to Don.

There was a moment of silence within the room before Sid spoke up. "I suppose you want to hear our story."

"We told her," Betsy said, petting him.

Claudia just sat there slowly shaking her head. *A frog actually talking,* she thought. *I'll never be the same.* "Claudia," Sid said, bringing her out of her thoughts. "Yes, yes - they did tell me, but I'd like to hear it from you two, if I could," she replied.

Sid started at the beginning when Mrs. Rose pulled up in front of the real estate agency with Theodore sitting on a suitcase full of money in the back seat of her car. Twenty minutes later, he ended his story with Willy carrying them out of the manor inside a jar. Claudia simply sighed not knowing what to say.

"Well," Betsy angrily said.

Betsy's tone of voice made Claudia mad. *Of all the lame brain ideas,* she thought. *How recklessly stupid can one be?* "You four," she yelled, shaking her head at them sitting there wearing frowns, "you're idiots for wanting to rob anyone." Betsy went to speak. Claudia raised her hand. "And furthermore," Claudia continued, "you're worse than those maggots upstairs for getting kids involved, especially that little girl."

Betsy almost fainted hearing that. *The sheer audacity,* she thought, peering into Claudia's eyes. She did not like what she saw. They were little balls of flames staring straight back at her. Betsy sighed feeling more than the heat from those eyes. She felt disgusted knowing that Claudia was right. To make herself feel a tad better she tried to blame it on their husbands. "Alright… OK… they were stupid for coming up with this idea."

"They were stupid," Claudia interrupted her. "You and Sue could have said *no* when they came up with this train wreck."

"That's enough," Sue angrily scolded. "It's over, so let's all just relax, shall we? We need to figure out what we're going to do now."

"We're going to do nothing," Sid said, glaring at Claudia. *That over sized bus has some nerve,* he thought.

"What do you mean nothing?" Betsy asked.

Sid turned sideways and looked up at his wife. "Don and I only have three more days and we'll return to normal. As far as I am concerned, I'd like to drop the whole thing right here and now and go on with our lives."

Betsy sighed.

"Betsy, look on the bright side, at least we're not sitting in jail," he added.

Claudia sat back listening to these fools.

"Go on with the rest of our lives?" Betsy fumed. "You'd like for us to just go on with our lives with that witch in town?"

"What else can we do? I mean look at us," Don spoke up.

"I'm with Betsy. However, I think we have a bigger problem," Claudia interrupted this little conversation.

They all stopped talking and looked over at Claudia.

Claudia sat up in her seat. "It's Molly we should be worried about right now." The four sat there pondering that. "Do you think she'll go to the Sheriff?" Sue asked.

"I don't know," Claudia replied. "I think it would be wise to talk to Willy and Bobby Ray first and hear if they've spoken to Molly. Besides, we may need those two boys down the road."

"If you're thinking Willy and Bobby Ray would want to get involved, I highly doubt it now. Not after that awful witch warned them both that she'd turn them into pumpkins every Halloween night for the rest of their lives if they spoke to anyone about this," Sue replied.

What the hell is going on here? Sid thought. "Am I missing something?" he asked.

The women stopped talking. "I guess you are," Betsy replied. "Well, fill me in please," Sid said.

"Claudia, Sue and I are thinking about reporting Mrs. Rose to the Sheriff for performing witchcraft," Betsy replied.

"Now wait a minute," Sid scolded. "I just told you that all I want is for us to just drop it right here and now. No one is going to the Sheriff."

"Sid is right," Don added. "How do we report this to the Sheriff without telling him that we went up there to steal her money? We could all end up in jail."

Once again, silence filled the air as the group sat there thinking. *How do you come forward with a story without saying you weren't involved?* Claudia thought. She sat back pondering that when an idea came to her. "Wait a minute," she said.

Everyone stared at her waiting to hear what she had to say.

"If we do report this," she continued," it'll be your word against Mrs. Rose."

"Our word against hers?" Don repeated.

"Yes," Claudia replied, seeing a way of catching that witch. "You two said that you looked up the Pennsylvania law on witchcraft, right?"

"Yes," Betsy replied. "It's from eighteen twelve."

"Eighteen twelve?" Sid laughed. "Really now… you honestly think they'd use that law to try and convict her?"

"They might," Claudia replied.

"Wait a minute," Don interrupted.

They stopped talking.

"You're not thinking of taking this to court, are you?" Don continued, looking at Sid.

"Why not? She's a witch and performing witchcraft is against the law in this state," Betsy replied.

"Do you honestly think we can get away with the break-in?" Sid asked.

"That's the biggest hurdle we have to get over, but if we can find a way, I think we have a case against her," Claudia replied.

"Our word against hers, I don't see that happening," Don pondered, glancing over at Sid again.

"Shut up, Don. I think we may be able to pull this off. Go on, I'm listening."

"Will you stop telling my husband to shut up!? Who do you think you are, anyway?" Sue blasted.

"Alright already," Betsy scolded. "Enough. Now… go on, Claudia. What were you thinking?"

"What if we say that you didn't go up there to rob Mrs. Rose, that you went there to see how she was doing?"

That thought gave Sid an idea. "Yeah, and when she opened the door and we walked in - surprise - the whole house was alive."

Don laughed. "Do you really think she'd just open the door while she was having a party with all her little friends?"

Claudia could see that idea wasn't going to work. However, it gave her a thought.

"Wait a minute you four," she said, with a scheming little gleam in her eyes. "You knock, Mrs. Rose opens the door and lets you in, and then Theodore comes down the stairs unaware of you being there."

"Yeah," Betsy interrupted her.

Claudia shook her head. It was her idea.

"Mrs. Rose then panics and instantly turns you two into frogs," Betsy continued.

The room fell silent once again.

"OK," Claudia spoke up, glancing over at Betsy. "Now, how do we go about doing this? I mean telling the Sheriff?"

"He'll have to see Don and Sid like this," Sue remarked.

"Are you two willing to go through with this?" Claudia asked them.

"I don't know. What do you think, Sid?" Don asked.

"Well," he started to say. "What about the rest of them? Willy and Bobby Ray, and Ernie and Arnold and that little weasel Molly Dutton?"

"Like I said before, let's talk to Willy and Bobby Ray first and set up a meeting with everyone without Molly. However, not knowing what's going on inside Molly's head, she may be convinced to help us." Claudia replied.

They all nodded.

"Alright," Claudia continued. "Let's just sit on this until tomorrow then we'll meet at my house when Bart's not there."

"What time?" Sue asked.

"Say about noon," Claudia replied.

They nodded.

"OK, get me home. Thanks for the drink," Claudia said, getting up.

After Sue and Betsy had dropped Claudia off at home, Claudia stood in the driveway until Sue's car was gone. She turned, and headed for the door. When she walked in, she went straight to the dining room. "I need another stiff drink," she said, opening the liquor cabinet. *I can't believe it, I just cannot believe it,* she thought, pulling out her bottle of rum. *That stuffed lion, the grandfather clock, the coat rack and that creepy moose head talking.* She poured herself a glass, drank it and then poured herself another. "I'll never step foot inside that manor ever again," she sighed, downing that entire glass.

34

Love in the Air

After Shaun went home, Abby strolled into the parlor and brought the house awake. Grandfather, Sir Henry and Boris opened their eyes to see her standing in the archway between the den and the parlor. Grandfather yawned. "What time is it?" he asked, checking at his hour and minute hands.

"It's just past noon," Abby replied, clutching something behind her back. "I have some great news today."

"You do?" Boris replied.

"Well," she said, looking up at him and then down at her mice. "I think one of them should tell you since I put them on a secret mission to finding it."

All eyes focused on Wilson, Cracker and Benjamin standing next to her feet. "Well," Benjamin said, puffing out his little chest. "Wait one minute," Wilson interrupted. "I'm the captain of the three musketeers. I should be telling 'em, right Abby?"

"Oh, here we go," Cracker said, folding his arms and shaking his head.

Abby laughed. "Why don't you all say it together?"

The three shrugged in agreement. "On the count of three, fellas,"

Benjamin said. "One, two, three - WE FOUND THE POTION AND SPELLS BOOK!" they shouted. "Well, *we* didn't find it. Shaun did," Wilson said, frowning.

Sir Henry rolled his eyes toward Grandfather. Grandfather lifted his brow. *So that was the secret mission Madam Rose gave them,* he thought. Right then, Theodore and Tasha strolled down the stairs. "I'm glad you two found time to come down," Abby said, eyeing up Theodore. He glanced over at Tasha. She gleefully smiled back at him with a twinkle in her golden-brown eyes. The whole house could feel the love in the air while admiring the two big cats. "Sorry, Madam Rose. I was just showing Tasha the rear property from the balcony," Theodore said, blushing.

"I'm sure you were," she replied. Now," she continued, "I have great news. Shaun found the Potion and Spells book."

Theodore cocked his head then majestically trotted down the remaining stairs. "Where was it?" he asked.

"Well," she replied. "Shaun accidentally discovered it while removing Wilfred's rumble seat to take off the gas tank."

Eye brows went up questioning the removal of Wilfred's tank.

"Shaun found a hole in it," she replied to their curious expressions.

"You don't say," Sir Henry, gasped. "When's the last time Wilfred's gas tank was filled?"

"Gee, I rightly don't remember," Abby replied, placing her finger to her chin. "I suppose the day my father purchased him. That was way back in nineteen hundred and seven," she continued.

They laughed.

After the laughter had settled, Grandfather asked, "You think Shaun suspects anything?"

"He hasn't a clue," she giggled.

"Speaking of Shaun," Benjamin questioned.

"Yes?" Abby replied.

"Are you going to marry him?"

Everyone shrieked. Wilson reached over and slapped his shoulder.

"Ouch," Benjamin screamed.

"How many times do we have to charge you with high treason giving up secrets like that?" Wilson scolded.

Abby let out a pleasant sigh humorously thinking that Benjamin would probably stand before the court of the three musketeers for the rest of his life for spilling the beans, or perhaps *peanuts* in his case. *However,* she thought, *it truly doesn't matter now if they all know my plans for capturing Shaun's heart. Besides, the cat was now out of the bag with his little outburst.*

She simply raised the book up to her face and looked at the cover. "It doesn't matter now with everyone knowing my intentions about Shaun. But let me say this," she continued, closing her eyes and feeling the power within her hands, "with this book I can do anything."

In that moment, they all stood there watching Abby float up toward the ceiling. The mice quickly stepped back covering their mouths with their little paws. Grandfather and Sir Henry slowly lifted their eyes upward as Abby reached the ceiling. She began twirling in a circle and started to sing,

"Somewhere... over the rainbow... skies are blue..."

Steinbeck heard the song and started playing the music to, *Somewhere Over the Rainbow* from the movie *The Wizard of OZ,* Abby's favorite song. Wilson, Cracker and Benjamin gazed at one another with delight. Wilson then bowed to Cracker. Cracker bowed in return and they began dancing with one another.

"Sometimes I wish I wasn't nailed over this mantle," Boris grumbled from the den, listening to all the merriment going on in the parlor.

Theodore glanced up at Tasha sitting on the landing with little hearts fluttering out of her eyes as she was watching Abby and listening to the music. It made him sigh. Tasha cast her eyes on him, delightfully smiled and then descended the stairs. Strolling over to her handsome prince, she laid her head against his beautiful white mane while watching Wilson and Cracker dancing together. She nudged Theodore to look at Benjamin standing there all by himself pouting. Theodore whispered in her ear. Tasha nodded and walked over to Benjamin. Benjamin looked up into her big brown eyes. "Care to dance with me?" she whispered, stretching out her paw to him. Benjamin shyly sighed. "Come, take my paw," she insisted. Benjamin took hold of her paw and began twirling and waltzing, from claw to claw.

Grandfather and Sir Henry stood there admiring everyone having a marvelous time. Without speaking a word, they felt this overwhelming bond. Abby's love made them feel like family.

When the song was over and she stopped singing, her feet slowly descended to the floor. In that short space of time amongst all that love, Abigail Von Haussler was changing. Her power was growing. She opened her eyes standing there holding the Potion and Spells book to her heart. Then suddenly, Benjamin noticed something strange. Abby's hands looked young again.

"Abby!" he shrieked.

She looked down at him. "What is it?"

"Your hands!"

She slowly released her right hand from the book and brought it up to her face. Her eyes began to sparkle. "Well, my word. Will you look at that?" she surprisingly said.

"Abby," Benjamin said, bringing her out of the moment.

"Yes, Benjamin?"

"May I be so inclined to ask…" his voice trailed off.

Abby laughed, looking up at Sir Henry.

He's finally learning proper English, Sir Henry thought. "Go on," Abby insisted.

"Seeing that you're changing, I mean…" his little voice trailed off.

"You mean my hands?" she said.

"Yes."

"Are you trying to say, do I have to marry Shaun in order to become fully young again?" she asked.

Benjamin nodded.

Abby stood there for a moment before answering him. *To be young and in love,* she thought. *I'd give up all my powers for that one gift.* With her thoughts floating in the clouds, she tenderly gazed at each of her friends. They could see something within her eyes that spoke more than words could say. She sighed, looking down at Benjamin again. He smiled up at her.

"Love is something truly special, Benjamin. We all have that wonderful passion within us. However, when two people are young and in love, there's nothing on the face of this earth that you can compare with it."

As her words drifted on the wind, Tasha sighed, glancing over at Theodore. All heads turned seeing the love between the two beautiful lions. In that moment, they all knew what Abby was trying to say, for within Tasha's eyes, they could see the immense love she had for Theodore. And Theodore, well… he looked like a giant white chocolate bar melted all over the floor. Benjamin, Wilson and Cracker all turned and slowly allowed their eyes to wander upward toward Abby, who was standing there mesmerized by Theodore and Tasha's longing stare.

Sir Henry cleared his throat to bring everyone out of the clouds. They all turned toward him. Grandfather thought a speech was coming.

"Enchanting - truly enchanting," Sir Henry said and then paused, taking his eyes off Theodore and Tasha and looking at Madam Rose. She slowly bowed her head for him to continue. "I remember a time when I stood there listening to a Knight speaking to his beautiful fair maiden. The Knight gracefully said… *If I were a captain of a tall sailing vessel, I'd sail into your harbor and carry you on board my ship - and together, we'd sail across the deep blue to paradise. To the land called love - to my kingdom by the sea, and there, my fair maiden, I would pronounce you my queen."*

A whispering sigh filled the parlor. Grandfather's brow went up as his mouth hung open. Boris looked across at Sir Henry in awe of his words. Tasha stood up and walked over to him. He looked down at her. "I never heard such words like that. That was truly heart touching, Sir Henry."

He delightfully smiled. "You, my dear, are a beautiful fair maiden yourself," he replied, slowly looking up from Tasha and catching Abby's eyes.

"And you, Madam Rose," he continued, "will once again be as beautiful as a summer garden in bloom when you marry Shaun."

If a pin had hit the floor in that moment, everyone would have heard it. Abby deeply sighed glancing down at Benjamin. A warm smile appeared on his cute little face.

"I wish I could just marry him, but I can't," she said, strolling over to the sofa and sitting down. She glanced up at her mother's portrait over the mantel.

"My father," she continued, looking into her mother's soft eyes, "placed this spell on me and then informed me that I could not interfere with making someone fall in love with me. They had to fall in love with me all on their own."

Tasha wrinkled her brow at Theodore confused at what Abby was saying.

"It was not my place to tell you, Tasha," he replied to her expression.

Tasha turned and strolled over to the sofa. Wilson, Benjamin and Cracker strolled over as well. They jumped up into Abby's lap.

"Madam Rose?" Tasha said. Abby took her eyes off her mother's portrait, "Yes, my dear," she replied to her longing gaze.

"Please tell me," Tasha asked.

"I suppose I should, since you just joined the family."

Tasha stood there waiting.

"It's a long story, but I'll keep it short." Ten minutes later, Abby finished.

Tasha nodded. "I am certain he will fall in love with you, Madam Rose."

Abby raised her brow.

"I'm serious. You are the most charming person I have ever met. I mean… her voice trailed off. "Not that I've come across many humans yet."

Abby laughed, interrupting Tasha.

"Well," she replied, lifting her chin and looking at Theodore. "I still say you will."

"I second that," Grandfather added.

"Me too," Cracker said.

"Thank you for all the flattery," Abby said, standing up. "Now, let's have some excitement."

"This isn't enough excitement?" Benjamin asked.

"No…." Abby laughed. "How about…." she continued, "a night of dazzling transformations."

"Dazzling transformations?" Benjamin repeated, scratching his head.

Abby laughed. "That's right. Tonight, Fanny is going to become a witch."

"Tonight!?" Wilson beamed.

"Yes, so we must start preparing. I need to set up the ballroom, cauldron and all."

"Oh, boy! Did you hear that, fellas? We're having a party," Benjamin shouted.

"I'll give you a party," Wilson fumed. "Now let's get moving. We've got a lot of work to do."

"That we do, gentlemen," Abby agreed.

35

Dazzling Transformation

With the ballroom all set up, the four chandeliers lit and the cauldron sitting in the center of the room, Abby slipped into her black hooded cape, Gertrude. With her broom, Isabella, standing alongside her, she raised the Potion and Spells book over her head. "Tonight, my friends, we call on Fanny," she gleefully announced.

The mice, along with Theodore and Tasha, were watching and waiting to see what was going to happen.

Abby pointed skyward as she opened the book and began her spell.

"Hailing winds from across the seas, up from the depths of darkened lees- cast this spell upon the one I call - let her come forth to the midnight ball.

After Abby finished her spell, she tossed herbs and spices into the boiling water. *"I call upon Fanny,"* she shouted, waving her hands over the cauldron.

Smoke began swirling up from the bubbling water. It magically separated, transforming into a dozen ghostly shaped crows flying about the room. The chandelier's candles flickered as they swooped through the air. Then suddenly the ballroom's rear patio doors opened and the crows flew out into the night.

"Did you see that?" Wilson gasped in shock.

"Yeah…" Cracker replied, seeing the smoke come alive and then forming into scary looking birds. He glanced over at Benjamin then quickly nudged Wilson to look. Benjamin was standing there completely frozen as if someone had just taken him out of a freezer; eyes bugged out, mouth draped open and two little knees rattling. Wilson laughed. Benjamin came out of his frantic stare and turned his head. "What's so funny?" he angrily asked.

"You."

"Me?"

"Yes. You looked as if those crows were going to come down and eat you."

Benjamin puffed out his little chest. He pointed at Theodore's leg. "Not with this brute standing next to me."

Theodore and Tasha looked down at the mice chatting. "Shh..." Theodore whispered.

On the other side of town, Fanny strolled into her bedroom and opened her windows before slipping into bed. The warm summer breeze felt good as she walked over, pulled down the covers and settled in for the night. With the covers all nestled up around her shoulders, she rolled over and fell asleep.

Under a full moon, in the midnight hour, the ghostly crows flew across town toward Fanny's house. One by one, they swooped down her street through the trees and then circled around to the back to where Fanny's bedroom was located.

Whoosh… whoosh… whoosh… one after another flew in through her open window. As the crows entered the room, each one magically exploded into a puff of smoke. The smoke twirled and then got bigger, materializing into a ghostly hooded figure. He gazed down at Fanny sound asleep. Extending his hand toward her, Fanny's covers began sliding off her body. "Wake up within your sleep and follow me," he whispered. Fanny sat up, turned sideways and got out of bed in her nightgown. Standing there still asleep, she followed the ghostly figure out of the room and down the stairs. The ghostly figure waved his hand at her door. It opened. They both walked outside. "Your car will take you to the manor," he said, pointing toward it. The car door opened. Fanny got in. The door closed and the engine started. The gearshift slipped into Reverse and backed out. The wheel turned, the gearshift slipped into Drive and the car drove down the street as Fanny sat there with her hands in her lap.

After Fanny left, the ghostly figure swooped into the air, transforming back into a dozen crows again. They followed the car all the way back to the manor.

When the car drove up the long driveway, the crows flew up and circled it. The car shut off, the door opened and Fanny got out still sound asleep. Her hair and nightgown were blowing in the breeze. The crows exploded once again transforming back into the ghostly figure. "Come," he said, waving his hand at the doors. The doors slowly opened. Grandfather and Sir Henry glanced back to see who it was. Their eyes grew wide as the ghostly hooded figure walked past them and then Fanny strolled in looking hauntingly beautiful while sleepwalking.

As the two entered the den, Grandfather and Sir Henry stared at one another. "We haven't witnessed anything like this since Derek's last Halloween Party," Grandfather whispered.

"You can say that again," Sir Henry replied, turning his head and watching them exiting the den toward the ballroom. "What I'd give for a set of legs right now," he continued.

"Me too," Grandfather replied. "I'd love to see what's going to happen to Fanny."

Boris watched the two walk by and then disappear down the corridor. "I hate missing parties," he grumbled, turning his head toward the parlor. "Hey, you two!"

"What?" Grandfather replied.

"You mind coming in here and getting me down? I don't want to miss the party."

Grandfather laughed. Sir Henry shook his head. *Why do I have to live with idiots?* he thought. "I think we're all a bit stuck, Boris. Maybe you'd like a little music instead?" he said.

"Well, if we're going to miss the party a little music would be nice."

"Steinbeck," Grandfathered shouted. "A little music, please."

Steinbeck's top lifted up, the bench scooted closer to the piano and Steinbeck began to play.

"Hey, isn't that the theme song from the 'Phantom of the Opera'?" Boris asked.

"It sure is," Grandfather laughed. "I guess Steinbeck is in the mood for a haunting evening."

"Oh joy," Boris fumed, feeling even worse than he already was.

The corridor ballroom doors slowly opened. The ghostly figure floated in with Fanny. Abby's eyes beaded on them. "Be gone," she ordered the ghostly figure. The ghostly figure exploded, transforming into twirling smoke again, engulfing the entire ballroom. The chandeliers swayed back and forth from the explosion causing the candles to flicker.

Benjamin placed his little paws over his face in fear. Wilson glanced over at him and smiled. "You have to see this," he whispered.

"I can't look," Benjamin replied.

"Shh," Theodore softly scolded.

"Come forth, my child," Abby said, placing the Potion and Spells book on a small podium next to her cauldron. Fanny walked over. Her nightgown was swaying in the breeze as the wind outside was blowing in through the rear ballroom doors. She stopped in front of Abby. Abby stared at her. "Tonight, while you remain asleep, you'll become one of us," she said, tossing herbs and spices over Fanny's head and shoulders. Fanny just stood there staring into space. Abby turned and walked behind the podium. Her head went down as she turned the pages. When she came to the spell she wanted, she raised her hands in the air and began to read. *"In the world beneath the sea - where the Oxbow whales are free - I cast this spell upon you Fanny,"* she said, pointing at her. *"From the realm of mystical creatures - from the realm of darkened seas,"* she said and then paused, as Fanny's body lifted off the ground and started floating in the air. Her body turned sideways as if lying in bed. Her hair was flowing outward from the wind.

"Oh my," Benjamin gasped, looking out between his paws.

Cracker and Wilson slowly stepped back behind Theodore's legs in fear.

Abby cast her eyes down on the book and continued reading. *"From the realm of mystical creatures, from the realm of darkened seas, open the gates of magic and become a witch like me."*

Fanny began spinning in the air. The smoke that had engulfed the room swooped toward Fanny encircling her, making her spin even faster. The wind outside picked up and rushed into the room. The long curtains blew upward. The chandeliers began swaying back and forth causing the candlelight to flicker once again upon the walls. Benjamin started to tremble. Wilson and Cracker hugged one another. Theodore and Tasha sat there completely mesmerized.

Abby raised her arms up toward Fanny. Fanny slowly floated down. Her body turned vertical as her feet touched the ground in front of Abby. Abby gazed into Fanny's glassy eyes. She then reached up and waved her hand over her head. *"Witch's stew, witch's brew - what kind of witch are you?"*

Fanny blinked and then came to. "Why… I'm a good witch," she replied, not knowing where she was.

Abby smiled and kissed her on the cheek making Fanny come fully awake. Fanny stood there utterly confused for a moment then she realized that she was standing in the ballroom when she knew she should be at home in bed. She slowly glanced down at her nightgown. Her eyes drifted upward meeting Abby's smile. "Welcome to the clan, Fanny," Abby beamed.

"The clan? How did I get here?" she asked.

"You were brought here simply by magic."

Fanny's brow grew wrinkles. Abby laughed. "Did you honestly think I could have performed this ritual on you while you were awake?"

Fanny's thoughts drifted back - back to when she walked into her bedroom and opened the windows before slipping into bed. That's all she could remember. She stepped out of her thoughts and said, "Did I walk here?"

"No. You drove."

"I drove?!"

"Well not actually. Your car drove you here," Abby laughed.

"You mean I just sat there sleeping while my car drove merrily down the street?"

"Yes," she replied, tossing her eyes back on her friends. "Come, welcome Fanny to the family."

The mice scampered over. "Wow, Fanny, you look beautiful," Benjamin gushed.

"In my nightgown?" she questioned and then laughed.

"Yes," Wilson and Cracker agreed.

As she turned to see where Theodore was, she almost lost her breath. There alongside him was her stuffed toy - well, not anymore. "Tasha!" she gasped. "I can't believe you did it," she screamed, turning toward Abby.

"Surprise!" Abby gleefully replied.

"Surprise?" Fanny shouted. "This is more than a surprise," she continued, watching Tasha walking over. "Oh, my word - oh my God - oh me oh my," Fanny went on and on gushing over Tasha. Tasha stopped in front of her.

"You are so beautiful. I…." Fanny's voice trailed off, looking into Tasha's gorgeous brown eyes.

"It's nice to meet you, Madam Chamberlin," Tasha greeted her.

Fanny completely lost it. "Oh my… you can talk," she gasped, turning and staring at everyone. They all started to laugh. She shifted her eyes back on Tasha. "You are absolutely adorable."

"Why, thank you."

"Welcome to the family, Madam Chamberlin," Theodore said, walking up.

"Thank you, Theodore. You can drop the Madam stuff. Just call me Fanny," she replied, turning toward Abby. "That's alright, isn't it? I mean, I'm not a princess or anything like that?"

"You're more than a princess, Fanny," Abby replied. "Nevertheless, we'll call you by whatever title you choose. Now," she continued, "come over here and take a look at this."

Before walking over, Fanny took one more look at Tasha and sighed. When she turned and saw what Abby wanted to show her, she was shocked seeing Abby lifting up the Potion and Spells book. "Where on earth did you find it?"

Abby told her how Shaun had discovered it. They both laughed. "Now," Abby said and then paused, "pick it up and hold it to your chest. Then close your eyes and turn in a circle three times."

Fanny wrinkled her brow confused.

"Go on," Abby insisted.

Fanny did what she asked. When she opened her eyes, she felt this overwhelming sensation wash over her. "Wow, can you feel that?" she whispered.

Abby smiled. "Yes, that's the power of magic."

"So that's what magic feels like."

"Yes, and you'd better get used to it. Now, I think you're missing a few things."

"I know - I should be wearing clothing right now. I feel…" she started to say, looking down at herself.

"You're close," Abby laughed, interrupting her. "Witch's apparel - like a cape and broom."

"Yes, but where will I get them?"

Abby smiled glancing down at the book. Fanny slowly cast her eyes upon it within her hands. She looked up at Abby. "What do I have to say?"

"It's all up to you."

"Really, it's up to me?"

"Go on, Fanny, think of something," Benjamin spoke up.

"Well," she replied, blushing. "Myself, I would just like to snap my fingers," she continued, raising her brow at Abby. Abby gave her an approving nod of her head. Fanny closed her eyes, thought of a cape and broom then quickly snapped her fingers. WHOOSH… they appeared. When Fanny opened her eyes, she noticed that she was wearing a black hooded cape and there was a broom standing alongside her. "Well, I'll be," she gasped, raising her arms and checking out the cape.

"Now think of names to give them," Abby said.

Fanny cocked her head thinking. "I'll name my cape Hilda after your great grandmother and my broom...," she continued, reaching up and tapping her chin. "Pandora... That's a lovely name, don'tcha think?"

"Those are splendid names, Fanny," Abby agreed. "Now, let's see you ride Pandora."

"Ride, Pandora? Are you kidding me? I can't even ride a bicycle."

"Come now, Fanny. Give it a try," Wilson goaded.

"Yeah, we'll even come with you," Benjamin delightfully said, smiling up at her.

"Oh… no you won't," Fanny scolded. "I wouldn't be able to live with myself if one of you fell off," she continued, bending over and rubbing his head.

"We'll hang on," Wilson said.

"Yeah, we're so light you won't even know we're there," Cracker added.

Fanny stood up. She cocked her head with a thought. She then turned and slyly winked at Abby. "How about," she continued, looking down at the mice, "before you all get on with me… I make you invisible and with that I won't even know you're there."

"Invisible?" Benjamin replied alarmed. "You mean make us disappear?"

Fanny nodded with an alluring smile. "Oh no," Benjamin said, waving his hands. "Not on your life," he continued, stepping back. He quickly turned and yelled, "Run for your lives, fellas."

Fanny laughed, shaking her head as Benjamin ran out of the ballroom.

"Poor, Benjamin. I just love his little antics," Abby said, walking over and hugging Fanny. "Welcome home."

"Oh… Abby, I feel like I *am* finally home."

"Stay the night?"

Fanny looked down at herself. "Well, since I'm already in my nightgown, yes," she laughed.

Abby nodded with a smile. "Come then. Let's go to bed," she said, walking toward the corridor doors.

Wilson nudged Cracker. "Well, my friend," he said to him, "let's go and find the *invisible mouse*, shall we," he continued, heading for the doors.

Tasha snuggled alongside Theodore as everyone was leaving. "Would you like to take a stroll with me?" she whispered, batting her eyes at him.

"That, my dear, would be better than a ride on a broom any day," he replied, swaying hip to hip with her toward the rear ballroom doors. The doors slowly closed all by themselves as Theodore and Tasha romantically strolled out into the moonlight.

36

The Plot Thickens

The following morning, Claudia was sitting in the lounge furiously waiting for Bart to leave for work. Oh… she was clever enough to look Bart in the eye, slip on a beautiful fake smile and tell him to have a wonderful day - all the while sitting there stewing like a plucked chicken simmering in a kettle of boiling hot water. After Bart had kissed her goodbye, he walked out the front door. Claudia waited to hear the door close and then she turned and stared out the window in a minefield of thoughts. *In all my days of running this town, I've never dealt with a woman such as Mrs. Rose.*

Claudia stood up and walked over to the windows. *Soothsayers, palm readers and those who toss cards on the table while telling you your future*. "It's funny… I used to laugh at them," she said aloud, looking down at her flowerbeds.

She turned from the window and sighed. "I cannot believe that witches are real," she continued, sitting back down. "What on earth am I to do?" She pondered. *If I leave it up to Betsy and Sue, those two will screw this up for sure. I must find Willy and Bobby Ray before Ernie and Arnold return to normal.* With that, she got up, grabbed her purse and headed for the door.

When Claudia drove into Cloverdale, she started looking for the two boys on Main Street. To her delight, she spotted two Stingray bicycles parked outside Captain Jack's Tropical Fish store. "I betcha that's them," she said, turning onto Garden Street and parking.

Walking through the door, she spotted Jack standing behind the counter watching Willy and Bobby Ray mulling around the fish food section. He turned his head as she entered.

"Good Morning, Mrs. Hornsby. How are you today?"

"Morning, Jack," she replied. "I'm fine," she continued, glancing over at the boys.

"What can I do for you?"

Willy turned to see her standing there. He nudged Bobby Ray. He looked over at her and then focused his attention back on the small fish tank filled with live mealworms. "How many should we get?" he whispered.

"We only have three dollars, Bobby Ray. We'll buy as many as we can, I guess."

Claudia walked up to the counter and smiled. "I was thinking of purchasing some fish," she said.

"What kind?"

"Well I'm not sure yet, Jack. Let me walk around and see what you have."

"Be my guest. When you're ready, just let me know."

Claudia nodded and strolled over to where the boys were standing. As she went to pass them, she glanced down at the fish tank they were looking into. "Do you think those are good for frogs?" she whispered. Willy slowly turned his head. She gleefully smiled at him. Bobby Ray just stood there without saying a word knowing Mrs. Hornsby knew what had happened.

"When you're done in here, boys, I'd like to speak with you outside. I'll be waiting on Garden Street," she whispered, turning and walking over to the rows of fish tanks along the wall. She looked inside each one and then circled back toward the counter. "Well, I think I'll speak to Bart, Jack. It was actually his idea. He wanted a tank set up in the lounge."

"When you two are ready, I'll walk you through the shop and I'll even set it up for you at home when you decide."

Claudia nodded. "That would be great. Thank you, Jack."

"My pleasure, Mrs. Hornsby. You have a nice day."

"We'll be talking soon," she replied, walking toward the door. Before stepping out, she glanced over at Willy and Bobby Ray. They looked at her. She smiled, opening the door and left. Bobby Ray locked eyes with Willy. "It had to be Betsy and Sue," he whispered.

"You got that right. Come on, let's get these mealworms and go," Willy replied, turning toward Jack. "We'll take three dollars worth of these."

Jack walked over, grabbed the plastic cup, and scooped a cup full into a bag. "OK," he said, heading back to the counter. "Now to keep 'em fresh just toss some water over them every morning."

"Thanks, Jack. We're planning on tossing a lot of water over them," Willy replied, smiling.

Jack stared at the boys. "Are you using these for fishing?"

"That we are."

"I know Bass and Perch love 'em. Just use small hooks."

"Got heaps of those," Bobby Ray replied, taking the bag.

"Have a nice day, boys," Jack said, watching them leave.

After gathering their bikes, they pushed them to the corner of Garden Street and Main. They spotted Mrs. Hornsby standing next to her car and walked over.

"Good morning," she said, observing their facial expressions, the same expression you'd see on young boys being marched off to church on Sunday. Willy looked up at the boxy woman with huge shoulders, large hips and a face only a bulldog could love. "Morning," he replied, knowing a line of questioning was about to start.

She placed her eyes on Bobby Ray. "Morning," he said. She nodded while glancing up to make sure they were alone and then got right down to business. "Where is your brother?" she asked Willy.

"I think you already know where he is," Bobby Ray replied.

"Where did you get your manners… out of a Cracker Jacks box?" she scolded.

"No, ma'am."

"Alright then. I asked Willy that question."

"Ernie and Arnold are inside a box in my parent's garage."

"Inside the garage?"

"Yes, my parents don't like when I bring snakes or frogs into the house."

"It was Betsy and Sue, wasn't it?" Bobby Ray nervously asked.

Claudia lifted her chin at him. "That's right, so let's not beat around the bush, shall we? How is Molly doing?"

"She's all done with us," Willy sighed.

"She is?"

"Yes, after seeing Ernie and Arnold down at Kessler's Dam, she wants to stay out of it."

"I see." Claudia replied, leaning over and eyeing them up, "She might think she's staying out of it, but she's up to her neck along with the rest of you."

"What do you mean?" Bobby Ray asked.

Claudia straightened up. "What I mean is last night your brother and Arnold committed a felony."

"A felony?!" Willy gasped. "They said that they're all done committing criminal activities."

"Oh, they are now, are they? Well, they took a gun to a robbery and that's fifteen years in the big house."

"It was a toy gun."

"It doesn't matter. A gun is a gun in the court's eye, which means, boys, they'll be spending lots of time behind bars."

Willy stared nervously at Bobby Ray. Claudia caught their facial expressions. *One more push and I got 'em,* she thought.

"Does that go for Sid and Don too?" Willy asked, focusing on her.

"Let's just leave them out of this for now. I'm actually more concerned about you two."

"Us two?" Bobby Ray replied confused.

"That's right. You're not so clean either. As I see it, you two could be heading off to reform school for a year or more."

"Reform school?" Willy gasped.

"That's right. All juvenile delinquents are sent to reform school. And count your lucky stars that you're not a tad older or you'd both be going off to juvenile hall."

"Look," Bobby Ray replied. "We don't want any trouble," he continued.

Claudia leaned over again. "Well, you have two choices then."

"What are they?" Willy asked.

"You can stand before a judge alongside your brother and Arnold, or," she said and then paused, "you can help me put Mrs. Rose before a judge."

"Mrs. Rose!? I ain't doing nothing of the sort," Willy fumed.

"Who taught you English? I ain't doing nothing of the sort," she repeated.

"It's… I will not do that," she continued and then went on. "However, you will do it, or you can go home and start packing your bags for reform school."

"But Mrs. Rose threatened us if we told anyone," Bobby Ray pleaded.

"That's all the more reason to send Mrs. Rose off to jail. Threatening children! The nerve of that woman. Well, I got news for Mrs. Rose… witchcraft's against the law in the state of Pennsylvania."

"It is?" Willy questioned.

"That's right! That witch will see her day in court or you two, along with your brother, Arnold, Sid and Don, will be standing before a Judge. Now you go home and tell your brother that. Tonight, I want you all to meet me at the little park next to Horseshoe Bridge at nine o'clock sharp."

"But..." Willy started to say.

"But nothing, young man," she interrupted. "You know who I am in this town?"

They both nodded.

"Well then, you do as I say or your parents will be the next folks I speak with. I'm sure they can pack your bags quicker than you can."

Bobby Ray swallowed. "We're done like a dinner, Willy."

"You'll be more then done like a dinner. You'll be sitting up in reform school learning proper English for a year if I don't see you all down there tonight," she scolded. "Now, I've got to go," she continued, turning and opening her car door. She looked back before getting in. "Tonight - nine sharp," she said, slipping behind the wheel and driving off.

Willy and Bobby Ray stood there watching her leave. They turned and looked at one another. "I feel like a cooked goose already, Willy."

"You can say that again. Hurry, let's get back. Ernie and Arnold must be hungry," he said, getting on his bike.

"I don't think they'll have the stomach to eat after we tell 'em where we'll be tonight," Bobby Ray replied.

Willy thought of that. He could already hear his brother croaking up a storm over Betsy and Sue telling Mrs. Hornsby, a woman who was a witch herself - believing she was the queen of Cloverdale.

37

Stewing Misfits

Willy and Bobby Ray rode up to the garage, got off their bikes and headed inside.

"About time you showed up," Ernie scolded. "What did you buy?"

"Mealworms."

"Mealworms!?" he sounded off. "Alright, go ahead and toss 'em in," Ernie continued, disgustedly shaking his head.

Willy opened the bag and poured some in the corner of the box. "You've got to be kidding me," Arnold spewed, staring at the nasty worms crawling around. "It's that or grasshoppers," Ernie replied, hopping over. Arnold watched him go in for the kill. His stomach turned sour. "Not bad," Ernie said, swallowing a few. Arnold almost heaved.

. "We've got some bad news," Willy interrupted.

"Bad news?" Ernie replied, swallowing. "What could be worse than this?" he continued, glancing back at Arnold who looked three shades greener than he already was. "Are you going to have some?"

Arnold sighed. He hopped over toward the pile.

"Just close your eyes and imagine you're eating a nice juicy hamburger," Ernie said with his mouth stuffed with worms.

"Close my eyes? That ain't going to help while I'm sitting here and smelling these awful things," Arnold spat, dipping into the pile and gobbling some up. Ernie sat there watching him chew. "Wow, they're not bad," he said, surprised.

"I told ya," Ernie beamed, eating a few more. After swallowing, he looked up at his brother. "So what's the bad news?"

"Betsy and Sue went and told Mrs. Hornsby. Ernie quickly spat out his worms. Arnold swallowed the ones in his mouth. They both locked eyes with one another. "Unbelievable," Ernie replied, shaking his little green head.

"Mrs. Hornsby cornered us at the fish store," Bobby Ray sighed.

"Is that right?" Arnold snidely remarked.

"She did, and then she dragged us around the corner and threatened us," Willy added.

"Threatened you?" Ernie questioned. "How?"

"She said that we'll be all standing before a judge if we don't do what she wants," Bobby Ray answered.

"What!?" Arnold yelled.

"That's right," Willy said, picking up a crate next to the box and sitting down. "She wants Mrs. Rose arrested for being a witch and if we don't help her you two are going to jail and Bobby Ray and I are off to reform school."

"Jail... reform school," Arnold laughed.

"She was serious, Arnold," Bobby Ray added. "I don't know if you know this, but she said that performing witchcraft is against the law in this state."

Arnold stopped laughing. He glanced over at Ernie. Ernie shook his head staring up at his little brother. "I don't care if it is against the law. You know that witch has us all in the palm of her hands. All she has to do is cast another spell and we'll be eating mealworms for the rest of our lives."

Silence filled the air. Willy then sighed. "Bobby Ray is telling the truth, you guys. Fat lady Hornsby said that it's either Mrs. Rose standing before a judge or we'll be standing before a judge," he said and then paused. "And you," he continued, staring at his brother, "you just had to bring a gun to a robbery. Mrs. Hornsby said that's a felony."

More silence filled the air.

"Listen to what you're saying, Willy. It was a toy gun," Arnold replied.

"That doesn't matter," Willy scolded.

Arnold looked at Ernie. "He's right," Ernie agreed. Arnold shook his head. "How stupid. How absolutely stupid bringing that silly toy pistol with us," he fumed.

Ernie stared down at the mealworms. *I'm not going to eat these for the rest of my life and I'm certainly not going to jail either,* he thought. "Alright," he said, stepping out of his thoughts. "What does the fat lady want?"

"We have to meet her down at Horseshoe Bridge tonight at nine," Bobby Ray replied.

"The old carriage bridge?" Arnold questioned.

"That's right," Willy replied.

"We'll be there," Ernie disgustedly sighed.

Once again, the garage fell silent as the four contemplated what was going to happen.

At around nine that night, Claudia, Betsy and Sue saw two bikes coming toward the bridge. "That's gotta be them," Betsy said.

"It better be them," Claudia replied, rounding her car.

Willy and Bobby Ray rode across the carriage bridge with Ernie and Arnold inside a bucket. They got off their bikes. "Hello, boys," Sue said, walking over. She glanced down at the two frogs.

"Hi, Sue," Arnold greeted her.

"Hello," she replied. "We're all going to sit down at the picnic table next to the river," she continued.

"Come on, we don't have all night," Claudia yelled under her breath.

"Don't forget Sid and Don," she continued over her shoulder walking toward the table.

Betsy looked over at Sue. Sue shook her head. *As if we could forget them,* she thought, opening her rear passenger door and taking them out of the box. She handed Sid to Betsy and carried Don over to the table.

Willy grabbed Ernie. Bobby Ray reached down and picked up Arnold. They walked over and took a seat. It was the first time the four; Ernie and Arnold, and Sid and Don, saw each other. "How many days did she give you?" Sid asked.

"Two," Ernie replied.

"Only two?"

"Yep, we'll be back to normal tomorrow sometime - I hope."

"You hope," Claudia interrupted.

They stopped talking. Sid then hopped over to her. "So, what's your plan?" he asked, staring up into a face he'd rather forget.

"Well," she said and then paused, sitting back, "I called Emmett Fisher."

"Emmett Fisher, the town's prosecutor? The one with syrup for brains!?" Sid replied, glancing over at Don.

"I've never heard of him," Willy spoke up.

"He's the head attorney for the district," Betsy remarked.

"That's right, and he should be here any minute now," Claudia interrupted.

"Are you half out of your mind?!" Sid shouted.

Claudia caught that slap. She bent over and glared at him. "How would you like to get tossed into that river?" she snarled.

Sid slowly looked toward the river. The current was running fast. Before he could speak, Betsy stepped in. "Claudia Hornsby…" Claudia beaded her eyes on Betsy. "Betsy," she quickly interrupted. "I'm running this show," she barked, shifting her focus on all the faces sitting there. "Now," she continued, "how else are we going to prove that Mrs. Rose is a witch if we don't show Emmett these four?"

Betsy leaned back, irritated.

Willy looked down at the table at Ernie. Ernie had nothing to say. *What could he say?* Willy thought. *It was Mrs. Hornsby's way or Ernie and Arnold would be going to jail.*

"You two just had to tell her," Don spat to his wife.

Claudia leaned over toward him. "Right after Sid hits the water, you'll be next, you got that!?" Don swallowed. "Alright," Claudia started to say, seeing a car crossing over the bridge. "That's got to be Emmett. Let me do the talking," she continued, getting up and walking back to the parking lot.

Everyone turned watching Emmett's car pull in. "Oh, this should be fun," Sid spat.

"Honey," Betsy interrupted him. He looked up at her. "Please, for once in your life, just shut up." Sid's eyes grew wide. "I mean it, Sid," she scolded. Sid let out a sigh.

"OK, so we screwed up by telling Claudia, but there's nothing we can do about it now, unless you four want to end up in jail," Betsy continued, shifting her eyes on the four fat frogs sitting there. Sid looked at Don. Don looked at Ernie. Ernie looked at Arnold. They all turned and shook their heads. "Alright then, we'll keep quiet and let Claudia handle this," Betsy said, glancing over at Willy and Bobby Ray. "I don't want to hear a peep out of you two either, understand?" They nodded.

"Now, Mrs. Hornsby, I honestly don't understand why we had to come all the way out here tonight so you could show me something. We could've done this at my house if you wanted to keep it a secret from Bart," Emmett said, walking up to the table. He looked at the group sitting there. He suddenly stopped when he noticed the bullfrogs sitting on top of the table. "What's going on?" he asked, turning toward Claudia.

"Please, have a seat, Emmett," Claudia calmly replied.

Emmett sat down studying the frogs. He glanced up at Betsy and Sue sitting there "Ladies," he greeted them, nodding his head. "Hello, Emmett. I haven't seen you in a while," Sue replied.

"I've been in New York."

"I see."

He looked over at Willy and Bobby Ray - both troublemakers. "Now that you have me here, what's going on?"

“Emmett,” Claudia said, sitting down next to the boys. “Before we start, I want to ask you as a lawyer what is your position on witchcraft?”

Emmett cocked his head confused. “I rightly can’t say I have one.”

“Is it against the law in this state to perform witchcraft?” Claudia asked.

“Not to my knowledge, why?”

“Pennsylvania Ordnance Thirty-Three, Section Ten…” Sue spoke up.

“Sue,” Claudia interrupted. Sue closed her mouth and sat back.

Emmett sighed and then laughed. “What year?” he asked.

Claudia looked at him and then at Sue.

“Eighteen twelve,” Sue replied.

Emmett shook his head. “Can you please tell me what’s going on?”

“We have a very mean witch living here in Cloverdale,” Claudia informed him.

“Really?” Emmett humorously replied, leaning up and folding his hands.

“That’s right, we do,” Sid said, looking up at him.

Emmett’s eyes glued on the frog. His face went flush. “Did you…. Did you just say something?”

“Why don’t you sing him a song, Sid,” Don said, “maybe then he’ll believe us.”

Emmett jumped back, falling off his seat. Claudia sternly wrinkled her brow at Sid and Don. “Emmett,” she scolded. “This is no time to have your face in the dirt. Get up here and sit down.”

“You know,” Ernie said and then paused, “maybe we should have discussed this before getting him involved.”

Emmett got up on his knees, eye level to the table, watching and listening to one of the bullfrogs talking to Claudia. “I’m losing my mind,” he gasped.

“You’ll be losing more than that if you don’t get up here and sit down,” Claudia scolded.

He stood up, brushed his clothes off and then nervously sat down. “In all my born days…” he drooled.

“You’re telling us,” Arnold sighed. “How’d you like to be turned into a frog?”

Emmett swallowed looking over at Claudia. “Her name is Mrs. Rose,” she said.

“Mrs. Rose…. Not that sweet old lady who just purchased the manor?”

“Yes, that’s the one,” Betsy chimed in.

Emmett eyed up the boys. “Cat got your tongue?” he asked.

"No. We were ordered to keep quiet."

"I see," he replied, turning toward Claudia. "You should have been a teacher, Mrs. Hornsby."

Claudia sighed. "Now look… That witch turned Sid and Don and Ernie and Arnold into bullfrogs..." she started to say.

"Is that you, Sid?" he interrupted.

"Emmett," Claudia scolded. "Is your head filled with woodchips or what?"

"Alright already, I'm listening."

"No - syrup," Sid snidely remarked.

Emmett looked down at him. "Did I miss something?"

"You're going to be missing some teeth if you don't shut up," Claudia shouted.

Willy and Bobby Ray laughed.

"OK… Let's just calm down, shall we?" Sue spoke up.

There was silence for a moment as they all sat there staring at one another. "First off, before we go any further with this, can you tell me why she turned you into frogs?" Emmett asked.

The table remained silent as all eyes shifted on someone to speak up.

"Sid," Claudia said.

"I knew it was going to be me."

"Well, you're the one who came up with the bright idea of ripping the old lady off," Claudia replied.

Sid glanced up at Emmett. He started his story with the suitcase full of money and ended it with Don and him hopping out of the manor. Emmett sat there for a moment. His mind was so in knots that he thought he just stepped off the planet and landed in OZ. He glanced across the table at the boys, then down at Ernie and Arnold and then shifted his eyes on Sid and Don. "Are you honestly telling me that everything in that manor came to life?" he asked the four.

"Yes," they all replied in unison.

"I'm still shaking just thinking about it," Bobby Ray added. "Especially Theodore, and her cape when it was chasing us," he continued.

"Yeah… that scared the daylights out of me too," Willy said, staring out into space.

Emmett looked into Willy's eyes. He could tell Willy was out there somewhere thinking of that. *That doesn't happen to a person unless they've seen something so surreal that they simply lose their mind.*

"Have you ever heard B.B. Cooper's story when he was a kid?" Bobby Ray asked, taking Emmett out of his thoughts.

Emmett blinked. He thought about that. "Yes, now that you mention it," he replied, focusing on Claudia.

Claudia raised her brow. Emmett sat back.

"Well I'll be damned," he sighed. "Old man Cooper has been telling the truth all this time."

"You think maybe we should get him involved?" Betsy asked.

Emmett nodded still in a whirlwind of thoughts. He shifted his attention back on the boys. "What about Molly?" he asked.

"She wants no part of this," Willy replied.

"Hmm…. That's bad," Emmett said. "If Mrs. Rose's defense attorney gets wind of her, they just might have her take the stand," he continued.

Claudia went to speak. Emmett raised his hand. "Give me a second, Claudia."

Everyone sat there waiting. "To nail her on the charge of witchcraft we'd have to bring these four in like this," he said.

"There's not enough time," Don replied. "Those two will be back to normal tomorrow and we only have two more days left."

Emmett sat there thinking. "Well, we can't take photos of frogs and then toss them before the court and say this is what she turned them into."

Photos, Claudia thought. "Wait a minute," she said. "Alright, so we can't take photos of them, but we could somehow get photos of all those things inside the manor."

The lights went on in each of their heads. "Now that's not a bad idea," Sid whispered.

Emmett looked down at him while gathering a plan. "We could get those two private investigators, Wayne Lawson and Eddie Hicks to sneak up there and take some photos."

"You want the Cloverdale caped crusaders to go up there?" Don sarcastically asked.

Ernie laughed. "We'd be better off sending Willy and Bobby Ray back up there instead of those two clowns."

"Not on your life," Willy scolded. "I'll never step one toe on that property ever again."

"I don't think we have any other choices," Claudia weighed in. "Call those two and have them come to your office tomorrow around noon. I'll be joining you," she said. "Until then, we keep our mouths shut, is that clear?"

Everyone nodded.

"Good. Now let's go home," she continued, standing up. "I'm sure Bart will have a million questions as to why I am out so late."

The group got up and left the table.

On the way home, Emmett knew he had one big problem - how to squeak past a preliminary hearing knowing that Sid, Don, Ernie and Arnold were as guilty as Mrs. Rose, but more so, Ernie and Arnold for being so stupid bringing a gun to a robbery. That's ten years in prison on its own, plus the robbery which adds five more years on top of that. He decided to wait and see what Wayne and Eddie came back with before worrying about anything else.

38

Eye Spy

After Fanny's eventful evening of becoming a witch, she stayed at the manor two full days learning and honing her skills in the art of witchcraft; mixing potions, reciting spells and moving things about with her fingers, or with a blink of an eye. Her only problem was riding Pandora. Not that she was unable to ride her broom - she was scared to death. With a little coaxing from Theodore and Tasha and encouraging words from the mice, Fanny finally got over her worries.

While Fanny was there, she even had the pleasure of getting to know Shaun better when he came up to reinstall Wilfred's gas tank. At the end of the second day, after Shaun left, Abby told Fanny a secret, a secret so big that it absolutely astounded her.

"Oh… Abby," she gushed, "So that's why you came back to purchase your father's manor."

"Yes."

"Shaun Stevenson," she beamed. "He's such a charming young man."

Abby contentedly nodded. "I knew the moment we met that he was the one."

Fanny laughed. "He almost knocked you over in the grocery store."

"Yes, isn't that a hoot?" Abby giggled.

"It sure is. And you know," Fanny replied, "I could see something in that boy's eyes every time he looked at you while he was here."

"It's called admiration."

"Oh… you go on with that nonsense. It's called love, Abby."

Abby blushed. "You think?"

"I don't think… I know, sweet child."

Abby laughed again. *Sweet child,* she thought, smiling at her. *You're going to turn out to be one beautiful witch.* "Well, I think you should be off. I'm sure Mitt is getting worried by now."

"Oh no…" she gasped, reaching into her purse and pulling out her phone. "I left it off," she cringed.

Abby raised her brow.

"He must be worried sick by now," Fanny said, walking over and taking her coat off Sir Henry. "Thank you for the dress. I'd hate to get pulled over with only my nightgown on."

Abby contentedly smiled. "No, we can't have that, can we? However, you just remember all your training. You'd be surprised what you can get away with now," she replied, tilting her head and winking.

Fanny sighed walking over to her. She gave Abby a warm hug. "I miss you already and I haven't even left." Abby kissed her on the cheek and saw her to the door. When the door shut, Abby sighed, "Two long days and nights with that girl."

"She'll be fine," Grandfather spoke up.

"I'm sure she will. However, you should have seen her riding Pandora around the ballroom last night. She flipped over twice in mid-air and ended up riding her upside down. She was screaming the whole time hoping she wouldn't fall off."

"I thought that screaming was laughter," Sir Henry remarked.

"I was laughing. Fanny wasn't." Abby quipped, walking over to the sofa.

"Where did those charming little mice go?"

"They're in the kitchen begging Hansel for some peanuts," Tasha replied.

Abby shook her head. "I seemed to have lost track of time today and I don't know how with Grandfather standing right here."

Grandfather rolled his eyes checking his hour and minute hand. "I must be getting old. It's six o'clock already," he said, glancing over at Sir Henry. Sir Henry raised his brow. "Don't even say a word," Grandfather scoffed.

That same evening, as darkness swept over Cherry Hill, two covert spies dressed in all black drove down Old Tiller Road with the car's headlights off.

"There, just up ahead. You see the barn?" Eddie said to his partner, Wayne.

"Yeah," Wayne whispered.

"There's a dirt path leading up to it. We'll hide your car inside."

Wayne nodded, slowing down. The car rocked back and forth, as he rolled up to the old structure and drove in. "Man, it's sure dark in here," Eddie said.

"It sure is. You got your pen light handy?" Wayne asked

"Yeah," Eddie replied, pulling it out and opening his door. He stood there shining the little light around the dilapidated barn. Wayne stepped out and rounded the backend. “OK, let’s grab our gear and get up there,” he whispered, opening the trunk.

“Do you really think we’ll see anything tonight?” Eddie asked, reaching down and grabbing his black surveillance bag.

Wayne looked at him in the light. “The question should be - do you honestly think witches are real?”

Eddie shook his head. “No… but what about Claudia and Emmett’s story?”

“I don’t know. Do you think that witches can turn people into frogs or make stuffed toys come alive?” Wayne asked.

“No.”

“Alright then, if those fools want to pay us to come up here and check it out, that’s fine by me,” Wayne said.

“This will be the easiest two hundred dollars we’ve ever made,” Eddie replied, grinning from ear to ear.

“Yeah… like taking candy from a baby, I’d say,” Wayne smirked, grabbing his gear and shutting the trunk. “OK, shut off that light and let’s get going.”

Down the trail, across the dirt road and up the hill they went. When they reached the top of the ridge, Eddie knelt down next to a tree. “Will you look at that?” he gasped, pulling out his night vision binoculars.

“I heard there are forty rooms inside that castle.”

“Forty?” Eddie replied, scanning the entire back. “It looks like Count Dracula’s home.”

Wayne laughed. Eddie dropped his glasses and stared at him. “Here, you take a peek,” he said. Wayne took the binoculars and scanned the back. He then raised them up and scanned the entire rooftop. “Count Dracula?” he quipped.

“I’d say this place looks more suitable for Frankenstein,” he continued, lowering the glasses. “Kind of spooky if you ask me. Are you sure you want to go up there?” he asked, feeling tingles.

“For two hundred dollars I’d kiss Frankenstein’s wife,” Eddie replied.

“That wretched thing in the movie?”

“That’s right. Now let’s go.”

Wayne cringed imagining planting his lips on that creature. *I’d rather kiss a snake,* he thought, getting up and following Eddie across the yard. They quickly ran toward the manor and holed up at the cement steps leading to the ballroom patio doors. “Hey,” Eddie whispered.

“What?”

“You remember B.B. Cooper’s story?”

“I don’t want to hear that crap now. Let’s just sneak up there and check out the ballroom, shall we?” Wayne replied, climbing the steps.

Eddie watched him go up. He looked down at the steps to follow. He could hardly see them in the dark of night. When he got to the top, he was amazed how large the ballroom patio was. When they crept up against the cement wall near the doors, Wayne whispered for the night vision glasses. Eddie handed them over while keeping his eyes peeled in every direction.

“Will you look at that?” Wayne gasped.

Eddie turned his head. “What cha see?”

“Here, take a look.”

Eddie took the glasses and stepped around him. Inside, he saw a cauldron sitting in the middle of the ballroom. Next to it was a small podium with a book sitting open. “Well, I’ll be,” he whispered.

“What cha think?” Wayne asked.

Eddie lowered the glasses. “I think there is a witch living here.”

“Me too.”

“What do you want to do now?”

“We’ll need a few photos of this,” Wayne replied, reaching down and opening his bag. He took out his night surveillance camera and started clicking away while Eddie continued scanning the room.

“Hold it,” Eddie whispered.

Wayne stopped. “What?”

“You’re not going to believe this.”

“What?” Wayne again asked.

“I thought I saw a white male lion just walk past the ballroom’s internal doors.”

“What?”

“Here, see for yourself,” Eddie said, handing him the glasses.

Wayne set his camera down, took the glasses and leaned out far enough to see the doors. His eyes filled with fear seeing Theodore entering the ballroom. He quickly pressed himself tight against the wall and sighed.

“You see it?” Eddie whispered.

Wayne looked at him. Eddie saw fear in his eyes. Wayne then pointed inside the ballroom. “He’s walking around right now,” he mouthed. Eddie leaned his back tight against the cement wall and sighed. He could feel his heart pounding a million miles per second. *Emmett and Claudia were telling us the truth,* he thought. “What are we going to do?” he whispered into Wayne’s ear.

Wayne shook his head and then peeked inside again. Theodore turned and started walking toward the corridor while making his nightly rounds. Wayne picked up his camera and clicked a few shots.

Tasha then strolled in before Theodore got to the door. Wayne kept clicking away. When the two lions had gone, Wayne took in a ton of air kneeling back. “There are two.”

“Two?” Eddie sighed.

“Yes, a female lioness just walked in and they left together.”

“Oh, that’s great. We better get the hell out of here before we’re lunch,” Eddie panicked.

“We’re not going anywhere.”

“What? Are you crazy? What if they’re on patrol and come outside?”

Wayne thought of that.

“It’s possible they could come out here and start patrolling the grounds,” Eddie added.

Wayne let that comment go as his thoughts were racing now. *Unbelievable… stuffed toys, a moose head, grandfather clock and a coat rack coming to life and talking. We need more photos of this.* “Let’s see if we can go around the front.”

“Did you hear a word I said?” Eddie scolded under his breath.

“Yes, but…”

“But nothing,” Eddie interrupted. “We’ve got to get the hell out of here.”

“Not yet.”

Eddie rolled his eyes. He looked back at the ridge and thought of his car. He felt a tap on his shoulder. It made him jump. “Come on. Let’s see if there are any hidey holes so we can peek into the front windows.”

Eddie frowned, picking up his bag. Thirty seconds later, they were kneeling at the front corner of the ballroom. “Let’s see if we can make it up to the first windows past the ballroom,” Wayne whispered.

“It was nice knowing you,” Eddie replied.

Wayne shook his head, got up and crept along the wall. After passing the ballroom, he knelt by the den windows. He felt Eddie creep up and kneel behind him. “The curtains are drawn, but there is a large enough gap to see in,” Wayne whispered.

Eddie glanced up seeing the gap. He then nodded his head for Wayne to peek in. Wayne smiled and then slightly stood up. Over the den fireplace mantle, he saw the moose head hanging there. He reached down and tapped Eddie for the camera. With camera in hand, he started clicking away.

Then suddenly, Theodore and Tasha strolled into the den. “Goodnight, Boris,” Theodore said.

Boris cast his eyes downward. “Goodnight, you two,” he replied.

Wayne kept clicking photos. After Theodore and Tasha had left, Wayne knelt back down again. “Did you hear that?” he gasped.

“Yeah.”

“It was the lion talking with the moose head.”

“No….” Eddie gasped, shaking his head.

“You said you wanted to leave?”

Eddie nodded with big wide eyes.

“Then let’s get the hell out of here,” he replied, tossing his gear inside the bag and heading toward the back of the property.

After making their way to the barn, they sat inside the car out of breath.

“My whole world feels like it’s upside down, Eddie.”

“You’re telling me. I think I need to speak to a doctor after seeing that.”

“You know any good ones?” Wayne replied, looking over and smiling at him.

“You’re crazy, absolutely crazy. Just start the car and let’s go. I’m sure Claudia and Emmett will want to see these photos as soon as possible.

39

Cunning Little Termites

At noon the following day, Emmett, Wayne and Eddie, were sitting inside Emmett's office waiting for Mrs. Hornsby. When the door opened, they all stood up. "Good afternoon, gentlemen. I hope I haven't kept you waiting," she said, strolling in.

"No... no," they replied, waiting for her to take a seat.

"Alright then, let's get right down to business," she insisted, sitting down in front of Emmett's desk. Wayne and Eddie took up seats next to her. "I guess I'll let these two fill you in," Emmett said, sitting back.

Claudia shifted her eyes on both men. "You were right," Wayne said.

"What do you mean I was right? You think we were lying to you?"

"No, no, we just thought...."

"Please," she interrupted, "save me the drama and tell me what happened last night."

Wayne looked at Eddie. He could tell Eddie wasn't about to step on her toes. "We saw it all, well at least the two lions and then the moose head talking," Wayne replied.

"Really now?" Claudia beamed. "Were you able to take some photos?"

"Yes," Eddie replied, reaching down and picking up his briefcase. He opened it up and took out a large yellow envelope. "It's all right here," he continued, handing it to her.

Claudia smiled taking it. Emmett leaned up on his desk. She quickly opened the envelope and pulled out the photos. "Unbelievable," she gasped, looking at a cauldron and a podium sitting in the center of the ballroom.

The next photo was a close-up of a book sitting open on the podium. She sighed again flipping the next one over. "Oh my," she said, staring at the photo of a male white lion walking around the ballroom.

"It gets a whole lot better," Wayne whispered, leaning over toward her.

Claudia slowly turned and looked at him. Her heart was already skipping beats. "Go on," he insisted. She flipped the next one over. The wind in her lungs gave way. In the photo was a female lioness walking into the ballroom. It appeared she was speaking to the male lion. "I think I'm losing my mind," Claudia said more to herself then the men sitting there. She flipped the next one.

It was the moose head over the fireplace in the den. Its head was cocked and its mouth appeared to be moving. "He was saying goodnight to the lions," Wayne commented.

"You don't say?" Claudia replied, looking up from the photo. She glanced across at Emmett leaning over his desk. He contently smiled. "I viewed them before you arrived."

"Well, well," Claudia drooled. "We have her right in the palms of our hands."

"I think so, but we do have one small problem," Emmett said.

Claudia sat back not liking the tone in his voice. "And what is that?" she gruffly asked.

Emmett sat back, picking up his pen. "There are steps in all legal procedures. Before we can haul Mrs. Rose before a court, she must be formally charged and have the right to an attorney. From there, you have what is called an arraignment where she goes before the Judge and pleads guilty or not guilty. I'm sure Mrs. Rose's attorney will have her plead not guilty which then it's up to the Judge. After he looks over the evidence to see if there is just cause to send her to trial, he may consider a preliminary hearing if he feels that it's a weak case against her."

"OK," Claudia replied, trying to take it all in.

"That's where it can get real sticky for us, Claudia," Emmett replied. "If the Judge orders a trial we'll be fine. However, if he orders a preliminary hearing then all witnesses and the evidence is brought before the court and the defense attorney, along with the judge, can question the witnesses and argue what evidence will stand or not stand up in court."

"We do have a problem then," Claudia replied, thinking.

"It's a risky move," he added to her thoughts.

"How risky?" Claudia asked.

"Those who make the complaint can wind up in jail themselves, especially if they're as guilty as Mrs. Rose - if you catch my drift," Emmett replied, eyeing her up.

Claudia cringed hearing that. She shifted her attention on Wayne and Eddie. "Mrs. Rose is a witch," Wayne said.

Claudia sighed shaking her head. *We all know she's a witch,* she thought. *I just wish those foolish men hadn't gone up there to steal her money.* "It's a risk I'm willing to take. So what now?" she quickly asked.

Emmett cocked his head. “Give me three days, which will be,” he replied, looking down at his calendar, “Thursday, that’s if I have all the statements in by then. With that, we can start the process.”

“How soon after that can she be arrested?”

“Hopefully, by Friday. Now, if you three don’t mind, I have a lot to prepare,” Emmett replied, standing up. “Oh, I almost forgot the money,” he continued, opening his top drawer and pulling out a check. As he went to hand it to Wayne, Claudia reached over and grabbed the check from Emmett’s hand. Wayne and Eddie sat there in shock.

“Before I let you have this, let me say just one thing,” Claudia warned.

They nodded, staring at the check in her hand.

“If I hear that you said one word to anyone, your days of working in Cloverdale will be over. I’ll order Bart to demand the remaining debt on your business, is that understood?”

Again, they nodded.

To ensure they’d keep their mouths shut, she made it quite clear. “That’s fifty thousand dollars, gentlemen.”

“We won’t say a word. Not one single word to anyone,” Eddie pleaded.

“Good.”

“Claudia,” Emmett intervened.

She turned her head toward him. “They’ll have to testify.”

“Alright,” she grumbled, “here is your check. Give your statement to Emmett today and I don’t want to see either of you until you take the stand to testify.”

“You have a deal,” Wayne replied, taking the check.

She stood up. Wayne and Eddie stood up. She handed the envelope with all the photos over to Emmett. “Good day, gentlemen,” she said, walking toward the door. She quickly turned around before opening it. “I’ll write my statement at the house and hand it over tomorrow.”

Emmett nodded. She turned and walked out. The men all looked at one another. “Now that’s a witch,” Eddie whispered.

“You can say that again,” Emmett agreed, “Mrs. Hornsby is downright evil when she wants to be.”

When Claudia returned home, she sat out on her back patio writing her statement. She made sure to keep it short and to the point. When she finished, she set her pen down, took off her glasses and sighed. “How am I going to tell Bart?” she said, drifting.

Bart spent his entire life here in Cloverdale. His father was a farmer, a life Bart never wanted. As a young man, Bart decided to go into the world of finance. Once educated, Bart returned in 1976 and took charge of overseeing the bank here in Cloverdale. He proposed to Claudia the very same year. They married the following spring.

Just his name and position alone wielded power, and without a doubt in anyone's mind, Bart Hornsby walked amongst the aristocrats in Cloverdale. That small, tight-knit group also had the honor of rubbing shoulders with the prominent Judge Robert T. Hollingsworth. It would be Judge Hollingsworth who'd be residing on the case against Mrs. Rose. That was Claudia's biggest worry of all. She surmised Bart would rip out every nail holding their house together once she told him what she was intending to do. *I must tell him tonight,* she thought, getting up and walking back inside.

It was around six that evening when Claudia heard the front door open. She got up from the back lounge and walked into the parlor. "Hello, sweetheart," she greeted him taking off his coat. "Supper is on the stove. Are you hungry?"

"Hi, honey. Yes, I am starving," Bart replied, wrapping his arms around his wife and kissing her on the cheek. "How was your day?"

She leaned back gazing into his eyes. "Well…" she replied, slightly cringing.

"Claudia," he said, letting her go. "I've seen that mischievous look before. I suspect you staying out late last night may have something to do with it."

"Now Bart, please hear me out …"

"Hear you out?" he interrupted.

She turned for the kitchen. He grabbed her hand. She sighed turning back around. "Alright, I wanted to at least have you sitting before I told you," she said, coaxing him into the kitchen.

"You want me sitting?" he asked, following her. "Now that has me worried," he continued, taking a seat at the table.

"Oh, will you stop it?" Claudia scolded, strolling over to the stove and fixing his plate. She set it in front of him and sat down on the other side of the table. "I'm listening," he said, picking up his fork and knife and slicing a piece of ham.

"I don't know how to say this."

"You never had a problem talking before, now what's going on?" he asked.

"Well…" she started to say. "We have a terrible witch living here in Cloverdale."

Bart set his knife and fork down. "I mean it," she said. He swallowed, staring into her eyes while thinking of her fine feathered friends down at Flo's Beauty Salon. *Ladies with too much time on their hands can always find trouble,* he thought.

"Are you just going to sit there?" she asked.

Bart cycled out of his thoughts and answered her. "You're the one telling the story, my dear," he replied with an uplifted chin.

"Alright, you want a story then I'll tell you one."

She started with Mrs. Rose coming to town with a suitcase full of money, all the things that had happened and then ended her story seeing Wayne and Eddie's photos. Bart calmly picked up his fork and knife again.

"Well?" she pushed.

He looked up from his plate. The pause was more than Claudia could stand. She got up and walked over to the sink. "OK, so you're telling me that all of Mrs. Rose's personal items are alive?"

Claudia spun around. "Were you listening? It's more than just those things all talking. What about Sid, Don, Ernie and Arnold? I saw them with my very own eyes. Mrs. Rose turned them into frogs. She's a witch, Bart. And…"

He could see it coming with that long drawn out AND… "And what?" he begged.

"Well… um, I contacted Emmett, and Emmett and I, along with Betsy and Sue, who brought Sid and Don, and the two boys, Willie and Bobby Ray, who brought Ernie and Arnold, we all met down by the Horseshoe Bridge. That's where I was last night. We wanted to show Emmett what Mrs. Rose had done to them."

Bart sat back from his plate. He wanted to laugh, but refrained. *My wife,* he thought. *I cannot believe that she'd fall for such a ridiculous scam. That group of lowlifes sure pulled it over her eyes bringing bullfrogs down to the small park and telling her they were Sid and Don, and Ernie and Arnold.* He shook his head. "I can't believe you could fall for their prank. I also cannot believe Sid and Don would team up with Ernie and Arnold to make you look like a real dill pickle either."

"Bart Hornsby," she scolded, folding her hands. "Let me say this real slow, so you hear it. They were sitting on top of the table talking to us."

"The frogs were actually talking?"

"If you don't believe me then call Emmett." she said and then paused,

"However, before you pick up that phone, I think I should inform you that Mrs. Rose will be arrested as soon as Emmett gathers all the witnesses' statements together."

That was the best line she said all night. It hit Bart straight in the face.

"You're not thinking..." he started to say.

"Yes. Mrs. Rose will be ushered into the Cloverdale courthouse and you know what that means."

Bart instantly thought of his dear friend Judge Hollingsworth. He could already hear Hollingsworth's laughter. It made Bart cringe sitting there. "Are you sure you want to bring her before Judge Hollingsworth?"

"Yes, now eat your meal," she politely replied.

"Eat my meal!? I just lost my appetite. Do you know what you're doing?" Bart grumbled.

"Yes, I am relieving Cloverdale of a very mean witch."

"Oh no, you don't," he replied, getting up from the table. "I've spent my whole life building up our name and now you want to destroy it with this nonsense."

Big, boxy and full of vinegar Claudia had had enough. "Go and put your coat on."

"What?"

"I said go and put your coat on. We're going for a drive."

"I'm not going anywhere."

"Oh yes you are. You need to see this for yourself."

Bart sighed. It was the last thing he wanted to do - to go over to Sid and Don's house and see them for *himself.* He looked at his wife knowing he had one more card to play before he was crowned 'The Fool of Cloverdale'. "If she is a real witch like you say she is, please tell me then, what law has she broken?"

Claudia contently smiled. "Pennsylvania Ordinance Thirty-Three, Section Ten: it's unlawful to use witchcraft, black magic, or the casting of spells within the state of Pennsylvania."

"Did Emmett tell you that?"

"No, Betsy and Sue looked it up. The ordinance is from the 1800s."

"Eighteen hundreds?" Bart spewed.

"I think you better call Emmett seeing you don't want to go over and look at Sid and Don."

He sat back down pondering that. *I had better get a handle on this mess before Judge Hollingsworth does.* "Yes, I'll call him now," he said, getting up and walking into the lounge.

Claudia sat down and waited. Bart came back into the kitchen fifteen minutes later looking stunned and bewildered. Claudia said nothing waiting to hear what he had to say to all this. "I can't believe it," he finally said, looking at his now cold plate of food.

"I can't either. That witch made my hair turn blue."

Bart glanced up from his plate. "Sid and Don," he said and then paused, "those two are not out of the woods for going up there with the intent of stealing her money."

Claudia sat back tilting her head. Bart knew what she was about to say before she even said it. "Yes, they did go up there to steal her money, however…"

He interrupted her by shaking his head.

"Alright, I didn't tell you this part. Sid and Don are going to say that they went up there to check on Mrs. Rose and that's when they saw all those things talking."

"So… they're going to lie in their statements?"

Claudia lifted her brow.

Bart shook his head. "I better go to the courthouse and see Judge Hollingsworth tomorrow."

"I don't think you should."

"Why not?"

"Look, Bart, if you're so worried about our name being destroyed in this town, I think you should just stay out of it."

Bart thought of that. *Maybe she's right. I'll wait and see how Hollingsworth handles this first.* "OK. I'll stay out of it."

"Good," she replied, standing up and rounding the table. She leaned over and kissed him on the cheek. "This will all be over before you know it," she whispered in his ear. He sighed wishing it was already all over and he and his wife were on a long trip to Europe.

40

Caught Blindsided

The days passed by like sands through an hourglass. On Friday afternoon, Abby asked Shaun to come back for dinner. It was around six that evening when he showed up. "Hello, Shaun," she greeted him, opening the door.

"Hi, Abigail," he said, walking in and hanging his jacket over Sir Henry.

"Tonight, I've fixed a nice lamb roast with dumplings and gravy. The kind my mother used to make."

"That sounds delicious," Shaun replied, taking a seat on the sofa.

"Will you move over?" Benjamin whispered to Wilson. "I can't see a thing," he continued, standing on the beam trying to look out from the hole under the staircase.

"OK, can you see now?" Wilson fumed.

"Yes," Benjamin replied, eyeing the two sitting on the sofa.

"You know, Abigail, I've never heard you actually play the piano," Shaun said.

Abby was surprised to hear that. "Now that you mention it, I never even gave it a thought. What kind of music do you like?" she asked, getting up and walking over to Steinbeck. She sat down on the bench and beckoned him over. Shaun got up and sat down beside her. "It sure is a beautiful piano," he said.

"Steinbeck is a grand piano. He's been in the family since I was a little girl. My mother taught me how to play. Now, what would you like to hear?"

Shaun looked up from the keys while thinking. "You may find this funny, but one of my favorite songs is '*Somewhere Over the Rainbow*' from the movie '*The Wizard of OZ*'."

Abby gazed into his eyes. *That is amazing,* she thought, *it's one of my favorite movies too.* "Well, let me see," she said, taking her eyes off him and looking down at the keys. She placed her hands upon them and closed her eyes.

Shaun sat back watching her fingers moving up and down the keys listening to a melody introduction before she started the song. He looked up as she began to sing. "Somewhere… over the rainbow… skies are blue…." It was heaven to his ears. When she finished, she opened her eyes and smiled at him.

"Wow," he gushed. "Has anyone told you how wonderful your voice is?"

"You just did," she teased. "Now, do you know how to waltz?" she asked, folding her hands in her lap.

"Waltz?" he said confused.

"It's a formal style of dancing."

"Oh, no, I don't know how to dance," he replied worried that she was going to have him get up and dance with her.

"Well it's high time you learned, young man. We have a few minutes before supper," she said, getting up and taking his hand.

"Now, Abigail," he cringed, feeling embarrassed.

"Oh now, it's quite simple," she said, pulling him up. "Here, take my hands."

Shaun nervously stood up, holding her hands. "Alright, now follow my lead," she said, taking a step sideways while humming '*Somewhere over the rainbow*'. Shaun followed her lead. "You see? It's easy," she laughed, waltzing him around the parlor.

"Will you look at that?" Cracker gasped.

"Yeah, the kid can dance," Benjamin whispered.

"Not as good as me," Wilson said, jumping down off the beam onto the floor. "Now watch," he continued, turning in a circle as if dancing with a partner under the stairs.

Cracker looked at Benjamin and laughed. Benjamin bowed to him as if asking him to dance. Cracker nodded then jumped down. Benjamin jumped down and took Cracker's hands. They began dancing in a circle listening to Abby humming the song. Wilson stopped dancing. He folded his arms staring at the two knuckleheads dancing together. He was just about to scold them when suddenly there was a knock on the front door.

Abby and Shaun stopped and looked at one another puzzled. "Who could that be?" she said, letting him go and walking toward the foyer. When she opened the door, she was startled to see Sheriff Roy Collins and Emmett Fisher standing there.

Before anyone could speak, a small moving van pulled up and parked right behind Emmett's car. Abby glanced at the men getting out. She turned her attention on Sheriff Collins. "Sheriff?" she said.

"Mrs. Rose," he interrupted here. "I am here to inform you that we have received an official complaint."

"An official complaint," she interrupted worried, knowing what he was about to say.

"That's right. We have statements from eyewitnesses that said they have seen you performing witchcraft, which is in violation of Pennsylvania Ordinance Thirty-Three, Section Ten. I also have a warrant here to search your house and take these items," he continued, handing her the warrant. She looked at Emmett. He stood there stone-faced. She glanced down at the warrant. The items listed were her two stuffed lions and the moose head, the items seen from Wayne and Eddie's photographs. *Sid and Don,* she thought. *They did not heed my warning.* She kept her composure. "I've been called many things in my day, but never a witch," she gruffly replied.

"We also have photographic evidence," Emmett spoke up.

Those scoundrels, she thought, *how could they be in possession of photos?* "Do I have the right to know who they are?" she asked already knowing their names.

Sheriff Collins looked at Emmett for the legalities of her request. Emmett reached up and loosened his tie. "The main complainants are Sid Peterson and Don Reed along with their wives, Betsy and Sue.

Abby laughed, masking her anger. "I think I should inform you," she started to say.

"Wait a minute Mrs. Rose," Shaun interrupted. "This is the most ridiculous thing I've ever heard."

"Shaun," Abby sighed. "I'm sorry I did not tell you," she said, focusing her attention on Sheriff Collins and Emmett. "Sid and Don along with Ernie and Arnold came up here trying to steal my money."

Sheriff Collins stepped back hearing that. He glanced over at Emmett. Emmett raised his brow.

"What are you talking about?" Shaun scolded, stepping out in front of her. She looked into his eyes and then focused her attention on the Sheriff. "I caught those two red-handed trying to steal my money the other night. If that isn't enough, then they lie to the authorities and hand over doctored photographs to have me arrested for being a witch."

"Mrs. Rose," Sheriff Collins said, alarmed by her statement.

"Don't Mrs. Rose me, Sheriff," she snapped. "You too would have turned into a witch if you had caught them red-handed breaking in to steal your money."

Sheriff Collins sighed. *She's right,* he thought, *I'd still be kicking their butts all over the state right now if they broke into my house.*

In the silence of the moment, Emmett was feeling the heat around his collar from her outburst, knowing that his clients, Sid and Don were as guilty as she was.

"This is all nonsense!" Shaun yelled, bringing everyone out of their thoughts.

"I've been up here a million times and never once have I seen anything out of the ordinary," he continued, turning and looking at her. "Why didn't you tell me?"

"I was trying to leave you out of it, Shaun," she sighed.

"Shaun Stevenson, please step aside," Sheriff Collins interrupted, taking the warrant from Abby and handing it to Emmett. "Now, Mrs. Rose, even though you have told me your side of the story, I still have to take you in."

"She's not going anywhere. It's Sid and Don you need to arrest for breaking and entering," Shaun insisted.

"Would you like to be arrested too?" Sheriff Collins softly replied. "If Mrs. Rose wants to make an official complaint on Sid and Don she can do so down at the police station."

"Shaun," Abby calmly intervened, "please do as he asks. I'll handle this."

"But, Abigail," he grumbled, turning toward her.

"Don't you worry. I'll be right back after I have a nice long talk with these men. I would like you to go see Fanny. She'll know what to do."

Shaun reluctantly stepped aside. Abby followed Sheriff Collins over to his patrol car. "Oh, I almost forgot," she said, turning around. "Shaun, please shut off the stove and have dinner."

"OK," he replied, glancing at Emmett standing there. "Be my guest," he said to him, waving his hand toward the doors.

"Alright, let's retrieve these items and get out of here," Emmett said to the two men.

Shaun followed the men inside. He watched them remove Abigail's personal items and take them out to the van. "This is utter madness," he said to Emmett as Emmett walked up to his car to leave.

"Have a good night, Shaun," Emmett shouted, getting in.

"Up yours, Emmett Fisher," Shaun yelled back, closing the doors behind him. After closing the doors, he suddenly remembered their dinner. "Damn," he swore, turning and racing through the parlor toward the kitchen.

Wilson, Benjamin and Cracker all stood there frightened under the stairs. They were speechless for the first time in their lives. They heard a muffling sound coming from the foyer. Wilson looked out the hole to see Sir Henry standing there with Shaun's jacket over his head. He turned and looked at his comrades. "We're in big trouble, fellas," he said.

"We're in big trouble? You mean Abby's in big trouble. What are we going to do?" Benjamin frantically replied. Wilson took a seat on the beam and began tapping his chin.

"Well?" Benjamin asked, seeing Wilson thinking of what to do next.

Wilson looked up. "I can't believe those bums told on her."

"I could just sock them right in the eye," Benjamin fumed, holding up his little fists.

"Me too," Cracker agreed.

Wilson sighed sitting there worried. Benjamin and Cracker glanced at each other then sat down beside Wilson with broken hearts.

"I sure hope Fanny gets here quick," Cracker said.

"Yeah, me too," Wilson replied, holding his chin in the palm of his hands.

Shaun quickly shut off the stove, pulled out the lamb roast and dumplings and set them on the counter. He ran back to the parlor, grabbed his coat and took off out the doors. Fifteen minutes later, he rode up to Fanny's house and knocked on her door. She opened it. "Fanny, I'm sorry for coming here so late," he said, hurrying in past her. She spun around confused. "What is it Shaun?" she asked worried.

"It's Abigail. She's been arrested for witchcraft."

"Oh my, God… by whom?" Fanny gasped, placing her hands over her mouth.

"Sheriff Collins, Emmett Fisher and the District Attorney."

"Come, sit down and tell me everything," she replied, escorting him in.

After he had told her, she sat back and sighed. *What am I going to do?* she thought. *I can't tell Shaun the truth that she is a witch.*

"I am so confused right now," Shaun said, sitting back on the couch.

Fanny stepped out of her thoughts, looking into his worried eyes. "I never once saw her using witchcraft, Fanny," Shaun continued, "sure, she has a funny way about her, you know, having names for all her personal items. But witchcraft?"

"I kind of liked that about her. And you're right, I never once saw her casting spells or stuff like that either," Fanny lied.

"Abby told me to come here and tell you. So, what do you think we should do?" he asked.

Fanny shook her head. "I guess all we can do now is to find her a good lawyer. Do you know of any?"

"Fred Akins. He's the best lawyer in town."

"Fred. Hmm," she replied. "You think it's too late to go see him?"

"I don't care if it were midnight. Abigail is down at the police station being questioned right now."

"OK," she replied, getting up. "We'll take my car."

After Fanny and Shaun woke up Fred and told him what had happened, Fred drove straight to the police station. When he walked in, he saw Deputy Oxford sitting at the dispatcher's desk. "Evening Fred," Deputy Oxford greeted him.

"Evening, Deputy. I'm here to inform you and Sheriff Collins that I am Mrs. Rose's attorney. I want to see my client right now." Deputy Oxford nodded.

"She's inside the sheriff's office with Emmett Fisher," he replied, standing up. "Please follow me."

Sheriff Collins looked up when he heard a knock on his office door. He sat back when Deputy Oxford walked in with Fred right behind him. "Good evening, gentlemen. Mrs. Rose," Fred greeted them, nodding to Abby. "I was informed that you're in need of a lawyer."

Abby smiled, thinking of Shaun. *He must have told Fanny and the two of them went and told Fred,* she thought. "As you can see, I am."

"Well, you heard her. The questions will stop until I speak with my client," Fred replied.

"Alright," Sheriff Collins replied, glancing across the table at Abby.

"Mrs. Rose, you are free to go. However, if you would like to press formal charges against Sid and Don, now is a good time," he said.

"Before you answer that, please fill me in," Fred asked her, taking a seat.

Abby sat back and sighed. After she told Fred what had happened, Fred looked at Sheriff Collins. "You can start the paperwork, Sheriff. We're pressing formal charges against those two, right here and now."

Emmett cringed hearing that. His thought of slipping past a preliminary hearing was all but over.

"OK, I'll start the paperwork," Sheriff Collins replied, standing up. "I've read the statements and saw the photos," he continued, shaking his head.

"Truthfully, I don't know what to believe. However, you can be assured that after I escort Sid and Don here, I will get to the bottom of this. In the meantime, Mrs. Rose you have been arrested and formally charged. Your arraignment will be on Tuesday morning at eight a.m. before Judge Hollingsworth."

Abby nodded, got up and walked out of the office with Fred. As they reached the front entrance to leave, she sighed seeing Shaun and Fanny standing outside next to Fanny's car.

"Abby!" Fanny shouted, running toward her with Shaun.

"Now don't worry, everything will be alright," Abby replied. The expression on Shaun's face was enough to make Abby cringe. "I'm truly sorry," she said. "I should have told you what happened, Shaun. I just thought…"

"Mrs. Rose...," Fred interrupted.

Abby looked at him. "Well I should have told someone. How foolish of me."

"Forget about it," Shaun said, "we're just glad nothing happened to you."

"Yes, that goes for me too," Fanny agreed. Abby sighed. *Such dear friends they are,* she thought.

Fred cleared his throat. The talking stopped. "I think Mrs. Rose should go home and get some sleep. We have a busy schedule coming up. Tomorrow I'll be requesting all the evidence from Emmett Fisher and then I'll come up to see you before your arraignment on Tuesday morning."

"Arraignment?" Shaun questioned. "What about Sid and Don? They're the ones who should be going to jail."

"Don't you worry, they're going to be charged," Fred replied. "I'll be talking to you soon, Mrs. Rose," he continued, turning and walking toward his car.

"Abigail…" Shaun started to say.

"Again, I'm sorry for not telling you, Shaun," she interrupted. "It's getting late. We'll talk more tomorrow, OK?"

"Alright," he replied, looking at Fanny.

"Come on, let's get you back to your motorcycle then I'll drive Abby home," Fanny said, wrapping her arm around Abby and escorting her over to the car.

41

A Manor Filled With Worries.

After Fanny had dropped Shaun off, she slowly drove back to the manor with Abby. Silence hung in the air like a stale loaf of bread as both women sat there all alone in their thoughts. Abby glanced over at Fanny and said that she was sorry again. “Forget about it,” Fanny replied.

“I can’t,” Abby sniffled. “Of all the people, I should have at least told you and I’m worried about Shaun. I know he’s upset.”

“I do wish you had told me. However, I wasn’t a witch then,” she replied, glancing over at her. “And as far as Shaun is concerned,” she continued, “he’s in love with you, Abby. Even a blind man can see that.”

Abby sat there for a moment. *A blind man,* she thought. *I might as well be blind not seeing it myself.*

“So,” Fanny said, taking Abby out of her thoughts. She sighed again knowing what Fanny was about to ask. She wanted to know what happened that night. “Well, it actually started when Sid and Don took me for ten thousand dollars,” she said.

“What?”

“Yes. They added that sum to the price of bringing the manor up to city code. I just figured they were telling me the truth.”

“Those dirty, little rats,” Fanny cursed.

“Well, like I said, that’s how it all started,” Abby continued.

By the time Fanny pulled up at the manor, she knew the whole story. It made her sick to her stomach. “They would have gotten a whole lot more from me than just being turned into frogs,” she said, sitting there.

“It’s not over yet,” Abby replied, smiling at her.

Fanny could see the devil in Abby’s eyes. She gleefully smiled back.

“It’s payback time.”

“Not just yet, my dear. We have the court to deal with first. If I can weasel my way out of this pickle jar, then we’ll see who’s going to have the last laugh,” she replied, opening her door.

Fanny got out and rounded the car. “Do you mind me staying the night?” she asked.

“I was just about to beg you to stay,” Abby said.

"Good," Fanny replied. "Let's get inside and find those mice. I am sure they're worried sick along with the rest of them by now."

"I'm sure you're right."

When Abby opened the door, she and Fanny heard a longing sigh in the foyer.

"Grandfather," Abby said.

"You have no idea how worried we were," he said. "So, what happened?"

"Yes, please tell us," Sir Henry added.

Before she could speak, the mice jumped off the bottom stair. "Abby.... Fanny...!" they yelled, scampering toward the foyer.

Abby knelt, gathering all three in the palm of her hand. "Where are Theodore, Tasha and Boris?" Wilson asked.

Abby frowned. "They're still down at the Sheriff's office.

"No...!" Benjamin gasped. "What are they being charged with?"

Wilson and Cracker shook their heads. "It's truly sad," Wilson then said.

"What's truly sad?" Fanny asked confused.

"Once you're made a full-fledged musketeer you can't be booted out," Wilson replied, nodding at Benjamin.

"Now, Wilson," Abby softly scolded. "Benjamin, there's nothing to worry about. They're not being charged. They took them in as evidence, that's all. They'll be back soon."

Benjamin shook his head while glaring at Wilson. "Booted out, you say. I'll boot you to the moon."

"Alright, you two" Abby intervened. "Are there any more questions?"

"No," Grandfather replied. "Gertrude and Isabella have gone back upstairs - where you should be heading."

"Thank you, Grandfather. I think we all need some sleep. Goodnight you two," she said, turning and walking toward the elevator.

"Goodnight Madam Rose, Fanny," Sir Henry and Grandfather replied.

Fanny waved over her shoulder following Abby into the corridor.

In the morning, Abby awoke feeling the length of Fanny's body snuggled up against her like a kitten. She turned her head to see the mice sound asleep next to her pillow on the other side. Slowly rolling over onto her back, Abby stared up at the ceiling. Theodore, Tasha and Boris cascaded through her thoughts. *At least they haven't a clue to where they are right now, down in the basement at the Sheriff's office - of all places.*

Fanny awoke rolling over. "What time is it?" she yawned.

"Too early to even ask," Abby replied.

"That early? Well, I wouldn't mind a bath if that's OK?" she said, slipping out of bed.

"Be my guest. I just want to lie here for a moment."

After Fanny's bath, she strolled out drying her hair. Abby placed a finger to her lip and then pointed down to the mice. Wilson and Cracker were up, but Benjamin was still in dreamland fighting with someone. Fanny carefully sat down at the side of the bed and watched.

"You lay one hand on Theodore and I'll wallop you," Benjamin said, turning this way and that in his sleep. "Don't do it - I'm warning you. I'll give you more than you can handle."

Abby softly chuckled glancing over at Fanny. "The heavy weight champion of the world," she giggled.

"You mean more like the feather weight champion of the world. Just look at that birdbrain," Wilson remarked, shaking his head.

"Shh..." Abby whispered, reaching down and rubbing Benjamin's stomach. "Benjamin," she softly said. Benjamin quickly grabbed her finger. "Oh, you want some too? Come get some of this," he said then suddenly awoke, looking at a finger he was holding onto. He glanced up with sleep-filled eyes to see Abby smiling down on him. "What's going on?" he asked.

"You were dreaming," Abby replied.

"I was?"

"Yes."

"Well let me get back there because I was just about to wallop Sheriff Collins."

"He's only doing his job," Fanny said.

Benjamin sat up, rubbing his eyes. "Well, if he had any noodles up in that stir fried, pea brain of his he'd know Sid and Don were lying."

"Stir fried?" Fanny questioned, never hearing him use that term before.

"After the Sheriff left, Hansel put the kitchen to work cooking us stir fried rice with roasted peanuts. I guess to make us feel better, seeing that we were in such an awful mood," Cracker replied.

Abby sighed. “I guess I’ll just have to thank Hansel when we go down. Now,” she said and then paused, “I know people will be coming over today and I want you three to go out and visit with Wilfred while they’re here. I’m sure he’d like some company.”

“That would be wonderful,” Fanny beamed. “We can all go out and visit with him.”

“OK, give me a minute to freshen up,” Abby said, getting out of bed.

After taking the elevator down, Fanny walked into the parlor toward Sir Henry.

“Good morning, Fanny. Did you sleep well?” he asked.

“Surprisingly, I slept like a rock. Tell me, when was the last time you saw the backyard?” she asked.

He looked at her confused then shifted his eyes on Grandfather. “Why… never,” he replied, looking back at her.

“Well, today is your lucky day,” she replied, picking him up. “We are all going out to visit with Wilfred this morning and there’s no sense in leaving you here,” she said shifting her eyes on Grandfather. “I hope you don’t mind, I’d take you too, but you’re too heavy.

“I don’t mind at all. I’m looking forward to the peaceful tranquility.”

“Peaceful tranquility?” Sir Henry grumbled. “Where did you go to school?” he continued.

“I have no time for this bickering,” Fanny interrupted, turning and walking through the parlor with Sir Henry.

“Oh no, I don’t like to be carried this way….” Sir Henry yelled, seeing the floor passing by as Fanny hurried down the corridor. “GRANDFATHER…!” he yelled. Grandfather laughed.

Wilfred was delighted to see Abby, Fanny, the mice, and surprisingly Sir Henry who was upside down in Fanny’s arms. “Good morning, Wilfred,” Abby greeted him.

“Morning,” he replied, looking at all the smiles. “Are we going for a drive?”

“No. Things have come up and I wanted the mice and… Sir Henry,” she said and then paused, glancing at Fanny, who gave her a contented smile back, “to stay with you today,” Abby replied. Fanny saw the look, but still enjoyed having Sir Henry with them.

Wilfred was worried seeing Sir Henry upside down in Fanny's arm. He knew something was wrong.

"The Sheriff was here last night," Sir Henry said. "They took everyone except me, Grandfather and the mice."

Wilfred cast his eyes upon Abby. "I'm in trouble," Abby said. When she finished telling him everything, Wilfred sighed, "Sometimes I think I am getting old. I'm sorry for not remembering."

"Remembering what?" Wilson asked.

"I saw the whole thing that night when they slipped up here and broke in through the basement window."

Fanny stepped back. "You saw them break in through the basement window?" she asked.

"Yes," Wilfred sighed again.

"I'll be…" Fanny said, staring at Abby.

"We'll keep that information under our bonnets for now," Abby remarked, nodding her head. "And you," she continued, eyeing up Wilfred. "Who said you were old." That made Wilfred feel better - he didn't get scolded.

Poor Wilfred, Benjamin thought. *Maybe he needs that longevity spell.*

At that time, a car pulled up in front of the manor. Flo, Karen and Albert got out. They raced up to the door and knocked. No one answered. Flo tried the handle, the door opened. "Hello," she shouted, walking into the parlor. "They must be still asleep," Karen said.

Grandfather slightly opened one eye and looked at the group.

"I'll go up, you two head to the back," Flo suggested, taking the stairs.

"Oh look," Fanny said, pointing at Karen and Albert walking out onto the kitchen patio. She watched Albert go back in. "I bet Flo is with them," Fanny continued, suspecting that's why Albert went back inside.

"Quick, you three hide," Abby said to the mice. The mice all scampered under the workbench. "We better hide Sir Henry too. Who in their right mind would have him out here?" Abby continued.

Fanny laughed. "No one, that's who," she replied, picking him up and frantically looking about the garage. She spotted Shaun's work jacket on the bench. She quickly walked over, set Sir Henry down and tossed the jacket over him. "Not that filthy thing," Sir Henry muffled underneath. "Shh… keep quiet," Fanny softly scolded, walking out of the garage.

Abby… Fanny…!" Karen shouted, walking up to them. They looked over Karen's shoulder at Albert and Flo walking down the patio steps.

"Morning, Karen," Abby replied.

Karen walked up and hugged her. "The whole town sounds like a turned over beehive with all the chattering about you being arrested last night," Karen said, letting her go.

"It's true, I *was* arrested last night. For witchcraft, no less."

"Witchcraft?!" Karen replied, shaking her head.

"Isn't that the most ridiculous thing you've ever heard?" Fanny stepped in, waving at Flo and Albert walking up.

"Morning you two," Flo greeted them.

"Good morning," they replied.

Albert greeted Abby and Fanny while glancing into the garage at Wilfred.

"Will you look at that? Now that's a classic if I ever saw one," he beamed, walking up to Wilfred. "Albert," Karen said in a tone of dismay. He looked at his wife and then at the women all standing there. "Right, right," he replied, walking out of the garage. "I spoke to the owner of the grocery store this morning. He filled me in on what happened last night," Albert continued.

Abby nodded and then sighed. "Oh, Abby," Flo gushed, hugging her.

"How could they do this to you?"

Abby stepped back. Before she could say another word, Fanny stepped in. "Sid and Don lied to Abby about the price for the manor. They added ten thousand dollars onto the sale of the manor and then they had the gall to come back and try to steal some more. Abby caught them red handed and now they've come up with this nonsense."

"You've got to be kidding me?" Karen said, stunned.

"Come, let's go inside and I'll tell you everything on the way," Abby said, walking back to the manor.

After they left, Sir Henry muffled, "Will somebody get this filthy jacket off of me?"

Wilfred rolled back to where Sir Henry was standing. "Wilson," he said, laughing, "Will you three help Sir Henry?"

Inside the manor, Flo and Fanny brought out glasses of lemonade for everyone sitting in the den. There was a moment of silence before the conversation continued.

"Why didn't you come and tell one of us when you found out that Sid and Don stole your money?" Flo asked, setting her glass down. "I don't know," Abby replied. "I guess I should have."

"If they had done that to us," Karen stepped in. "I would have gone straight to Sheriff Collins."

"Enough," Fanny interrupted. "It doesn't matter now. We have to help Abby get through all this nonsense. Also," she continued, "Abby made an official complaint against Sid and Don last night for breaking in. Sheriff Collins will be charging them today."

Albert nodded then realized something odd. "We're missing somebody," he said. The women dropped their thoughts looking at Albert. *He's right, where is Claudia?* Flo thought. "You don't think Claudia has taken Sid and Don's side, do ya?"

Abby sat there fuming. *I'd bet a shiny penny that Claudia has, in fact, sided with Sid and Don.*

Suddenly, they heard a car pulling up out front. "Sit, Abby, I'll see who it is," Fanny said, getting up.

"It's probably Claudia," Karen whispered.

Fanny opened the door. It was Fred and Mayor Bumpkin. Abby stood up.

"Good morning," Fred greeted everyone.

"Good morning," they said in unison.

"Mayor Bumpkin?" Abby said in a questioning manner to why he was there.

"Morning, Mrs. Rose. I thought I'd come up and see how you were doing."

"Under the circumstances, I'm holding up."

"I'm sure that's enough to even try to do under these circumstances," Mayor Bumpkin replied. "Look," he continued, "I just wanted to tell ya that after I went down and spoke with Sheriff Collins and heard the whole story, you have my full support."

"Thank you, Mayor. Have you seen Claudia today?"

Mayor Bumpkin cocked his head in dismay. "I'm sorry to say this, but Claudia has made an official complaint against you too."

"What?" Fanny shouted.

"That's right," Fred stepped in. "She's written out a statement claiming that you turned her hair blue, Abby."

Flo stood up and laughed. "I did that. I used the wrong bottle that day," she said.

Fred nodded. "I'll need that in writing," he replied. "Now," he continued, "let's sit down and I'll go over all the evidence and statements with you."

"Abby," Mayor Bumpkin said. She turned and looked at him. "I have to get back. I just wanted to come up and tell ya my feelings, and also, from what I am hearing on the street, most of the town folks are behind you as well."

"Well that's nice to know. Thank you for coming, Mayor," she replied, walking him to the door. After she seen him out, they all sat in the den listening to Fred going over the case with Abby.

"Alright, here are the names: Sid and Don, Claudia and Ernie and Arnold."

"Before you go on," Fanny interrupted. "we've discovered how Sid and Don got in that night."

Abby looked at her surprised. She had forgotten what Wilfred had said.

"How?" Fred replied.

"They came in through the basement window on the west side of the manor."

"Really?" Fred replied, happy to hear that. "Well, I don't know too many people who'd come through a basement window to see how you are doing. I'll have a fingerprint expert come over and see if they can lift some prints off the window. If they did, in fact, come in that way, I'll nail them during the preliminary hearing," he continued, looking through the statements in his file.

He pulled out Sid's statement and scanned down the paragraphs. "Here is what Sid had stated in his sworn affidavit. He said that Don and he came to the door around eight in the evening. You let them in then a white male lion came down the stairs. You panicked and turned them into frogs."

Abby laughed. Her friends joined in and laughed along with her.

"I know it sounds funny. I laughed too when I heard it. However, I saw the photos they have," he said, pulling one out, "This is not your stuffed lion. Your lion only stands ten inches in height. This is a real male lion in the photo."

Abby glanced over at Fanny. Fanny could see the joy in Abby's eyes hearing that.

"Even though it's not Theodore in the photo, do any of you truly believe that I could make that stuffed toy come to life or turn people into frogs?" Abby asked, gazing at everyone.

"Oh now, Abby," Karen, gushed. Those fruit loops are reaching for the stars. Who in their right mind could even believe such baloney?"

Fanny sat back relieved. She could tell Albert and Flo were thinking the same thing.

Abby focused her attention on Fred. "So, what do Ernie and Arnold say in their statements, besides the truth?"

"They said that they came up here looking for Willy and Bobby Ray, who came up here looking for Molly. Apparently, Molly came here that night to visit with you, and Willy and Bobby Ray got worried. That's when Ernie and Arnold said they saw the lion."

Abby giggled. "As you all know, Ernie and Arnold came up here with Willy's toy gun to rob me before Sid and Don could get their hands on my money. That's the truth, and I know Molly can testify to that because she did, in fact, come up here that night. Not to visit, but to warn me they were coming."

"She's not testifying. Nor are Willy and Bobby Ray," Fred replied.

"They're not?" Fanny questioned.

"They could… that's if Mrs. Rose wants to make an official complaint against them."

"No, and the reason why is I believe that Willy and Bobby Ray were conned by Sid and Don to come up here and help them. I gave those two boys a good scolding and sent them on their way."

"I can just imagine those two slimy dogs baiting those kids," Fred replied and then paused, "But just to let you know, I spoke to all three. It was off the record due to their age. Those three pretty much said what you're telling us right now, Mrs. Rose. Willy and Bobby Ray came up here with Sid and Don to steal your money. Molly said that she came up here to warn you, and that's when Ernie and Arnold showed up at the front door with Willy's toy gun."

"You have to make an official complaint, Abby," Fanny said. "They must testify."

"That's enough, Fanny," Abby scolded. "I don't want those boys in trouble. They still have a long life ahead of them and you know a charge like that will ruin them for sure."

"Maybe Abby is right," Karen remarked. "But can't the court at least order them to take the stand without them getting into any trouble?" she continued.

"I could ask the Judge during the preliminary hearing," Fred replied.

Abby shook her head. “Let’s just drop that argument, shall we? At least you all know the truth.”

“We never doubted you for a second,” Flo replied.

Abby pleasantly smiled. “Thank you. I’m so glad I have friends like you,” she said.

“So now what?” Fanny asked, getting back to the problem.

“There’s no way this will get past a preliminary hearing,” Fred said.

“That’s when we go over all the statements and evidence. I’ll have a chance then to cross-examine each witness as they come forward. The finger prints alone might do it, however, I’ll also have a computer graphic designer in the courtroom that day to go over the doctored photos if I have to,” Fred continued.

Abby sat back and sighed knowing it was still going to be a tormenting week ahead regardless if Fred had all the nails to seal those vultures inside their own coffins.

42

Judgment Day

Tuesday morning came in with rolling dark clouds over the landscape as Abby just sat in silence while Fred drove her to the courthouse. Cloverdale was a town built on its history - proud from its beginnings with so many historical places. The courthouse was at the top of the list as one of its main attractions: a white washed Victorian style structure with beautiful wooden entrance doors and a vestibule with stairs leading up on both sides to the balcony. The room below was small, separated into two sections by a dark hardwood guardrail, one side for the court proceedings and the other for spectators.

By the time Fred and Abby arrived, they saw hoards of people gathered out front. “It looks as if the circus has come to town,” Fred remarked, driving around to the rear parking lot.

“It might as well be a circus,” Abby replied. “And the show is about to start.”

“Oh now, stop worrying, Mrs. Rose. You’ll be up before the judge for only a minute or so and then I’ll whisk you back to the manor.”

Abby sighed opening her door. They walked into the rear entrance and strolled down the corridor. A courthouse guard spotted them. “Good Morning Fred, Mrs. Rose. You two may have a seat in the waiting room. I’ll call you when Judge Hollingsworth is ready.” Fred nodded and proceeded on.

After they had entered the small room, Abby sat there staring at the walls. *I could use a bit of magic about now,* she thought. That made her think of her father, Derek Von Haussler. *What would he do in a situation like this?* She smiled thinking he’d probably just disappear and reappear on the other side of the planet, a place she wished she were right now.

The door opened. Fred stood up. “Judge Hollingsworth is ready,” the guard said.

Abby wrung her hands getting up. She nervously followed Fred into the courtroom full of people staring at her. She smiled seeing Fanny and Mitt, Karen and Albert, and Flo sitting up front.

“All rise for the Honorable Judge Hollingsworth from the District of Cloverdale County,” the Court Bailiff called out, bringing the congregation to attention. Judge Hollingsworth's chamber door opened and the tall prominent Judge entered the courtroom dressed in his black gown. "Please be seated," he said, walking up to his chair.

"This court is now in session on this day, the tenth of May," the Bailiff said.

Abby sat there clutching her purse. Fred looked over at her and smiled while they waited for the judge to look over the court documents. "Fred, will you and your client please stand?"

They both stood up. "Mrs. Rose, I have here on my desk a formal document charging you with the use of witchcraft here in the state of Pennsylvania, which is in violation of Ordinance Thirty-Three, Section Ten. How do you plead, guilty or not guilty?"

"I am innocent of the charge, Your Honor."

Judge Hollingsworth sat back in his chair. He took off his glasses, wiped them off and then placed them back onto his nose. "Let it be known that Mrs. Rose is pleading not guilty," Judge Hollingsworth said to the court reporter.

She nodded, typing.

"Now, with your plea, I'll set the pretrial motion date on," he continued and then paused, looking down at his calendar, "the Fifteenth of May, at eight a.m. Do you have any questions?" he asked.

"No." Fred replied.

"Is the prosecution side requesting bail?"

"No, Your Honor," Emmett replied.

"That will be all then. You're dismissed, Mrs. Rose," Judge Hollingsworth said, standing up.

"All rise for the Honorable Judge Hollingsworth," the Bailiff bellowed. The congregation rose to their feet. Judge Hollingsworth walked out. Fanny leaned over the separation barrier. "You did wonderful," she whispered.

Abby smiled at Fanny then gazed over Fanny's shoulder at all the people gawking at her. She spotted Claudia in the back row sitting next to Betsy and Sue. The look in Claudia's eyes said it all - she was on fire. *Your day is coming, my dear,* Abby thought, focusing her attention on Fanny again. "Have everyone come over for tea this afternoon. Tell Shaun to come too," she whispered.

"I will."

Fred tapped her arm. Abby turned and followed him out.

By the time Fred pulled up at the manor, Abby felt spent. The turmoil and worry were taking its toll. "This will be over before you know it, Mrs. Rose," he said, getting out and rounding the car. He walked her to the door. "I'll be in touch after the pretrial motion hearing and tell you where we stand. I can assure you this case will not get past a preliminary trial. So just relax and take it easy."

"I'll try," she replied, opening the door. Fred stood there until she closed it behind her. *How can anyone do this to such a wonderful person?* he thought, walking back to his car.

That same afternoon, Abby's spirits lifted when her friends came over with Shaun. They had a lovely day together chatting and having fun. Only on several occasions did the trial even come up in conversation. When everyone stood up to leave, she whispered in Shaun's ear to stay for dinner. He said yes. She then saw her friends out and turned toward him. "I didn't prepare anything tonight," she confessed, walking alongside him through the parlor.

"That's alright. I just wanted to be alone with you anyway." Abby turned and smiled, "Me too," she replied, strolling into the kitchen. "Now, what would you like?"

"How about a ham sandwich and a cold glass of milk?"

"That I can do," she replied, opening Simon and getting the ham and milk out.

Abby sat there watching him eat his sandwich and then finish drinking his glass of milk. "Feel better?" she asked. "Yes," Shaun replied, looking at her from across the table. He could tell by her smile throughout the day that this whole mess was making her sick.

"You know, Abigail," he started to say.

"What?"

"There is no way this will last one full day in court. The whole town is in an uproar over this and most folks think the other side has lost their minds."

"The other side, you mean Sid and Don and their flock of vultures?"

Shaun laughed. "Yes, and I can't imagine what Bart Hornsby is thinking with his charming wife smack dab in the middle of it."

Abby cocked her head pondering that. She never thought of how Bart was handling all this. "Have you heard anything?" she asked.

"No, but Mr. Olson from the service station said that Bart is keeping a low profile."

"I can just imagine," she quipped.

"So,x what are you going to do when this is over? I mean you're not going to leave, are you?" he asked.

That question caught her off guard. She thought of an answer. "Why no, I never ran from anyone or anything. I am staying put. This is my home now."

Shaun sighed. "I'm so glad to hear that, Abigail," he replied and then paused. She could tell he wanted to say something. "What's cooking inside that head of yours?" she asked.

"Well…." he said and then paused, "would you mind waltzing with me again? I kind of liked it."

Abby sat up. "Kind of liked it?" she teased.

"Yes - sort of," he replied, blushing.

"Come now," she said, getting up and taking his plate and glass. "Let me put these in the sink and we'll go out into the parlor."

"Will you play something first?"

"Why of course."

She played a few melodies and then they spent the rest of the evening dancing. Once he got the hang of waltzing with her, she showed him the Charleston, a favorite dance in the 1920s. Around 10:00 that evening, Shaun had to leave. She saw him to the door. "Thank you for coming, Shaun. I sure enjoyed dancing with you. It took my mind off…" she started to say.

"That's what I was hoping," he interrupted her and then without a thought, he leaned over and kissed her on the cheek. It startled her, making her blush. She wanted to kiss him back, but refrained. "Goodnight, Shaun. Thank you for coming over."

He nodded, opened the door and left. After the door had closed, she leaned on it and sighed.

"Wow, that was some kiss," Benjamin said, coming out of the hole under the staircase.

She turned around. "Oh now, I've been wondering where you three were hiding," she replied, watching Wilson and Cracker walking out.

"Madam Rose," Sir Henry said.

She turned and looked at him. "You have something to say on the subject?" she questioned, placing her hands on her hips.

He looked at her for a moment and then jumped in. "It was truly a beautiful kiss."

"Oh now," she gushed. "You're all being silly," she continued, walking toward the elevator. "Goodnight, Sir Henry, Grandfather."

"Goodnight, Madam Rose," they replied, looking down at the mice. Sir Henry gave them a wink. They winked back, turned around and raced after Abby.

Grandfather waited until they had gone. He glanced over at Sir Henry. "It was truly a beautiful kiss," he said and then puckered up and blew Sir Henry one.

"My word," Sir Henry grumbled. "You'll give me nightmares if you keep that up," he continued.

Grandfather winked at him and then closed his eyes. All he heard was a long sigh in return.

43

Courthouse Proposal

On the day of the preliminary hearing, Fanny and Flo drove Abby to the courthouse. "I'm so sorry that Mitt had to go away on business. He really wanted to be here today," Fanny said.

"That's alright," Abby replied. "However, I am glad Fred was OK with you two driving me in this morning," Abby replied, buckling up.

"He's a fine lawyer," Flo commented from the back seat.

"Yes, he sure is," Fanny agreed, taking Abby's hand. "I think he's going to blow them right out of the water today."

"Let's hope," Abby replied.

Fanny looked up into the rearview mirror at Flo. Flo shook her head hearing the sadness in Abby's voice. Fanny softly sighed and proceeded down the driveway. The short trip to Cloverdale was quicker than Abby wanted. When Fanny turned onto Main Street, Abby gasped seeing all the people. They looked like a horde of army ants marching toward the courthouse on the outskirts of town. "Can you believe this?" Flo said, reading the signs supporting Abby.

"I'm shocked. I hardly know anyone here," Abby said. "Just look at those signs they're carrying and waving about."

"I told you, Abby," Fanny quipped.

"We've all told her," Flo added.

"Oh no, will you look at that?" Abby cut in, seeing a group of people in front of the courthouse holding up signs - "Burn the Witch."

"Well… I am not surprised," Fanny snidely remarked, taking the corner and driving around to the rear parking lot. "Now you know how many friends Claudia actually has. There were only five people standing there," she continued and then laughed.

Flo also laughed, but Abby remained silent. It made her angry. *In all my days of living,* she thought, *have I never wanted to see harm come to another human being, except for today. I would sure like to see Claudia, Sid and Don, and their darling little wives thrown into a slimy mud pit before they were hauled off to jail.*

After parking, Fanny got out and rounded the car. Abby opened her door. Fanny could see the dismay in Abby's expression. *Claudia's going to be paid back in full before this day is over,* Fanny thought, escorting Abby to the rear courthouse doors.

As they entered, Abby noticed Fred pacing up and down the small corridor. He turned and sighed upon seeing her. "Mrs. Rose, there you are," he bellowed, walking up to the women. "Good morning, Fred," they said. "Good morning, ladies. You two go ahead and take your seats. I need to get Abby down to the waiting room."

Flo and Fanny hugged Abby and wished her luck. Abby then followed Fred down the corridor to the waiting room where she sat the previous day. "We have about ten minutes to wait so with this time I'd like to tell you what happened during the pretrial motion's hearing," Fred said.

"I'm all ears," she sighed.

"It's good news, Abby."

She let go of her frown. "My fingerprint expert, John Cobs, lifted some real good prints off the basement window."

Abby wrinkled her brow. "John was going to knock, but decided not to disturb you."

Abby nodded.

"I had the fingerprints submitted as evidence. In addition, I took Emmett's photo evidence of the lions and your moose head to my photographer, Bill Gibson's office. Bill showed me how easy it is to doctor a photo using a digital camera and a laptop computer. He quickly snapped a photo of me, downloaded it into his computer and then brought up a photo of a guy surfing on his computer screen," Fred said and then paused. "You're not going to believe this, but it took Bill about five minutes to cut out the image of the guy surfing from the picture and then he replaced it with the one he just took of me. It looked so funny because I was wearing a suit coat and tie riding that surfboard," he continued with a smile.

Abby lightly laughed, seeing the image inside her head. "You really think we have them over a barrel?" she asked.

"Not over a barrel, Mrs. Rose, we have them inside the darn thing, and they haven't a clue that we're about to push them over Niagara Falls today." Before she could reply, there was a knock on the door. It opened. "Judge Hollingsworth is ready," a guard said.

Abby slowly stood up and followed Fred out. When she walked into the courtroom, the first thing she noticed were all the people sitting there. Even the balcony above her looked as if a flock of pigeons had landed and had taken it over. People were standing, sitting and some were leaning over the railing looking down at her. She glanced back to see Shaun and his parents sitting alongside Karen and Albert who had saved seats for Fanny and Flo. Shaun smiled at her. She smiled back and then shifted her eyes on his parents. Mrs. Stevenson smiled. Mr. Stevenson nodded his head. *That's a good sign,* she thought, sitting down and focusing her attention on Judge Hollingsworth's chamber door.

Emmett and Fred took a moment to greet one another and then turned in their seats.

"All rise for the Honorable Judge Hollingsworth for the District of Cloverdale. This court is now in session on this day the twenty-seventh of May," the Bailiff said. Judge Hollingsworth entered the courtroom and sat down. "You may be seated," he said. The spectators anxiously sat down waiting for the show to begin.

"I want to start out by saying we have selected a jury for this case and they can be called upon today to render a verdict. Or, it could be settled by me if I find that there is insignificant evidence," Judge Hollingsworth said and then paused, "The state can now begin the proceedings," he continued, looking at Emmett.

Emmet got up buttoning his suit coat. *Whatever happens today, I am not going to end up in jail for siding with criminals,* he thought, focusing his attention on Judge Hollingsworth. "Thank you, Your Honor. Good morning ladies and gentlemen of the jury," he greeted them, walking over to the jury box. They all nodded. "The state believes we have more than enough evidence to settle this today with a conviction by you, the jury.

"This morning I'm going to break this case down into chronological order. First off, I will have an expert on witches take the stand and discuss in detail the craft of placing spells on people.

"Next, I'll have eyewitnesses come forward and describe to you what they saw and then I'll bring out the physical evidence to show you," he started his longwinded opening statement. "Now, today is not just your average day here in Cloverdale, this town has not had a case like this in nearly a century."

Abby glanced at the jurors sitting there listening to Emmett. She shifted her eyes up at Judge Hollingsworth, who had leaned back in his chair listening too.

"I know it seems rather hard to believe that we have witches in our midst here in the twenty-first century, but we do, and today… I am going to prove to you beyond a reasonable doubt that Abigail Rose is, in fact, a witch. I have irrefutable eyewitness testimony, from those who actually saw with their very own eyes, Mrs. Rose placing people under spells. In addition, I will produce before this court strong evidence to substantiate these findings for the state," Emmett continued, pacing back and forth in front of the jury box. "So… at this time, I'd like to call my first witness, Jane Bellingham, the Cloverdale Librarian."

Whispering could be heard throughout the courtroom. Fred glanced over at Abby. She wrinkled her brow questioning Jane taking the stand. Fred slightly shook his head.

After Jane had been sworn in, she sat down in the witness stand. Emmett walked over and greeted her.

"Good morning, Mr. Fisher, Your Honor," she replied, looking up at him. The Judge nodded.

"Jane," Emmett said, starting his questioning. "How long have you been the Cloverdale librarian?"

"Ten years."

Emmett nodded. "And how long have you been studying witchcraft during that time as the librarian?"

"The whole time."

"Do you consider yourself an expert on the subject of witchcraft?" Emmett asked, turning toward the jurors.

"I suppose," Jane replied.

Emmett turned and faced her.

"I think anyone who has studied witchcraft as long as I have rightly should be."

Laughter erupted. Judge Hollingsworth sat up looking back at the people. The laughter stopped.

Before Emmett continued, he waited for the courtroom to settle down.

"Jane, can you please inform the jurors how magic is performed by witches?"

Jane looked over at the six women and six men. "They use a mixture of potions and spells."

Abby slightly cringed hearing that. She kept a straight face sitting there as if she didn't have a care in the world.

"Does the person have to be in the same room with a witch when the witch mixes a potion or casts a spell over them?" Emmett asked.

"Sometimes and sometimes not, it all depends on how powerful the witch is," Jane replied.

Emmett turned and faced the jurors. "Can you tell us what types of things witches use in creating a potion?" he asked, turning and looking at her.

"They use all kinds of nasty things."

Laughter again erupted from the crowd. Judge Hollingsworth raised his hand. The laughter stopped.

"Like what?" Emmett continued.

"They use vinegar, weeds, old bones, dead frogs, crushed bat droppings," she replied and then paused, hearing Judge Hollingsworth clearing his throat. She turned in her seat toward the judge. He kept a straight face. "May I?" he then asked, Emmett.

"Yes, Your Honor" he replied.

"Mrs. Bellingham," Judge Hollingsworth said. "I'm sure the prosecutor has informed you that this is a preliminary hearing."

"Yes, sir."

"Mrs. Bellingham, in a preliminary hearing, the Defense and the Judge can ask questions too.

"Yes, sir. Mr. Fisher made me aware of that."

"Good. Now tell me, Mrs. Bellingham, from what section in the library do you gather your research?"

Jane wrinkled her brow and then cast her eyes on Emmett. Emmett nodded for her to answer. "The fiction section, your Honor."

Laughter erupted. Judge Hollingsworth placed his hand to his chin to hide his smile. Fred humorously sighed sitting back. Abby looked over at the jurors, they were all smiling too. Emmett was not. He was melting inside his shoes. Jane had just excused her testimony with that ridiculous answer. "I have no further questions for this witness, Emmett." Judge Hollingsworth said.

"I have no further questions for Mrs. Bellingham either," Emmett replied in a disgruntled tone, walking back to his seat.

Judge Hollingsworth looked at Fred. "I have no questions for the witness," Fred said to the Judge.

"You may step down, Mrs. Bellingham," Judge Hollingsworth requested.

"Did I say something wrong?" Jane asked.

"No," the Judge replied.

Jane got up and left the witness stand. Judge Hollingsworth looked at Emmett. *I'd hate to be in his shoes right now,* the Judge thought.

"I call Claudia Hornsby to take the stand," Emmett said, feeling the stares from the jurors.

Fred leaned over to Abby and whispered, "Here we go."

Claudia entered the courtroom. She raised her right hand and was sworn in before sitting down. She looked over the crowd and then cast her eyes on Abby. They were dead and lifeless. "Good morning, Mrs. Hornsby," Emmett greeted her.

"Morning," she replied, tossing a glance at the jurors.

"Can you first start off by telling us what happened on the fifth of April down at the beauty parlor here in Cloverdale?" Emmett started his questions.

"Why certainly. I was there having my hair done."

"By whom?"

"Why Flo, she owns the place."

"And what happened while you were there?"

"Well, if I recall, Harriett Brown, Karen Bloom and I were all there having our hair done when Mrs. Rose and Fanny Chamberlin walked in."

Emmett nodded for her to continue.

"Well… we were all shocked to see Fanny looking like a million dollars."

"What do you mean by that phrase, a million dollars?"

"If anyone knows Fanny, Fanny could never dress herself right and…" she said and then paused when laughter and talking erupted from the crowd. Judge Hollingsworth tapped his gavel on the sound block. The room became quiet.

"What I'm trying to say, in a nice sort of way is, before Mrs. Rose came to town, Fanny looked like an old book worm," Claudia continued. No one laughed this time. Abby, however, coiled in her seat to that remark. *What a cruel and disdainful woman,* she thought, looking at Claudia in her pink dress. *If that color doesn't make you look fatter than you already are, I don't know what would,* she snarled in thought.

"Please go on," Emmett said.

"Fanny went off as if she were queen of the ball, giving Mrs. Rose lavishing praises for fixing her up. No one could fix her up like that, but a witch."

A stunning sigh went out through the spectators.

"That's a very harsh word," he said.

"I'm sorry, but that's not all that happened,"

"Please tell us," Emmett pushed.

"After Fanny spewed all that attention on Mrs. Rose, Fanny said that Mrs. Rose also cut her hair. Flo was ecstatic by that revelation and asked Mrs. Rose to show her how she cuts hair. Mrs. Rose declined. I can only imagine why," she replied, looking at the jurors and seeing if they'd give a response to that remark. They just calmly sat there listening to her.

"Then what happened," Emmett kept leading his witness.

"I said something smart trying to goad Mrs. Rose to show us how she cuts hair and Mrs. Rose beaded her eyes at me then blinked. After that, she gave an excuse that she had to run along to do some grocery shopping. Then the next thing I know, everyone is laughing at me. When I turned and looked into the mirror, I almost fainted seeing the color of my hair."

"What color was it?"

"It was blue," Claudia replied in a scornful manner, folding her arms.

The courtroom erupted with laughter once again. Even Judge Hollingsworth smiled, tapping his gavel. The crowd settled down.

"Do you think Mrs. Rose made your hair turn blue?" Emmett asked.

"Why of course. I've been going to Flo's Hair Dresser for years now and never once did that ever happen."

The jurors all sat up hearing that answer. They looked at Abby as if she were sitting in a park on a warm summer's day.

"Is there anything else that makes you believe that Mrs. Rose is a witch?"

"Yes, I saw it with my very own eyes."

The spectators sat up intently listening now.

"What happened?" Emmett asked.

It was on a Wednesday, I think. Betsy Peterson and Sue Reed came over to my house with the most ridiculous story. They said that their husbands, Sid and Don, who work for Meek's Realtors in town, went up to see how Mrs. Rose was doing. They sold her the place."

"And?" Emmett pushed.

“Well… when they got there and were invited in, a white male lion came down the stairs into the parlor. Betsy and Sue said Mrs. Rose panicked and turned Sid and Don into frogs.”

Whispering and talking was heard in the back.

“Order,” Judge Hollingsworth called out.

“Go on, Mrs. Hornsby,” Emmett said.

“After they told me, I thought they were just pulling my leg. So, they took me over to Betsy’s house to see for myself. I couldn’t believe my eyes - there they were, sitting inside Betsy’s tub.”

Everyone laughed - even Judge Hollingsworth.

“I am not kidding,” Claudia said, looking into the crowd.

Judge Hollingsworth tapped his gavel. Claudia waited for the people to settle down. “Go on,” Emmett said.

“Well that’s it,” Claudia replied, raising her brow waiting for him to give her another question.

“Did you think they were pulling your leg when you saw the two frogs?” Emmett asked.

“You know, when I was standing there looking at those bullfrogs I thought maybe it was a prank. Then those frogs started talking. I knew by the sound of their little voices that it was Sid and Don.”

“She’s been nipping with old man Cooper behind Charlie’s pub,” someone yelled out.

The entire courthouse broke out in laughter and talking.

Claudia stared out at the crowd. Judge Hollingsworth stood up. The courtroom settled down.

Claudia then looked over at the jurors again. “I don’t care what they think. I’m telling you the truth, and if that isn’t bad enough, Sid and Don told me that Ernie Meyers and Arnold Gilbert were turned into frogs as well by Mrs. Rose.”

Emmett wasn’t going to allow the spectators to turn this into a three-ring circus. He quickly asked his next question. “Did you see Ernie Meyers and Arnold Gilbert as frogs?”

Claudia knew she had to lie to this question because Emmett had warned her not to get herself involved with Ernie and Arnold because of them bringing a gun to a robbery. “No, and I am glad I didn’t. Just seeing Sid and Don has given me nightmares.”

"I have no further questions, Your Honor," Emmett said, turning and sitting down.

Whispering and talking went on in the back when Fred stood up. He unbuttoned his suit coat walking up to the witness stand. "Good morning, Mrs. Hornsby."

"Morning," she replied, shifting in her seat.

"That was some story," Fred said, shaking his head.

"It isn't a story. I did see them as frogs."

Fred let that pass. He had another angle to trap Claudia. "Before we get into that, let's start at the beginning of your statement," he said, turning toward the jurors. "First off, do you have actual proof that Mrs. Rose performed some kind of witchcraft on you that day at Flo's?"

"No, but what else could it be?" Claudia replied in a tone of defiance.

"How about Flo using the wrong bottle of hair coloring," he suggested, walking back to his desk. He picked up a sworn affidavit and approached the witness stand.

"Flo told me that she didn't. That's why I came to the conclusion that it had to be Mrs. Rose, wouldn't you? Especially after seeing what she did to Sid and Don?" she replied, trying to keep their names in front of the jurors.

"No, I wouldn't have thought it was Mrs. Rose," he sharply replied, "but I can say this much. This here is Flo's sworn affidavit, which, if I need her, she'll be called to testify." "Now," he continued, walking over to the jurors, "this is what Flo stated happened on that day: '*I told Claudia that I did not use the wrong hair coloring because I was afraid she'd clobber me. In truth - I did use the wrong bottle.*' Fred read aloud. He turned and looked at Claudia. "It appears you have a lot of people afraid of you in this town," he continued, trying to bait her into anger.

"She sure does," someone yelled out.

Judge Hollingsworth sat up looking over the crowd. Fred smiled inside from that outburst seeing Claudia sitting there ready to blow her top like a volcano, and she did. "Why I never…" Claudia spat. "You undoubtedly must be half out of your mind, Fred, along with that fool who just shouted, to speak to me in such a demeaning and distasteful manner. I deserve respect in this town."

Abby was more than delighted; she was over the moon seeing Claudia in full stride, showing her true colors - mean, nasty and downright ugly.

"Respect?" Fred replied. "You sit here today and tell me that you deserve respect from the good people of this town?" he replied, turning toward the jurors.

"So, you're saying that people should just bow down to you? Is that correct?" he continued, turning to face her.

Claudia caught a lump in her throat seeing Fred getting the upper hand with his questioning. "I didn't mean it like that," she replied.

"She thinks she's the queen of Cloverdale," someone shouted.

Judge Hollingsworth leaned up and tapped his gavel. "Order, please."

"Your Honor," Claudia bellowed, turning in her chair, "are you just going to sit there and allow this overbearing little twit of a man speak to me like this?"

Judge Hollingsworth heard it in her tone and saw it on her face - that was a slap. He leaned over toward her. "Mrs. Hornsby, are you talking *to* me or *at* me?" he sharply inquired.

"That's the Claudia Hornsby I know. Now she's disrespecting the judge," someone yelled.

Judge Hollingsworth slammed his gavel. "The next person who yells out in this courtroom will get two days in the county lock up. Is that understood!?"

Claudia melted in her chair feeling like a real buffoon. *I'd better do something quick or I am finished,* she thought, realizing she had just chastised the Judge in front of everyone, including the jury, and now the town folk were calling for her head.

"I have no further questions," Fred said, turning to sit down.

"Wait," Claudia said, stepping out of her thoughts.

Fred turned and looked at her.

"Aren't you going to ask me any questions about Sid and Don?"

"Mrs. Hornsby, I think everyone sitting here right now knows how much you hate Mrs. Rose. You hate her because she has more money than you do. You hate her because, in your mind, she has taken all your friends away. So, to get back at her you came up with this outlandish lie about her being a witch when rightfully…" he started to say.

"Fred," Abby, spoke up from behind him. Fred caught his tongue and sighed. He almost said it - 'the real witch is you, Mrs. Hornsby'.

The jurors all looked over at Abby sitting there. They felt sorry for her, and yet, they felt proud of what she had just done - she stopped her lawyer from going over the edge.

Fred glanced up at the Judge. "I have no more further questions, Your Honor."

"But…" Claudia started to say, standing up.

"I have no further questions, Your Honor," Fred interrupted her, sitting down.

"That will be all, Mrs. Hornsby," Judge Hollingsworth said in a stern manner.

"But…" she said again, staring at Emmett sitting there with his chin resting in the palm of his hands. The expression on his face said it all, 'you imbecile'.

Claudia stepped down from the witness stand. She slowly proceeded across the wooden floor toward the gate. A guard opened it. She walked through keeping her eyes straight ahead. It was the hardest thing she had ever done, to have to walk through a crowd of people who had nothing but contempt for her.

Fanny, Flo, Karen and Albert gazed up at her as she passed them. Shaun and his parents sat there with frowns. Mayor Bumpkin and his wife slowly shook their heads in the back row as Claudia opened the double doors and walked out.

She stood there in the late morning sun, and deeply sighed knowing her rein was over in Cloverdale. *I'm finished. I'm completely finished in this town,* she thought, walking over to her car. When she got in and slammed the door shut, her next thought was of Bart. *I hope he still wants to take that trip to Europe.*

Back inside the courtroom, Judge Hollingsworth looked at Emmett. It was his turn at bat again. Emmett slowly stood up and faced the jurors. "At this time, I would like to present to the court some evidence."

"Bailiff," Judge Hollingsworth said. The Bailiff walked over to Emmett.

"Bring in the two stuffed lions and the moose head, please," Emmett whispered. The Bailiff nodded and left. Five minutes later, he and a few guards came back with Theodore, Tasha and Boris. They set them on a table before the jury box. The jurors amusingly gazed at the two stuffed toy animals and the large moose head.

"Now for the record, Exhibit A, the white stuffed lion, Exhibit B, the brown, stuffed lioness and Exhibit C, the moose head were all taken from Mrs. Rose's house," Emmett said, walking over to his desk and picking up the photos Wayne and Edie had taken on the night they slipped up to the manor. He handed the photos to one of the jurors. "Please pass them around," he continued then waited. When the last female juror viewed all the photos, she handed them back to Emmett.

"Do you see any resemblance between the ones in the photos and the ones now sitting before you on the table?" he asked the jurors. They all nodded.

"Objection," Fred interrupted, standing up.

Emmett spun around. Judge Hollingsworth cocked his head wondering why he was objecting.

"Your Honor, I would like to have it stated for the record that the photos are of real lions and the ones on the table are toys. The only resemblance within two of the photos is the real male lion and the stuffed toy lion are white."

"Sustained," Judge Hollingsworth said and then turned toward the jurors. "Is that why you all nodded?"

The jurors said yes with a nod of their heads.

"OK, you may continue, Emmett," Judge Hollingsworth said.

Emmett locked eyes with Fred. *I almost got away with that,* Emmett thought, turning and facing the jurors. "At this point I would like to call my next witness." Judge Hollingsworth nodded. "I call Sid Peterson to the stand."

Fred leaned over toward Abby. "How are you holding up?" he whispered.

"Good. I loved what you did to Claudia."

He slightly smiled. "Now it's Sid's turn to get pushed over the falls."

Abby sighed with hope, watching Sid take the witness stand.

Before Emmett started his questions, Judge Hollingsworth leaned over to Sid. "Mr. Peterson, I want to make it perfectly clear to you that since you've been officially charged with an offense and have been read your rights, anything you say or do today in this hearing could be used against you. Do you understand?"

"Yes, your Honor."

"Alright," Judge Hollingsworth said, sitting up. He looked at the jurors.

"Understand ladies and gentlemen of this jury, one is innocent until proven guilty. They nodded, looking at Sid.

"Emmett," Judge Hollingsworth said, waving his hand for him to proceed.

"Thank you, Your Honor. Good morning, Mr. Peterson," Emmett greeted him.

"Good morning," Sid replied, wondering how Claudia did. By the look in Emmett's eyes, he thought it didn't go well with her.

"Can you please give the court a little background regarding your relationship with Mrs. Rose?"

Sid explained to the jurors Mrs. Rose buying the manor through Meek's real estate agency in Cloverdale and the condition of the manor on the day she purchased it. This bit of information gave Emmett the lead into his first question. "In your affidavit, you stated that you and Mr. Don Reed went up to the manor that night to see how Mrs. Rose was doing?"

"Yes, we heard that the manor was up and running and we just wanted to make sure, since we sold her the place, that she was happy."

"That's a bald-faced lie," Abby leaned over and whispered to Fred.

Fred placed his hand over hers. Abby settled back in her seat.

"And after Mrs. Rose let you in what happened?" Emmett asked.

"After walking through the foyer, a white male lion came down the staircase."

Emmett showed Sid the photo. "Is this the lion you saw?"

"Yes," he replied, looking toward the jurors.

"Then what happened?" Emmett asked.

"Mrs. Rose spun around, saw the lion and then spun back around and looked at us. The next thing I know is I'm hopping out of my pants as a frog."

The entire courtroom fell out with laughter.

Judge Hollingsworth tapped his gavel while hiding his smile. The courtroom settled down.

By the expression on Emmett's face, Sid could tell that Emmett wanted him to answer the questions straight without trying to be funny.

"Now… is this the same lion?" Emmett asked him, pointing at the stuffed toy sitting on the table."

Giggles and whispers went out from the crowd.

"Yes, she calls him Theodore."

"So, you saw Theodore as a real lion?"

"Yes."

"Objection, Your Honor," Fred interrupted, standing up.

"Sustained," Judge Hollingsworth said, turning in his chair toward Sid.

"Did you actually see her perform some kind of witchcraft over the stuffed toy to bring it to life, Mr. Peterson?"

"No, but it's the same lion. Look at those eyes," he replied, pointing at Theodore sitting there. "Now look at that photo," he continued, "they're the same lion."

"Mr. Peterson, I do have eyes," Judge Hollingsworth replied. "However, if you did not actually see her perform some kind of witchcraft over that stuffed toy, then you cannot be one hundred percent certain that it is the same lion, can you?"

"No, Your Honor, but regardless of that fact, it scared me to death when it came down those stairs," Sid replied.

As Judge Hollingsworth was questioning Sid, Emmett glanced over at the jurors. He thought they were leaning toward Sid's side of the argument.

Judge Hollingsworth sat back and waved his hand for Emmett to continue.

"I'd like, at this time, to enter into the records that Mr. Peterson did not actually see Mrs. Rose place a spell over the stuffed toy lion, however, both lions do look identical," he said, turning toward Fred.

Fred nodded.

"OK," Emmett continued, turning toward his witness, "let's talk about what happened after Mrs. Rose turned you and Mr. Reed into frogs."

"She brought out some sawdust in a box and then cast a spell over the box. The sawdust turned into maggots. She then told us that's what we'd be eating for four days."

Some jurors glanced over at Abby. She was slowly shaking her head at Sid.

"I see. So why do you think she did this to you?" Emmett asked.

"Objection," Fred said, standing up.

"Sustained," Judge Hollingsworth agreed. "Hearing someone's opinion is not admissible, Emmett," Judge Hollingsworth commented.

Emmett nodded. "Let me rephrase that. Did she tell you why she did it?"

Sid glanced up at Judge Hollingsworth. "She said that she was worried about us going to the police," Sid replied, shifting his eyes on Abby.

They locked eyes on one another. Sid knew he was lying and Abby knew he was lying also, but she could not do anything about it because she was as guilty as he was.

Emmett turned and faced the jurors. "I guess that didn't work out so well for Mrs. Rose because you did tell the police," he replied, smiling at the men and women sitting there. Some on the jury smiled back. Others just sat there stone-faced.

Abby sat there studying the smiles. It made her mad. *This isn't the least bit funny,* she thought. *I'd sure like to get up and tell everyone how you two stole ten thousand dollars from me.* With that thought, she froze. *Wait a minute... This might be the ideal time to push Sid right over the Niagara Falls,* she thought, tapping Fred's arm. Fred looked at her. She leaned in and whispered in his ear.

"Why didn't you tell me that before?"

"It slipped my mind."

"Ten thousand dollars slipped your mind?"

She raised her brow.

"Do you still have the receipt?"

"Yes, why of course. The Mayor has one too. If we can show the court both receipts, the Judge will see the difference in both prices."

"How do you know this?"

"Because Mayor Bumpkin informed me during the county fair that the total price on the purchase of the manor and bringing it up to city code was five hundred and ten thousand dollars. I paid Sid and Don five hundred and twenty thousand dollars."

Fred cringed hearing that. He quickly turned in his seat and waved to his female assistant to come over. She knelt behind Fred. "Tell Mayor Bumpkin to come up here please and then tell Fanny to race over to Mrs. Rose's house and get the receipt she has for the purchase of the manor," he said and then paused. "Where do you keep your receipts?"

"In the kitchen, there's a small wooden box on the counter."

The female staff member nodded.

Fred looked up at the Judge eyeing their little conversation. Judge Hollingsworth knew Fred was up to something as he watched his staff member go over and whisper something to Mayor Bumpkin and then Mayor Bumpkin got up and proceeded up to Fred.

Emmett missed the whole conversation at the defense table while gas bagging up by the witness stand. "In the time you were a frog, did you see Ernie Meyers and Arnold Gilbert at all."

"No, I just heard they went up there to find Willy and Bobby Ray."

"Why did Willy Meyers and Bobby Ray go up there?" Emmett asked.

"They went up there to get Molly. Apparently, Molly went up there to visit with Mrs. Rose and they were afraid for Molly."

Mayor Bumpkin walked up and tapped Fred on the shoulder. Fred turned in his seat. "How much was the total price on the sale of the manor?"

Mayor Bumpkin wrinkled his brow and then glanced over at Abby. "It was five hundred and ten thousand dollars, why?"

"I need that receipt, fast."

"Sure, sure, what's going on?" Mayor Bumpkin asked worried.

"You'll see, please hurry," Fred replied.

At the time, Emmett stated that he had no further questions and sat down.

I have to stall as long as I can, Fred thought, standing up. "Mr. Peterson, let me get this right, you went up there with Mr. Reed in the evening to see how Mrs. Rose was doing, is that correct?"

"Yes."

"And she let you in?"

"Yes."

"And that's when you saw a huge white male lion coming down the stairs, correct?"

"Yes," Sid again replied.

"I see," Fred remarked. "Have you ever seen Mrs. Rose carrying her white lion while she's in town?"

"Yes, Mrs. Rose carries it where ever she goes. Everyone in town knows that," Sid replied, glancing over at Abby.

You're a lowdown, dirty rat, she thought, staring back at him.

"It wouldn't be by chance that you made this all up and added a white lion because she carries her stuffed toy with her?"

"That's ridiculous. Why would I do something like that?" Sid gruffly answered.

"Well," Fred said and then paused, walking back to his desk. He picked up a file with the fingerprints his expert removed from the manor's basement window. "Do you know who these may belong to?" he asked, walking up to the witness stand.

He opened it up and showed Sid the fingerprints.

"I'm not God. Only He would know by looking at these," Sid replied. A burst of laughter from the crowd followed.

Fred took the file from Sid and held it up in the air for all to see. "These fingerprints were removed from the basement window of Mrs. Rose's house," he said.

Sid knew this line of questioning was coming. Emmett had informed him on what to say when Fred started asking about the prints discovered on the window.

"Are you sure you did not come through the basement window that night instead of knocking on the front door, Mr. Peterson?" Fred asked, turning to face him.

Sid sat back cocking his head. "How stupid would that be?"

"Well, Mr. Peterson, that would be exceedingly stupid if you went into the house through a basement window to see how Mrs. Rose was doing," he replied and then paused, glancing at the courthouse doors and wishing Mayor Bumpkin and Fanny would show up. "Now, can you tell me, Mr. Peterson, when was the last time you went down into the basement?" he asked.

"Gee, I don't know. Maybe six months ago, I think."

"You think?" Fred quickly commented.

"Yes."

"What if I told you that not only were there prints on the window but there were also bootprints left on the dust covered floor?" he lied to see if that would make Sid squirm in his seat.

"Objection," Emmett interrupted, standing up. Judge Hollingsworth looked at Emmett.

"Your Honor, footprints discovered on the basement floor were never brought up in the motion hearing."

"Sustained," Judge Hollingsworth agreed.

"Alright," Fred replied to that. As he went to speak, he heard the courtroom doors behind him. He quickly turned and sighed, seeing Mayor Bumpkin and Fanny walking in. "If you will excuse me for one second, please," Fred said, walking back and taking the receipts. He turned and smiled at Sid. "At this time, Your Honor, I would like to present to the court two receipts."

"Objection," Emmett shouted, standing up.

"Your Honor, I was just informed a few minutes ago that Mr. Peterson and Mr. Reed, charged ten thousand dollars more for the price of bringing the manor up to city code and these documents will prove it."

"The court room filled with chatter. Judge Hollingsworth tapped his gavel. "Order, order in the court!" he shouted. "Fred - Emmett, front and center," he sternly said.

Sid sat there shaking in his pants. He knew what was about to happen, once the Judge saw those receipts.

"What's going on Fred?" Judge Hollingsworth whispered.

"Your Honor, I just learned from Mrs. Rose that Sid and Don had ripped her off of ten thousand dollars. Mayor Bumpkin came up and confirmed that by telling me the price she was supposed to pay on the manor and work needed done before she could move in. Here is the city's receipt," he said handing it to the Judge. "Now here is the receipt that Mr. Peterson and Mr. Reed gave Mrs. Rose to sign for the purchase of the manor," he continued, handing that receipt to the Judge. "As you can see, there is a difference in price. A ten-thousand-dollar difference," he finished, turning his head and staring at Emmett.

Judge Hollingsworth studied the receipts. "Well now," he spat, handing the receipts over to Emmett. Emmett slowly looked down at the receipts and saw the price difference. *Game over,* he thought, knowing Sid and Don would be living in an eight by four cell for a very long time.

As the spectators remained silent while the two lawyers were up talking to the Judge, the courtroom doors opened. Everyone turned to see who just walked in. A sigh went out from the crowd when little Molly Dutton and her father walked up the aisle. Judge Hollingsworth looked up to see what the commotion was about and then spotted Molly and her father standing at the gate. Fred turned around, Emmett turned too, and poor Abby almost fell right out of her chair seeing Molly and her father.

"Is there something you want to say, Mr. Dutton?" Judge Hollingsworth asked.

Molly cast her swollen eyes up at her father. Mr. Dutton nodded to the Judge. Molly turned and looked up at Judge Hollingsworth. "I know everything, sir," she said. The people sitting there gasped. Judge Hollingsworth leaned back taking off his glasses and rubbing his eyes. It was the first time in his entire career that anyone simply walked into his courtroom and said that to him. What struck him the most it was little Molly Dutton. Before he said anything to Molly, he looked over at Sid. "I have in my hand two receipts; one from you to Mrs. Rose, and one from the Mayor's office. The one from you shows that she paid you ten thousand dollars more than the Mayor's receipt."

Sid looked down and sighed.

"Sid Peterson," Judge Hollingsworth then said. "I am charging you with grand theft and also for breaking and entering into the home of Mrs. Rose," he continued, looking at the courthouse guard. "Bailiff, escort Mr. Peterson to the holding cell below, in handcuffs if need be. Then escort Mr. Reed from the waiting room down there, as well."

Everyone in the courtroom was stunned. Judge Hollingsworth waited until Sid was escorted out of the room. Betsy and Sue sat there cringing in the back row. They knew they were in serious trouble too.

Judge Hollingsworth focused his attention on Emmett. “Sit down, Mr. Fisher,” he ordered.

Emmett turned and walked over to his seat. He knew he was also in trouble. What kind of trouble he did not know, but trouble all the same.

“You too, Fred, please take your seat,” Judge Hollingsworth said.

Fred turned and looked at Abby. If he could have run over and hugged her right then, he would have.

“Mr. Dutton,” Judge Hollingsworth said.

“Yes, your Honor.”

“Is Molly here to testify?”

“Yes, your Honor.”

“Come here Molly,” Judge Hollingsworth replied, leaning up on his desk. A guard opened the gate. Molly walked through. “Now raise your right hand,” the guard said.

After being sworn in, Molly took her seat on the witness stand. The jurors all sat there heartbroken seeing the sorrow within Molly’s eyes.

“Now Molly,” Judge Hollingsworth said in a soft reassuring tone. “I’m the only one who’ll be asking you questions, OK?”

“Yes, sir,” she replied, fidgeting with her hands.

“I want you to sit there and relax and please take your time, Molly.”

“OK,” she replied.

“In your own words, tell us what happened that night.”

Molly told the court everything - from the moment Sid and Don and their wives confronted them at the county fair and bribed them to go up to Mrs. Rose’s house to help in stealing her money. The only part she left out of her story was the part about Mrs. Rose turning Sid and Don, and Ernie and Arnold into frogs. In her mind, she was not lying. She never saw Mrs. Rose do that to them. She went to sleep somehow. When she finished her story, she started to cry.

“Now, Molly,” Judge Hollingsworth softly said. “There is no need to cry. I would have been scared too, and so would all these people sitting here today.”

Molly looked out into the crowd. “I was really scared, but I knew I had to warn Mrs. Rose,” she replied, wiping her eyes.

Tears rolled down Fanny’s cheeks. Flo was wiping her nose listening to Molly. Shaun, on the other hand, was angry. He wished Abigail had told him.

“Molly,” Judge Hollingsworth said. Molly turned toward him. “Is there anything else you’d like to say?”

“Yes,” she replied, “what about Willy and Bobby Ray? Will they be going to reform school like Mrs. Hornsby threatened?" she sniffled.

Mrs. Hornsby, Judge Hollingsworth angrily thought. *I never liked that woman from the moment I met her.* He stepped out of his thought and answered Molly. "No, nothing will happen to Willy or Bobby Ray, not unless Mrs. Rose wants to make an official complaint against them," he replied, glancing over at Abby.

Abby stood up. "No, I do not your Honor. I think those two boys, along with Ernie and Arnold - understand full well now that trouble is something you run from, not chase after."

Judge Hollingsworth cocked his head hearing that from her. "Thank you, Mrs. Rose. If anything was learned here today, that was it. Trouble is something you run from - not chase after."

Everyone sat there staring at Abby while contemplating what she had just said, and more so, what she just did by allowing those boys to grow up and become fine men within the community.

As the courtroom remained silent, Shaun felt this overwhelming urge to stand up. Judge Hollingsworth saw him get up. "I would like to say something, Your Honor," Shaun said.

Abby quickly turned in her seat hearing his voice. She glanced over at Fanny and Flo. They both had a puzzled look too.

"Shaun Stevenson, there is no need for you to testify. This court is about to make a decision."

"No, your Honor," Shaun replied, stepping out into the aisle.

"Shaun," his mother whispered, extending her hand to him.

Shaun turned and looked at her. She waved for him to sit down. He shook his head and turned toward the Judge. "After listening to all that was said today, I think the whole town needs to hear what I have to say."

Judge Hollingsworth studied the boy and weighed up his comment.

"Alright, son. Come forward," he replied, turning toward Molly. "Thank you, Molly. It was a brave thing you did today and I am proud of you. You may step down."

Molly wiped her tears, got down from the witness stand and walked up to the gate. She stopped in front of Fred and Abby. "I'm really sorry, Mrs. Rose that I didn't come to you sooner with this," she sniffled.

"That's OK, Molly. Please come up and visit with me anytime. Bring Willy and Bobby Ray with you if you'd like." Molly smiled, nodded and then walked out to her father.

As Shaun proceeded through the gate, he slightly turned toward Abby. She wrinkled her brow, questioning his reasoning for wanting to speak. His facial expression remained blank. When he sat down, everyone in the courtroom waited to hear what he had to say.

"OK, son," Judge Hollingsworth said. "Tell us what's on your mind."

Shaun nodded, turned and focused his attention on the jurors, and then allowed his eyes to roam the entire courthouse. "I wanted to say that," he said and then paused, feeling a lump growing inside his throat. He swallowed staring at Abby. She presented a soft small smile while worrying.

"I wanted to say," he started again, "that Mrs. Rose is one of the kindest persons I have ever met." Judge Hollingsworth sat back, feeling Shaun's words.

"She is sweet and gentle with a heart of gold. I know this because I have spent many hours with her while working on her car," he said and then paused again.

"I… um…." his words sounded shaky. "I'm in love with her. I don't know how it happened, but it did. I guess when you meet a person and they simply sweep you off your feet, where you lose your breath every time you see them, you know in your heart that that person is the one."

"Shaun," his mother shouted, standing up and clasping her hands to her chest. His father stood up and took hold of his wife. "Shaun Stevenson…" he started to say.

"Dad, Mom, I know what I am doing. Please sit down."

"Are you sure about that, son?" Judge Hollingsworth asked, thinking Shaun was about to propose to Mrs. Rose.

"Yes, your Honor. I have given this much thought," he replied, turning and looking at Abby. "Abigail, will you marry me?"

The entire courtroom erupted in sighs. Mrs. Stevenson passed out. Mr. Stevenson caught her falling and assisted her gently to the floor. Abby looked at Shaun utterly stunned. Fanny and Flo beamed with excitement, holding onto one another. Karen and Albert, on the other hand, sat there like tree stumps not knowing what to think.

"Will you marry me, Abigail?" Shaun again asked her.

"Shaun," Abby replied, standing up. Fred stood up too to make sure she didn't drop to the floor herself. "I am almost one hundred years old," Abby continued, clutching her hands together.

"If I had you for only one year, Abigail, I'd be the happiest man in the world," Shaun replied.

Abby cocked her head. She looked up at Judge Hollingsworth. He raised his brow and gave her a contented smile. Abby shook her head and sighed.

"Shaun Stevenson… at my age, I never thought that I'd fall in love with anyone, that is until you almost ran me over inside the grocery store," she said and then paused as laughter filled the room. In that moment, while waiting for the courtroom to settle down, she had her answer, "Yes, I will marry you."

Everyone stood up and cheered. Judge Hollingsworth leaned over and shook Shaun's hand. Shaun stepped down from the witness stand and walked over to her. She rounded the table and stood there gazing at him. "I love you more then you'll ever know," he whispered. That brought tears of joy to Abby's eyes. Fred sighed rubbing her shoulder. He looked at Shaun and extended his hand. "Congratulations," he said, stepping aside. Abby turned, thanked Fred, then turned and hugged Shaun.

Judge Hollingsworth was so caught up in the moment that he had entirely forgotten to end the proceedings. The Bailiff walked up to his desk. Judge Hollingsworth looked at him then realized he had to bring this to a close. He tapped his gavel on the sound block. "Order, please," he said. "May I have order in this courtroom?"

The room became silent. Abby and Shaun turned and looked up at him.

"Now, as to the findings of this court - I find Mrs. Rose innocent of all charges. You are free to go, and we'll be transporting your personal items back to your house," he continued, shifting his eyes on the Bailiff. "I want Mrs. Reed and Mrs. Peterson arrested before they leave this courthouse, and…," he said and then paused, "please locate Ernie Meyers and Arnold Gilbert and bring them to my chambers. Mrs. Rose may have let them off the hook, but I want to have a little chit-chat with those two to make sure that in the future, they run from trouble and not chase after it."

"Yes, sir," the Bailiff replied, smiling.

"Emmett," Judge Hollingsworth said. "I'll see you in my chambers ASAP. This court is now adjourned," Judge Hollingsworth continued, standing up and walking out.

Emmett slowly turned in his seat toward Mrs. Rose standing there with Shaun and Fred. He knew that Mrs. Rose was a witch. There was no mistaking that. *Maybe not all witches are evil,* he thought. *Maybe there are some witches who are sweet and gentle like Shaun just said,* his thoughts continued, glancing over at Judge Hollingsworth's chambers door. He deeply sighed, stood up and proceeded toward it knowing he was about to be chastised or worse.

After everyone had left the courthouse and an empty silence filled the air, a little old man stood up in the back row of the balcony. He took off his hat, walked out to the railing and looked down to where Abby had been sitting.

"Abigail Rose," B.B. Cooper whispered, thinking back in time and remembering a little girl he once saw in the middle of the night. "Abigail Rose… yes… she was that little girl I saw sitting out on the ballroom patio listening to those two pumpkins talking when my friends and I snuck up there on Halloween night," he said, slowly putting on his hat and drawing it down over his brow. "Sid and Don, and Ernie and Arnold are very lucky that Abigail Rose, whom I know is really Abigail Von Haussler, did not turn them into snakes," he continued, walking toward the balcony staircase down to the vestibule.

Before opening the door to the little courthouse on the outskirts of town, he pulled his coat collar up, lowered his head and stepped out into a warm summer's day. As he slowly walked the side streets to his little shack in the foothills of Cloverdale, B.B. Cooper thought back to that night when he actually saw those witches flying over the back lawn and landing on the ballroom patio to enter Derek Von Haussler's Halloween party.

His friends and he had slipped up to the ballroom steps and hide within the bushes. It was there that he saw little Abigail, wearing a beautiful black dress and a witch's hat standing there listening to those two pumpkins talking to one another. He smiled now remembering what she had said to them.

"I hope you two have learned your lesson of getting too drunk at my father's parties. You can't even fly your own brooms home now."

"We won't be flying anywhere, not like this," one moaned.

44

Magical Love and Romance

A week after the hearing, and with plenty of discussions between Shaun and his parents, they finally put their differences aside. Shaun and Abigail were married in the ballroom with just their closest friends attending. Fanny, Flo and Karen had the room looking spectacular with one very big surprise for Shaun and Abby when they entered. Shaun was the first to discover that it would be Judge Hollingsworth performing the ceremony. When Albert escorted Abby in, her smile lit up the room seeing the distinguished Judge standing up at the podium.

After the ceremony and with Shaun finally kissing Abby on the lips, the catering personnel went to work bringing out all the dishes of food, drinks and desserts. There was much laughter, dancing and singing throughout the entire evening as everyone had a real good time. Before Shaun and Abby's guests started to leave, Abby found Fanny alone inside the women's bathroom. "I am so happy for you, Abby," Fanny beamed, walking up to the sink and washing her hands.

"Fanny," Abby replied in a tone for Fanny to be quiet and listen. Fanny turned off the water and looked at her. "I would like for you to come back here at four in the morning." Fanny stood there gazing at Abby trying to guess why.

"No sooner. No later. Four on the dot," Abby continued to Fanny's questioning stare.

"Alright, I'll be here, but aren't you going to tell me why?"

"Shaun and I will be leaving in the wee hours before the town wakes up. That's all I'm going to say."

Fanny said nothing.

"I guess I can tell you this much, we're going on a long extended honeymoon," Abby continued.

Fanny cocked her head as to where.

"I have a nice cottage right on the beach in South Carolina."

That brought Fanny's tongue into action. "You never told me you had a cottage on the ocean."

Abby raised her brow. "I also have a mansion in Laurence, Maine."

Fanny slowly shook her head. *How rich is this woman?* she thought.

"I can see it in your eyes, Fanny. Money is no object. It never has been in my family. Now, listen," she said and then paused, "your time is at hand. I will be turning over the manor to you while we're away. I'll be taking Theodore, Tasha and the mice. You'll have the rest of the house to keep you company, but remember… you must never forget to water our tree."

Fanny slowly nodded. *I guess my working days are over too,* she thought, knowing that Abby was leaving the little money tree behind. "Alright, I'll be here at four on the dot. I promise."

"Good," she replied. "Now I must see to my guests; some are getting ready to leave.

After everyone left for the evening, Abby strolled alongside Shaun to the elevator. Before pushing the button, she told him that she wanted to freshen up.

"OK, I'll be up in awhile," he replied, kissing her.

She walked into the elevator, pushed the button and smiled at him. When the door closed, Shaun stood there listening to the elevator. He sighed knowing that the moment had finally arrived for him to go to be with his new bride, his almost one-hundred-year-old - new bride.

He nervously walked into the kitchen and set his champagne glass on the counter. Turning on the faucet, he washed his hands while staring out the window. A full moon was sitting high overhead bathing the entire back lawn in moonlight. He dried off his hands and walked out.

As he stood there in front of the elevator, he felt his heart pounding. *It's now or never,* he thought, glancing down at the elevator button. Before pushing it, he thought of the staircase. That would take him a bit longer to get up to the master's chambers.

Shaun turned, headed down the corridor and slowly took the stairs up. When he got to the third-floor landing and was just about to round the staircase to go up to the fourth floor, he heard a female singing. He stood there for a moment listening. The voice sounded so young and gay. It startled him.

When he got to the fourth-floor hallway, he looked at the closed master's chambers door. The singing was coming from within the room. He slowly walked up, opened the door and saw no one. Walking over to the bed, he noticed the bathroom light streaming into the bedroom from underneath the closed door.

He sat down on the bed and waited for the door to open. When it did, his face went blank. Standing in the glow of the bathroom light was a beautiful young woman wearing a white nightgown. “Shaun,” Abby said, surprised to see him sitting there.

“Who… are you?” his voice wavered. “And where is Abigail?”

Abby took in a huge breath slowly walking up to him. “Shaun,” she started to say.

“How do you know my name?” he asked, looking around her body into the bathroom. He shifted his eyes upon her face. “And where is my wife?”

“Now, I really don’t know how to say this to you, Shaun,” Abby hesitantly replied. “I am Abigail. It’s me, Shaun.”

The color in Shaun’s face washed out. He quickly stood up. “I’m not buying this little prank for a second. “Abigail,” he shouted toward the bathroom.

“You can come out now, sweetheart.”

Abby sighed, placing her hand on Shaun’s arm. He looked at her then felt something strange while gazing into her eyes. Abby cocked her head and slightly smiled. “Oh...my...God,” Shaun gasped, backing up and falling onto the bed. He knew the young woman was Abigail by her smile. He’d seen it a hundred times before. He quickly covered his face as his mind tried desperately to comprehend what was happening.

“Oh, Shaun, I’m sorry I…” Abby’s voice trailed off.

“You’re a witch,” he muffled between his fingers.

The tone in his voice caught her off guard. “But I’m a good witch.”

Shaun spread his fingers open and looked up at her. “Did you turn them into frogs?”

Abby placed her hands on her hips and sharply replied, “Yes, they deserved it, Shaun.”

“Oh, geez,” he sighed, covering his eyes.

“Shaun, please,” she said and then paused, “take your hands from off your face and look at me.”

He lowered his hands placing them in his lap.

“Look at me,” she again said.

He looked up at this beautiful young woman with her long black hair and beautiful brown eyes, dressed in that nightgown. “Will you let me explain?” she continued.

Shaun nodded while patting the bed.

“This might take some time,” she said, sitting alongside him.

“Well, my dear, I’ve got the rest of my life to hear it,” he sighed.

"Oh… now, Shaun. It's not the end of the world, you know" she replied, nudging him.

"Go ahead, I'm listening."

Shaun sat there listening to her whirlwind story, which went all the way back to the 1700's with her great uncle the Black Knight, and how he received the Potion and Spells book and brought it back to his small Village of Nome. She then spoke of her father, Derek Von Haussler, and how he used his magic to become a famous magician… and on she continued telling him her story, which ended with her moving back to Cloverdale. After telling him everything, she sat there staring at the floor.

"So, you're really not Mrs. Rose?"

She slowly shook her head still staring at the floor. "No. Like I said, my real name is Abigail Von Haussler. I changed my name to hide my identity when I left my mother and father. My father was too well known and I wanted to make my own way through life - if you can understand that."

"So why didn't you cast a spell over me to have me fall in love with you?"

"I couldn't," she replied, looking up from the floor at him. "You had to fall in love with me all on your own or, the spell my father placed on me would not come true."

Shaun reached over and placed his hand over hers. She looked into his eyes.

"Are you mad?" she asked.

"No, I'm just a bit shocked, that's all," he replied, leaning over to kiss her cheek.

"Shaun, wait," she said, leaning away from him. He looked at her confused. "There's more."

He sat up straight. "After that unbelievable story you just told me - there's more?"

"Well…," she replied, biting her lip.

"Abigail," he said in a manly tone.

"You must come downstairs with me."

"Downstairs?"

"Yes," she replied, standing up and nervously taking his hand.

Shaun said nothing following her to the elevator. When the door opened to the main floor, she escorted him into the parlor. "Now I want you to sit here on the sofa and I'm going to sit over there," she said, pointing for him to sit down. Shaun sat down opposite her and waited. Abby looked at him for a moment and then said, "Now, from here on out I want you to look straight into my eyes. Do not look away from me for any reason, understand?"

"Yes," he slowly replied, feeling butterflies in his stomach.

"I mean it, Shaun. Keep your eyes on me the whole time."

He nodded staring at her.

Abby sat back in her seat and with a heavy sigh, she called Theodore to come in.

Theodore walked out and sat down beside her. Shaun could see from the corner of his eyes this beautiful white male lion stroll in and sit down next to her. He went completely numb.

Abby kept her eyes on Shaun and called Tasha to come in.
Tasha walked in and sat down on the other side of her. Shaun felt himself losing it seeing the lions looking at him.

"Just keep your eyes on me, Shaun," Abby said.

His eyes immediately glued onto hers. "Wilson, Cracker and Benjamin," she called out.

The three mice scampered out from underneath the stairs. When they approached Abby, she picked them up and placed them on her knee. Even with his eyes glued onto her's, he could see the mice standing there gazing up at him. He slightly glanced at both lions and then he totally lost it. Tears began welling up in the corner of his eyes and then it happened. He clasped his hands to his face and began to cry.

"Shaun!" Abby gasped.

Benjamin looked back at her. Abby looked down to see his little worried expression. She nodded her head toward Shaun. Benjamin turned and looked up at Shaun. "Hello, Shaun," Benjamin said. "It's really nice to meet you."

Shaun opened his fingers and through his tears looked down at the little mouse standing there smiling up at him. "Oh no," Shaun whispered.

"I'm Benjamin."

"Hello, Shaun, I'm Wilson."

"Hi, Shaun, I'm Cracker. It's nice to meet you."

"We're the three musketeers," Benjamin then added.

"Will you stop with the nonsense?" Wilson fumed.

"Gentlemen," Abby softly scolded.

They looked back at her. She lifted her chin. They slowly turned toward Shaun again.

"Honey… Sweetheart…" Abby whispered.

The words honey and sweetheart caught Shaun off guard. She never called him those names before. He opened his hands and gazed into her eyes. She slightly turned her head toward Theodore.

"Good evening, Master Stevenson," the white male lion greeted him in a deep husky voice.

Shaun's knees began to shake hearing the lion speak. *My world is spinning out of control,* he thought, looking into the most dazzling blue eyes he had ever seen.

Abby shifted her eyes on Tasha.

"Hello, Master Stevenson," Tasha greeted him.

Shaun almost melted right into his shoes.

"If I may?" Tasha said to Abby.

Abby nodded thinking maybe Tasha could settle Shaun's nerves. "Master Stevenson," Tasha continued, getting up from her haunches and walking over to him. Shaun quickly leaned back frightened of the big cat. *It's not every day that a lion walks up to you.*

"In the world of magic, one can find themselves overwhelmed with such a display as us, but let it be known that in this world of magic one can find themselves in the most happiest of places. For with friends like us, who'll always love you and keep you safe, you'll find no better world."

Shaun was mystified by her words, so gentle and soothing. "I'm… I'm overwhelmed with all of you. I just don't know what to say," he replied, staring at her and then casting his eyes on the rest of them.

Abby set the mice on the floor and got up. She walked up to him, leaned over and took his hands. Shaun stood up. "Before you get too overwhelmed, let me introduce to you the rest of my friends," she said, turning toward the grand piano. "Steinbeck," she said.

Shaun watched the bench scoot up closer to the piano and sweet music started to play. "Well I'll be," he gasped, glancing back at Abby. "Is the whole manor alive?"

"Pretty much," she replied, smiling

That answer made Shaun think of Wilfred. He had to ask her.

"Yes, Wilfred too, and I suspect that hole in his gas tank has been there for some time now. He doesn't run on gas."

Shaun slowly shook his head thinking back to the time when he discovered the Potion and Spells book under Wilfred's rumble seat and was reading a spell aloud when Wilfred's horn sounded. *So that's why,* he thought, *Wilfred was trying to stop me from saying it.*

"Now... are you ready?" Abby said, taking him out of his thoughts.

"Yes," he replied, following her into the foyer.

"Grandfather," she said, "I want you to meet Shaun."

Grandfather opened his eyes. Shaun stepped back surprised.

"Good evening, Master Stevenson. I am the timekeeper here."

"The timekeeper," Shaun repeated, looking at the mystical old man with bushy white eyebrows and white flowing beard.

"According to my minute and hour hand - I am."

"Oh, now Grandfather," Abby laughed.

"You'll have to forgive him," Sir Henry spoke up from behind Shaun. Shaun quickly turned and looked at the coat rack. "Did you say something?"

"Yes, Master Stevenson. My name is Sir Henry of Knotting Wood. I was first servant to King Louie the Third of England before Derek brought me over to live with him. It's nice to meet you."

"Oh, here we go," Grandfather spewed.

"Gentlemen, this is neither the time nor the place," Abby scolded.

"What's going on?" Shaun asked.

"These two fight night and day. I don't know what I can do to have them stop."

"I know," Benjamin spoke up.

Shaun knelt and picked him up. "You have an idea?" he asked.

Benjamin waved his paw for Shaun to lower himself so he could whisper in his ear. After Benjamin told Shaun, Shaun glanced over at Abby and winked. She smiled wondering what Benjamin had said. He handed Benjamin to her and then turned toward Grandfather and Sir Henry. "Gentlemen?" he started in on them.

"Yes, Master Stevenson," they replied in unison.

"Am I now Lord of this manor?"

"Yes, Master Stevenson," they both said.

"Then I order you both to become friends."

"Wha.." Grandfather started to say.

"Grandfather," Shaun interrupted him, placing his hands on his hips, as Abby always did. Grandfather lowered his eyes to the floor. "Sir Henry," Shaun then said, staring at him. Sir Henry lowered his eyes to the floor too. "If I have to place you both out on the back patio until this fighting is over, I will. You'll stand out there all day and all night as long as it takes - you're not coming back in. Now… am I making myself clear?" Shaun scolded. Grandfather and Sir Henry slowly looked up at one another.

"I'm sorry," Grandfather said.

"I'm sorry too," Sir Henry replied.

Shaun looked from one to the other. "Friends?" he asked.

Grandfather sighed. "Yes, I've always considered Sir Henry as my friend, but…" his voice trailed off.

"But what?" Shaun pushed.

"I just couldn't tell Sir Henry that," he replied, looking down at the floor again.

Sir Henry stared at Grandfather. "You mean….?" his voice trailed off.

"Yes, I've always liked you, Sir Henry. I just didn't …." Grandfather said and then paused.

"You didn't know how to say it," Shaun stepped in.

"That's right," Grandfather replied.

"Well… I'll be," Sir Henry gasped. "I've always felt the same way about you."

"You have?" Grandfather questioned.

"Yes, you just made life miserable for me, and I… well, I wanted to tell you, except I was mad."

"I'll be," Grandfather gushed. "I thought you hated me."

"No, I've never hated you. I've always wanted to be friends."

Shaun turned toward Abby as the two went on and on. She sighed, shaking her head. "You are my prince, my handsome prince," she purred, walking into his arms and kissing him on the lips.

All her friends stood there admiring the moment when suddenly Boris cleared his throat. Abby let go of Shaun. "Oh no," she said, ushering him into the den. "I'm sorry, Boris," she said, looking up at him. Shaun stood there amazed seeing the moose head on the wall talking. "Good evening, Master Stevenson," Boris greeted him.

"Unbelievable," Shaun gasped, walking over to the fireplace. "Hello there. I suppose you have a story to tell too?"

"That I have, but right now, shouldn't you two be going upstairs…?" Boris replied with a wink.

Abby smiled looking at Shaun. Their hearts started fluttering thinking romantic thoughts. “Last one upstairs is a rotten egg,” Abby laughed, turning and running for the staircase.

“Abigail Stevenson!” Shaun shouted after her.

“Oh… I like the sound of that already. Goodnight you all,” she yelled, dashing up.

“Oh, that beautiful wife of mine - teasing me already,” Shaun mused.

“Wait for me!” he shouted, running toward the staircase. “Goodnight everyone,” he continued, racing after Abby.

The group all stood there looking at the staircase after Shaun went racing up chasing after Abby. “The house will never be the same I suspect,” Theodore said.

“Yeah, I think it’s going to be a lot of fun with Shaun living here,” Benjamin added. Cracker and Wilson gathered by his side, still gazing up the stairs. “You think he likes peanuts?” Wilson asked. “I’m sure he does,” Cracker replied, nodding.

Theodore nudged Tasha sitting there still admiring the moment. “Do you remember our first night together?” he asked, raising his lofty brow. She slowly turned her head from the staircase. “Well, if you stroll with me in the moonlight I just might remember,” she replied, smiling at him. “You’re just like Madam Stevenson,” Theodore replied, shaking his head. “That I am. Now let’s see how fast you can run,” she teased, quickly turning and dashing through the den, down the ballroom corridor toward the back patio doors.

After Theodore ran off chasing Tasha, Wilson looked at his comrades.

“Well, fellas, where are we going to sleep tonight?”

“I know,” Cracker said, winking at him. “How about we all go up and sleep in the bell tower.”

“Not on your life,” Benjamin spat, walking toward the den. “You two can go up there. I’m going to stay right here and sleep with Boris.”

“But Benjamin, don’t you want to stay up all night reading spells with us?”

Benjamin waved his hand at him.

Cracker glanced over at Wilson and devilishly smiled at him. They both turned toward Benjamin walking away.

"*Ooga Booga – Ooga Boo, flames from a dragon - who said who – storms in a teacup, storms in a pail - get on your belly and crawl like a snail.*" Cracker and Wilson said together and then laughed.

A Touching Ending

That morning when Shaun woke up with Abby snuggled alongside him, he rolled over and kissed her on the cheek. "It's time, honey," he whispered.

"That time already?" she yawned.

"Yes."

"Before we get out of bed I have something to tell you."

Shaun leaned back on his elbow placing his hand under his chin.

"Fanny," Abby said and then paused, yawning again. "She's a witch too."

Shaun broke down and laughed. "No, I mean it. I turned her into a witch," Abby replied to his laughter.

Shaun stopped laughing. "She found out and I had no other choice."

"She found out about what?"

"That I was Abigail Von Haussler."

"I see," he replied slowly nodding. "Does she like being a witch?" he humorously asked.

"Shaun," she replied, slapping his arm. "Of course she does. She even has her own broom."

Shaun looked at her then rolled over laughing.

"Go ahead and laugh," Abby fumed, glancing over at the closet.

"Gertrude - Isabella," she called, waving her hand at the closet door.

Shaun stopped laughing when he saw the closet door opening and Abby's cape and broom came floating out.

"Gertrude, say hello to Shaun, dear." Gertrude nodded her hood. "Isabella come over here and say hello too."

Shaun moved up on the bed when Isabella walked over and curtsied to him. He sighed, glancing over at Abby. Before he could speak, they heard a car pulling up.

"It's Fanny, hurry and get dressed," Abby said. "Gertrude, Isabella - back in the closet, please."

It was four a.m. on the dot when Fanny knocked on the door. Shaun opened it wearing his blue robe. "Good morning, Fanny. You sleep well?" he greeted her, stepping aside.

"I wish I could say that I slept like a sailor at sea, but I don't think I slept at all," Fanny yawned, walking into the parlor. "Where's Abby?"

"She'll be right down. Now before she does, I must tell you

something." Before he could say it, the elevator door opened. Fanny turned toward the corridor. Her mouth immediately dropped open seeing Abby strolling into the parlor.

"I was just about to tell her, Abigail," Shaun said.

"Abbbyyy…!" Fanny gasped.

"Good morning, Fanny," she replied with a big bright smile.

"Abbbyyy!" Fanny again gasped, seeing this beautiful young woman standing there. "I can't believe it - I just can't believe it. You're…" she started to say.

"Young," Abby interrupted.

Fanny was so overwhelmed that she didn't know what to say or do. She turned and grabbed Shaun. "Shaun, Shaun will you look at her?" she gushed all over him. Shaun stepped back while glancing over at Abby who was standing there trying to take this all in. Fanny let go of Shaun. She dashed into the foyer.

"Oh, my word," she yelled. "Grandfather, Sir Henry have you seen…?" she said, turning and running into the den. "Wake up Boris you have to come and take a look," she shouted running back into the parlor.

"See what? I'm nailed up here on the wall," Boris replied.

Shaun and Abby stood there flabbergasted watching Fanny running in circles and screaming her head off. When Fanny ran back into the parlor, she took hold of the banister completely out of breath. "Shaun!" she gasped.

Shaun rushed over to her side. "What, what?" he asked.

"I think I'm going to…." was all Fanny replied before passing out in Shaun's arms. Shaun lowered her to the floor. Abby walked over. "This isn't the first time she's done this. Go get a glass of water, please."

Shaun took off and then quickly returned with a glass. Abby sat down on the stairs and tossed the water on Fanny's face. Fanny jerked her head. She looked up at Abby sitting there. "Tell me I'm still in bed dreaming," she slurred still floating in space.

"You're not dreaming, Fanny," Abby replied.

"I'm not?"

"No."

"Then how?" she asked, feeling light headed.

"It was a part of the spell my father spoke over me."

Fanny sat there spinning trying to think. "You mean…" she said and then paused, "that if you found a young man to marry you that you too would turn young again?"

"Yes."

Fanny glanced up at Shaun standing over her. "How lucky can you be?" she asked, not wanting an answer.

Shaun laughed. "We're both very lucky," he replied. "Now, are you going to be alright?"

"Yes, I think so," she replied, rubbing her forehead.

"Good," Abby said, standing up. "Now Shaun and I need to go upstairs and get dressed so we can leave."

Fanny nodded, sitting up. "I'll be right here."

"I'm sure you will," Abby said, turning and walking toward the corridor with Shaun.

Twenty minutes later, they both came down carrying Theodore and Tasha along with their luggage. "OK now, I left the Potion and Spells book up on my nightstand, and please, do not forget to water our little tree."

"I won't."

"Now where are those mice?" Abby said, looking about.

"We're ready," they yelled, walking out from underneath the stairs carrying little suitcases.

"What are you three bringing?" Shaun musingly asked.

They looked at one another thinking Shaun was on cloud nine.

"In your suitcases?" Shaun added.

"We're heading to the beach, right?" Wilson said confused.

"That's right," Shaun replied.

"Well, we packed our sunglasses, towels and lotion," Benjamin said, surprised he'd ask such a stupid question like that.

Fanny started to laugh which made Abby laugh too. "I suppose," Shaun giggling.

"Alright," Abby said, breaking up the merriment. "Let's walk out front while Shaun brings Wilfred out to meet us."

Outside, they handed Fanny the keys to the manor and kissed her goodbye.

Fanny waited until Wilfred turned onto Daisy Lane and headed off into the sunset before reaching into her pocket and pulling out her mobile phone.

"Hello?" Flo yawned into the phone.

"Flo…" Fanny beamed. "I'm sorry for waking you up so early."

"What's happening? Is there something wrong?" Flo replied, worried.

"No, no. Everything is fine. Shaun and Abby just left on their honeymoon, and they handed me the keys to the manor."

"No…"

"Yeah… now look. I want you to pack some things and spend the night with me."

"What?"

"Yes, I want to show you something very special."

"Fanny Chamberlin, are you playing with me?"

Fanny smiled, she was more than playing with Flo, she was going to turn Flo into a witch. "You know I'm not into games, Flo," she replied with a smirk.

"Now just pack something nice to wear. We're going to spend the entire evening in the ballroom."

"The ballroom?" Flo questioned. "Alright, I'll see you around seven."

"Great," Fanny replied. After placing her phone inside her pocket, she looked up into the morning sky and gently sighed, *Fanny and Flo - the witches of Cloverdale.* Hey… that doesn't sound bad at all," she continued, turning and opening the door. "Good morning, Grandfather, Sir Henry, she greeted them as if nothing had just happened.

"Good morning, Madam Chamberlin," they replied, glancing over at one another.

Grandfather waited until she exited the parlor. "I think we're going to have a real good time with Fanny here."

"I think you're right," Sir Henry replied.

After Fanny walked up to the elevator, she pushed the button and waited for the door to open. "Now Abby said that the Potion and Spells book was up on her nightstand and don't forget to water the little tree," she said, stepping in.

"Now who could ever forget to water that little tree?" she continued, with a smile.

The End

Wonderful Spells From The Story

1. **The spell for the little money tree to sprout money…**

   Red belly frog legs jump over me – when you're in need of money - just sing to the tree. "Now sing a song"

2. **The spell Abby used to make herself look beautiful…**

   Gailing winds and soaring tides - honey from a bumblebee hive. Teardrops welling up on a cliff - bring back the beauty of this fine witch.

3. **The spell to wake up the house…**

   Dreamtime dandies wishes and bandies - wakeup, wakeup to the land of candy.

4. **The spell to put the house to sleep…**

   Lullaby blue, lullaby red - lullabies that's all that needs to be said… now sleep.

5. **The spell to put Theodore to sleep…**

   Moonlight, starlight - just say goodnight, Theodore.

6. **Cracker and Wilson's prank spell on Benjamin…**

   Ooga Booga – Ooga Boo, flames from a dragon - who said who – storms in a teacup, storms in a pail - get on your belly and crawl like a snail.

7. Longevity spell…

Dribble drabble, dribble drum - a cork barrel full of rum. Now go to sleep, and dreams will come – the rainbow's promise will keep you young.

8. The spell to turn Sid and Don, and Ernie and Arnold into frogs…

Whispering winds from a den of fools - slithering through a slimy pool - up from a muddy river bog - you two will now become big fat bullfrogs.

9. The spell to turn sawdust into maggots…

Up from the depth after a thousand years, slimy maggots slithered out from their lairs. One day juicy - one day not - you have four days before they all rot.

10. The spell to bring Tasha alive…

Clouds of darkness, clouds of light, bring me the power that will ignite. Cast these words up on the wind and let life begin.

11. The spell to bring Fanny to the manor to become a witch…

Hailing winds from across the seas, up from the depths of darkened lees- cast this spell upon the one I call - let her come forth to the midnight ball.

12. The spell to make Fanny a witch…

In the world beneath the sea - where the Oxbow whales are free - I cast this spell upon you Fanny... from the realm of mystical creatures, from the realm of darkened seas, open the gates of magic and become a witch like me.

ABOUT THE AUTHOR

There is no better MAGIC than a story that captivates your imagination. I've always wanted to write a children's story, but not just any story - a story for all ages to read and enjoy.

I truly hope '*The Mysterious Abigail Rose*'
becomes one of your favorites too.

81052936R00226

Made in the USA
Columbia, SC
25 November 2017